Transitions

Narratives in Modern Irish Culture

Doras feasa fiafraighe
'The door of knowledge is questioning'
(Irish proverb)

'We do not want uniformity in our culture, but the balancing of our diversities in a wide tolerance. The moment we had complete uniformity our national life would be stagnant.' (AE)

By the same author

Dialogues with Contemporary Continental Thinkers
(Manchester U.P. 1984)
Poétique du Possible (Beauchesne, Paris, 1984)
Myth and Motherland (Field Day Publications, 1984)
Modern Movements in European Philosophy (Manchester U.P. 1986)
The Wake of Imagination (Hutchinson, 1987)

Edited and coedited by the same author

The Black Book: An Analysis of 3rd level Education
(Denam Press, Dublin, 1977)
Heidegger et la Question de Dieu (Grasset, Paris, 1981)
The Crane Bag Book of Irish Studies (Blackwater Press, Dublin, 1982)
The Irish Mind: Exploring Intellectual Traditions (Wolfhound Press, 1985)
The Crane Bag Book of Irish Studies, Volume 2 (Wolfhound Press, 1987)

For my godchildren, Emma, Luke and Claire.

Transitions

Narratives in Modern Irish Culture

Richard Kearney

Manchester University Press

Published by Manchester University Press
Oxford Road, Manchester M13 9PL, UK
Distributed exclusively in the USA and Canada
by St. Martin's Press, Inc.,
Room 400, 175 Fifth Avenue, New York, NY 10010, USA
Published in Ireland by Wolfhound Press

British Library Cataloguing in Publication Data
Kearney, Richard
  Transitions: narratives in modern Irish culture
  1. Ireland – Civilization – 20th Century
  I. Title
941.5082'4   DA959.1
  ISBN 0-7190-1926-5

Library of Congress cataloging in publication data applied for

Hum
PR
8753
K43
1988

Acknowledgements

I wish to acknowledge the following journals and collections where
earlier versions of various studies in this book were published: *The
Crane Bag, Studies, Esprit, Third Degree, Screen, The Irish
Literary Supplement, The Honest Ulsterman, The Irish
Philosophical Journal, The Irish Theological Quarterly, Mythes
et Histoire, Cahier de l'Herne, Keltisches Bewusstsein, Toward
the Reconciliation of Histories and Irishness in a Changing
Society.* Quotations from various writers cited are credited in the
notes or text and are gratefully acknowledged. The kind assistance
of the Academic Publications Committee of University College,
Dublin is also gratefully acknowledged.

Cover design: Jan de Fouw
Cover illustration: Anne Madden, 'Door into the Dark, II'
  by kind permission.
Typesetting: Design & Art Ltd., Dublin.
Printed by Billings & Sons Ltd., Worcester, Great Britain.

CONTENTS

PART III: VISUAL NARRATIVES

PART IV: IDEOLOGICAL NARRATIVES

PART V: CONCLUSION

PREFACE

The studies published here have a common aim – to argue that the real strength of Irish culture lies not in its uniformity but in its plurality. While *The Irish Mind*, edited in 1984, illustrated this model of cultural diversity from the point of view of the historical genesis of intellectual traditions in this island, the present publication focuses more exclusively on the modern period. *Transitions* might be seen as a companion piece to *The Irish Mind* in that it explores the critical relationship between past and present, between the heritage of cultural memory and the shock of the new. But *Transitions* could also be said to complement *The Irish Mind* in suggesting the possibility of a third perspective – the postmodern – from which to reassess the rival claims of tradition and modernity. Furthermore, *Transitions* extends the cultural critique beyond the limits of conceptual and literary discourse to include analysis of visual art, cinema and political symbolism. The basic approach of both works remains, however, largely the same: a philosophical analysis of culture rather than a social history or an aesthetic critique. Each publication investigates how creative minds have grappled with the specific circumstances and complexities of Irish culture.

The view that 'national culture' is a guarantor of homogeneous identiy is no longer tenable. A living culture – national or otherwise – fosters a multiplicity of voices. It keeps history open, encouraging us always to think, to imagine and to live *otherwise*. Authentic culture is not a matter of ourselves alone. It is most true to itself when it is open to others, an exercise in dialogue, a way of welcoming the difference *(dia-legein)*, a question rather than merely a response.

Most of the studies collected here – under the headings of *literary, visual, dramatic* and *ideological* narratives – have appeared in earlier versions in a number of periodicals, most particularly *The Crane Bag* and *Studies*. What they have in common, and this is why they are called narratives, is a determination to interrogate specific texts, images and symbols which tell the story of modern Irish culture as it makes and remakes history.

Finally, I wish to thank both allies and adversaries in the contemporary cultural debate who, with their challenging comments, helped me develop my own ideas and kept me always open to question.

INTRODUCTION: THE TRANSITIONAL PARADIGM

'The appeal to thought arises in the odd in-between period which sometimes inserts itself into historical time when not only the later historians but the actors and witnesses, the living themselves, become aware of an *interval in time* which is altogether determined by things which are no longer and by things which are not yet. In history, these intervals have shown more than once that they may contain the moment of truth.' (Hannah Arendt, *Between Past and Future*).

In our century Ireland has witnessed a crisis of culture. This has often been experienced as a conflict between the claims of tradition and modernity. Such an experience of residing between two worlds – one dying, the other struggling to be born – has given rise in turn to a crisis of consciousness. How is one to confront the prevailing sense of discontinuity, the absence of a coherent identity, the breakdown of inherited ideologies and beliefs, the insecurities of fragmentation? Is it possible to make the *transition* between past and future, between that which is familiar to us and that which is foreign?

Irish people have, in this century, experienced fundamental changes in their political and economic status. The South has become a post-colonial independent Republic with a hugely urbanised population and an expanding industrial sector. Traditional mores have been challenged. And the 'filthy modern tide' which Yeats deplored as a threat to indigenous Irish culture, has turned, during the sixties and seventies at least, into the 'rising tide' of multinational prosperity – a tide which the advocates of the Lemass Era announced would 'lift all boats'. Moreover, the traditional ideology of cultural nationalism which claimed Gaelic to be Ireland's first language, Catholicism its first religion and the reunification of North and South its first political priority, has been increasingly eroded by the demands of present day reality. The Irish Republic is becoming, in spite of resistance to constitutional change, a secular state of the

European Community. And needless to add, the dominant ideology of the Northern Irish state (political and cultural unionism) has been subjected by the tumultuous events of recent years to an even more unsettling crisis of identity. In short, both the 'unitarist' ideology of the South and the 'unionist' ideology of the North are proving more and more untenable in the face of the growing pressures of current history. The tensions between traditional aspirations and modern realities have combined to make some kind of transition, however resisted, inevitable.

This work offers a number of studies of the transitional crisis in Irish culture. It analyzes different attempts – in our literature, drama, art and ideologies – to *narrate* the problematic relationship between tradition and modernity. Such a narrative impulse has been described by Seamus Heaney as a 'search for symbols and images adequate to our predicament'. In this respect, one might say that the narratives examined in this volume represent a dialogue of sorts, however conflictual, between various Irish minds and the traditions from which they derive, and which they often seek to transcend or transform. Every cultural narrative – be it a poem, play, painting, film, novel or political ideology – is in some sense a reinterpretation of its own history; an attempt to retell the story of the past as it relates to the present; an act of understanding otherwise the *subworld of symbols* which informs our consciousness of our society. Narrative, in short, is where the text of imagination interweaves with the context of history[1]. It is a point of transit between past and future.

Some narrative reinterpretations seek to revive the past; others choose to rewrite or repudiate it altogether. Apropos of Irish culture in this century, we call the former option *revivalism* and the latter *modernism*. Since most of the narratives featured in this book mark, to a greater or lesser degree, a transitional tension between revivalist and modernist perspectives, it may be useful to begin with an introductory sketch of these two cultural paradigms.

*   *   *

Revivalism is a well established phenomenon. It became something of a cultural orthodoxy in the early decades of this century, playing a powerful role in the debate about identity inaugurated by Hyde, Pearse, Yeats and other exponents of the Irish Cultural Revival (in both languages). Revivalism often took the form of 'cultural nationalism'. Hyde epitomised this attitude when he called for the deanglicization of Irish culture. The basic argument of the Gaelic League, founded by Hyde, was that Ireland must cease to be a mere 'province' of England and become instead an independent nation through the restoration of its ancient Gaelic traditions and, of course, its language. 'The bulk of Irish minds', wrote Hyde, 'as the

Gaelic League has proved, can only be emotionalised through our own ancestral culture. . . .' Hyde saw the Gaelic Revival as an 'intellectual movement' which would make 'Ireland interesting for the Irish' by making the 'present a rational continuation of the past'. Once the education system was 'intellectually nationalised', then Ireland's economic and political systems would follow suit and Irish people once again 'desire to live in Ireland and to develop it'. Pearse added more grist to the revivalist mill when he denounced the 'alien' system of education practised in Ireland: he called it a 'murder machine' which quenched every spark of national pride, prohibited the teaching of the 'true history' of the people, discouraged the playing of Gaelic games and made the speaking of the 'native language' an offence punishable by law. Pearse's remedy was to promote a general rehabilitation of Ireland's repressed National Heritage, one which would lead in turn, he believed, to the political restoration of a nation 'Gaelic and free'.

Yeats, AE and Lady Gregory prescribed a similar campaign within the distinct terms of the Anglo-Irish Literary Revival. AE affirmed that to 'create the Ireland in the heart, is the province of a national literature. Other arts would add to this ideal hereafter, and social life and politics must in the end be in harmony'. The exponents of the Celtic Twilight movement held that Ireland could only be redeemed from the prevailing spiritlessness of modernity, and reborn into its proper destiny, by retrieving the myths of the Celtic past. A mythological renaissance of the national spirit was what was most needed. 'We are yet before our dawn', wrote AE, but 'we can see as the ideal of Ireland grows from mind to mind, it tends to assume the character of a sacred land. The Dark Rosaleen . . . expresses an almost religious adoration. . . '. It was Yeats and Lady Gregory, however, who brought this revivalist tendency in Irish literature into sharpest relief by founding an indigenous theatre, the Abbey, where the ideals of both the Anglo-Irish Ascendancy and the Gaelic peasantry could find common cause in a shared reliving of their ancient Celtic heritage. A primary purpose of this Literary Revival was to offset the influence of bourgeois Enlightenment materialism by restoring a sense of spiritual continuity with the past. Only by returning to what Yeats called the 'proper dark' of pre-Enlightenment Celtic mythology could Irish culture begin to repossess its true identity. It was, no doubt, with such sentiments in mind that Yeats wrote in *The Statues*:

> We Irish, born into that ancient sect
> But thrown upon this filthy modern tide
> And by its formless spawning fury wrecked,
> Climb to our proper dark, that we may trace
> The lineaments of a plummet-measured face.

The revivalist project to renew the link with tradition in order to rescue Ireland from spiritual homelessness and colonial dependency, was also endorsed in large part by the nationalist tendency within the Irish Catholic Church and by the Irish Republican movement of 1916 and Sinn Féin. Thus we witness a number of revivalist currents – literary, linguistic, religious and political – converging in the early decades of this century in response to a common cultural crisis. Desmond Fennell records the basic motivations of this revivalist tendency as follows: '"Modern" has always meant what is in vogue, in the way of life-styles, technology and opinions, in the power-centres of the capitalist world – in London, Paris, New York etc. Secondary nations have had the choice either of aping that, provincially, and finding themselves always lagging, or of striking out on their own for a better-than-modern life. Ireland . . . at the beginning of this century (was a) secondary nation which opted to attempt the latter course . . Pearse in the educational field . . Russell and Yeats by working for the restoration of myth and sacredness, the Catholic clergy by building a Holy Ireland to convert the world, almost all the leading revolutionaries by exalting rural civilisation, set their faces against the "filthy modern tide" and aimed to create a new . . . truly human life which would radiate from Ireland and transform the age'[2]. Revivalism may be characterised, accordingly, as a movement from cultural provincialism (the experience of being a secondary or dispossessed culture) to cultural nationalism (the experience of being a primary or self-possessed culture).

* * *

Modernism rejects both the aims and idioms of revivalism. It affirms a radical break with tradition and endorses a practice of cultural self-reflection where inherited concepts of identity are subjected to question. Modernism is essentially a 'critical' movement in the philosophical sense of questioning the very notion of *origins.* And as such it challenges the *ideology of identity* which revivalism presupposes. The modernist mind prefers discontinuity to continuity, diversity to unity, conflict to harmony, novelty to heritage. Rimbaud offers one of the earliest manifestos of this modernist attitude in his *Lettre du Voyant:* (Newcomers are free to condemn their ancestors.) . . The poet makes himself a seer by a long, gigantic and rational derangement of all the senses . . . he leaps through unheard of and unnameable things. . . . Let us ask the poet for the *new'.*

Modernism is, consequently, suspicious of attempts to re-establish national literatures or resurrect cultural traditions. And most of those we might call Irish modernists deny the possibility of sustaining a continuous link between past and present. The contemporary crisis of culture is, as it were, their point of departure, their *raison d'être*. It is something to be exploited, not resolved.

The modernist tendency in Irish culture is characterised by a determination to *demythologize* the orthodox heritage of tradition in so far as it lays constraints upon the openness and plurality of experience. Joyce's Stephen Dedalus exemplifies this impulse when he speaks of trying to awaken from the 'nightmare of history'. He refuses to serve that in which he no longer believes, whether it call itself 'home, fatherland or church'. The revivalist credos of 'nationality, language and religion' are derided as nets which hold the creative spirit back from flight. For Stephen the 'conscience of his race' is not something inherited from the past but something still 'uncreated' and therefore, by definition, still to be invented. Repudiating revivalist nationalism as a 'pale afterthought of Europe', Joyce went into exile and chose an experimental aesthetic. Beckett too rejected the myths of the Irish Literary Revival concentrating instead on the modernist problematic of language itself – what he termed 'the breakdown of the lines of communication'. The privileged province of his exploration was to be the no-man's-land of the author's own interior existence: an existence condemned to perpetual disorientation.

For Joyce and Beckett – and the Irish modernists who succeeded them – it is not what one writes about that is of primary importance but the process of writing itself. Or as Beckett said of Joyce, 'his writing is not *about* something, it *is* that something'. What matters, in other words, is less the content than the form of language. The modes of communication are more significant than the message communicated, since there no longer exists any inherited reservoir of meaning which can be taken for granted. Not surprisingly then, the very notion of culture as a transmission of collective experience is itself at issue. Language becomes self-conscious, reflexive; it begins to question its own conditions of possibility. It is in this context that we may best understand John Banville's recent claim that there is no such thing as an Irish national literature, only Irish writers engaged in the practice of writing. We might say that the modernist tendency of certain Irish writers, artists and intellectuals generally represents a shift away from the cultural nationalism of the Revival to a cultural internationalism committed to formal and critical experimentation. Turning its back on the political agenda of national revival, modernism espouses an aesthetic 'revolution of the word'. Seamus Deane puts this point well: 'In the place of political ideology we discover a whole series of ideologies of writing – those of Joyce, Beckett, Francis Stuart . . . and others – in which politics is regarded as a threat to artistic integrity; the heroics of the spirit which formerly were indulged for the sake of the Yeatsian "Unity of Being" become a doctrinaire aesthetic of privacy, insulation, isolation and exile'.[3]

Instead of attempting to rekindle tradition, the modernist

movement in Irish culture disassembles it by critically exploring language itself as the privileged site of innovation and difference. The contemporary sense of 'homelessness' which revivalism sought to remedy by the reinstatement of a lost homeland, becomes for modernism the irrevocable condition not only of Irish culture but of world culture. The 'filthy modern tide' is here to stay. At worst, one must attest to its divisive ravages, without alibi or illusion. At best, one might discover in the flotsam and jetsam of its wake, the still floating possibilities of other, postmodern, modes of consciousness. Either way, the modernist prefers, as Brecht put it, to begin with 'the bad new things' rather than the 'good old ones'.

*   *   *

Most of the narratives analysed in this book bear witness to a tension between revivalism and modernism. There are, of course, different degrees of attraction towards either pole. Some narratives largely gravitate towards tradition and the past: an attitude that might be described, paradoxically, as 'revivalist modernism'. Others veer in the opposite direction, resisting the pull of tradition and its attendant idioms of national revival: this attitude may be described as 'radicalist modernism'. Others again comprise a third set of narratives occupying a middle position in the transitional compass: a position which we might call 'mediational modernism' – or perhaps 'postmodernism'.* But whatever their individual leanings, all of the narratives examined in this work reflect, to one degree or another, a *transitional crisis*.[4]

The transitional paradigm exemplifies the essentially conflictual nature of contemporary Irish experience; it expresses the multiple complexities and paradoxes which inform our sense of history. It is striking how many modern Irish authors have spoken of being in transit between two worlds, divided between opposing allegiances. They often write as *émigrés* of the imagination, conveying the feeling of being both part and not part of their culture, of being estranged from the very traditions to which they belong, of being in exile even while at home. Joyce described his own work as a dual fidelity to the 'familiar' and the 'foreign', inhabiting a sort of liminal space between 'twosome twiminds'. And Heaney defines his poetry as 'journeywork' – a migrant preoccupation with threshold and

---

*Precisely as a *collage* of modern and traditional motifs, this third narrative tendency cannot strictly be confined to either modernist or revivalist categories. It may be termed postmodern to the extent that it borrows freely from the idioms of both modernity and tradition, one moment endorsing a deconstruction of tradition, another reinventing and rewriting the stories of the past transmitted by cultural memory.

transit, passage and pilgrimage, with the crossing over of frontiers and divisions. The chosen emblems of his work are, accordingly, Terminus (the god of boundaries), Sweeney Astray (the displaced, wandering king) and Janus (the double-faced god who looks simultaneously backward to the myths of indigenous culture and forward to the horizons of the future). But Heaney's journeywork is nowhere more evident than in his relentless probings of the hidden ambiguities and duplicities which enseam the very language he writes. While this preoccupation with language is a common feature of international modernism in general, it carries a singular resonance for those Irish writers who remain aware of their dual linguistic heritage. Modern Irish literature often dwells on the medium in which it is written because 'it is difficult not be self-conscious about a language which has become simultaneously native and foreign'.[5]

Brian Friel marks yet another inflection in the transitional paradigm when he affirms that his plays are concerned with 'man in society, in conflict with community, government, academy, church, family – and essentially in conflict with himself'. A consequence of this recognition of conflict is the impulse to negotiate between the terms of the opposition, to mediate between the split selves – in short, the need for translation. The problem of transition thus becomes a problem of *translation* (*transferere-translatum*, meaning to carry over or across). The schoolmaster of Friel's play *Translations* recognizes the necessity of transition, poised as he is between the vanishing ancestral order and the emerging new one. 'It is not the literal past, the "facts" of history, that shape us', he acknowledges, 'but the images of the past embodied in language. We must never cease renewing those images because once we do we fossilize'. But Friel is aware that one does not cross the frontiers dividing cultures with ease or impunity. The translation from the old set of images to the new is frequently seen as a *transgression* – even as betrayal. As another of Friel's characters observes: 'You don't cross those borders casually – both sides get very angry'. Our transitional culture has its share of victims as well as its survivors. While some manage a successful translation from the traditional to the modern order of images, there are many who fail to do so. In one 'Diary Entry' on *Translations* (18 June, 1979), Friel describes the casualties of transition as follows: 'The cultural climate is a dying climate – no longer quickened by its past, about to be plunged almost overnight into an alien future. The victims in this situation are the transitional generation. The old can retreat into and find immunity in the past. The young acquire some facility with the new cultural implements. The in-between ages become lost, wandering around in a strange land. Strays'. The winners and the losers of the transitional crisis are, as it were, two sides of the same dialectic, siamese twins of the migratory imagination.

A central problem facing contemporary Irish culture is how to mediate between the images of past and future; how to avoid the petrification of tradition and the alienation of modernity; how, in short, to obviate the extremes of either a reactionary Re-Evangelization or a multi-national Los-Angelisation of society. In a study entitled 'Universal Civilisation and National Cultures', the French philosopher, Paul Ricoeur provides a relevant account of this dilemma facing many post-colonial societies. Acknowledging that the contemporary phenomenon of universalization generally represents an advancement for mankind, he notes how it sometimes constitutes a subtle attrition not only of traditional cultures – which he admits might not be an irreparable loss – but also of what he calls 'the creative, mythical and ethical nucleus of all great cultures': the nucleus on the basis of which we interpret our history and make sense of our lives. Ricoeur describes the resulting conflict of conscience:

> In order to get onto the road towards modernisation, is it necessary to jettison the old cultural past which has been the *raison d'être* of a nation? . . . Whence, the paradox: on the one hand, it has to root itself in the soil of its past, forge a national spirit and unfurl this spiritual and cultural revindication before the colonialist's personality. But in order to take part in modern civilization, it is necessary to take part in scientific, technical and political rationality, something which very often requires the pure and simple abandonment of a whole cultural past. There is the paradox: how to become modern and return to sources; how to respect an old dormant civilization and take part in universal civilization [6].

*   *   *

The thirteen studies featured in this volume offer a variety of responses to the above paradox. One of our main objectives is to analyse certain representative texts – ranging from poetry, fiction, drama, painting and film to ideological debates on the 'national question' – which have reflected the transitional crisis in diverse ways. Considered as a whole, there is much evidence here to counter the received wisdom that Irish culture constitutes a single entity. These texts suggest, on the contrary, that our culture may be more properly understood as a manifold of narratives which resist the uniformity of a closed system. There is no unitary master narrative of Irish cultural history, but a plurality of transitions between different perspectives. Moreover, this very plurality is perhaps our greatest cultural asset; something to be celebrated rather than censored.

*   *   *

As I have suggested elsewhere, the notion of an 'Irish mind' should be comprehended in terms of a multiplicity of Irish minds.[7] This tension between unity and difference is crucial. And it must be preserved in the face of ideological reductionism. Modern Irish culture is larger than the distinct ideological traditions – nationalist, unionist or otherwise – from which it derives and which it critically reinterprets.* And it is this *surplus* of cultural meaning which makes it possible for contemporary Irish minds to engage in a dialogue which resists both the tyranny of a single dominant identity and the sectarianism of embattled tribes. Such dialogue has the beneficial effect of encouraging us to reinvent the past as a living transmission of meaning rather than revere it as a deposit of unchangeable truth. It is only when we abandon what AE called the 'infantile simplicity of a single idea' that we can properly affirm cultural diversity.

The commitment to a transitional model of open-endedness has meant, furthermore, that the narratives analyzed in this collection not only attest to an interplay between familiar (national) and foreign (international) ideas, but also lend themselves to the kinds of reading I have attempted here. I see no good reason why the critical methods of contemporary European thought – hermeneutics, existentialism, structuralism, psychoanalysis, dialectics or

---

* Our particular selection of narratives does not claim to be comprehensive. Apart from our chapter on 'Nationalism and Irish Cinema', there is little mention, for example, of the decisive influence of the technological media and popular culture generally on contemporary Irish life. Nor is there any analysis of those cultural narratives which address the problem of the 'unionist' culture or tradition. Most of our discussion of the transitional paradigm concentrates on texts engaged, directly or indirectly, in the debate concerning Irish 'nationalist' culture – in the broadest sense of the phrase. However critical Joyce, Flann O'Brien, Heaney, Friel, Jordan or Murphy may be apropos of tradition, it is largely the nationalist tradition that is in question. I have no doubt that similar tensions between tradition and modernity exist for those contemporary Irish writers who seek to revoke or revise what we might term, by way of distinction, Irish unionist culture. Some obvious examples would be the work of Hewitt, Mahon, Longley, Paulin, Simmons, Parker and Reid. Transitional paradigms are also at work here; though admittedly the opposition between revivalist and modernist tendencies has not been as explicit. And this for the reason, perhaps, that the mythological past of the 'planter' (to borrow Hewitt's term) has rarely been invoked by Ulster poets to compensate at a *cultural* level for the historical experience of *political* failure or dispossession. Nevertheless, both traditions of Irish culture, nationalist and unionist (in the sense of traditions which the modernist impulse interrogates, demythologizes or rewrites), have produced literary works preoccupied with the transition from past to present. And at times, of course, these two traditions have overlapped and complemented each other.

One must be wary, too, of hasty oppositions. For just as it is a mistake to conceive of Irish culture as a seamless continuum, it would be equally erroneous to posit two or more Irish cultures which are absolutely polarized or mutually exclusive by virtue of their differences. Here again, Irish culture is best conceived as a complex web of interweaving narratives which refuse the facility of an homogeneous totality.

deconstruction – cannot be usefully employed in the interpretation of the texts of Irish culture. And so I have not hesitated to read Joyce and Beckett, for example, in the light of Derrida or the structuralists; Heaney in the light of Heidegger and Freud; Friel and Jordan in the light of Lévi-Strauss or Saussure; le Brocquy in the light of Marcuse; or the ideology of Irish Republicanism in the light of Ricoeur or Sartre. These readings stem from the conviction that it is neither necessary nor always illuminating to interpret Irish culture exclusively in terms of Ireland, literary works exclusively in terms of literature, political ideologies exclusively in terms of politics. The interdisciplinary character of this work is intended to resist the academic habit of consigning the multiple and cross-referential discourses of intellectual life to ghettoes of specialization. Against such academic apartheid, I have sought to inscribe a series of transitions between Irish and European culture, between thinking and writing, between politics and art. Such boundaries, I believe, cannot be sustained in any absolute fashion without leading to cultural indifference, or worse, dogmatism. And if the crossing of boundaries causes some degree of interference, maybe it is an interference worth experiencing[8].

I
LITERARY NARRATIVES

1
YEATS AND THE CONFLICT OF IMAGINATIONS

'No mind can engender till divided into two'.
(*The Trembling of the Veil*).

Yeats often canvassed the view that poets should seek inspiration in some great tradition of imaginary heroes. A question which appears to have obsessed Yeats throughout his lifetime, however, was whether it is tradition which shapes the poet's imagination or the poet's imagination which shapes tradition. In his *Autobiographical Writings,* Yeats informs us that already at the age of seventeen he had formulated the doctrine that 'because those imaginary people are created . . . to be man's measure and his norm, whatever I can imagine those mouths speaking may be the nearest I can go to truth'. This statement can be read in two ways: either this imaginative norm refers to a power immanent in the individual poet; or it refers to an attitude of visionary obedience to a transcendent truth which comes from beyond the human mind. Otherwise put, either man is the measure of his imagination or he is not.

Yeats was well versed in the philosophical debates on images.[1] He was particularly impressed by the neo-Platonic notion of the *Anima Mundi* – a cosmic storehouse of symbols, based on Plato's world of Eternal Forms and reformulated in Carl Jung's psychology of a 'collective unconscious'. The main attraction of this notion for Yeats was that against the Enlightenment philosophies of individualism and empiricism, it set the theory of a Great Tradition still in contact with the accumulated memories of generations: 'Pre-natal memory, like Plato's assertion that all knowledge is recollection, also supports the doctrine of reincarnation. The *Anima Mundi* . . . is the sum of human wisdom, to which the individual gains access through the symbols of dream and reverie, or through deliberate magical invocation. We are thus organically linked to each other, to the dead, and to our former and future selves: the history of the world is a stream of souls, and not a catalogue of facts'.[2]

The fascination which the old philosophical debate on imagination exerted on Yeats was not of course unrelated to the particular historical circumstances of modern Ireland. Yeats longed for a tradition which might transcend the bitter divisions which had bedevilled Irish life since the seventeenth century – most notably, the sectarian strife between Catholic and Protestant and the colonial strife between Gael and Planter. A 'Unity of Culture' was needed, Yeats was convinced, to offset the 'filthy modern tide' of fragmentation and conflict.

And yet the matter is not so simple. For if Yeats is powerfully drawn to the unifying idioms of tradition, mythology and collective memory, he is also, in some measure, a proto-modernist who refuses to abandon the contrasting idioms of individual creativity, autonomy, desire, play and will. Yeats's complex attitude to the Irish national revival is an apt reminder of this collision of fidelities. While he championed a return to the pieties of a collective national culture he also prided himself on being a perpetual dissident committed to the principles of intellectual freedom, cultural diversity and political pluralism. In short, if Yeats's desire to obviate the divisive ruptures of Ireland's colonial history found refuge in the mythic timelessness of the *Anima Mundi*, it was no more than provisional – a refuge repeatedly harrassed by the intrusions of history. 'A colony', as Seamus Deane has remarked, 'always wants to escape from history. It longs for its own authenticity, the element it had before history came to disfigure it'.[3] Thus, if Yeats set out to invent an Ireland amenable to his imagination, he was to be confronted by an Ireland inhospitable to it.[4] Yeats's entire work may be viewed in this wise as an endless vacillation between the rival claims of myth and history, that is, between the ideal of a timeless unifying tradition and the reality of a divisive and fragmenting modernity.

I: The Imagination of Desire

In the essay, *Ireland After Parnell* (1922) Yeats makes a telling distinction between what he calls 'images of desire' and 'images of vision'.[5]

The *imagination of desire* is characteristic of the romantic artist who seeks to construct an anti-self or Mask to complete the halfness of his natural self.

The *imagination of vision*, by contrast, is described as the sacramental property of those 'who seek no image of desire, but await that which lies beyond their mind – unities not of the mind, but unities of nature, unities of God'.[6]

But where is Yeats himself to be situated in terms of this divide? Most critics tend to corroborate R.P. Blackmur's claim in *Anni Mirabiles* (1956) that Yeats is an 'erotic' rather than a 'sacramental' poet (a contrast corresponding to the distinction between images of desire and images of vision). In *The Romantic Image* (1957), Frank Kermode places Yeats in the 'central Romantic tradition' which held that the creative imagination must don a mask in order to ward off passive acceptance of any principle transcending, and thereby threatening, the sovereignty of its own dramatic energies. And Denis Donoghue (*Yeats*, 1971) enlarges the argument when he explains that 'the romantic imagination' which Yeats embodies, is to be understood as 'exercising its freedom by playing widely ranging roles in a continuous drama: the poet is playwright and actor in his own play. The self is the object of its own attention . . . creates and extends itself by a continuous act of imagination; thus it evades the penury of the given'. According to this reading Yeats belongs to that romantic movement, which runs from the German Idealists, Coleridge and Nietzsche to several of the early modernists, 'where imagination is deemed a creative faculty and the self its final concern'[7]. A list of the operative terms of such a *romantic* imagination would read as follows: desire, will, drama, conflict, energy, tension, style, personality, mimesis, mask, power, self and self-transformation.[7a]

According to the romantic canons of modern humanism, 'active virtue, as distinguished from the passive acceptance of a code, is . . . theatrical, consciously dramatic, the wearing of a mask'[8]. The romantic imagination always assumes postures of belligerence before the exteriority of the world. Its habitual attitude is warmongering and divisive. Indeed, Yeats tells in his *Autobiographies* of how he was accustomed to plan 'some great gesture, putting the whole world into one scale of the balance and my soul into the other, imagining that the whole world somehow kicked the beam'[9]. This is the Yeats who exchanged the traditional notion of *character* (epitomized by man's obedience to a naturally or divinely given vocation) for the modern notion of *personality* (e.g. wilful self-determination). Poetry thus becomes *mimesis*, the imitation of a mask or *persona*. The aim of the genuine poet, Yeats proclaimed, is the 'birth, the growth and the expansion of everlasting personalities'[10]. Art, or at least romantic art, is the transmutation of character into the free play of personality. For, Yeats insists, 'we have all something within ourselves to batter down and we get our power from this fighting'. Moreover, 'without this conflict we have no passion', that is, no energy for artistic creation[11]. This accounts for the artist's fascination for what's difficult: the war of self on self waged by Yeats in *Deirdre*; the will to 'make the truth' out of one's struggle with oneself which his imaginary Cuchulain embodies. Yeats sums up the aesthetic of modern romanticism in a letter to Russell in 1904, – the artist 'possesses nothing but the will . . . '

Hence Yeats's enthusiasm for the medium of drama. 'Drama's end', he insists, 'is to turn the imagination in upon itself'[12]. Religion, being the opposite of drama, is denounced by Yeats accordingly as a denial of creative liberty 'An enforced peace is set up among the warring feelings . . . that is why the true poet is neither moral nor religious'[13]. Thus it comes as no surprise to find Yeats on one occasion advocating a move away from *vision* toward *self-portraiture*; a move which suspends anything that does not concern the self, anything that does not testify to the 'presence of man, thinking and feeling'[14]. In this mood, the French poets, Mallarmé, Ronsard and Villon, became his models, those who 'created marvellous drama out of their own lives'[15]. Mallarmé's typically modernist lines on Hérodiade especially intrigued Yeats – 'All about me lives but in mine own/Image, the idolatrous mirror of my pride'. In *The Tragic Generation* he candidly admits that 'there was something in myself compelling me to attempt creation of an art as separate from everything heterogeneous . . . as some Hérodiade of our theatre, dancing seemingly alone in her narrow moving luminous circle'[16].

It was this persuasion, abetted by a reading of Nietzsche, which prompted Yeats towards his celebrated formulation that poetry is created out of the quarrel with ourselves.[17] According to this reading even the transcendental Images of the *Anima Mundi* are construed as dramatic antithetical inventions of man which can best rouse 'the will to full intensity'; for Yeats firmly believed that 'no mind can engender till divided into two'[18]. This romantic fascination with self-conflict is perhaps most vividly expressed in *The Tower* where Yeats commends that 'excited, passionate, fantastical imagination' which stems from a 'troubled heart' and 'expects the impossible'. The romantic imagination is imperious; it *calls* images from the ruin of the surrounding world so that the artist may 'dream and so create translunar paradise'. This is the Yeats that 'mocks' the transcendental 'vision' of Plato and Plotinus, concluding that 'death and life were not, till man made up the whole'.

The romantic in Yeats cultivates genius in defiance of all constraints. The best art, he writes, occurs when 'propinquity has brought/Imagination to that pitch where it casts out/All that is not itself'[19]. Thus while Yeats deplores 'the saint and sage' in the Irish philosopher, Bishop Berkeley, he is 'attracted beyond expression' to him as sponsor of the 'intellectual fire' of creative imagination: that which he saw as the only genuine 'substitute for the old symbol God'[20] Yeats hails here the Promethean Berkeley who shocked the elders of traditional belief by opening 'once more the great box of toys'. It is insofar as Berkeley's philosophy of imagination resists man's servility to reality and usurps the creative function of the traditional god, that Yeats invokes it as the epistemological equivalent of Mallarmé's modernist doctrine of the artist as Priest of the Eternal Imagination. Yeats expresses here his preference for an aesthetic of play over one of prayer. He endorses the symbolist maxim, *le style c'est l'homme*. The best art is one of 'style and personality, deliberately adopted'[21].

One final aspect of Yeats's commitment to the romantic imagination is its relevance to Irish politics. Here we might cite his model of an 'Irish Imagination' fuelled by the 'romantic dreaming' of a group of isolated poets – including Russell, Synge and himself – who had fled the sordid reality of post-Parnellite Ireland and created an imaginary Ireland to correspond with their affronted desires.[22] In brief, when Yeats interprets the notion of an Irish Tradition as the expression of a visionary imagination, he sees it as a specific set of archetypal images which reveal themselves to the poetic seers of the Nation; but when he interprets it as the expression of the romantic imagination he sees it as a deliberate invention of the defiant dreamer who insists on creating himself what history refuses to grant. This latter version is evidenced in Yeats's contention in *First Principles* that poets must *create the illusion* of a national tradition; and that in so doing they will do the people of history the honour of naming after them the inventions of their own imaginings. Yeats gives as example Shakespeare's creation of Richard II: 'He is typical not because he ever existed, but because he has made us know of something in our own minds we had never known of had he never been imagined'[23]. It is no great leap of fancy from Shakespeare's Richard II to the brilliant inventions of Yeats's own historical drama: Deirdre, Cuchulain, Maud Gonne or Parnell. Indeed, it is in just such a mood that Yeats espouses the romantic cult of the shaping individual imagination in the conclusion to *First Principles* (1904): 'In Ireland, where the tide of life is rising we turn . . . to the imagination of personality – to drama, gesture'.

II: The Imagination of Vision

But while the imagination of will, personality and desire accounts for a good part of Yeats's aesthetic, it by no means tells the whole story. At times, we witness Yeats's poetic notion of the *self*, for example, moving from the romantic idiom of self-transformation back to the sacramental idiom of self-abnegation, preferring a peace treaty between self and transcendence to a proclamation of the self's omnipotence. In this mood, Yeats pleads for an imagination of mystical vision which 'seeks unity with a life beyond the individual being'[24]. Citing the religious examples of Saint Simon on his pillar and Saint Anthony in his cavern, Yeats praises such receptive and obedient imaginations 'whose preoccupation is to seem nothing; to hollow their hearts till they are void and without form, to summon a creator by revealing chaos, to become the lamp for another's wick and oil'. So that imagining becomes a matter of passive vigil rather than of active formation. 'For such men', explains Yeats, 'must cast all Masks away and fly the Image, till that Image, transfigured because of their cruelties of self-abasement, becomes itself some Image or epitome of the whole natural or supernatural world, and itself pursues.'[25] The guiding Image of the shaping imagination – that of the 'perfectly proportioned human body' – suffers crucifixion in the saintly imagination; it becomes instead the contrary Image of the crucified God, the sacrificed and emptied heart, *Kenosis*.

But Yeats does not deny that this visionary or saintly imagination is capable of poetry as well as prayer. He explicitly acknowledges that 'images of vision' inspired the religious poetry of George Herbert, Francis Thompson and George Russell (A.E.): 'those whose imaginations grow more vivid in the expression of something *they have not themselves created*, some historical religion or cause'[26]. But as soon as this visionary imagination abandons its passive vocation and aspires instead to become pursuer and hunter (as in the case of poets like Morris and Henley) then Yeats maintains that their art degenerates into a mere 'repetition of thoughts and images that have no relation to experience'. Yeats expresses disappointment with visionaries who permitted their sacramental imagination to be misled by 'modern subjective Romanticism' away from the bedrock of 'traditional belief'. For such a fidelity to tradition, Yeats now argues, would have eliminated all those 'images of desire' which 'Romanticism admires and praises', and redirected attention back to 'the images of his vision'. In pronouncing thus Yeats was, of course, also pronouncing on himself.

In a telling passage in *The Trembling of The Veil*, Yeats claims that visionary art can only occur when the inclinations of romantic will have been laid aside. And this requires that the poet 'exhausts personal emotion in action and desire so completely that something *impersonal*, something that has nothing to do with action and desire, suddenly starts into its place, something which is as unforeseen . . . as the images that pass before the mind between sleeping and waking'[27]. The sacramental imagination thus emerges as an *involuntary* agency. At extreme moments, this notion prompted Yeats to plan a mystical order of contemplation on the Castle Rock in Roscommon where he intended to re-establish Celtic mysteries like those of Eleusis and Samothrace. This project, both religious and aesthetic in inspiration, was a clear expression of the *revivalist* tendency in Yeats: 'I had an unshakeable conviction . . . that invisible gates would open as they opened for Blake . . . Swedenborg . . . and for Boehme, and that this philosophy would find its manual of devotion in all imaginative literature, and set before Irishmen for special manual an Irish literature which, though made by many minds, would seem the work of a single mind, and turn our places of beauty or legendary association into holy symbols'[28].

The single mind spoken of here is that *Anima Mundi* or Great Memory from which individual poets would receive a set of collective images. These images would be archetypal and mythological in contrast to the personal and psychological images fashioned by the romantic imagination. Yeats identifies them in mystical fashion with the 'strange things said by God to the bright hearts of those long dead'[29]. Other times, he suggests that these archetypal images can be embodied in the mythic transmutation, often through terror or violent crisis, of certain national heroes such as the 1916 leaders or Maud Gonne McBride. 'Are not such as she', Yeats comments of the latter, 'aware at moments of great crisis, of some power beyond their own minds . . . there was an element in her beauty that moved minds full of old gaelic stories and poems, for she looked as though she lived in an ancient civilization where all superiorities whether of the body or the mind were a part of public ceremonial'[30].

For the most part, Yeats's concern with the images of the *Anima Mundi* was less religious than literary. Due to the fact that these collective images are engendered by a 'memory independent of individual memories', Yeats saw them as constituting a *Unity of Image* which could ultimately serve as the originating symbol of a national literature.[31] It was thus the sacramental imagination which revealed to Yeats the possibility of a Unity of Culture.[32] This encouraged him in turn to privilege the primordial images of ancient Celtic mythology which predated all subsequent historical divisions into different religious (Catholic/Protestant) or political (Nationalist/Unionist) beliefs. Yeats maintained that certain folk-images of ancient Ireland came to him in the waking visions which inspired much of his writing.[33] It was with such experiences in mind that Yeats confessed in a letter to the Fenian leader, John O'Leary, in 1892: 'The mystical life is the centre of all that I do and all that I think and all that I write.' On such occasions, Yeats tends to favour the in-voluntary and trans-personal characteristics of the sacramental imagination over the wilful energies of the romantic imagination.[34] He renounces the modern aesthetic of mastery in deference to a mystical vision wherein images are *given* rather than *chosen.*[35] Consequently, while the romantic poet in Yeats celebrated self-possession in life and style in art as products of a 'deliberate shaping of all things', the visionary in him recognized that in sacred or mystic experiences, the poet's 'imagination began to move of itself and to bring before (him) vivid images that . . . though never too vivid to be imagination . . . had yet a motion of their own, a life I could not change or shape'[36].

*   *   *

Yeats's commentaries on other 'visionary' artists of the Irish literary revival (in particular George Russell and John Millington Synge), convey a similar scruple concerning the origin of images. In *From Ireland After Parnell*[37], he recalls how he had quarrelled with Russell (A.E.) because the latter refused to examine rationally his visions and record them as they occurred. Yeats had at first insisted that they were symbols of the subconscious whereas A.E. claimed for them an objective exterior reality. So keenly attuned was A.E. to the primordial images of the *Anima Mundi* that he saw 'all life as a mythological system'[38]. Russell's influence on Yeats was strong, so strong, in fact, that in *A Symbolic Artist and the Coming of Symbolist Art* (1898), Yeats asserts that to write of literature in Ireland is to write 'about a company of Irish mystics' whose 'religious philosophy' has changed both poet and non-poet alike into 'ecstatics and visionaries'. Under this influence, Yeats even subscribed to the doctrine that the source of literary inspiration was a 'divine flame' which revealed itself as a motion in the 'imagination of the world', thus affecting change in any specific culture through its impact on 'one or two' visionary individuals[39]. The imagination in question here is transcendent of the individual artist and speaks to, or through, him.

The commentaries on Synge reinforce the sacramental interpretation. Yeats confesses in *Autobiographies* that Synge's writing had persuaded him to renounce 'the deliberate creation' of imagination. But this did not mean that Yeats felt compelled to abandon imagination altogether. On the contrary, he saw in Synge a further testimony to that visionary imagination which repudiates the controlling will or personality in favour of a more vigilant attitude to the images of a language and community other and older than the author's own. In *The Tragic Generation*, Yeats commends Synge's renunciation of 'power and joy' which are generated by 'subjective dreaming'. He praises him as one who 'judged the images of his mind as if they had been created by some other mind'[40]. Thus Synge is enlisted in Yeats's inventory of visionary revivalists who remained faithful to the sacramental source of their inspiration. For such men, Yeats affirmed, this inspiration stemmed from the mystical 'earth' which had become 'not in rhetorical metaphor, but in reality, *sacred*'[41].

But one could also give a political reading to Yeats's revivalist hankering after a transcendental 'Unity of Culture'. It has been argued that Yeats mythologized the revolutionary dynamic of the Irish nationalist rebellion – directed in part against the Anglo-Irish Ascendancy to which Yeats and many other advocates of the Celtic Revival belonged – in order to take the subversive harm out of it. By gathering the anarchic energies of history into the 'artifice of eternity', he contrived to defuse the disruptive potential of the rebellion in the very act of mythologizing[42]. According to this reading, Yeats's urge to reinstate sacred myths is informed by a political motivation to reconcile the historical antinomies of class and creed – which the revolutionary drive of Irish nationalism threatened to expose – within a timeless and seamless tradition. But the more spiritually idealized the collective memory of the nation becomes the more it assumes the form of a death cult erected upon the dual fetishization of the Past (the golden age of Celtic myth) and the Motherland (Caitlín ní Houlihán and the sacrificial Rosaleen). Yeats's revivalist nostalgia for a tradition guaranteeing a prehistorical Unity of Culture may be construed accordingly as a regressive death drive towards an imaginary reunification with the mythological mother. In short, the *Anima Mundi* of the collective unconscious becomes identical with the *Magna Mater* of the nation. Terry Eagleton summarizes the main aspects of this ideological reading of Yeats's revivalism as follows:

> Adherents of aristocratic ideology like Yeats are committed... to the values of order, ceremony, peace, stability and tradition –that is to say, to an impersonal organic hierarchy to which the individual subject is – precisely – subjected... The desire to merge gracefully into the impersonal matrix of an aristocratic matriarch is woman as desexualized, defused, rendered safe, and so an appropriate symbol of a non-violent, courteous social order. But this process of sublimation is inescapably a kind of castration: by depleting your libidinal virility it renders you vulnerable to the forces of death which are equally associated with the woman... When your aristocratic order is threatened with violence from the people... you can turn to the ideal of womanhood, defending yourself against the grubby-handed plebs by unity, ceremony, innocence, Nature, rootedness and associated ideological illusions[43].

We will be exploring the related ideological connotations of Yeats's 1916 poems –and particularly his symbolism of blood sacrifice – in our 'Myth and Martyrdom I' study in the final section of this book.

Conclusion

Yeats's endless vacillation between the rival claims of 'vision' and 'desire' would seem to indicate a fundamental incompatibility between the 'sacramental' and 'romantic' impulses of imagination[44]. In several passages, however, Yeats expresses the conviction that these imaginative impulses may function as a kind of dialectic where vision is *revealed* to the poet and *invented* by him at one and the same time.[45]

In *Discoveries* Yeats suggests that the great artist will have his share of *both* 'the sadness that the Saints have known' *and* the 'promethean fire' which engenders active desire. In *Poetry and Tradition* he contends that the finest poetry is one-half the 'self-surrender of sorrow' which characterizes tragedy, and one-half 'the freedom of self-delight', which is the expression of comedy. Tragedy is for Yeats closely identified with the ecstasy of the saint in that it leads beyond the wilful personality to that 'sorrowful calm' which epitomizes the sacramental imagination[46]. Comedy, by contrast, is the genuine articulation of the romantic spirit in that it fosters the personality and will of deliberate creation; the comic attitude celebrates, as Nietzsche taught Yeats, a gaiety which transfigures dread and transforms the nay-saying into yea-saying.[47] On the final count, Yeats is prepared to compromise, dividing the spoils judiciously between the rival imaginative tendencies. And so he writes that while comic desire, 'because it must be always making and mastering, remains in the hands and in the tongue of the artist, with his eyes (the faculties of tragic vision) he enters upon a submissive, sorrowful contemplation of the great irremediable things'.[48] In such passages, Yeats seems to acknowledge that the two imaginations can function together in creative dialectic and indeed *must* do so, if the art is to be excellent. Yeats's ultimate position would appear to be that the best literature arises from a dialectical tension between the imaginations of saint and artist: 'The shaping joy has kept the sorrow pure . . . *for the nobleness of the arts is in the mingling of contraries,* the extremity of sorrow, the extremity of joy, perfection of personality, the perfection of its surrender, overflowing turbulent energy, and marmorean stillness; and its red rose opens at the meeting of the beams of the cross, and at the trysting-place of mortal and immortal, time and eternity'[49].

It was a despondent Yeats who finally admitted that 'outside of myth . . . the union cannot be'[50]. In the Irish context, this meant that Yeats came to realize that the myths of the Irish Literary Revival which promised to reconcile the rival impulses of vision and desire – and by implication the opposing claims of tradition and modernity – were themselves imaginative constructs. In short, the revivalist myth of a Unity of Culture could not be translated into reality. Faced with the 'filthy modern tide', Yeats acknowledged that the sacramental need for harmony and the romantic need for adversity could not be reconciled *within history*. Perhaps this was the greatness of Yeats's achievement – to have carried this impossibility of synthesis to its ultimate crisis, registering its full consequences in that dialectical conflict of imaginations which his work as a totality embodies. Indeed this very conflict is Yeats's own eloquent testimony to the transitional tension between revivalism and modernism.

Appendix: The Byzantine Imagination

Yeats's advocacy of a dialectical mingling of contraries may *itself* be interpreted according to either the sacramental or romantic perspective. If the sacramental reading prevails the dialectic is seen as a reconciliation of contraries, as a process of pacification. By contrast, the romantic reading construes this dialectic of the two imaginations as itself merely another expression of the human need for dramatic conflict and tension. But it would be a mistake to favour this reading, as most critics have done, at the total expense of the sacramental. To do so is to reduce the rich bi-polarity of Yeats's art to just one of its terms; it is to ignore the independent validity of the sacramental imagination, to deny it the power, in itself, to engender

its own specific form of art, its own 'pacifying' dialectic of contraries. Such a view caricatures the sacramental imagination as but a
pale self-alienation of the romantic imagination, as little more than a
prop or plaything in its own comic drama.

Yeats does recognize a specific and autonomous form of
sacramental art which dates from the artisans of Byzantine Christen-
dom, Dante and the metaphysical poets to such visionary modern
poets as Shelley, Synge, AE and of course, at times, himself. By
overestimating the significance of the romantic imagination in Yeats,
critical opinion has tended to completely ignore its visionary
counterpart; or, at best, to dismiss it as the infrequent outburst of the
occultist dabbler in him. The mistakenness of this assessment
becomes evident as soon as we turn from the poetry of imperious
desire – arguably much of his best – and try to account for the self-
abnegation of *Supernatural Songs,* the sorrowful calm of *Wisdom
with Time,* the humility of *A Coat, Hightalk* or *Among School
Children,* the tragic acquiescence of *The Circus Animals'
Desertion.* It is the sacramental and religious imagination in Yeats
which regrets that it was but a 'dream', 'players and painted stage'
that 'took all (his) love, and not the things that they were emblems
of'. It is the same Yeats who acknowledges that 'masterful images'
shaped by the mind amounted to little more than 'refuse or the
sweepings of a street'; that 'the soul cannot take until her master
give'; or that as a solitary man of fifty, he could sit in a London cafe
and contemplate a street until in ecstasy he 'was blessed and could
bless'. How but in terms of the sacramental perspective can we
explain the motive of an imagination, as featured in *Among School
Children,* capable of repudiating the 'self-born' *images of desire*,
that is, images revered by the same desire that created them in the
first place: a nun's piety, a mother's affection or a lover's passion?
Or an imagination able to embrace such archetypal and impersonal
images of vision as the harmonious chestnut tree or the dancer that
is inseparable from the dance? In short, the sacramental imagination
habitually expresses itself as at once iconoclastic (concerning all
images of desire) and utopian (concerning images of vision).

Perhaps the most representative example is to be found in the
Byzantium poems. Byzantine art epitomized for Yeats a sacramental
imagination based on the obedient reception and imitation of a single
Image – that of Christ and his Kingdom – before which the will and
personality of the artist sacrificed itself: 'the work of many that
seemed the work of one, that made building, picture, pattern, metal
work of rail or lamp, seem but a single image' (*Selected Prose,*
p. 244). He described such art as a 'vision' which proclaimed 'its
invisible master', testifying to the conviction of an early, and
still genuine, platonic Christianity that 'god's messengers . . . who
show His will in dreams or announce it in visionary speech, were
never men' (*ibid.* p. 239). Yeats even insists that anyone today
still capable of Vision can recognize in the mosaics of Ravenna or

Sicily the work of a sacramental imagination: an imagination dying unto itself in imitation of the Galilean whose 'assent to a full Divinity made possible this sinking in upon a supernatural splendour' (*ibid*. p. 245).

In the Holy City of Byzantium the artist *was* saint; the sages 'standing in holy fire' could effectively serve as 'singing-masters' and thus transform 'the heart of desire' into the 'artifice of eternity'. The Song of Parnassus and Prayer of Galilee were reconciled here, for it was a privileged time and place – timeless and u-topic – combining Judaeo-Christian *holiness* with Greek *culture*. It was the place 'where religious and aesthetic life were one, as never before or since in recorded history' (*ibid*. p. 244). This qualifying admission is significant. It clearly foreshadows Yeats's final realisation in *Byzantium* (1930) that the miraculous images of vision which 'scorn . . . all complexities of mire and blood', cannot in our time be reconciled with images of desire: 'those images that yet/Fresh images beget,/That dolphin-torn, that gong-tormented sea'. It was with a similar sense of reluctance that he renounced, in his 1925 preface to *A Vision*, the sacramental ideal of a new age when 'men will no longer separate the idea of God from that of human genius, human productivity in all its forms'. Such a Beatific Vision would have to remain merely a *vision*, a myth, a sacramental image for the sacramental poet. The time was not yet ripe for it to become a *reality*. Only in the refuge of a few visionary images could such a sacramental aspiration to reconcile man's contrary instincts find asylum. The question for those coming after Yeats was: is it *there* that such a visionary aspiration must remain?

2
JOYCE: QUESTIONING NARRATIVES

Joyce responded to the crisis of modernity in a manner very different to Yeats and the Irish revivalists. Instead of seeking to transcend the fragmentation of modern consciousness by invoking a timeless mythic past, Joyce embraced the 'filthy modern tide' and resolved to create in its wake altogether different possibilities of experience. Whereas Yeats moved back towards a pre-modern culture, Joyce moved forward to a post-modern one. He opted for a radicalist rather than revivalist version of modernism; a version which revolted against traditional notions of both cultural identity and literary narrative.

*   *   *

Joyce had little patience with the revivalist dream of a unitary cultural identity. He scorned the very idea of an Irish literary tradition (Anglo-Irish or Gaelic) and was particularly dismissive of the Celtic Twilight. As Yeats records in his account of their meeting in Dublin in 1902: 'He began to explain all his objections to everything I had ever done. Why had I concerned myself with politics, with folklore . . . and so on? These were (for Joyce) all signs of the cooling of the iron, of the fading out of inspiration'. Joyce was even less charitable when he characterised Yeats and Gogarty elsewhere as the 'blacklegs of literature'. The revivalism of Douglas Hyde and the Gaelic League he found equally unattractive. He most probably agreed with the young artist in *Stephen Hero* who remarked indignantly to his nationalist classmate, Madden: 'It seems to me you do not care what banality a man expresses so long as he expresses it in Irish'.

Unlike most of his Irish literary contemporaries Joyce did not champion the cause of an indigenous revival. Stephen Dedalus seems to have been rehearsing Joyce's own sentiments when he declared in *A Portrait* that he would no longer 'serve' that in which he no longer 'believed' whether it call itself home, father-land or church: 'You talk to me of nationality, language and religion.

I shall try to fly by these nets'. These terms are, curiously, almost an exact paraphrase of those advanced by Padraig Pearse when he wrote: 'Patriotism is at once a faith and a service . . . and it is not sufficient to say "I believe" unless one can say also "I serve"'[1]. Joyce's refusal of this kind of revivalist patriotism is also evident in his devasting parodies of the Fenian shibboleths of Owen Roe, Proud Spain, Dark Rosaleen and Earl Gerard's Steed etc. in the 'Citizen' episode of *Ulysses*. He would no doubt have sympathised with Stephen who, when asked if he would be remembered by Ireland, replied that Ireland would be remembered because of him! The Irish nationalist ideology, he maintained, was but a 'pale afterthought of Europe'. Even the 1916 uprising and subsequent establishment of the Irish Free State failed to impress Joyce as he made plain in refusing to carry a passport from what he called an 'Upstart Republic'. In short, Joyce resisted the various efforts of the Irish Revival, both literary and political, to reread history in terms of a *continuous* tradition. As Seamus Deane has observed: 'Yeats created an Anglo-Irish tradition out of Swift, Burke, Berkeley, Goldsmith. Pearse created a heroic revolutionary tradition out of Tone, Emmet, Mitchel, Lalor. Joyce created a tradition of repudiation. What was a principle of continuity to others was a principle of betrayal to Stephen Dedalus'[2]. Instead of cultural revival, Joyce chose cultural revolt. He preferred to deconstruct rather than reconstruct the myth of a Unity of Culture.

But if Joyce held no brief for 'Irishness' in the revivalist sense he by no means turned his back on Ireland. While he felt oppressed by his nation as an inhabitant, he was obsessed by it as an émigré. Like Wilde and Shaw before him, Joyce was no less sceptical of the allurements of imperial British culture than he was of national Irish culture. This resistance to all forms of cultural hegemony was best expressed at the level of *language*. While Joyce chose to use the English language, he did so as an alien, an iconoclast, a subversive. He worked inside the language as an outsider, forever mindful of the confusions, ambiguities and discontinuities which this language of Empire – like most hegemonic languages of the European nation-states – sought to conceal in order to preserve the veneer of a pure homogeneous identity. English could never be his own as Stephen pointed out in his famous exchange with the English Dean of Studies in *A Portrait* 'The language in which we are speaking is his before it is mine. How different are the words home, Christ, ale, master on his lips and mine! I cannot speak or write these words without unrest of spirit. His language, so familiar and so foreign, will always be for me an acquired speech. I have not made nor accepted its words. My voice holds them at bay. My soul frets in the shadow of his language'. It is primarily in this sense of linguistic dissidence that Joyce may be called an 'Irish' writer.

Joyce's writing rendered the English language self-reflexive and challenged its historic claim to a continuous literary tradition running from Chaucer and Milton to Fielding and Hardy. His linguistic restiveness was in itself a formal revolt against the presumed continuity of this august tradition (as evidenced in the 'Oxen of the Sun' episode in *Ulysses* when he parodies the 'artificial' nine-stage evolution of the English tradition of prose writing by contrasting it with the 'organic' nine-month evolution of Mrs. Beaufoy-Purefoy's embryo).

Joyce's deconstructive approach to literary traditions was, however, motivated by other scruples besides that of the post-colonial rebel. He fully subscribed to the modernist motto of Eugene Jolas, his Paris friend and editor of the avant-garde literary journal *transition*, that 'the real metaphysical problem today is the *word*'. He resolved accordingly to commit himself to what Jolas called *the revolution of the word*[3]. The very process and problem of writing would become Joyce's overriding concern.

*   *   *

For Joyce language was that enigmatic medium which, as *Finnegans Wake* 'retales', first entered the world in the form of the biblical *logos* and subsequently fell into non-meaning with the fall of Adam and Eve and the construction of the Tower of Babel. Indeed, Joyce declared to Frank Budgen that to write or read the *Wake* was to come to understand the story of Babel – that is, the genesis and evolution of the 'polygutteral' nature of language.

Finnegans Wake takes the form of a chronicle of human babbling. It is, in the author's own words, a 'collideorscape' of 'comparative accoustomology' which attests, by a play on language as *lapsus*, to the 'fallen' character of words. Joyce's language might be described accordingly as *lapsarian*, built as it is on lapses of pen and tongue, embodied in the legendary figures of falling – Humpty Dumpty who fell off the wall, Old Tim Finnegan who fell off the ladder, and of course Adam and Eve who fell out of paradise[4]. The transgression of the First Parents was a *felix culpa* not only because it ultimately enabled the Word to become flesh in the incarnation but also because it enabled the Word to become multiple, that is, to enter into *histoire* (in the dual sense of both history and story). The *Wake* reminds us that Adam was the one who invented naming by first saying 'goo to a goose', and that Eve, the instigator of the fall of language, is the 'grandmère of grammaires'. But modern European man, puffed up by his own sense of cultural purity or racial superiority, prefers to ignore the multilinguistic genesis of western civilisation; he does not want to think that 'his grandson's grandson will stammer up in Peruvian' or that 'his grandmother's grandmother coughed Russky in suchky husky accent (which) means I once was *otherwise*'. As the *Wake* makes plain, Joyce gave no quarter to ethnocentric imperialism with its smug illusion of cultural homogeneity and its refusal to accept that each society is composed of 'diversed tonguesed . . . antagonisms'. Behind the postures of imperial *consensus* Joyce's writings expose a cultural *conflict* expressive of the underlying polyvalence of language itself.

Writing thus became for Joyce a sort of linguistic psychoanalysis of the repressed genesis of western culture. In the *Wake* he proposes to 'psoakoonaloose' the multi-voiced unconscious of language, to trace the original sin of the Word back to its fall from univocal meaning into a medley of different equivocal languages. This linguistic fall gave rise to what Joyce calls the 'law of the Jungerl' – a verbal play on the triple connotation of *jungle* (the aboriginal chaos from which modern man has sprung), *Jung* (a founder of the psychoanalytic method of exploring the unconscious through word-play, symbol and myth) and *young girl* (Anna Livia's young daughter, Issy, promises to reveal the secret formula of creation in the 'nightlessons' of the *Wake*). By composing a language which discloses this unconscious 'law of the jungerl', Joyce dismantles the conventional notion of narrative as a transparent representation of some univocal mental message. Against this representational model of language as mere instrument of the author's conscious intentions, the Joycean text shows – some fifty years before Lacan and the post-structuralists – how language is (i) stuctured like the unconscious, and (ii) thus operates according to a deeper and more complex logic which allows for at least 'two thinks at a time'. Joyce called this the logic of 'nighttime consciousness' in contrast to the 'daytime consciousness' of formal logic based on the laws of identity and non-contradiction (see Appendix). By exposing the unconscious structure of language as an interplay of 'intermisunderstanding' minds – where *I* becomes *other* – Joyce defied the classic myth of narrative as a one-dimensional communication of some fixed predetermined meaning. Consequently, his mischievous definition of the *Wake* as 'crums of trektalk' and 'messes of mottage and quashed quotatoes' should not be read as a biographical allusion to Nora Joyce's cuisine but as a comment on the pluralising structures of language itself. Indeed Joyce's text provides an excellent illustration of Mikhail Bakhtin's notion of the 'dialogical imagination' as a carnivalesque rupturing and dispersal of the official norms of narration[4a].

Finnegans Wake is a deconstructing, or rather self-deconstructing, narrative which reveals language to be an infinite interplay of multiple meanings, a 'bringer of plurabilities' which serves as the matrix of all human culture. 'In writing of the night', as Joyce explained, 'I felt I could not use words in their ordinary relations and connections. Used that way, they do not express how things are in the night, in the different stages – conscious, then semi-conscious, then unconscious'. And this is why the *Wake* is a text where 'the forms prolong and multiply themselves, where the visions pass from the trivial to the apocalyptic, where the brain uses the roots of vocables to make others from them which will be capable of naming its phantasms, its allegories, its allusions'[5]. Suspending the established relation between author and text and, by extension, author and reader, Joyce refuses the traditional autonomy of narrative and demonstrates its inextricable dependence on *language*. The reader of *Finnegans Wake* is compelled to acknowledge this text as 'writing which is calling attention to its written nature'[6].

*   *   *

Joyce's deconstruction of the classical conventions of narrative did not confine itself, however, to *Finnegans Wake*. It was already under way in *A Portrait* and *Ulysses*. When *Ulysses* was published in 1922 it seemed to many writers of the time that the resources of the traditional novel had been exhausted. D.H. Lawrence and Virginia Woolf declared it a literary scandal; F. Scott Fitzgerald offered to jump out of his hotel window to prove his admiration; and Hemingway hailed it as a 'goddam wonderful book'. No serious novelist could afford to ignore Joyce's revolt against both the narrative form and content of the 'classical realist' novel. From its emergence in the eighteenth century, the novel genre exhibited a specific structure of *quest*. This quest-structure was related to several dominant paradigms of modern European culture, in particular Cartesian idealism, bourgeois individualism and Reformational subjectivism. The quest-structure generally took the form of an individual subject's search for value in an alienated world. Its conventional theme was that of a journey from meaning-lessness to meaning, from the insufficiency of the surrounding social environment to some new vision of things. The quest-structure thus presupposed the experience of a rupture between the internal imagination of the hero and the external reality which he is trying to explore or transcend. The novel of quest was characterised by a psychological preoccupation with the hero's solitary ego as it struggled with an alien world.

This quest-structure of the novel has been comprehensively analysed by such diverse critics as Lucien Goldmann, René Girard and George Lukács[7]. The bourgeois genre of the novel differs from the old genre of the epic, as Lukács explains in *Theory of the Novel*, in that it narrates a quest without the guaranteed resolution of a providential deity. The hero of the novel must invest meaning *ex nihilo*, drawing exclusively from the resources of his own subjective desire, for meaning has fled from the modern world and can no longer be expected as a miraculous gift from the gods. Hence the recurring theme of the great 'classical realist' novels: the attempt by an isolated human consciousness to provide a narrative coherence for its fragmented existence in a society devoid of value. The quest-structure operates on the basis of a radical discrepancy between the subjective desire of the hero and the objective reality of the historical world: a discrepancy between 'essence' and 'life' (to borrow Lukács' terms) which the narrative fails to overcome except as a *subjective project*. The contemporary Czech novelist, Milan Kundera, provides the following useful account of the development of the modern novel from Richardson's discovery of confessional narrative in the eighteenth century to Joyce's dissolution of such narrative in our own century:

> Richardson launched the novel on the path of the exploration of the interior life of man. . . . What is the self? How can the self be grasped? This is the fundamental question on which the novel as such is based. By the different responses to this question one can distinguish different tendencies and periods in the history of the novel. . . . But (with Joyce) the quest for the self finishes in a paradox: under the great Joycean lens which decomposes the soul into atoms, each one of us resembles everyone else'[8].

We may say, accordingly, that Joyce deconstructs the quest-structure of the novel by dissolving its *egological* constituents (i.e. the subjective ego of the author and his fictional characters) into an *ecological* system (i.e. the unconscious structures of the text as a language process). In other words, the Joycean transition from 'classical' to 'critical' forms of narrative is characterized by a surpassing of the ecology of the bourgeois novel, typified by the narrator's psychological exploration of himself and his world, towards an ecology where the language system assimilates the narrator's subjective consciousness to itself. Consequently, 'plot and theme, those elements which produce the story, are to be subdued, even abolished and replaced by language. Even though language will inevitably carry the traces of these story patterns, it will not allow them to dominate'[9].

* * *

Joyce's first novel *A Portrait of the Artist as a Young Man* is, as the self-reflexive title suggests, a parody of the quest-structure of the traditional bourgeois novel. Stephen is the alienated artist in search of beauty in a hostile world. He defines beauty in terms of the meta-physical triad of *integritas/consonantia/claritas* and pretentiously affirms the transcendental and quasi-divine status of art. Stephen aspires towards the condition of a Platonic demiurge who might transmute the dross of his surrounding reality in the 'silver womb of the imagination'. Like the 'fabulous artificer' he is named after, Dedalus seeks to forge the conscience of his race in the smithy of his own soul (in Greek mythology Dedalus was said to have invented the instruments of sculpture and forgery which enabled him to imitate the gods by creating human-like figures from amorphous spiritual mediation between father and son through the agency of the Ghost, finds its closest parallel in the theological Trinity of Father, Son and Holy Ghost which in itself constitutes an all-male self-generative process of creation beyond the female principle of historical generation (see Appendix).

In order mutually to recreate each other as 'artistic' father and 'artistic' son, Bloom and Stephen believe it necessary to abandon *memory* – that 'agenbite of inwit' which binds them to the procreative principles of history. It is Stephen's guilt-ridden memory which keeps him chained to mother Church, mother Ireland and mother Dedalus, just as it is Bloom's paranoid memory which feeds his obsession with an unfaithful wife and deceased son. Stephen and Bloom seek to bypass the oppressive 'mothers of memory' towards the liberating power of creative imagination. Through an art that transcends history, through an imagination that creates *ex nihilo*, they aspire to a transcendental condition of consubstantiality.

*   *   *

In similar fashion, Stephen is trying to move beyond the constraints of historical filiality towards an aesthetic principle of creation. Stephen has abandoned his allegiance both to his natural father, Mr. Dedalus, and to his natural mother whose death bed request for prayers he rejected. But this refusal of his inherited filial condition is most vividly manifest in his repeated efforts to evade the threatening 'mothers of memory'. Thus in the opening chapters of *Ulysses*, Joyce portrays Stephen attempting to escape his oppressive matriarchal origins, as he seeks to awake from the 'nightmare of history' which he identifies with the three mother-figures of the determining past: mother-nature (his biological mother); mother-church (the Virgin mother); and mother-Ireland (the Sean-Bhean-Bhocht Milkwoman or Caitlín ní Houlihán variously derided as an 'Old Gummy Granny' or a 'sow that eats her own farrow'). Joyce reinforces this son-versus-mother structure by means of a clever introductory *leitmotif* of omphalic signifiers: the shaving-bowl, sacrificial bowl, vomiting bowl, the bowl of Dublin bay, the hollow tower, etc. The suggestion seems to be that before Stephen can embark upon his journey toward a metaphysical father he must first transcend his bonds to the historical mothers of memory (a suggestion reinforced by Buck Mulligan's description of Stephen as a 'Japhet in search of a father').

Both Bloom and Stephen, then, construe art as an 'eternal spirit' which promises to unite father and son in a new communion, one which transcends the oppressive transience of history and the sexual-maternal cycles of nature. Louis Gillet, Joyce's Parisian friend, confirmed the centrality of this theme in the Joycean aesthetic when he declared in 1949 that 'the problem of paternity . . . is the essential basis of the Joyce problem' [11]. But it is Haines, in the very first chapter of *Ulysses*, who already provides us with the key to this narrative structure: 'the father and the son idea. The son striving to be atoned with the father'. Stephen and Bloom. Telemachus and Ulysses. Prince Hamlet and King Hamlet. Christ the son and God the Father.

This quest to discover in art a supra-historical rapport between father and son finds most explicit expression in the celebrated scene in the National Library (Chapter 9). Here the trajectories of Stephen and Bloom briefly converge. Stephen poses the problem of how Shakespeare sought to recreate himself by 'writing and reading the book of himself'. Just as God was the original artist who 'wrote the folio of this world', so too Shakespeare/Hamlet, sought to become a divine artist by creating an artistic world in which he could find 'as actual what was within his world as possible'. Thus Stephen demonstrates that the Godlike artist compounded of father and son and ghost is 'all in all, the father of his own grandfather' – and of everyone else, but most importantly, 'himself his own father' (i.e. a self-creation from nothing). Shakespeare's desire in *Hamlet* for a stone). But Stephen's seeking becomes self-conscious and ultimately self-parodying. Thus while *A Portrait* ostensibly conforms to the quest-structure of the traditional novel to the extent that it recounts the efforts of an heroic imagination to redeem the degraded world from which it is severed, Joyce is in fact subtly mocking this very paradigm of quest. Stephen's romantic desire to become an 'eternal priest of the imagination' who will transform the squalor of history into art, is treated ironically by Joyce. The 'sluggish matter of the earth' proves refractory to Dedalus' alchemical designs. As his friend Lynch exclaims: 'What do you mean by prating about beauty in this miserable god-forsaken land'.

Already in *A Portrait* we witness Joyce's modernist strategy of making writing reflect upon its own condition of possibility. The quest-structure of conventional narrative begins to scrutinize itself: fiction becomes meta-fiction. Joyce the artist-author writes about himself as the artist-hero, Stephen, who in turn writes about himself as the artist-*manqué* (e.g. Stephen's confessional portrayal of himself in his introspective journal and 'dewy-wet' doggerel). Moreover, the artist's self-portrait as a Byronic pedant citing Aquinas and Newman in support of his own romantic aesthetic further accentuates this sense of the narrative as critical self-reflexiveness. In *A Portrait* the text as a closed product to be passively consumed by the reader is already being replaced by a text which represents itself as an open-ended process in which the reader may actively participate. And in this modernist impulse towards critical self-representation we find the *novel of quest* being subverted by the *novel of question* – or to be more precise, of *self-questioning* [10].

The *Portrait* ends with Stephen invoking the assistance of his mythic namesake Dedalus, the 'old father, old artificer'. In *Ulysses* the narrative quest of the 'artist' son (Stephen) for his 'artificer' father (Bloom) is brought to its absurd conclusion. It is significant that Stephen and Bloom journey towards each other in search of an *aesthetic* father-son relationship, rather than a *real* one. History has let them down, so they look towards art for their salvation.

Bloom's 'real' son, Rudi, died as soon as he entered life and his wife, Molly, is unfaithful. His alimentary condition (Joyce makes much of his corporeal infelicities, in chapters 5, 6 and 7) is as poor as his sexual condition (he is a cuckold 'adorer of the adultress rump') and his social condition (a Jew in anti-semitic Dublin). In brief, Bloom feels himself a failure in reality and so seeks to recreate himself in the artifice of eternity. Time and again Bloom fantasises about himself as a great prophet-artist. He inscribes the words 'I am A' on the Dollymount sand – a cryptic cabalist formula which may signify Artist, Alpha, Adonai, Abba (*Heb*. Father) or I Am who Am (Yahweh). Bloom uses fantasy to free himself from the 'accumulation of the past'. As Lenihan says of him: 'There's a touch of the artist about old Bloom'. In short, Bloom strives to relinquish his temporal familial bonds – both to his wife, Molly, and his dead but remembered son, Rudi – in order to achieve an aesthetic 'atonement' with an 'eternal son'.

But the hope for such an aesthetic communion is exposed as illusory in the final 'Ithaca' chapter. Here Stephen-Telemachus and Bloom-Ulysses reach their journey's end (Eccles St.,/Itacha), only to find it is a *cul de sac*. This episode is presumably intended to demonstrate the impossibility of communication between Stephen and Bloom. The sheer encyclopaedic abstruseness of their dialogue – what Joyce referred to as the 'dry rocks' of 'mathematical catechism' – belies the dream of an exclusively aesthetic alliance. The auto-creative imagination proves to be sterile, devoid of all genuine creativity, all intimacy and life. And so memory reasserts itself at last when the early morning chimes of St. George's bell make Stephen remember the mother he thought himself rid of and make Bloom recall the dead. The 'Ithaca' chapter concludes with an acknowledgement of the futility of any artistic creation which seeks to censure the nightmare of history. The point seems to be that imagination must incorporate memory, opening itself to the fluxile temporality of history as it does in Molly's final soliloquy. Bloom reaches towards such an intuition, accepting his past in a spirit of equanimity: 'If it was it was. He bore no hate'. He curls up at Molly's feet, a 'childman weary, the man-child in the womb'. Stephen too ultimately assents to the reality of history he had previously scorned; he agrees to meet Molly, to trust in what 'he must come to ineluctably'. Stephen and Bloom cannot commune without Molly. She is the life-giving flesh to the skeleton of Ithaca.

As Joyce himself put it in a letter to Valéry Larbaud: 'Ithaca is alien, Penelope the last word'. The world of creation cannot ignore the world of procreation. Art which excludes history cuts its own throat[12].

In Molly's soliloquy the fertile chaos of everyday historical time coincides with the structuring principle of art. Joyce resists the temptation to reduce Molly to some *Magna Mater* archetype who is all matter and no mind. Molly is both a procreator and a creator, (she is a mother, a lover and an opera singer). Her stream-of-consciousness epilogue is *both* a welling up of suppressed images from memory *and* an aesthetic shaping of a new vision of things. It exemplifies how language may be liberated from a closed 'egological' narrative into an open 'ecological' system of textual play – one where conscious *imagination* which leads beyond history and unconscious *memory* which leads back to history become one and the same.

By thus conjoining the aesthetic principle of imagination and the reality principle of history, Joyce dismantles the linearity of the search-structure, so indispensable to the traditional novel. Molly's mind moves in circles; it allows for no journey from one point to another. Her epilogue is therefore a sort of anti-novel. For once the two poles of the journey – the subjective pole of the ordering imagination and the objective pole of disordering reality – are superimposed, the novel would appear to forfeit its very *raison d'être*. It is exposed as *writing*: the textual play of language as an open-ended process of signification.

Joyce differs principally from Yeats in his belief that the dualistic opposition between creative desire and recreative memory can be overcome. This entails for Joyce a deconstruction of both the traditional quest structure of narrative desire and the traditional constraints of oppressive memory – including the monolith of tradition itself. Thus while Yeats conceived of memory as a sacramental refuge from history, a Great Tradition of timeless myths restoring the dream of a lost Unity of Culture, Joyce redefines memory as a 'nightmare of history' – something to be interrogated and creatively explored so as to open up new possibilities of historical meaning. For Yeats memory offers the promise of cultural *identity* based on the retrieval of tradition; for Joyce it opens the possibility of cultural *difference*, of being always *otherwise*. Caithlín ní Houlihán, the matriarch of national unity, is supplanted by Molly and Anna Livia, 'bringers of plurabilities'.

APPENDIX I:
Joyce and Derrida

In *Writing and Difference*, Jacques Derrida offers the following comment on *Ulysses*: 'Are we Jews? Are we Greeks? We reside in the difference between Jew and Greek, which is perhaps the unity of what we call history. . . . What is the legitimacy or the meaning of (Joyce's) proposition – *'Jewgreek is greekjew. Extremes meet'*?' In a footnote, Derrida elaborates: 'In constructing Bloom and Stephen (Jew-Greek), Joyce showed great interest in the thesis of Victor Bérard who saw Ulysses as a semite. . . . Furthermore, this proposition is attributed to feminine logic: 'Woman's reason. Jewgreek is greekjew'.'[1]

Derrida is suggesting here that Joyce's *Ulysses* is a narrative replay of the historical relationship between the two primary cultural movements that make up modern Western civilisation: *Greek metaphysics* (represented by the Aristotelian Stephen), and *Biblical messianism* (represented by the semitic-prophetic Bloom). Both cultures have remained dualistically opposed in Western history to the extent that they propounded rival 'logocentric' systems which excluded the mediating principle of 'woman's reason' (represented by Molly).

In the light of Derrida's hypothesis, let us briefly isolate and re-examine some of the philosophical implications of our preceding analysis. Bloom, the surrogate Hebraic father, sought 'atonement' with Stephen the surrogate Hellenic son, through the holy ghost of an aesthetic discourse totally devoid of feminine creativity or procreativity. Quite appropriately, Stephen formulates his version of atonement with the eternal father, transcending the sexual-maternal chains of nature, in the idiom of Greek metaphysics. Already in *A Portrait* Stephen had coveted art's 'silver womb of the imagination' capable of dispensing with the corporeal womb of maternity, by creating quasi-mystical images of *consonantia*, *integritas* and *claritas*. It is not insignificant that Stephen's theory of aesthetic epiphany is derived here from Thomistic metaphysics. Thomas Aquinas originally advanced this triadic definition of beauty to account for the spiritual rapport of *similitudo* or consubstantiality between God the Son and God the Father[2]. In *Ulysses* Stephen frequently invokes the teaching of 'the bulldog of Aquin' and prides himself on reading his 'gorbellied works . . . in the original'. Stephen's meditations on the Aristotelian-Thomistic model of a self-creating, self-thinking *Logos* beyond time, history and matter (the mothers of memory) reach their most conspicuous expression in the National Library scene. Here Stephen employs the model of metaphysical paternity to explain how Shakespeare essayed to recreate himself out of himself, in emulation of the divine *creatio ex nihilo*, by 'writing and reading the book of himself' – *Hamlet*. Thus, as we noted, the god-like artist assumes the metaphysical status of a self-identical trinity (an Ens Causi Sui), becoming 'all in all the father of his own grandfather . . . himself his own father. . . . It is a mystical estate, an apostolic succession, from only begetter to only begotten'. This idea of a patriarchal *Logos* in silent dialogue with itself through its exclusive self-creation as divine son, recurs in the 'Circe' episode when Stephen muses: 'What went forth to the ends of the world to traverse not itself. God, the Sun, Shakespeare, a commercial traveller, having itself traversed in reality itself, becomes that self'. It is in this context that we must interpret Stephen's search in the 'Proteus' chapter for the secret 'signature of things' (Boehme) and the 'form of forms' (Aristotle/Aquinas) which will serve as the divine-artistic Word of creation. (See the Dalkey meditiation in Chapter III).

*   *   *

In *Ulysses*, this self-deconstructive language of substitution is epitomised by Molly's 'woman's reason'. In contrast to the logocentric principles of identity and non-contradiction (the traditional metaphysical logic of *either/or*), Molly advances a deconstructive logic which allows for 'two thinks at a time'. Opposites are no longer dualistically opposed, as in the paternal logic, but are subversively played off against one another until the opposition is undone. 'Jewgreek is greekjew': this ambivalence is accessible to the traditionally repressed 'woman's reason' (as we see in Molly's final soliloquy); but, it is incompatible with the phallogocentric fiction of self-presence coveted by Bloom and Stephen.

The projected atonement between the Hebraic father and the Hellenic son is, as we noted, humourously dismantled in the incomprehensible dialogue of 'Ithaca'. And it is certainly a clear reminder that the silver womb of the exclusively male imagination begets not a divine *creatio ex nihilo* but a *nihil ex creatione*: a slow slump into intellectual nothingness. By contrast, Molly's concluding 'anamnetic' soliloquy recollects the fragmented events of the day; her stream of consciousness serves as a 'chapter of accidents' which synchronises the contrary and irreconcilable claims of Greek and Jew, of father and son. Stephen implicitly subscribes to Molly's 'woman's reason' by accepting 'what he must come to ineluctably' (i.e. history is transformed from a curse to the condition of existence); while Bloom explicitly acknowledges it when he faces up to his past history of betrayal and persecution, in a spirit 'less of envy than equanimity'. In short, Bloom the 'jewgreek' can only hope to be atoned with Stephen, 'the greekjew', through the historically mediating consciousness of Molly who is *both* a creator faithful to her imaginative vocation as chanteuse *and* a procreator (mother, wife and lover) devoted to the everyday claims of history. Her affirmative 'yes' transcends the nihilistic theology of father and son.

In *Finnegans Wake* the *both/and* logic of 'woman's reason' re-emerges in the equally deconstructing, equivocating, decentering language of Anna Livia Plurabelle. In this 'mistresspiece' Joyce leaves us in little doubt as to where his intellectual and linguistic sympathies lie: 'In the name of Annah the Allmaziful, the Everliving, the Bringer of Plurabilities, haloed be her eve, her signtime sung, her rill be run, unhemmed as it is in heaven'. Anna's language ruptures the logocentric principles of *identity* (a is a), *non-contradiction* (a is not non a), *excluded middle* (truth is *either* a *or* b, but not *both* at once) and *linear causality* (a causes b). ALP reverses the traditional metaphysical censure of the polyvalence of language. Her word-play debunks the fallacy that language could ever be a 'pure dialect of the tribe', a vehicle for transmitting some homogeneous cultural or racial identity. It disinherits the patrimony of the word. This 'woman's reason' is what Derrida calls 'undecid-ability', adding that if a meaning is *both/and* it is also *neither/nor*. Once the accredited world of *either/or* is disrupted, new possibilities of meaning emerge from the irresolvable indeterminacies and unforseen diversities of language. Beyond, or behind, the secure veneer of binary opposition, there resides a world of 'excluded middles' revealing 'another mode of meaning beyond the obvious one' (as Tom Pynchon remarks in *The Crying of Lot 49)*. And this undecidable play of meaning is what *Finnegans Wake* aptly nominates as the interface 'between twosome twiminds'.

Finnegans Wake thus testifies to the fall of the metaphysical and biblical *Logos* into the babel of history. It is a 'mamafesta' which retells how Anna (the Celtic mother-goddess who reconciles the father-god, Manaanan, and the son-god Aengus Og) and Eve (the temptress who first challenged patriarchal self-sufficiency and self-presence) inaugurated the history of human creation and procreation. As such, Anna and Eve have become identified in western consciousness with the subconscious and suppressed depths of language. Joyce seems to be saying that it is only by attending to this *other* language which subtends our logocentric culture – the 'nighttime' language of the *Wake* which sabotages 'the wideawake language of cut and dry grammar and go-ahead plot' – that we can become aware of the polyphonic legacy of 'woman's reason'.

* * *

This metaphysical relationship of *identity* between father and son is what Derrida calls *logocentrism*. Western metaphysics is fundamentally logocentric, Derrida explains, because it is founded on the ideal of a perfect self-presence or self-immediacy which the

Greeks called the *Logos* or the *Arche*. From these founding notions
the cardinal metaphysical terms of reason, logic and transcendent
intellect were derived. Because the transcendent *Logos* was thought
to reside beyond historical time and matter, and by extension
beyond the so-called 'feminine' principles of desire and procreation,
the logocentric era of the West, dating from Plato and Aristotle to
the present, is also characterised by Derrida as *'phallogocentric'*.
Consequently, the platonic *Logos* of self-presence became
synonymous with an all-male self-referential relationship between
father and son. As Derrida observes in *Dissemination*: 'The
absolute invisibility of the origin of the visible, of the God-Sun-
Father, Platonism, is the general rehearsal of this family scene and
the most powerful effort . . . to conceal it by drawing the curtains
over the dawning of the West'[3]. Thus, for example, when the
Stranger in Plato's *Theaetetus* (241–242) 'dares to lay unfilial hands
on the paternal pronouncement' of the *Logos* (*toi patrikoi logoi*), he
is accused of parricide.

Platonic metaphysics defined the paternal *Logos* as a 'silent
dialogue of the soul with itself'; and it deemed language and writing
to be an adulteration of this original self-presence. Accordingly, in
the *Phaedrus*, Plato condemned writing because it acted as an
intermediary detour of inscription which interrupted the monological
dialogue of Father with Son, i.e. because it 'claimed to do without
the Father of *Logos'*[4]. In short, once language is written and thus
recollected and recorded, it no longer requires the unmediated
speaking presence of the paternal *Logos*. Writing disrupts the *Logos*
because it breaks from the original self-identity of the father and
assumes a life of its own, an existence *other than the father*. The
language of writing, as Derrida concludes, is the 'father's other', it
'cannot be assigned a fixed spot . . . sly, slippery and masked . . . a
joker, a floating signifier, a wild card (which) puts play into play'[5].
This 'floating indetermination' and 'unstable ambivalence' which
characterises the written form of language, deconstructs the paternal
Logos of identity by permitting the play of *substitution*, i.e. the play
of a re-presentation standing in for self-presence, of the derived
replacing the original, the mediated replacing the immediate, the
temporal replacing the eternal, the different replacing the same.

*   *   *

By dispensing with all quotation marks or 'perverted commas' in
the *Wake*, Joyce shattered the illusion of the author as some extra-
linguistic identity. In similar fashion, he demonstrated that language
is not derived from some original, prelapsarian Word, but from
compound multivocal 'thunderwords' made up from a wide variety
of tongues. *Finnegans Wake*, as noted, proposes to reveal the secret
'law of the Jungerl' (*Jung's* law of the synchronistic and non-causal

order of the unconscious) enunciated in Issy's 'nightlessons' (Anna's *young-girl*)[5a]. The nighttime logic of Anna and Issy discloses language as a fecund interplay between different meanings. The discourse of 'woman's reason' invites us to experience language itself *as language* through the destruction of the conventional model of language as a servile mirroring of some univocal, pre-existing presence (residing *a priori* in the mind, in reality or in some transcendental world of Ideas). As Colin McCabe points out in his deconstructionist reading of Joyce: 'Through its constant demonstration of the differences and absences with which language is constituted, writing allows a constant openness to the feminine. *Finnegans Wake* lets the unconscious speak by investigating the very act of writing, it tells us the mother's secrets . . . it suggests that there is a totally different attitude to language which can be characterised as female'[6].

Anna and Issy destroy the myth of the father's phallic omnipotence (Persse O'Reilly/HCE/Tim Finnegan). They do so by frustrating the father's efforts to narrate a centralising, linear story of identity ('to identifine the individuone' per se). ALP deconstructs HCE's phallogocentric claim to be 'constantly the same and equal to himself'; she shows him to be a 'multiplicity of personalities'. Anna is a 'site of salvoceon' for she permits the voices of feminine desire to speak and thus liberates language into its differing discourses. She thereby redeems not only herself and Issy from patriarchal dominance, but also her guilt-ridden husband (we are told 'she made him able') and her schizophrenic sons, Shem and Shaun.

The quasi-divine father of *Ulysses* inscribing 'I am A' in the sand has become in the *Wake* 'mushame' (myself, mise-same, my shame)[7]. Shaun is portrayed as a Christ-like son who 'usupps' the paternal word by falling into the Liffey in a barrel, thus reducing his eschatological father to a scatological 'popodownapapa'. This passage ends significantly with the verbal deconstruction of the son's prayer to the omnipotent father; 'ah, mean' (Amen, Ah men, I mean). Shem and Shaun, the wielders of the authorial literary pen and of authoritative legal power respectively, attempt to take over the patriarchal *logos* – by becoming 'two in one': an interchangeable, self-identical *Ens Causa Sui*. Because he admits to 'talking to myself' and to being 'me atar's ego in miniature', the judge accuses Shaun of homosexual narcissism: "You have homosexual cathesis of empathy between narcissicism of the expert and stetopygic invertedness. Get yourself psychoanalised!' Moreover, the fact that Shem and Shaun metamorphose into Cain and Abel, Adam's sons, further highlights the Joycean critique of the established models of patriarchy[8]. In this way, the *Wake* rehearses the age-old 'family scene' of parricide which Derrida traced back to the Platonic metaphysics of language.

But if Shem and Shaun are to accede to the logocentric throne, they must first steal the secret letters of ALP; they must incestuously violate the mother's word, for she is that 'New Tree Woman with novel inside'. The salvation she offers is not that of a return to some prelinguistic presence but of an endless cycle of ressurrection through language, through words 'returnally reproductive of themselves'. In the concluding pages of the *Wake*, Anna recovers her own voice; she celebrates her 'golden wending' with HCE, not by dying into his fiction of paternal identity, but by rejuvenating herself as the river of Life – the Liffey – flowing back to the sea only to recur again in her 'rain/reign'. This cyclical return of the prodigal mother disrupts the conventions of literary architectonics, founded on the illusion of a centering, authorial *arche*, and replaces it with anarchic, ex-centric discourse. Anna's repetitive word-flux reminds us that life, like language, can never end, can never even 'start to finish'. The logocentric promise to possess an original *arche* or final *telos*, outside of the fallen language of time, history and female desire, is thus indefinitely deferred. And as a result, the very notion of hierarchy – be it patriarchy or indeed matriarchy – is debunked. As Anna declares with stoic but prophetic calm: 'We'll lave it so' (meaning both we'll leave it so and we'll resolve the guilt so, *lavé* is also a poetic term for to wash or cleanse).

There can be no definitive conclusion to the *Wake*. It can only end as it begins, in its own endless wake. Redemption for human kind, Joyce suggests, must be sought by embracing, not eschewing, the temporal recurrences and differences of language itself; it must be sought in the woman's word uttered by the washerwomen: 'talk save us!'

*   *   *

It is no accident, finally, that *Finnegans Wake* is largely written about the city of 'doublin' and presents itself as a self-confessed forgery or fake – an 'epical forged cheque' whose 'last word is stollentelling'. The *Wake* teaches us that history is not derived from some preorginal identity which precedes language, but is a multi-layered story (the French have the same word, *histoire*, for both history and story), a palimpsest of ever-repeatable textual erasures and revisions. Thus history is revealed to be a text of language; not some linear, causal teleology, but a 'circumbendibus' which, like Vico's road, 'goes round and round to end where time begins'. As Maud Ellmann remarked: 'origin exists only in the wake of its own betrayal. . . . Here instead of presence is a wake: a prelude, a waking – or a wake, an aftermath. . . . The *Wake* is never to be present, but is always *coming into*, or *dying out* of being. . . . The word is literally made flesh: the flesh made literal'[9].

Joyce gave expression to his anti-phallocentric sentiments when he defended Ibsen's feminist writings to Arthur Power: 'You ignore the spirit which animated him. The purpose of the *Dolls House*, for instance, was the emancipation of women, which has caused the greatest revolution in our time in the most important relationship there is – that between men and women; the revolt of women against the idea that they are the mere instruments of men'. Joyce recognised that any genuine revolution in our socio-political or literary culture would have to begin with a deconstruction of the 'phallogocentric fallacy'. The fact that Joyce was himself a male writer did not in the least disqualify him from participating in such a critique. For one of the crucial tenets of 'woman's reason' is its ability to surpass the old metaphysical oppositions and to champion the creative coexistence of contraries, differences and ambivalences: it knows that truth is *both* female *and* male, nighttime *and* daytime, Hellenic *and* Hebraic. And this implies in turn, as Derrida notes, that truth is *neither* one *nor* the other. As such, Joyce's 'woman's reason' does not seek to dissolve patriarchy into matriarchy but to *deconstruct* the kind of metaphysical thinking upon which such dualistic oppositions rest. As Joyce makes clear, Anna Livia Plurabelle, the 'bringer of plurabilities', is a chiasmus of opposites: 'Every person, place, and thing in the chaosmos of alle . . . moving and changing every part of the time'.

APPENDIX II:
Joyce and Borges: Modernism and The Irish Mind

(Richard Kearney and Seamus Heaney in conversation with Jorge Luis Borges)

The following interview took place in Dublin on the 16th June, 1982, Bloomsday. Borges had been invited to Dublin by the Joyce Centenary Committee to honour Ireland's writer one hundred years after his birth. Borges first read Joyce in 1922 when a friend presented him with a first edition copy of *Ulysses*. In 1925 he published a remarkable essay on Joyce and a translation of a fragment from this work in the Argentine journal *Proa*, entitled *El Ulises de Joyce/Traducción de James Joyce, La última hoja del Ulises*.

For some sixty years Borges had, as he puts it, 'walked the imaginary landscape' of Dublin portrayed by Joyce in *Ulysses*. He had experienced Dublin as the exiled Joyce had fictively recreated it – not as a literal but as an imaginative presence. Now that he finally set foot in this labyrinthine city, 'at the ripe old age of 82', he was blind, still compelled to represent its visual contours in his mind, tip-tapping his way through its streets with his probing stick, like the blind man of the 'Sirens' episode. Here he was, reliving Dublin just as the aging Joyce had done – as a blind man's memory. 'Maybe my trip to Ireland is just a dream', he mused. Borges savoured the irony of this impish, almost Joycean, coincidence.

But the similarity between Borges and Joyce does not end, nor begin, with this Bloomsday coincidence. Both are modernist masters of the word, avant-garde non-conformists who pioneered new forms of literary creation (the compressed, parabolic fiction of Borges, the expansive, epic prose of Joyce); both promoted the paradox that an international literary consciousness may be forged from the vernacular and lived experiences of its authors; and both believed in a cyclical metaphysics of time, convinced that the worlds of reality and fiction continually intertwine, the meaning of human history revealing itself like the Vico road, in *Finnegans Wake*, turning round and round 'to end where terms begin'. Finally, Joyce and Borges both subscribed to the notion of the artist as *émigré*. Borges insists on the importance of his extended journeys abroad as a young man, and particularly his sojourn in Geneva (1914–1921) where he first discovered Conrad, Baudelaire and Joyce and joined, as he put it, the 'international modernism of letters'. This discovery of European culture was, he insists, really a rediscovery of himself as an 'expatriated European'. His own experiments in writing, he decided, would try to remain faithful to the rich multiplicity of European culture as experienced by the European-in-exile which he considered himself to be. If something specifically Argentine remains in his work, it is, he reminds us, because he believes, as Joyce did before him, that the universal can be reached by an abiding, if not always apparent, fidelity to the genesis-glance of the particular.

*   *   *

Kearney: I think it would be appropriate, since today is Bloomsday and since you are here in Dublin for the Joyce Centenary celebrations, if you could begin by talking about your literary relationship with Joyce. In 1925 you declared yourself proud to be the 'first Hispanic adventurer to undertake the conquest of James Joyce'. How would you describe this adventure?

Borges: Let us go back to the early nineteen twenties. A friend of mine gave me a first edition of *Ulysses* which had just been published by Sylvia Beach in Paris. I did my best to leaf through it. I failed, of course. However, I did recognize from the beginning that I had before me a marvellously tortuous book. But a book of what? I asked myself. Every time I thought of *Ulysses*, it was not the *characters* – Stephen, Bloom or Molly – that first came to mind, but the *words* which produced these characters. This convinced me that Joyce was first and foremost a poet. He was forging poetry out of prose. My subsequent discovery of *Finnegans Wake* and *Pomes Penyeach* confirmed me in this opinion. When I consider novelists such as Tolstoy, Conrad or Dickens, I think of their powerful characters or plots, of the content matter of their narratives. But with

Joyce the focus has shifted to the forms and words of the language itself, to those unforgettably musical sentences that strive towards the condition of poetry. Looking back on my own writings sixty years after my first encounter with Joyce, I must admit that I have always shared Joyce's fascination with words, and have always worked at my language within an essentially poetic framework, savouring the multiple meanings of words, their etymological echoes and endless resonances. My own characters are often no more than excuses to play with words, to enter the fictional world of language. Joyce's obsession with language makes him very difficult if not impossible to translate. Especially into Spanish – as I discovered when I first translated a passage from Molly's soliloquy in 1925. The translations of Joyce into the Hispanic or Romance languages have been very poor to date. His symphonically compound words work best in Anglo-Saxon or Germanic languages. Joyce used prose to produce poetry. And I think all of his works should be read as poetry.

Heaney: I have often wondered about what constitutes the difference between Joyce's use of language in his poems, *Chamber Music* for example, and in his prose works, *A Portrait* or *Ulysses*. It seems to me that in the former Joyce is approaching language as a sort of ventriloquist, he remains its obedient servant, he rehearses a note caught from literature. Whereas in the prose, something cuts loose and comes alive in a new way. Whenever he tried to approach verse directly he seems to have been hampered. Yet it was the inveterate struggling poet in him which enabled him to play with prose in unprecedentedly creative forms.

Kearney: In an essay in 1941 you praised Joyce for having written some of the 'most accomplished pages in matters of style'. Do you think Joyce has influenced your own style as a writer?

Borges: I was very struck by the way in which Joyce dared in *Ulysses* to write each chapter or episode in a different style. My own work also uses a plurality of styles. I'm not sure however that there is a direct influence here. Or if there is it is an unconscious one. The writers whose literary influence I consciously assimilated were Stevenson, Chesterton, Kipling and Shaw, authors I read when I was still a young boy growing up in Buenos Aires and spending a considerable amount of my time in my father's library which contained a remarkable collection of English books. I spent my childhood dreaming with these authors, with Kipling in India, with Coleridge in Kubla Khan, with Dickens in London. This is perhaps where I first experienced literature as an adventure into an endless variety of styles. The library was like a single mind with many tongues. I have been fascinated by libraries ever since (as have many of my fictional characters). I longed, for instance, to work in the National Library of Buenos Aires which possesses over 900,000 volumes. But the year in which I was finally appointed director of this library – 1955 after the fall of Peron – was the year I went blind. There I was surrounded by books I could no longer read. Sometimes I used to pretend I could still see. Even to this day, I occasionally go into a bookshop and buy some volumes so as to deceive myself that I can still read. But I feel uneasy when talking about influences on my 'writing' for I do not consider myself as a writer. I don't write very good stuff and whatever I do write I cannot bear to reread. Nor have I ever read a commentary on my work. My library does not contain one such commentary. I have become famous, it seems to me, in spite of what I've written, not because of it. There must be some mistake, I say to myself. Perhaps people mistake me for somebody else, for some other writer?

Heaney: Perhaps it is Borges rather than you who writes your works?

Borges: Perhaps indeed! There seems to be two of us, at least. The shy, private man and the celebrated, talkative, public man.

Kearney: In the *Argentine Writer and Tradition* you said you felt yourself to be an author 'outside of a cultural mainstream'. Joyce expressed a similar sentiment when he described 'home, fatherland and church' as restrictive nets he would try to fly by, or when he had Stephen admit that he could never feel at home in the English language, that he could never speak or write its words 'without unrest of spirit'. Do you experience such a cultural or post-colonial alienation in your use of the Spanish language?

Borges: It is true that as an Argentine I feel a certain distance from the Spanish mainstream. I was brought up in Argentina with as much familiarity with the English and French cultures as with the Spanish. So I suppose I am doubly alien – for even Spanish, the language I write precisely as an outsider, is itself already on the margin of the mainstream European literary tradition.

Heaney: Do you think there exists such a thing as a Hispanic-American tradition – accepting the fact that all traditions have to be imagined before they emerge?

Borges: It is true that the notion of tradition involves an act of faith. Our imaginations alter and reinvent the past all of the time. I must confess however that I was never very convinced by the idea of a Hispanic-American tradition. When I travelled to Mexico, for example, I delighted in their rich culture and literature. But I felt I had nothing in common with it. I could not identify with their cult of the Indian past. Argentina and Uruguay differ from most other Latin-American countries in that they possess a mixture of Spanish, Italian and Portugese cultures which has made for a more European-style climate. Most of our coloquial or slang words in Argentine, for instance, are of Italian origin. I myself am descended from Portugese, Spanish, Jewish and English ancestors. And the English, as Lord Tennyson reminds us, are themselves a mixture of many races: 'Saxon and Celt and Dane are we'. There is no such thing as a racial or national purity. And even if there were, the imagination would transcend such limits. Nationalism and literature are therefore natural enemies. I do not believe that there exists a specifically Argentine culture which could be called 'Latin-American' or 'Hispanic-American'. The only real Americans are the Indians. The rest are Europeans. I like to think of myself therefore as a European writer in exile. Neither Hispanic nor American, nor Hispanic-American, but an expatriate European.

Heaney: T.S. Eliot spoke of the 'whole mind of Europe'. Do you feel you have inherited something of this mind through the Spanish detour?

Borges: In the Argentine, we have no exclusive allegiance to any single European culture. We can draw, as I said, from several different European languages and literatures – perhaps even from the 'whole mind of Europe', if such a thing exists. But precisely because of our distance from Europe we also have the cultural or imaginative freedom to look beyond Europe to Asia and other cultures.

Kearney: As you do in your own fiction when you frequently invoke the mystical doctrines of Buddhism and the Far East.

Borges: Not to belong to an homogeneous 'national' culture is perhaps not a poverty but a richness. In this sense I am an 'international' writer who resides in Buenos Aires. My ancestors came from several different nations and races – as I mentioned – and I spent much of my youth travelling through Europe, particularly Geneva, Madrid and London, where I learned several new languages, German, Old English and Latin. This multi-national apprenticeship enables me to play with words as beautiful toys, to enter, as Browning put it, the 'great game of language'.

Heaney: I find it very interesting that your immersion in several languages in early childhood – and particularly Spanish and English – gave you that sense of language as a toy. I know that my own fascination with words was keenly related to my learning of Latin as a young boy. And the way words travelled and changed between languages, the Latin roots, the etymological drama; all that verbal phantasmagoria in Joyce also seems to be deeply involved with his conventional classical education.

Kearney: Are there other Irish writers, besides Joyce, that you particularly admired?

Borges: When I was still a young man in Buenos Aires I read George Bernard Shaw's *The Quintessence of Ibsenism*. I was so impressed that I went on to read all of his plays and essays and discovered there a writer of deep philosophical curiosity and a great believer in the transfiguring power of the will and of the mind. Shaw possesses that typically Irish sense of mischievous fun and laughter. Oscar Wilde is another Irish author who had that rare ability to mix humour and frivolity with intellectual depth. He wrote some purple passages, of course, but I believe that every word he wrote is true. . . .

Kearney: Wilde once said that a 'truth in art is that whose contrary is also true'.

Borges: Yes, this is just what I meant by *comic truth*, the truth of fiction which is able to tolerate cyclical and contradictory representations of reality. This is why I say that every word that Wilde wrote is true. I too believe in comic truth. Perhaps it is no accident that my first literary venture as a young man was a translation of Wilde's fairy tales. But there is another Irishman who also fired my imagination at an early age – George Moore. Moore invented a new kind of book, a new way of writing fiction, nourished by anecdotal conversations which he overheard in streets and then transformed into a fictive order. I learned from him too.

Kearney: And what of Beckett – perhaps Joyce's closest Irish literary disciple? He seems to share with you an obsession with fiction as a self-scrutinising labyrinth of the mind, as an eternally recurring parody of itself?

Borges: Samuel Beckett is a bore. I saw his *Waiting for Godot* and that was enough for me. I thought it was a very poor work. Why bother waiting for Godot if he never comes? Tedious stuff. I had no desire to go on to read his novels after that.

Kearney: Your works are peppered with metaphysical allusions and reflections. What is your relationship with philosophy?

Borges: For me Schopenhauer is the greatest philosopher. He knew the power of fiction in ideas. This conviction I share, of course, with Shaw. Both Schopenhauer and Shaw exposed the deceptive division between the writer and the thinker. They were both great writers and great thinkers. The other philosopher who fascinated me greatly was George Berkeley – another Irishman! Berkeley knew that metaphysics is no less a product of the creative mind than is poetry. He was no civil servant of ideas, like so many other philosophers. Plato and the pre-Socratic thinkers knew that philosophical logic and poetic mythologising were inseparably linked, complementary partners. Plato could do both. But after Plato the Western world seems to have opposed these activities declaring that we either dream or reason, use arguments or metaphors. Whereas the truth is that we use both at once. Many hermetic and mystical thinkers resisted this opposition; but it was not until the emergence of modern idealism in Berkeley, Schelling, Schopenhauer and Bradley (whose wonderful book *Appearance and Reality* actually mentioned me in its Foreword: I was so flattered to be taken seriously as a thinker!) that philosophers began to explicitly recognize once again their dependence upon the creative and shaping powers of the mind.

Kearney: How did you first become interested in Berkeley's metaphysics?

Borges: My father introduced me to Berkeley's philosophy at the age of ten. Before I was even able to read or write properly he taught me to think. He was a professor of psychology and every day after dinner he would give me a philosophy lesson. I remember very well how he first introduced me to Berkeley's idealist metaphysics and particularly his doctrine that the material or empirical world is an invention of the creative mind: to be is to be perceived/*Esse est Percipi*. It was one day after a good lunch when my father took an orange in his hand and asked me: 'What colour is this fruit?' 'Orange' I replied. 'Is this colour in the orange or in your perception of it?' he continued. 'And the taste of sweetness – is that in the orange itself or is it the sensation on your tongue that makes it sweet?' This was a revelation to me: that the outside world is as we perceive or imagine it to be. It does not exist independently of our minds. From that day forth, I realised that reality and fiction were betrothed to each other, that even our ideas are creative fictions. I have always believed that metaphysics, religion and literature all have a common source.

Kearney: Berkeley insisted that his idealism was not to be confounded with British empiricism and protested against Locke: 'We Irish think otherwise'. Yeats hailed this phrase as 'the birth of the national intellect'. Do you think it is just a happy accident that your early discovery of the creative power of the mind coincided with your admiration for Irish writers and thinkers such as Berkeley, Shaw, Wilde and Joyce, who had also made such a discovery. How would you account for this shared empathy?

Borges: Perhaps nothing is an accident? Perhaps all such coincidences obey some hidden law, the unfolding of some inscrutable design? The principle of Eternal Return? of a Universal Logos? of a Holy Ghost? Who knows. But as an outsider looking on successive Irish thinkers I have sometimes been struck by unusual and remarkable repetitions. Berkeley was the first Irish philosopher I read, from the *Principles* and the *Three Dialogues* to *Siris*, and even his messianic poem about the future of the Americas: 'The course of Empire takes its sway . . . etc'. Then followed my fascination for Wilde, Shaw and Joyce. And finally there was John Scotus Erigena, the Irish metaphysician of the 9th century. I loved to read Erigena, especially his *De Divisone Naturae*, which taught that God creates himself through the creation of his creatures in nature. I have all of his books in my library. I discovered that Berkeley's doctrine of the creative power of the mind was already anticipated by Erigena's metaphysics of creation and that this in turn recurred in several other Irish writers: in the last two pages of the foreward to *Back to Methuselah* we find Shaw outlining a philosophical system remarkably akin to Erigena's system of things coming from the mind of God and returning to him. In short, what Shaw calls the life-force plays the same role in his system as God does in Erigena's. I was also very struck by the fact that both Shaw and Erigena held that all genuine creation stems from a metaphysical nothingness, what Erigena called the 'Nihil' of God, which resided at the heart of our existence. I doubt that Shaw ever read Erigena; he certainly showed very little interest in medieval philosophy. And yet the coincidence of thought is there. I suspect it has less to do with nationalism than with metaphysics.

Kearney: Your own writing displays a continuous obsession with the world of fiction and dream, a universe of subconscious labyrinths. So dream-like is it on occasion that it becomes impossible to distinguish between the author (yourself), the characters of the fiction and the reader (ourselves).

Heaney: This interplay between fiction and reality seems central to your work. How does the world of your dreams affect your work? Do you consciously use dream material?

Borges: Every morning when I wake up I recall dreams and have them recorded or written down. Sometimes I wonder whether I am awake or dreaming. Am I dreaming now? Who can tell? We are dreaming each other all of the time. Berkeley held that it was God who was dreaming us. Perhaps he was right. But how tedious for poor God! To have to dream every chink and every piece of dust on every teacup and every letter in every alphabet and every thought in every head. He must be exhausted!

Kearney: Several characters in your fictions suggest the possibility of a single Divine mind or Alphabet which conjures up the universe as an author conjures up his imaginary world. In *Aleph*, for example, you seem to be challenging the conventional notion of an individual ego or subject, implying that all human beings may be no more than the *dramatis personae* of a universal play. The hero of this fiction declares at one point: 'I have been Homer . . . shortly I shall be all men'. And in *Tlön* it is even stated that 'it has been established that all works are the creation of one author who is atemporal and anonymous'.

Borges: Schopenhauer spoke of '*die traumhaft Wesen des Lebens*' – the dreamlike being of life. He wasn't referring to some oneiric unconscious sublimation as modern psychology might like us to believe. He was referring to the restless mind in its search for imaginative fulfilment. Though I discovered this metaphysical doctrine in Berkeley and Schopenhauer, I later learned, on reading Koeppea's *Die Lehre des Budda*, that it was a central teaching of Eastern philosophy. This Buddhist teaching that reality is the recurring dream of a Godhead prompted me to write *Circular Ruins*.

Heaney: I would like to come back to the relationship between your dreams and your fictions. Does your dream world actually nourish your writing in a direct fashion? Do you actually borrow and transpose the *content* of your dreams into literature? Or is it a narrative skill that gives the images their shape and form?

Borges: The fictional retelling brings an order to the disorder of the dream material. But I cannot say whether the order is imposed or is already latent within the disorder merely waiting to be highlighted by its repetition in fiction. Does the writer of fiction invent an entirely new order *ex nihilo*? I suppose if I could answer such questions, I would not write fiction at all!

Heaney: Could you give us some actual examples of what you mean?

Borges: Yes. I will tell you of a recurring dream which interested me greatly. A little nephew of mine who often stayed with me and told me his dreams every morning, experienced the following recurring motif. He was lost and then came to a clearing where he saw me coming out of a white wooden house. At that point he would break off his summary of the dream and ask me 'Uncle, what were you doing in that house?'. 'I was looking for a book,' I replied. And he was quite happy with that. As a child he was still able to slide from the logic of his dream to the logic of my explanation. Perhaps this is the way my own fictions work?

Heaney: Is it then the *mode* rather than the actual *material* of dreams that primarily inspires and influences your work?

Borges: I would say that it is both. I have had several recurring dreams over the years that have left their imprint on my fiction in one form or another. The symbols often differ, but the patterns and the structures remain the same. I have frequently dreamt, for example, that I am trapped in a room. I try to get out. But I find myself back in a room. Is it the same room? I ask myself. Or am I escaping into an outer room? or returning into an inner one? Am I in Buenos Aires or Montevideo? In the city or in the country? I touch the wall to try to discover the truth of my whereabouts, to find an answer to these questions. But the wall is part of the dream! So the question eternally returns, like the questioner, into his room. This dream provided me with the motif of the maze or labyrinth which occurs so often in my fictions. I am also obsessed by a dream in which I see myself in a looking glass with several masks or faces each superimposed on the other; I peel them off successively and address the face before me in the glass; but it doesn't answer, it cannot hear me or doesn't listen, impossible to know.

Heaney: What kind of truth do you think Carl Jung was trying to explore in his analyses of symbols and myths? Do you think the Jungian archetypes are valid explanations of what we experience in the subconscious worlds of dream and fiction?

Borges: I have read Jung with great interest but with no conviction. At best he was an imaginative, exploratory writer. More than one can say for Freud: such rubbish!

Kearney: Your suggestion here that psychoanalysis has worth as an imaginative stimulant rather than as a scientific method, reminds me of your claim that all philosophical thought is "a branch of fantastic literature".

Borges: Yes, I believe that metaphysics is no less a product of imagination than is poetry. After all, the ontological idea of god is the most splendid invention of imagination.

Kearney: But do we invent God or does God invent us? Is the primary creative imagination divine or human?

Borges: Ah, that is *the* question. It might be both.

Heaney: Did your childhood experience of the Catholic religion nourish your sensibility in any lasting way? I'm thinking more of its rites and mysteries than its theological precepts. Is there such a thing as a Catholic imagination, which might express itself in works of literature as it did in Dante for example?

Borges: In the Argentine, being a Catholic is a social rather than a spiritual matter. It means you align yourself with the right class, party or social group. This aspect of religion never interested me. Only the women seemed to take religion seriously. As a young boy, when my mother would take me to mass, I rarely saw a man in the church. My mother had a great faith. She believed in heaven; and maybe her belief means that she is there now. Though I am no longer a practising Catholic and cannot share her faith, I still go into her bedroom at four o'clock every morning – the hour of her death four years ago (she was 99 and dreaded being a hundred!) – to sprinkle holy water and recite the Lord's prayer as she requested. Why not? Immortality is no more strange or incredible than death. As my agnostic father used to say: "reality being what it is – the product of our perception – everything is possible, even the Trinity". I do believe in ethics, that things in our universe are good or bad. But I cannot believe in a personal God. As Shaw says in *Major Barbara*: "I have left behind the Bride of Heaven". I continue to be fascinated by metaphysical and alchemical notions of the sacred. But this fascination is aesthetic rather than theological.

Kearney: In *Tlön, Uqbar and Orbis Tertius*, you spoke about the eternal repetition of chaos gradually giving rise to, or disclosing a metaphysical pattern of order. What did you have in mind?

Borges: I enjoyed myself very much in writing that. I never stopped laughing from beginning to end. It was all one huge metaphysical joke. The idea of the eternal return is of course an old idea of the Stoics. St. Augustine condemned this idea in the *Civitas Dei*, when he contrasts the pagan belief in a cyclical order of time – the City of Babylon – with the linear, prophetic and messianic notion of time to be found in the City of God, Jerusalem. This latter notion has prevailed in our Western culture since Augustine. But I think there may be some truth in the old idea that behind the apparent disorder of the universe and the words we use to speak about our universe, a hidden order might emerge – an order of repetition or coincidence.

Kearney: You once wrote that even though this hidden cyclical order cannot be proved it remains for you "an elegant hope".

Borges: Did I write that? That's good, yes, very good. I suppose that in 82 years I am entitled to have written a few memorable lines. The rest can "go to pot", as my grandmother used to say.

Heaney: You spoke of laughing while writing. Your books are certainly full of fun and mischief. Have you always found writing an enjoyable task or has it ever been for you a difficult or painful experience?

Borges: You know, when I still had my sight, I loved writing, every moment, every sentence. Words were like magic playthings that I would toy with and move about in all sorts of ways. Since I lost my sight in the fifties, I have not been able to exult in writing in this casual manner. I have had to dictate everything, to become a dictator rather than a playboy of words. It is hard to play with toys when one is blind.

Heaney: I suppose that the physical absence of pen and being hooped to the desk makes a big difference . . .

Borges: Yes, it does. But I miss being able to read even more than being able to write. Sometimes I treat myself to a little deceit, surrounding myself with all sorts of books – particularly dictionaries – English, Spanish, German, Italian, Icelandic. They become like living beings for me, whispering to me in the dark.

Heaney: Only a Borges could practise such an act of fiction! Your dreams have, quite obviously, always been important to you. Would you say that your capacity or need to inhabit the world of fiction and dream was in any way increased by your loss of sight?

Borges: Since I went blind all I have left is the joy of dreaming, of imagining that I can see. Sometimes my dreams extend beyond sleep into my waking world. Often, before I go to sleep or after I wake up, I find myself dreaming, babbling obscure and inscrutable sentences. This experience simply confirms my conviction that the creative mind is always at work, is always more or less dimly dreaming. Sleeping is like dreaming death. Just as waking is like dreaming life. Sometimes I can no longer tell which is which!

(From *The Crane Bag,* Vol. 6, no. 2, 1982).

3
BECKETT: THE END OF THE STORY?

I: Beckett the Irish Writer: A Contradiction in Terms?

(a) Beckett and The Revival

Samuel Beckett considers himself not as an Irish writer belonging to a specifically Anglo-Irish literary tradition, but as an Irishman engaged in the universal problem of writing. While Yeats, Synge and O'Casey had championed an indigenous literary renaissance and succeeded in founding a national theatre – the Abbey – Beckett grew up in the secluded Dublin suburbs of Foxrock, was educated at Portora in Northern Ireland, studied French at Trinity College, wrote convoluted Italianate poetry and dreamt of getting away to Europe. His early intellectual sympathies were clearly those of 'radicalist modernism'. He sided with the Joycean revolt rather than the Celtic revival.

Beckett bemoaned the insular introspectiveness of most Anglo-Irish literature. He showed scant sympathy for those who chose to write in their native Gaelic and derided the triumphalism of the 1916 Rising. Quite typical is his remark that if all the Irishmen who claimed to be in the General Post Office in Dublin during the Rising had actually been there, the building would have burst at the seams. In an early essay, 'Censorship in the Saorstat' (1929), Beckett accused the Free State government of a 'sterilisation of the mind', exemplified in the removal of every nude from the National Gallery. Furthermore, those contemporary writers committed to specifically indigenous concerns frequently earned Beckett's contempt. He dismissed Arland Ussher's project to translate *Utopia* into Gaelic as a 'futile exercise'; and Austin Clarke, one of the few Irish poets willing and able to continue the Yeatsian preoccupation with Celtic mythology and tradition, was ridiculed in Beckett's first novel *Murphy* (1938) as 'Austin Ticklepenny . . . a distinguished indigenous drunken Irish bard' [1]. 'Not for me all these Deirdres and Maeves and Cathleens', declares Beckett caustically. And in his critical essay of 1934, 'Recent Irish Poetry', the young author is even more unequivocal in his condemnation of the mythologising that had fired the literary imaginations of the National Revival: he pooh-poohs the legends of Cuchulain and Oisin as no more than 'segment after segment of cut and dried sanctity'.

In this same essay Beckett first pronounces, after the manner of Stephen Dedalus, his own aesthetic manifesto: rather than losing himself in antique lore, the artist must cut the cords that tie him to the world that shaped him, to his nation, his family, his tradition. Only by means of such a 'rupture of the lines of communication' can the artist expose and interrogate that 'space that intervenes between him and the world of objects'. Against the *naturalist* thesis which highlights literature's debt to 'objective' environmental factors, Beckett calls in typical modernist fashion for 'the breakdown of the object'. And against the *nationalist* thesis which urged the subordination of the individual subject to a pre-existing mythological tradition, Beckett pleads for a return to the 'existence of the author', to that freedom from any given identity which he calls 'no-man's-land, Hellespont or vacuum'. Henceforth Beckett's writing evinces a systematic suspension of his origins, of that which has determined him at the national, religious or linguistic levels. The Irish Protestant writing in English becomes a nomadic agnostic writing in French. *The vacuum of the author's own interior existence* becomes the singular focus of his work.

A graduate of Trinity College Dublin, Beckett was named *lecteur* at the *École Normale Supérieure* in Paris in 1928. This was to prove Beckett's long awaited opportunity to follow Joyce into exile and escape the prevailing ethos of cultural revivalism. George Moore, an influential revivalist in his own right, had suggested that 'whoever casts off tradition is like a tree transplanted into uncongenial soil'. And in 1922 George Russell, another leading intellectual of the Revival, declared that 'the Irish genius is coming out of its seclusion and Yeats, Synge, Moore, Shaw, Joyce and others are forerunners. The Irish imagination is virgin soil and virgin soil is immensely productive when cultivated'. Beckett, however, would hear nothing of it. The 'virgin soil' of a productive Irish imagination would not be his chosen theme, but the 'uncongenial soil' of his own solipsistic voice. He would write as an inmate in the asylum of the *solus ipse* rather than as an Irishman in his native tradition. His explicit rejection of this national heritage is humorously, if acerbically, evoked in the following passage from *First Love*: 'What constitutes the charm of our country, apart of course from its scant population, and this without the help of the meanest contraceptive, is that all is derelict, with the sole exception of history's ancient faeces. These are ardently sought after, stuffed and carried in procession. Wherever nauseated time has dropped a nice fat turd you will find our patriots, sniffing it up, on all fours, their faces on fire. Elysium of the roofless'[2]. It is little wonder that Beckett refused to return from exile to his native land declaring that he preferred 'France in war to Ireland in peace'.

But it would be a mistake to suppose that Beckett rejected *Irishness* in all its aspects. There were many features of the Irish mentality that fascinated Beckett and found original and often comic expression in his writings. What Beckett could not accept was the revivalist idea of a predetermining, inherited identity. Had he been born in France, – or any other nation, for that matter, with a powerful sense of cultural continuity – Beckett would no doubt have been equally impatient with its particular version of cultural nationalism.

(b) Beckett and Joyce: Asylum and Exile

Shortly after his arrival in Paris, Beckett was introduced by the Irish poet Thomas MacGreevy to the Joyce circle. Indeed he became such a devoted disciple that he was referred to by some cynical observers as 'James Joyce's white boy'. Beckett fully acknowledged that his early work had 'adopted the Joyce method . . . with original results'[3]; and he contributed an enthusiastic appraisal of his modernist mentor (entitled, 'Dante . . . Bruno. Vico . . . Joyce') to the famous critical collection, *Our Exagmination round his Factification for the Incamination of Work in Progress* published in Paris in 1929. But the young protégé soon felt compelled to declare his right to independence. In 1932, Beckett presented Joyce with the poem 'Home Olga' (with its play on *Homo Logos*) in which he announces the termination of his literary apprenticeship. Each line in the poem begins with a letter of Joyce's name and develops an analogy between Joyce and the betrayed Christ. The concluding words '*ecce* himself and the picthank agnus' leave us in little doubt as to Beckett's identification with the peccable and ungrateful lamb who abandons the flock of his Saviour-Rabbi (*Ecce Homo*).

But given their shared commitment to experimental modernism, what was it in the Joycean aesthetic that Beckett sought to avoid? First, at the level of subject matter, it seems that Beckett wished to surmount the Joycean preoccupation with 'exile' which continued to link the author (albeit in a negative manner) to his national origins. Though written or published abroad, *Ulysses* and *Finnegans Wake* were explicitly concerned with Dublin, Joyce's 'first and only love', and with the local and mythic lore surrounding it. Nor did Joyce ever completely deny his allegiance to Ireland, however radically he modified it for his own aesthetic purposes. This sense of allegiance is candidly stated, for example, in his advice to Arthur Power: 'Borrowed styles are no good. You must write what is in your blood and not what is in your brain. . . . For myself, I always write about Dublin because if I can get to the heart of Dublin I can get to the heart of all the cities of the world. In the particular is contained the universal'.

Beckett too would search for the universal. But his search would not express itself in a fidelity to his native place; and even though some of his prose writings in the thirties – *More Pricks than Kicks*

(1934), *Dream of Fair to Middling Women* (unpublished) and *Murphy* (1938) – still carry satiric allusions to Irish characters and placenames, the movement of interest is clearly away from the historical island of Hibernia and towards the metaphysical island of inwardness. Already in *Murphy*, Beckett voices his own conviction that 'asylum (after a point) is better than exile'. The vertical descent into the void of the self, or non-self, is more challenging for Beckett than the horizontal detour of geographical exile from, and imaginative return to, one's beloved homeland. The Beckettian journey is an inner exodus rather than an epic odyssey; his anti-hero is styled more on the Hebraic Job than on the Hellenic Ulysses.

In *Finnegans Wake*, Joyce prophesied Beckett's literary vocation as follows: 'Sam knows miles bettern me how to work the miracle . . . illstarred punster, lipstering cowknucks. . . . He'll prisckly soon hand tune your Erin's ear for you'. While Beckett would indeed fulfil his role as 'illstarred punster', it was not necessarily with a language attuned to 'Erin's ear'. He would write with as much ease and eloquence in French as in English, practising a kind of 'neutralized' language typical of European modernism[4]. The problem of language was truly to be his abiding obsession. But this invariably took the form of a relentless investigation, at once anguished and playful, into the *universal problematic of writing itself*. The questions which haunt Beckett are: How is it possible to continue writing after the 'revolution of the word' which Joyce's radical modernism brought about? What are the conditions of possibility of literary communication given the collapse of traditional systems of meaning which our century has witnessed? Or more particularly, how can modernist writers in the post-war period even begin to express in fictional narrative the insufferable anguish and alienation of contemporary man. 'After Auschwitz, who can write poetry?' asked the German philosopher, Theodor Adorno. This question was also one of Beckett's abiding obsessions. In comparison all efforts to revive national literatures or purify tribal dialects appeared insignificant, if not insupportable.

(c) An Art of Impotence

The difference between the modernist approaches of Joyce and Beckett is, however, perhaps most evident in their respective interpretations of authorial narrative. In his controversial exchange with Israel Shenker in 1956 Beckett is reported to have acknowledged the following contrast between Joyce's writing and his own: 'Joyce was a superb manipulator of material, perhaps the greatest. He was making words do the absolute maximum of work. There isn't a syllable that's superfluous. The kind of work I do is one in which I am not master of my material. The more Joyce knew the more he could. His tendency is toward . . . omnipotence as an artist. I'm working with impotence, ignorance. I don't think that impotence has been exploited in the past. There seems to be a kind of aesthetic axiom that expression is an achievement – must be an achievement. My little exploration is that whole zone of being which has always been set aside by artists as something unusable – as something by definition incompatible with art'. Thus while the Joycean aesthetic aspires towards an omniscient narrator (compared in *A Portrait*, to 'the god of creation . . . invisible, refined out of existence, indifferent'), the Beckettian narrator is one who continually acknowledges his own irredeemable failure.

The narrator in *Dream of Fair to Middling Women*, for example, rebukes the author as absolute master and confesses that 'the only unity in this story is, please god, an involuntary unity', for 'the reality of the individual . . . is an incoherent reality and must be expressed incoherently'. Similarly, in *More Pricks than Kicks*, Beckett cleverly undermines the omniscient stance by making obtrusive critical cross-references from one story to the next. In 'What a Misfortune', he introduces Abba Perdue reminding us that 'she was the nice little girl in a 'Wet Night' '. And in the same story the author even makes disparaging references to his other unpublished work: 'The powers of evocation of this Italianate Irishman were simply immense, and if *Dream of Fair to Middling Women*, held up in the limae labor stage for the past ten or fifteen years, ever reaches the public . . . we ought to be sure to get it and have a look at it anyway'. Later again he breaks off his narrative in a highly self-conscious aside which affirms that it is 'up to the reader to determine' the meaning and he includes a footnote to the effect that one of his concluding phrases constitutes 'a most foully false analogy'. This auto-critique of narrative omniscience is further developed in Beckett's novel *Malone Dies* where the hero-narrator frequently intrudes into his own story with such self-depreciating comments as: 'What a misfortune, the pencil must have slipped from my fingers', or 'This is awful', or 'This should all be rewritten in the pluperfect' etc. Malone, the ailing author, rails against the 'whole sorry business, I mean the business of Malone (since that is what I am now called)'.

But nowhere does Beckett express his rejection of the controlling omnipotent narrator more emphatically than in his *Proust* essay (1931). Here Beckett distinguishes sharply between *involuntary memory* which gives access to the revelation of being on the one hand, and what he calls *voluntary memory* or 'imagination' on the other. Voluntary memory, Beckett claims, 'is of no value as an instrument of evocation and provides an image as far-removed from the real as the myth of imagination'. Involuntary memory, by contrast, suspends our wilful inventions and brings us face to face with the real *suffering of being*. Whereas the images which convention chooses 'are as arbitrary as those chosen by imagination and are equally remote from reality', involuntary memory constitutes a 'mystic experience' irreducible to the self-projecting subjective will. Just as Swann in Proust's novel decomposes the reality of others in the acid of his fantasising ego, so too the fiction-writer runs the risk of reducing the *otherness* of reality to his own hermetic imagination. 'Art is the apotheosis of solitude', Beckett acknowledges stoically. 'There is no communication because there are no vehicles of communication'. Like Proust's Swann, the fiction-writer comes to the realisation that the 'art which he had for so long believed the one ideal and inviolate element in a corruptible world [is] as unreal and sterile as the construction of a demented imagination' – 'that insane barrel-organ that always keeps the wrong tune'[4a].

Beckett thus appears reluctantly to confirm Proust's conviction that the imagination cannot create without projecting its prejudices onto the world. The creative act, he concedes, tends to dismiss as an intruder whatever cannot be fitted into its preconceived pattern, even though 'the essence of any new experience is contained precisely in [that] mysterious element that the vigilant will rejects as an anachronism'. No amount of imaginative manipulation can recreate a genuine experience of the real world. All fiction is in some sense voluntary and therefore a falsification. The *suffering of being* is as unsayable as it is insurmountable; and art is no more than the 'dream of a madman', finding no solace outside of itself or even within itself. Beckett sums up his attitude of sceptical modernism thus: 'Reality whether approached imaginatively or empirically, remains a surface, hermetic. Imagination, applied *a priori* to what is absent, is exercised *in vacuo* and cannot tolerate the limits of the real'.

Beckett resolves accordingly to debunk the narrative strategies of omniscient will by exposing the impotence of human consciousness before the void of existence. This necessitates a rejection of the Joycean hegemony of the word. 'I can do anything with language I want', boasted Joyce after the completion of *Ulysses*. By contrast Beckett, in the last of his dialogues with George Duthuit published in *transition* in 1949, affirmed that the *failure* of his writing is its very *raison d'être*: 'To be an artist is to fail, as no other dare fail, that failure is his world and to shrink from it desertion . . . I know that all that is required now . . . is to make of this submission, this admission, this fidelity to failure, a new term of revelation, and of the act which unable to act, he makes, an expressive act, even if only of itself, of its impossibility, of its obligation'. This aesthetic of submission to the suffering of being, with its disclosure of the impotence of language, constitutes the originality of Beckett's writing and signals its departure from the Joycean aesthetic of omniscience. Beckett's Malone epitomizes this departure when he begs to be released from the 'gossip of lies' that flows from his fiction-spinning mind.

(d) Desophisticating language
But if Beckett refused the Joycean emphasis on narrative

omnipotence, he nevertheless recognised in the master's *Work in Progress* a radically new and challenging approach to *language*. In his 1929 essay on Joyce ('Dante . . . Bruno. Vico . . . Joyce'), the twenty-three year old Beckett formulated what must be considered one of the guiding principles of his own writing: 'Here is direct expression – pages and pages of it. And if you do not understand it, Ladies and Gentlemen, it is because you are too decadent to receive it. You are not satisfied unless form is so strictly divorced from content that you can comprehend the one almost without bothering to read the other. This rapid skimming and absorption of the scant cream of sense is made possible by what I may call a continuous process of copious intellectual salivation'. To avoid such intellectual salivation, and to properly appreciate the force of Joyce's writing, it is imperative, retorts Beckett, not to concentrate on the literal sense or psychological content of writing to the exclusion of the writing itself. 'Here form *is* content, content *is* form', insists Beckett. Joyce's 'writing is not *about* something; it is that *something itself*'[5].

As both critic and author, Beckett fully endorsed Joyce's modernist preoccupation with language *as language*. If Husserl and the phenomenologists announced a philosophical revolution in this century with the maxim 'back to the things themselves', Beckett and Joyce announced its literary counterpart with the maxim 'back to the words themselves'. But while the modernist 'revolution of the word' (to borrow the *transition* formula) expressed itself in Joyce's writing as a triumphal manipulation of language, it becomes with Beckett, in contrast, a stoical subversion of language.

It is significant that when the young Beckett wrote about Joyce in 1929, the question of his Irish origin or his position in the Anglo-Irish tradition did not concern him for a moment. The company in which he placed Joyce comprised not Yeats, Synge or A.E. but Dante, Bruno and Vico – and these, it must be added, only to the extent that they shed light on Joyce's particular concern with language. 'Joyce has desophisticated language', enthuses Beckett, 'And it is worth while remarking that no language is so sophisticated as English. It is abstracted to death'. Beckett's own writing, and particularly his prose writing, testifies to a similar determination to desophisticate the English language. The great lesson he learned from his mentor, Shem the Penman, before taking his French leave, was to show 'how worn out and threadbare was the conventional language of cunning literary artificers', to turn our habitual attitude to language inside out and expose the very working of words themselves. Such was Joyce's invaluable bequest to Beckett.

But what exactly is the habitual attitude – 'the language of cunning literary artificers' – that Beckett and Joyce were so determined to challenge? This attitude is best exemplified by what is known as *classical realism*: a narrative practice employed by most traditional novelists which presumed the literary text to be a medium which carries a message about reality from the author to the reader. This *representational* model, as we noted in our preceding chapter, operated on the assumption that there is a given *reality* and that the narrative discourse of the author functions as a mirror reflecting it. The text is thus treated as an homogeneous, definable *representation* for the reader to translate into a paraphrase of 'intended meaning'. The modernist narratives of Joyce and Beckett, by contrast, insist on the breakdown of representation and thereby expose the complex process of language itself that intervenes between the writer and reality. Exploding the realist illusions of 'cunning literary artificers', modernist fiction deconstructs the conventional notion of the text as a transparent *object*; and, by the same token, it dispenses with the classical realist pretence that the author is an autonomous ego enjoying a privileged hold over reality and deploying the text as a means of representing this reality to others. The Joycean or Beckettian texts serve to undo this supposed *correspondence* between the word and the world. Rather than using language to represent experience, they enable us to experience language through a dismantling of representation[6]. Modernist writers put language itself in question. Trojan horses in the city of the Word, they deconstruct it from within.

Beckett, it may be said, replaces the self-sufficient author of a single discourse with the self-differentiating author of a plurality of discourses. The Beckettian narrator discovers that he is nothing more than the sum of his own fictive discourses. Thus the narrator of *The Unnamable* (1958), for example, exclaims: 'All these Murphys, Molloys and Malones do not fool me. They have made me waste my time, suffer for nothing, speak of them when, in order to stop speaking, I should have spoken of me and me alone'. Yet the narrator realises that the ideal 'me alone' is itself a mere verbal fiction and that as long as he speaks he must always speak in the voice of another, or rather in a multiplicity of voices. For Beckett, as for Rimbaud before him, *'Je est un autre'*. To change one's language, just as to change one's national abode or narrative voice, is not therefore a betrayal of identity – for there is no *identity* to betray. And the very idea of an 'Irish' or 'French' writer is a contradiction in terms, for national identities and traditions are themselves no more than impostures of language. We are the voices that speak us. Language precedes existence. It determines who and what we are. Beckett's entire literary corpus may be seen accordingly as a relentless deconstruction of the fiction of identity which underpins our traditional attitudes to language and, by extension, to literature. But where Joyce's deconstruction was one of rebellion, Beckett's is one of resignation. He has, he believes, no choice in the matter. In the second part of this chapter we offer a detailed analysis of this deconstructive practice as it progressively unfolds in Beckett's prose writings. (The impact of this practice on his drama is examined separately in an appendix to this chapter).

II: Beckett and The Deconstruction of Fiction

(a) The Early Novels: Beyond The Fiction of Self-Identity
    Already in his first published novel, *Murphy* (1938), Beckett
satirises the illusion of self-identity. Beckett's literary and philosophical preoccupations are so intimately connected that one cannot
fully appreciate the originality of his writing without some grasp of
the metaphysical ideas it rehearses and challenges[7]. Western
metaphysics, from Plato onwards (as noted in the appendix to our
previous chapter), has defined the ideal state of Being as a timeless
'presence' which is self-sufficient and self-identical. Thus God, the
Supreme Being, is referred to as *Ens Causa Sui, Ipsum Esse
Subsistens* or *Nunc Aeternum* – an entity existing above and beyond
the human world of temporal flux and movement. The intellectual
dimension of the human subject is deemed to participate in this
Divine Being to the extent that it rises above its mortal physical
existence, that is, transcends time so as to become absolutely self-
present, at one with itself. This is the essence of the Cartesian
attempt to found a self-contained thinking subject (or *Cogito*) which
Beckett exposes to ridicule[7a].
    Murphy wishes to be alive and dead simultaneously: to be
atemporal while existing temporally, to jump out of his own skin. He
refers to this post-mortem mortality as his 'Belacqua bliss', alluding
thereby to the Dantesque vision of a timeless paradise (a vision
which Beckett denounced in his Joyce essay as 'the static lifelessness of unrelieved immaculation'). Thus Murphy aspires to a Divine
condition of absolute self-sufficiency. Though he is desired and
needed by others – Celia, Miss Counihan, Neary, Wylie – Murphy
desires and needs no one. For human desire, as Aristotle pointed
out, already implies movement beyond the *self* towards the *other*;
and Murphy's whole existence is modelled on the Aristotelian ideal
of a Divine 'Unmoved Mover' (represented by his rocking chair).
Murphy wishes to reduce the world to the sealed-off cloister of his
own 'ipssimosity'. Hence the appropriateness of his death in a
lunatic asylum totally sequestered from the outside world. Murphy's
project is to become absolutely present to himself by excluding all
that is other than himself. In the nirvana of the isolated ego he
expects to accomplish his eternal self-realisation.
    But Beckett satirically exposes the folly of this endeavour. In
chapter six, Murphy's Leibnizean ideal of splendid self-adequacy is
subjected to parody: 'Murphy's mind pictured itself as a large hollow
sphere, heremetically closed to the universe without. . . . Nothing
ever had been, was or would be in the universe outside it but was
already present as virtual, or actual, or virtual rising into actual, or
actual falling into virtual, in the universe inside it . . . his mind was a
closed system, subject to no principle of change but its own, self-
sufficient and impermeable to the vicissitudes of the body'. Beckett

introduces the chapter with the heading, *Amor intellectualis quo Murphy se ipsum amat*, an explicit reference to the metaphysical definition of God, in common currency since Augustine, as that Love which is sufficient unto itself (*Amor quo Deus se Ipsum amat*). This definition is modelled, in turn, on the Aristotelian ideal of an incorporeal self-thinking thought (*noesis tes noeseos*), an ideal which the author of *Murphy* never ceases to satirically undermine.

In *What Is Literature?* Sartre argued that a writer's style or technique refers us back, implicitly or explicitly, to his metaphysics. This is certainly true of Beckett. Like many of the great modern novelists, from Tolstoy and Dostoevsky to Mann and Camus, Beckett's literary inventions are inseparable from fundamental philosophical projects. His project in *Murphy* is to challenge the traditional doctrine, advanced by the eponymous anti-hero himself, that man can be identified as a timeless, silent and immutable consciousness. Already in this first novel, he wittily demonstrates that we are bodily beings bound irremediably to speech, movement and time.

Beckett's assault on the fiction of identity becomes more explicit in his subsequent novel *Watt* (1944). Here Beckett engages in a painstaking, and at times mischievous, critique of the conventional notion of language as a naming process. Language has been traditionally defined as a set of proper names corresponding to a correlative set of univocal objects or essences. Watt's endeavour to establish a fool-proof logic of names reiterates the metaphysical ideal of a perfectly transparent language. But the enigmatic events in Mr. Knott's house prove refractory to Watt's naming system. His method for transmuting 'disturbance into words' is far from infallible. By the end of the novel the reader is made painfully aware, even if the tone is playful, of Watt's utter inability to establish language as a self-sufficient totality capable of explaining or containing reality. Language unveils itself as the irreducible reminder of man's tragic-comic fallibility[8].

As the novel proceeds the comforting illusion that there exists an authorial language able to classify reality is progressively undermined. In Mr. Knott's house, for example, Watt discovers a world resistant to the fixities of naming. 'Looking at a pot, for example, or thinking of a pot, at one of Mr. Knott's pots, of one of Mr. Knott's pots, it was in vain that Watt said, Pot, pot . . . . it resembled a pot, it was almost a pot, but it was not a pot of which one could say, Pot, pot and be comforted.' Mr. Knott, as his name suggests, exemplifies that force of nothingness which, as the existentialists have argued, shocks us out of our habitual attitude to things and, filling us with 'dread', reveals the world in all its unassailable otherness. The elusive Mr. Knott, like Malone after him, illustrates the enigmatic maxim of Beckettian philosophy that 'nothing is more real than nothing'[9]. The more Watt pursues his goal of explaining the nothingness at the heart of existence, the more he becomes aware of the impossibility of ever finding names for the unnamable. Thus Watt is forced to acknowledge that the self is no more self-contained than the square root of two. Just as the ideal language of mathematics can be exploded from within by the recurring decimal $52.285714....$, so too the so-called 'identity' of the self is irreparably subject to the haemorrhage of differentiation. The human self bleeds into the void of language.

What we traditionally took to be a pre-established harmony between words and things is in truth, Watt discovers, no more than a 'pre-established arbitrary'. Language itself is a shifting process of differentiation which we seek to conceal and stabilize by granting it an origin outside of time. But Watt's reflections on the temporal anomalies of the comings and goings of Mr. Knott's three servants Tom, Dick and Harry, brilliantly serve to highlight the tortuous paradox of *time*, the fallaciousness of that eternal 'freedom of indifference' so ardently coveted by Watt, Murphy and other Beckettian narrators. 'It is useless not to seek, not to want' (confesses another of Knott's servants, Arsène) for we are condemned to desire, to exist in time, transcending what we are not (Knott). Thus are we condemned to speak our *failure to be*. In the *Addenda* to the novel, Beckett goes so far in his liquidation of self-identity as to exhort the reader to 'change all the names'. And lest we presume to equate his writing with some fixed symbolic meaning referring to something *outside* of the text, he adds his much quoted caveat: 'no symbols where none intended'.

(b) Molloy: The Demise of the Narrative Ego

In *Molloy* (1955), the first and most accomplished novel of his trilogy, Beckett intensifies his attack on the classical notion of the authorial subject (thus fulfilling his early promise to explore the problematic 'existence of the author'). Since Molloy, the book's garrulous narrator, is unable to discover a stable ego either in himself or in his fictive pseudo-selves, the whole structure of a traditional plot with a beginning, middle and end has to be abandoned. Molloy's narrative turns in a vicious circle and thereby excludes the possibility of a linear sequence. The end of the novel is in fact the writer writing the beginning: the narrator alone in his room narrating and re-narrating for some unknown author 'who gives him money and takes away the pages'.

Beckett's intention in the trilogy is twofold: to debunk the classical structure of the novel as a linear quest wherein a subject progresses towards the discovery of a real or transcendental self; and to dismantle the idea of a privileged meta-language (usually that of an omniscient narrator) serving to assess and situate the various other discourses in the text. By parodying Molloy's authorial discourse, Beckett sabotages the standard claim of 'classical realism' to a 'representable' meaning. Words never correspond to reality –

Molloy admits that 'what really happened was quite different'.

The narrating ego is thus doomed from the outset. Beckett creates Molloy who confesses to have 'spoken of himself as [he] would have of another'; Molloy creates a sub-self Malone, who in turn regenerates himself in an endless series of 'vice-existers'. The author, as Beckett demonstrates with his characteristic passion for narrative anarchy, can enjoy no controlling meta-discourse which would permit him to identify himself *outside* of the text as original source of the story. The author has no identity apart from that of his characters; and his characters have no identity. The writer *is* his writing and his writing is arbitrary, without beginning or end, impotent. The omniscient narrators of the classical novel have had their day, as one of Molloy's vice-narrators complains, 'those old craftsmen whose race is extinct and the mould broken'. Beckett's own confession of authorial impotence to George Duthuit gives us a further chilling insight into this dilemma: 'There is nothing to express, nothing with which to express, together with the obligation to express'.

In something of a love-hate manner, Beckett presents Molloy as an author in search of a story which might furnish him with a new-found sense of selfhood. Through fiction, Molloy hopes to tell the tale of himself, to remember himself, his name, his birthplace, to retrace his existence back to its origins, to his deaf blind mother Mag with whom he could only communicate by knocking on her skull ('one knock meant yes, two no, three I don't know, four money, five goodbye'). It is precisely this kind of deflationary humour which flouts the very seriousness of Molloy's enterprise. Moreover, the narrator himself is all too aware that in writing of his origins he is merely spinning an elaborate myth: 'I speak in the present tense, it is so easy to speak in the present tense when speaking of the past. It is the mythological present, don't mind it'.

Furthermore, Beckett doesn't allow us to forget for a moment that Molloy has as many *selves* as he has *stories* to tell of himself, each from a different perspective: 'Chameleon in spite of himself, there you have Molloy, viewed from a certain angle'. Though Molloy's reason for recounting his past is 'to be a little less in the end, the creature you were in the beginning, and the middle', he realises that the idea of a developing self-identity is itself a mere invention of words. This terrifying realisation is expressed in one of the most iconoclastic prose passages composed by Beckett:

> Even my sense of identity was wrapped in a namelessness often hard to penetrate . . . there could be no things but nameless things, no names but thingless names. I can say that now, but after all what do I know now about then, now when the icy words hail down upon me, the icy meanings, and the world dies too, foully named. All I know is what the words know, and the dead things, and that makes a handsome little sum,

with a beginning, a middle and an end as in the well-built phrase and the long sonata of the dead. And truly it little matters what I say, this or that or any other thing. Saying is inventing.

But to make matters worse – and Beckett simply thrives on making matters worse – it appears that it is not we who invent words but words that invent us. Whether we will or not we are condemned to language. 'You invent nothing, you think you are inventing, you think you are escaping, and all you do is stammer out a lesson, the remnants of a pensum one day got by heart and long forgotten, life without tears, as it is wept.'

Beckett's obsession with the *suffering of being* springs from his awareness that language – and more particularly writing – is a process of dying. Language brings us face to face with our own mortality by making us aware that we can never escape from time so as to become fully present to ourselves. We are finite, temporal, de-centred beings who, as the structuralists declare, are *spoken by* language before we choose to *speak* it[10]. This dissolution of the autonomous humanist subject (or the 'disappearance of man' in Foucault's phrase) into the shifting, impersonalising structure of language, is what Beckett refers to as the 'deanthropomorphization of the artist'[11].

(c) Malone Dies: Somewhere in the Void

In the second novel of the trilogy, *Malone Dies*, (1956) Beckett's chosen theme is, once again, the writer trapped in the purgatory of fiction. Malone, like all the other Beckettian authors, writes in order to absolve himself from the obligation of writing. He speaks in order to stop speaking. But the circle is more vicious here than in any of the previous novels.

Malone begins by telling himself four stories 'almost lifeless, like the teller'. But unlike Molloy before him, Malone is absolutely with-out illusions. He realises from the outset that he 'shall not succeed any better than hitherto', and shall only end up finding himself 'abandoned in the dark, without anything to play with'. So that no sooner has he begun his first story (about a boy named Sapo) than he retracts it and goes on to the next: 'Already I forget what I have said. That is not how to play . . . perhaps I had better abandon this story and go on to the second, or even the third . . .'. Malone is helpless before the flux of language: 'Words and images run riot in my head, pursuing, flying, clashing, merging, endlessly'. He seeks to get beyond this textual tumult to a calm, a silence, a self. This, however, is not permitted for 'when I stop, as just now, the noises begin again, strangely loud, those whose turn it is'. The narrator is unable to represent any credible reality; but he is equally incapable of abstaining from the activity of writing. 'I did not want to write, but I had to resign myself to it in the end', confesses Malone. What is more, Malone is disturbingly aware that he himself is just one *persona* in another narrator's play of words. 'You may say it is all in my head', he interjects, 'and indeed sometimes it seems to me I am in a head and that these eight, no six, these six planes that enclose me are of solid bone'. Not surprisingly, Malone also revokes his own stories (those of Sapo, the Lamberts, Macmann). 'My stories are all in vain', he repeats, self-consciously rebuffing his own style as 'innumerable babble'. Thus, once more, the classical myth of narrative as an adequate representational correspondence between narrating subject and narrated object is exposed in mock-heroic fashion: 'The subject falls far from the verb and the object lands somewhere in the void'. And as the illusion of representation dissolves, language itself, as that irrepressible process of signifying without origin or end, forces itself to the forefront of the reader's attention. Beckett's narrators are perpetual transients of the word, migrants incapable of receding from that endless play of language which Lévi-Strauss has called the 'superabundance of signifiers'.

Subtly undermining our accredited notions of plot, character and even punctuation, Beckett obliges us to acknowledge that meaning is not something originating from an extra-textual world to be subsequently reproduced by language. Meaning can only be produced through the labour of speaking, writing and reading, through the interminable differentiation of signs. Incapable of bringing the Beckettian text to a close the reader discovers that there is no pre-linguistic identity to return to. The self covered by the mask of fiction is itself but a mask; each mask being the mask of a mask just as each story is the story of a story. In this way Beckett *implicates* the reader in the text itself; he makes him aware that there is no authentic or 'original' version of a text, only endless translations; no single factual meaning, only interpretations; no truth, only parodies. We are thereby revealed to ourselves, in fear and trembling, *as language*, as continuous dispersion into multiple discourses, as beings who are always *other* than what we say we are, irremediably exposed to the metamorphosis of language.

To read Beckett is therefore to discover that the meaning of our existence is not *literal* but *figurative*; and this discovery, brought about by the self-dissassembling of the Beckettian narrative disrupts our established vision of things. His radical *technics* of formal experimentation – to borrow Sartre's formula – refer us to an equally radical *metaphysics*[12].

(d) The Unnamable: A Hell of Stories

The Unnamable (1958) begins where *Malone Dies* left off – with the admission that we can never forestall the disseminating play of language. But the admission has become more vehement and more uncompromising by virtue of its repetition. (And *repetition* or 'supplementarity' is, as Derrida notes, the *modus operandi* of the self-deconstructing writing process). The very *contents* of writing, those vibrant flesh and blood characters and events that make fiction so satisfying, have not survived the purges of the previous novels. Only the metaphysical *problem* of writing remains. 'Whereof I cannot speak, thereof I will be silent', Wittgenstein once asserted. But Beckett, a less quietistic philosopher of language, cannot be silent though he has no longer anything of which to speak. For even if the author stops inventing new stories the old ones repeat themselves. He will go on trying to name the unnamable. 'I seem to speak', declares the narrator whom Beckett leaves without name, 'it is not I, about me . . . I shall have to speak of things of which I cannot speak . . . I shall never be silent – never'.

This final novel of the Trilogy is in fact a never-ending preliminary to a novel that never begins. Here the narrator passes in review all of his previous narrators – Malone, Molloy, Murphy etc. – commenting on their successive failures. Once again we witness a baffling interchangeability of narrator and narrated: 'Malone is there. . . . He passes before me at doubtless regular intervals, unless it is I who pass before him. . . . I like to think I occupy the centre but nothing is less certain'. The decentered narrator tries desperately to 'attribute a beginning', a definitive and definable origin, to himself; but he cannot, he remains unnamed and unnamable. And yet he is cruelly condemned to go on *searching* for names, for that ultimate conclusion which would grant him an identity and permit silence. 'I hope this preamble will soon come to an end', exclaims the author after thousands of faltering fine-spun words, 'and the statement begin that will dispose of me'. But in the inevitable absence of such a statement he is doomed to go on – 'murmuring my stories, my old story, as if it were for the first time'. The writer thus finally comes face to face with the brutal metaphysical truth that his world is merely a fiction of language which in turn sustains the fiction of himself as author. The only solution – which of course is no solution – is to accept, with a sort of perverse *amor fati* the ineluctable 'hell of stories', relinquishing one's will to power, one's will to be oneself. Beckett has rarely expressed the stoic hopelessness of the authorial quest so movingly:

> This voice that speaks, knowing that it lies, indifferent to what it says, too old perhaps and too abused ever to succeed in saying the words that would be its last, knowing itself useless and its uselessness in vain. . . . I can't stop it, I can't prevent it, from tearing me, racking me, assailing me. It is not mine, I have none, I have no voice and must speak, that is all I know . . . of what I must speak, with this voice that is not mine, but can only be mine . . . in obedience to the unintelligible terms of an incomprehensible damnation.'

(e) How It Is: The Obituary of the Novel

In 1961 Beckett published what appears to be his last attempt at a full length novel, *Comment C'est* (published in English in 1964 as *How It Is*). The original French title is an ironic pun on *commencer*, meaning to begin, or in context, to begin all over again. Composing a magnificently poignant and torrential prose, bereft of plot, character, syntax and punctuation, Beckett was to pen here his obituary of the novel form. In a letter to Jack Schwartz in 1959, Beckett admitted that the bottomless pit of *How It Is* is 'as dumb of light as the Fifth Canto of Hell' (an admission that recalls the definition of hell in his early Joyce essay as 'the static lifelessness of unrelieved viciousness')[13].

Here the narrator inhabits the subterranean darkness of a Platonic cave – the original starting point of Western metaphysics; but, in contradistinction to Plato's optimistic allegory, the nostalgic desire for the world of truth 'up there in the light' is forever unfulfilled. This denial is ingeniously expressed in Beckett's very style of writing. The words are meticulously defused by the author and exposed as artifices; they fold back upon themselves and refuse to serve as metaphors pointing beyond (*meta-phorein*) language to some transcedent meaning. In this way the very structure of the narrative belies the traditional illusion of language as a journey *progressing* upwards toward an ultimate transcendental meaning (*logos*). By reducing writing to a language without names, without the redemptive magic of transcendence or light (as ultimate metaphysical origin prior to language), Beckett pronounces a mordant critique of the 'logocentric' philosophy of Western humanist civilization.

How It Is parodies the classical quest-structure of the novel as a linear journey wherein the hero progresses from ignorance to insight[14]. Beckett achieves this with habitual comic cruelty by portraying the narrator as an abandoned vagabond, crawling through slime and darkness, ten yards at a time, trailing after him a sack of sardine tins (his daily sustenance) and muttering meaningless ditties 'qua qua'. Death would represent a satisfactory termination to this *navigatio* that goes nowhere; but even this, alas, is indefinitely postponed. And so the narrator's discourse turns in a circle, returning to the beginning to end, symmetrically but absurdly, with the pun *comment c'est*. Beckett's deconstructive approach to the traditional novel of quest remains unswervingly consistent from start to finish.

(f) The Shorter Prose: Textes Manqués of Another Voice

Having apparently exhausted the traditional resources of the novel, Beckett has had increasing recourse to what may prove to be (along with drama) the most resilient genre of his literary corpus: the shorter prose experiments. Here there is nothing to be proved, nothing to be done; the texts are anti-texts, 'texts for nothing'. In these *écrits manqués*, which Beckett also refers to as his *nouvelles* or *residua*, the self-negation of language seems capable of persevering indefinitely. The collected shorter prose (1945-1966) is entitled, appropriately, *No's Knife* (1967).

The shorter prose texts – ranging from *Texts for Nothing* (1954), *Enough* (1966), *Imagination Dead Imagine* (1965), *Ping* (1967) and *Lessness* (1969) to the recent *Company* (1980) – do not, and cannot it seems, depart from the fundamental Beckettian obsession with the deconstruction of the writing process. The title of *Imagination Dead Imagine* concisely reiterates the essential contradiction involved in narrative's attempt to obviate its own narrative activity. To destroy fiction we must resort to fiction. The word is as inescapable as it is insufferable. Unable to go beyond the paralysing conclusions of *The Unnamable*, Beckett is nevertheless compelled to go on writing, to say and unsay himself again and again. *Company* (1980) is a further reaffirmation of the impossibility of rediscovering some adequate 'correspondance' in or by means of fiction. The first line – 'A voice reaches someone in the dark. To Imagine.' – announces the fiction of companionship which the last word of the text – 'alone' – erases. And the text itself is a replay of this unique theme. The 'other', the companion, who might witness the author's existence, justify his narrative quest and restore his identity, as he lies in the mud, on his back, in the dark, is no more than a ghost of language, as he is himself, one amongst many, a voice uttering a voice uttering a voice . . .

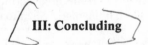

III: Concluding

With Beckett the classical forms of fictional narrative, of telling a story with a beginning, middle and end appear to have been utterly negated. It is, one might say, the end of the story. Nothing remains to be represented in the plot and characterization of traditional narration. So why does Beckett go on writing? Why does the reader go on reading?

The answer perhaps lies in the 'radical modernist' – or perhaps even 'postmodernist' – appeal of Beckett's literary enterprise. Beckett's writing reveals that the story-telling function of language is not just to relay messages or revive memories but to critically explore and expose the fundamental quest structure of human existence. This structure, as we pointed out, is an endless transcending towards meaning. The particular character of Beckett's quest structure is that it leads towards nothing. There is no longer a transcendent meaning that could furnish the narrative self with a fixed identity. The human subject is abandoned to its own devices and desires, marooned on the island of language with no reference beyond itself. In Beckett's texts the metaphorizing of language, therefore, functions less as a means to an end than as an end in itself. And this is, strangely, the power of Beckett's writing. As Geoffrey Hartman has observed in *Deconstruction and Criticism* (1979), the force of modern literature is to reveal 'the priority of language to meaning. Literary language foregrounds language itself as something not reducible to meaning'[15]. Once the transcendental aspirations of language are revealed as misguided – since there is no identifiable transcendence to which it can aspire – the human *quest* is transmuted into *passion* (in the etymological sense of 'patience' and 'suffering', *patior pati passus*). Language is exposed accordingly as the *suffering of being*. In this respect, the Beckettian text can be described as *passionate* writing: a writing which insists on waiting for a meaning which refuses to show up, an absent meaning which leaves traces but cannot be traced, signifies but cannot be signified.

In all this Beckett bears an uncanny resemblance to his counterpart from Prague, Franz Kafka. Kafka described the world of writing as a hell with its good moments. For both of these authors language is a labyrinth where the path leads on indefinitely without ever reaching sanctuary. Indeed a Beckettian narrator might well have uttered the exhortation of the accused in *The Trial*: 'Once you have started on a path, stick to it under all circumstances. . . . And if you fail in the end that is better than if you fail at the beginning, as you certainly would if you retraced your steps. . . . As long as you don't stop climbing, the steps will not come to an end. . . .' One is reminded of Beckett's unnameable narrator concluding his monologue with the equally poignant and paradoxical words – 'I can't go on, I'll go on'. Beckett's fidelity to paradox conveys the hope that the hell of language can perhaps have its comic moments, its happy days. There is a serenity in the failure to find meaning which itself constitutes a strange beauty, the beauty of impossibility, perhaps the kind most suited to Beckett's own particular brand of post-war modernism. Far from being an acquiescent nilhilist, Beckett traverses human suffering and despair in an obsessive commitment to language as a passionate, if always unrequited, waiting.

APPENDIX: WRITING UNDER ERASURE
I: Ending Narrative

Beckett's narrator in *Molloy* ends his story where he began, behind his desk, concluding with the same lines that open the story – 'It is midnight. The rain is beating on the windows' – still subordinate to the impersonal dictates of language, to the 'voice telling [him] things'. The only difference is that time has passed and the original meaning has cancelled itself out. The narrator adds – 'it was *not* midnight. It was *not* raining'.

This double strategy of affirmation and denial is what Jacques Derrida calls writing 'under erasure' (*sous rature*). Meaning is cancelled out by the very language that produces it to the extent that it purports to tell us of something existing *before* language – and there is no such thing. There is no *hors texte*. Language itself is disclosed as a self-effacing or self-erasing process which simultaneously points towards and precludes some pre-linguistic origin of meaning. There is no meaning before or beyond the words that articulate it. For Derrida, as for Beckett, the world is itself a text.

But Beckett, unlike Derrida, will not take no for an answer. He skilfully compels his narrator and reader to go on searching for an absolute origin of meaning *in spite of its non-existence*. His writing thus unfurls sedulously and cunningly, like Penelope's tapestry, weaving and unweaving itself in ever finer, ever more intricate patterns. Indeed, it is a token of Beckett's extraordinary literary talent that he can so deftly spin his web of words as to sustain the reader's interest and excitement in a self-defeating project.

The narrator of *The Unnamable* persists in reiterating the view of his predecessors that the great metaphysical problem is 'how to get back to me, back to where I was waiting for me'. He reckons that if he can re-establish the origin of himself, rediscover his family, his birthplace, 'that unthinkable ancestor of whom nothing can be said', then, at last, he will transcend words. Yet the absurd paradox remains that in trying to name his origin the narrator is forced to speak with alien, borrowed voices. So that, in desperation, he resigns himself to telling 'another of Mahood's stories and no more about it', to make it his 'last story' so as to bring the whole sorry business to a full stop. No sooner begun, however, than the narrator breaks off and censures his own deceit – 'This story is no good, I'm beginning almost to believe it'. Yet after this interruption, he cannot go on because he has no memory of what he has already said. Consequently the story is suspended in mid-course and he has to begin all over again. Amidst all this confusion and indecision – at once fascinating and frustrating for the reader – all we can know for certain is that 'it all boils down to a question of words . . . a question of voices'.

And still for all that certainty, the voices keep on trying to deceive the narrator 'till I hear myself saying, myself at last, to myself at last, that it can't be they speaking thus, that it can only be I speaking thus. If only I could find a voice of my own, in all this babble, it would be the end of their troubles, and of mine'. But there is no single voice that he can call his own and be sure that it is his. 'The subject doesn't matter there is none'.

It also becomes abundantly clear in *The Unnamable* that for Beckett language is naked, utterly devoid of images and things, *incommunicado*. There is no longer any transfer of meaning possible. The words are blank, as the author explains:

That's all words they taught me . . . all the words they showed me, there were columns of them, oh the strange glow all of a sudden, they were on lists, with images opposite, I must have forgotten them, I must have mixed them up, these nameless images I have, these imageless names, these windows I should perhaps rather call doors, at least by some other name, and this word man which is perhaps not the right one for the thing I see when I hear it, but an instant, an hour, and so on, how can they be represented, a life, how could that be made clear to me, here, in the dark, I call that the dark, perhaps it's azure, blank words, but I use them . . . I need them all, to be able to go on, it's a lie.

By describing his imageless names as 'doors' and 'windows', the author is suggesting to himself that they might somehow become referential *meta-phors*, carrying (*phorein*) the self out of (*meta*) itself towards some external reality. 'If only there were a thing somewhere to talk about', sighs the rueful author. But the 'thing' that metaphor is supposed to talk about is itself no more than a metaphor, a figure of speech, a lie. The so called window-doors of words are really hollow metaphors referring to nothing beyond themselves. They are quite impotent to carry the self to some higher being and merely 'open on the void'.

The longed for silence of *self-identity*, where language could supposedly 'correspond' with reality or with the subjective ego, is forever deferred[1]. One story leads into another, one narrator into his opposite, and so on *ad vitam aeternam*. This infinite regress of language (towards some non-existent origin) is what Derrida has referred to as the *palimpsest*, meaning by this that behind every text lies another that has been erased or written over, and behind that yet another, etc. Thus Beckett's nameless narrator exclaims that if only he could synchronize these various stories, voices and pronouns into a single 'original' subject, 'then I could stop, I'd be he, I'd be silence, I'd be back in the silence, we'd be reunited, his story the story to be told, but he has no story, he hasn't been in my story, it's not certain, he's in his own story, unimaginable, unspeakable, that doesn't matter, the attempt must be made, in the old stories incomprehensibly mine, to find his. . . .' In the final analysis, there is only language which asserts and then erases itself, boldly exposing itself as a multi-layered palimpsest of narratives[2]. The conclusion to *The Unnamable* is an apt statement of such self-erasing exposure: '. . . Where I am, I don't know, I'll never know, in the silence you don't know, you must go on, I can't go on, I'll go on'.

But the very impossibility of ending the story is itself part of the life-history of narrative. Kermode makes this point in his study of 'schismatic modernism' in *The Sense of an Ending* when he argues that 'crisis is inescapably a central element in our endeavours towards making sense of our world'[3]. The 'shift towards schism', which Kermode identifies with Beckett's deconstructive approach to traditional narrative forms, retains nevertheless a relationship with narrative paradigms albeit in the form of parody and irony. The schism is devoid of meaning once deprived of all reference to the anterior conditons of narrative: "The absolutely new is simply unintelligible, even by virtue of its very novelty . . . novelty itself implies the existence of that which is not new – a past'[4]. The very notion of a radical novelty presupposes the totality of the traditional paradigms which it seeks to surpass or deconstruct. Nothing, by virtue of a reference to itself only, can ever be *new*. The 'innocent eye sees nothing'. In short, one cannot speak of the *end* of the story without presupposing the prior existence of the story.

Paul Ricoeur develops this point in his philosophical study of the modernist anti-novel in *Time and Narrative* (Vol. 2). He argues that whereas the birth of the novel coincided with the security of 'representational realism' (which masked the insecurity of writing itself as a formal process of composition), the end of the novel exposes the insecurity of ordered composition by shattering the traditional conviction that fiction is a mimetic representation of an externally ordered reality. Thus 'L'écriture devient son propre problème et sa propre impossibilite'[5]. The total refusal of narrative order or coherence would mean the death of the narrative paradigm of storytelling. The end of the story in this sense would signify that modern man has no longer a common experience to narrate. While Ricoeur acknowledges that the anti-novels of Beckett's 'schismatic modernism' or the *nouveaux romans* of post-modernism seem to point towards such an apocalyptic conclusion, he issues the following thought-provoking caveat:

'Peut-être, en effet, sommes-nous les témoins – et les artisans – d'une certaine mort, celle de l'art de conter, d'où procède celui de raconter sous toutes ses formes. Peut-être le roman est-il en train lui aussi de mourir en tant que narration. Rien en effet ne permet d'exclure que l'expérience cumulative qui, au moins dans l'aire culturelle de l'Occident, a offert un style historique identifiable soit aujourd'hui frappée de mort. Les paradigmes dont il a été parlé auparavant ne sont eux-mêmes que les dépôts sédimentés de la tradition. Rien donc n'exclut que la métamorphose de l'intrigue rencontre quelque part une borne au-delà de laquelle on ne peut plus reconnaître le principe formel de configuration temporelle qui fait de l'histoire racontée une histoire une et complète. Et pourtant. . . . Et pourtant. Peut-être faut-il, *malgré tout*, faire confiance à la demande de concordance qui structure aujourd'hui encore l'attente des lecteurs et croire que de nouvelles formes narratives, que nous ne savons pas encore nommer, sont déjà en train de naître, qui attesteront que la fonction narrative peut se métamorphoser, mais non pas mourir. Car nous n'avons aucune idé de ce que serait une culture où l'on ne saurait plus ce que signifie *raconter*'[6].

II: Ending Play

In *Waiting for Godot* (1952), his first play, Beckett pursues his deconstruction of the linguistic fictions which hide us from the *suffering of being*. The genre and idiom of drama offered some release from the dwindling resources of the novel form (i.e. fictional narrative). By supplementing words with the actions, gestures and movements of physical characters on a stage, Beckett was afforded a certain distance from the paradigms of verbal narration. But this in its way indicated a departure from his central obsession with the mortality of meaning – the terminal illness of language. In short, the movement from fiction to drama signalled a renewed assault on the strategies of story-telling.

Waiting for Godot shows how language is 'deadened' by human 'habit' so as to preserve the illusion of commonplace meaning. Vladimir and Estragon tell each other stories in order 'to pass the time'. They are terrified by the passing of time, by the process of dying. 'Will you stop tormenting me with your accursed time', wails Pozzo, reiterating in cogent dramatic terms Beckett's denunciation of the 'time cancer' in his early Proust essay. For time is the reminder that we are transient beings who cannot re-collect our existence into some *original* beginning or *final* end. There is only the passing out – from nowhere to nowhere: the journey is thus transformed into a waiting, an endless, motiveless vigilance. Hence the appositeness of Vivian Mercier's description of *Godot* as a two act play in which 'nothing happens – twice'.

Estragon is the poet who cannot remember. Past events are for him merely traces receding into infinity; they *represent* nothing and might as well be dreams as memories. Pozzo and Godot's messenger deny at each encounter that the previous encounter has taken place. Indeed, all Vladimir and Estragon possess of the past is their story of it. 'To have lived is not enough for them, they have to talk about it'. But they cannot even know if it is really *their* story or merely a repetition of 'all the dead voices' that assail them and speak through them.

Here again Derrida's palimpsest analogy is helpful for an understanding of Beckett's literary designs. It is not only in Beckett's novels that the phrases and characters refer back to each other in a series of internally receding traces; the plays too participate in this regressive game of superimposition and erasure. Vladimir, for example, repeats phrases from Malone and Molloy; Pozzo's orders reiterate Moran's; Godot is a fourth-generation replica of Mahood, Basil and Youdi; and Lucky's diatribe resumes the Unnamable's endless twaddle. This indicates that the entire Beckettian corpus constitutes a cross-textual play of traces where each text refers to a predecessor. The words spoken by Beckett's protagonists do not refer forward to some *symbolized* extra-textual reality. They refer back to some former instance of themselves, some previous textual attempt to get beyond the game of language. 'No symbols where none intended'. We must take the author at his word.

This play of language as relentless repetition is alluded to in the gaelic pun on the name 'godot' itself, *'go deo'* meaning 'forever' or 'interminably'. The theological parody of the play's title is particularly significant with regard to the theme of deconstructing the word, for as Derrida observes in *De la Grammatologie (Of Grammatology*, tr. Spivak, J. Hopkins U.P., 1974): 'The sign and divinity have the same place and time of birth. The age of the sign is essentially theological. Perhaps it will never *end*. Its historical *closure* is, however, outlined' (p. 14). The internal repetitiveness of *Godot* can be read accordingly as a symptom of the 'ending' of the theological model of the sign as a re-presentation of some divine origin of meaning (i.e. presence or the *logos*). This 'ending' can only express itself as *play*. Derrida explains: 'From the moment that there is meaning there are nothing but signs. We think only in *signs*. Which amounts to ruining the notion of sign at the very moment when, as in Nietzsche, its exigency is recognized in the absoluteness of its rights. One could call *play* the absence of the transcendental signified as limitnessness of play, that is to say as the destruction of onto-theology and the metaphysics of presence' (p. 50). In the *Phaedrus* Socrates condemned writing as mere play – *paidia* – and saw it as a threat to the self-sufficient speech of the *logos* which was celebrated as 'being its own father', that is, the source of itself as absolute foundation. If Godot is for Beckett the inevitable absence and impossibility of some transcendental signified, then the play, as a play of different and differing signifiers, can only be a waiting without end, a perpetual deferment of accomplishment through time and space. The characters of Beckett's play are all victims crippled by what onto-theology considered to be the 'original sin of language' (Derrida); for language is ultimately a writing which operates as a sign without a signified, that is, a sign which annuls its own *raison d'être* as linear and accumulative movement towards some teleological signified of final meaning (*Ibid* pp. 86). Beckett's work is perhaps the most challenging literary instance of this contemporary deconstruction of the sign announced by Derrida: ' 'Signifier of the signifier' describes . . . the movement of language: in its origin, to be sure, but one can already suspect that an origin whose structure can be expressed as 'signifier of the signifier' conceals and erases itself in its own production. There the signified always already functions as a signifier. The secondarity that it seemed possible to ascribe to writing alone affects all signifieds in general, affects them always already, the moment they enter the game. There is not a single signified that escapes, even if recaptured, the play of signifying references that constitute language. The advent of writing is the advent of this play; today such a play is coming into its own, effacing the limit starting from which one had thought to regulate the circulation of signs, drawing along with it all the reassuring signifieds, reducing all the strong-holds, all the out-of-bounds shelters that watched over the field of language. This, strictly speaking, amounts to destroying the concept of 'sign' and its entire logic. Undoubtedly it is not by chance that this *overwhelming* supervenes at the moment when the extension of the concept of language effaces its own limits' (*ibid*, p. 7).

In *Endgame* (1957), Beckett's second major play, the critique of language as 'sign' becomes even more radical. Here there is not even the pretence of a journey, of linear progress towards truth. The world is reduced to a single cell inhabited by four characters, only one of whom (Clov) is capable of movement. Nagg and Nell, cripples in dustbins, 'tell stories' of their past in order, like Vladimir and Estragon before them, to pass the time. Hamm, the king piece in this stalemate, and his mindless pawn, Clov, both refer back nostalgically to some original preexistence when language had, if they remember correctly, meaning. But now that language is denuded there is no longer even the illusion of communication. There is only the 'suffering of being' and the irrevocable duty, as Clov reminds us, to learn to 'suffer better'. Hamm undoes the play from the inside by making self-conscious critical comments such as 'This is deadly', 'Not an underplot I trust' or 'I'm warming up for my last soliloquy': comments which express the awareness that he is no more than a chess piece in the endgame of language. It is for this reason that Beckett insisted that the original French title *Fin de Partie* be translated as *Endgame* and not as 'End of the Game' as some suggested. Ending is itself a game. One might even add an *endless* game, to fully savour Beckett's paradox. For Beckett (a keen chess player) is alluding to the technical concept of 'endgame' which is that stage of a chess match where the forces are reduced to such a minimum that stalemate is almost inevitable. Endgame is a game that cannot end, an irresolvable tension between irreconcilable forces.

Endgame is a play within a play: the actors realise that their dialogues are lines written by a dramatist, who is himself merely reiterating his own scenario. Here drama is self-referring, without exit. Beckett admits that in writing *Endgame* he felt 'all dried up, with nothing left but self-translation'. This explains why it is a play 'based on repetitions' and entirely devoid of symbolic references to some ulterior or hidden meaning. As Beckett protested to Alan Schneider after the first French performance in 1957: 'When it comes to journalists, I feel the only line is to refuse to be involved in exegesis of any kind. ... If people want to have headaches among the overtones, let them. And provide their own aspirin. Hamm as stated, and Clov as stated, *nec tecum nec sine te*, in such a place, and in such a world, that's all I can manage, more than I could'. In short, *Endgame* is impotence, but it is, ironically, perhaps Beckett's most perfectly constructed and experimentally successful drama.

Beckett's subsequent plays are progressively futile – if daring – attempts to justify their own existence. Drama, despite its incarnation in gesture and act – which is undoubtedly the main reason Beckett chose it – proves ultimately no more immune to the mortal disease of language than the novel. And drama, it must be recalled, is also a form of language: as Aristotle realised, it is the aesthetic imitation (*mimesis*) of an action. As soon as the action is on stage it is already *re-presented* and *interpreted* by an author, director, actor(s) and audience. Action on stage is itself a *sign*, a semiotic carrier of meaning. Dramatic action is not pure action, pure presence, but is invariably contaminated by the signifying process of language. Drama too is writing.

Each of Beckett's remaining plays features, in ever diminishing detail, the absurd strategies of different narrator-actors to establish their literal but lost identity, to '*be* again' by obsessively re-telling the story of some illusory existence (what Winnie in *Happy Days* (1961) calls her 'happy days'; what Krapp in *Krapp's Last Tape* (1958) calls his 'never to be forgotten' vision; what the characters of *Play* (1963) refer to as the silence of their pre-existence). They seek an identity which might redeem them from the erosion of time and speech. But their supposedly *literal* identities can only be recaptured through the figurative detour of language, which, of course, amounts to saying they cannot be recaptured at all. Krapp cannot catch up with his past self even with the aid of his numerous tape-recordings; and Winnie's 'happy days' are no more than the fabricated ventriloquist sounds which assail her: 'Yes, those are happy days when there are sounds'.

Beckett has declared that 'the best possible play is one in which there are no actors, only the text' (letter to Deirdre Bair, 1973, quoted in her biography of Beckett, 1978, p. 513). In *Play* the three protagonists are reduced to mouths uttering from urns. In *Breath* (1969) (thirty-five seconds of anti-dramatic, plotless, speechless breathing) there are no protagonists at all; only a voice reduced to a trace of itself, an inarticulate whisper. Here Beckett's art seems to go too far, to reach the apogée of its self-negation, the prophetic words of his Proust essay being thoroughly vindicated: 'The artistic tendency is not expansive, but a contraction. And art is the apotheosis of solitude. There is no communication because there are no vehicles of communication'. And when the voice hesitantly returns again in *Not I* (1972), it is only to reiterate one last time, during fifteen minutes of meaningless, actorless repetition, that the I cannot represent itself for it is never present to itself: self-identity is nonsense. With *Not I* and the mime plays (*Acts without Words*) in the seventies and his subsequent TV plays and dance plays for *Süddeutcher Rundfunk* in the eighties (*Quad* 1 and 2), Beckett's revolutionary crusade to 'de-anthropomorphise' the writing process would seem, as nearly as possible, accomplished.

4

A CRISIS OF FICTION:
Flann O'Brien, Francis Stuart, John Banville

What was to become of the Irish novel after Joyce and Beckett? How would it be possible to go on writing fiction once its basic narrative quest-structure had been radically overhauled by *Ulysses* and the *Trilogy*? The fact of the matter is that the majority of Irish novelists continued, as did the majority of novelists elsewhere, in the classical tradition of fiction-writing in spite of the challenge issued by the radical modernism of Joyce and Beckett. In this mainstream tradition of Irish novelists figure such celebrated authors as Liam O'Flaherty, Sean O'Faolain, Kate O'Brien, Jennifer Johnston, Edna O'Brien, James Plunkett, Bernard McLaverty, John McGahern, Brian Moore and others. These writers broadly conform to the structural requirements of classical realism unflustered by the modernist problematic of fiction (though some did, on occasion, incorporate aspects of its interrogative character[1]). A small number of modern Irish novelists, however, explicitly chose to pre-occupy themselves with the modernist critique of writing. In this 'critical' movement of fiction, which we could even call a 'counter-tradition', we might place the experimental works of Flann O'Brien, Aidan Higgins, John Banville and the later Francis Stuart. These authors believe that they can no longer take the novel for granted. Writing in the wake of Joyce and Beckett, they feel compelled to interrogate the very possibility of writing.

In this chapter I want to examine a representative sample of works by some of the major novelists of the Irish counter-tradition – in particular O'Brien, Stuart and Banville. My purpose is to indicate how their writing becomes self-reflexive as it explores fundamental tensions between imagination and memory, narration and history, self and language. In short, I propose to show how these authors share with Joyce and Beckett the basic modernist project of transforming the traditional narrative of *quest* into a critical narrative of *self-questioning*.

I: Flann O'Brien

Flann O'Brien belongs with Beckett to what might be described as the first generation of 'critical' Irish novelists. Like Beckett he

tended to view Joyce's deconstruction of the quest-structure of conventional narrative as a total *subordination of reality to
imagination.* Writing becomes problematic accordingly in that the
writer appears to be a prisoner of his own fiction. We saw, in the
previous chapter, how this aesthetic reduction of the historical world
to the ploys of imagination posed all kinds of dilemmas for Beckett's
narrators as they tried to break free from the tyranny of their own
fiction in order to confront the 'suffering of being'. We also saw how
these narrative attempts to undo narrative, to move from voluntary
imagination to involuntary memory, resulted in failure. Nowhere is
this failure more explicit than in Beckett's late short prose piece,
Imagination Dead Imagine.

Here the narration takes the form, significantly, of a monologue,
in which the narrator finds himself trapped inside a plain white
rotunda which reduces the outside world to a hot white light that
comes and goes. This rotunda is the imagination itself, and Beckett's
point seems to be that even death ('imagination dead') is no panacea
to the solipsism of fiction which simply goes on imagining.
Imagination is the 'eye of prey' which converts all exterior life to its
own currency, which reduces the multi-faceted world to its own
point of view; and for the writer *there is no other*: 'No trace
anywhere of life, you say, pah, no difficulty there, imagination not
dead yet, yes, dead, good, imagination dead imagine . . . world still
proof against ending tumult. Rediscovered miraculously after what
absence in perfect voids it is no longer the same, from this point of
view, but there is no other'.

In Flann O'Brien's fiction the imagination also reigns supreme;
history is no more than a figment of the narrator's own comic
designs. Since imagination consumes everything it imagines there is
no exit from the process of writing itself. O'Brien's novels – or
perhaps post-novels is the more appropriate term – express their
creator's mock-heroic efforts to jump out of his own skin or, like
Pygmalion, to breathe real life into his fictional characters.
Narrative becomes for O'Brien, as for Joyce and Beckett, a
questioning of its own conditions of possibility.

O'Brien shares Beckett's modernist dilemma as a practitioner of
experimental fiction. But his 'critical' approach to writing is also
informed by his own profound experience of social alienation and
depression in modern urban Irish society put into quarantine by the
Second World War and the isolationist policies of the new Republic.
While Beckett depicted the modern ethos of the absurd within the
confines of a nihilistic limbo, O'Brien's novels explore this ethos in
the more localized phantasmagoria of upstart undergraduates,
pseudo-intellectual civil servants and eccentric policemen
confronted with the squalid inertia of Dublin life in the thirties and
forties. Such fictional characters, as De Selby remarks in *The Third
Policeman*, reside in the 'permanent hallucination known

conventionally as 'life', with its innumberable concomitant limitations, afflictions and anomalies'.

Joyce hailed O'Brien as a 'real writer, with the true comic spirit'. There can be no doubt that O'Brien inherited the master's deconstructive approach to the inherited narratives of both classical realism and cultural revivalism. *At Swim-Two-Birds*, published in 1939, is a parody of heroic linear narrative from beginning to end. As with Joyce's *Ulysses* or Beckett's *Trilogy*, the novel here becomes its own critical self-representation, a novel about novelwriting, a narrative which puts itself in question. The opening paragraph is illustrative of this approach:'

> Having placed in my mouth sufficient bread for three minutes chewing, I withdrew my powers of sensual perception and retired in to the privacy of my mind, my eyes and face assuming a vacant, preoccupied expression. I reflected on the subject of my sparetime literary activities. One beginning and one ending for a book was a thing I did not agree with. A good book may have three openings entirely dissimilar and inter-related only in the prescience of the author, or for that matter one hundred times as many endings.

The author having thus included himself in his own novel then proceeds to comment upon the 'examples of three separate openings', directing the reader with the obtrusive editorial headings – 'First opening', 'Second opening', 'Third opening', etc.

At Swim-Two-Birds is as much a mimicry of the conventions of the novel as is *Ulysses* or *The Unnamable*. The traditional queststructure is ridiculed in the aimless wanderings of such Irish legendary heroes as Finn McCool, Sweeney or the pseudo-bardic Pooka Mac Phellimey. By transforming these mythic heroes of cultural nationalism into modernist anti-heroes O'Brien succeeds in undermining the orthodox structures of realist and revivalist narrative. His various permutating characters slide into each other, self-elide, and ultimately expose themselves for what they are – expendable experiments of the author. Such dismantling of the 'individuated' characterization of the traditional novel together with the recurrence of conspicuous editorial interruptions in the text, reminds the reader that he is witnessing not a story but the problematic creation (and destruction) of a story. We are not permitted to forget that character and plot are but figments devoid of all *rapport* with the real world. Indeed Trellis, the writer, is so attracted by one of his own female creations that he ravishes her and produces a son of a 'quasi-illusory sort'. But the 'literary' son conspires with the other characters and together they revolt against their patriarchal author by writing an alternative fiction in which he is arrested, tortured and put on trial. Rather than cohere in a plausible sequence of events, the diverse characters turn against their own creator – Trellis/Flann O'Brien – and transform him also into a fiction.

The narrator's attempt to reach reality via fiction thus constitutes an infinite regress. At the conclusion of the novel, Sarah the maid discovers that Furriskey and his friends are but inventions of her master Trellis: 'It happened that these same pages were those of the master's novel'. O'Brien's Trellis like Beckett's Malone, seems to have become a victim of his own inner voices – 'Was Trellis mad? ... Was he a victim of hard-to-explain hallucinations?' Indeed at this point we begin to realize that Trellis himself is but a fictional creation of another author, Flann O'Brien (who is, of course, himself a fictional creation – a pseudonym – of the 'real' author and Dublin civil servant Brian O'Nolan). We thus understand, in retrospect, that the admonitory notice which prefaced the novel is perhaps a self-description of this solipsism of writing: 'All the characters represented in this book, including the first person singular, are entirely fictitious and bear no relation to any person living and dead'.

Flann O'Brien takes Joyce's identification of imagination and reality to mean that writing is all imagination and no reality. Despite countless ingenious strategies, the author cannot make contact with the outside world. The real congeals into the imaginary like Midas' food into gold. The *search-structure* of traditional narrative is therefore shown to be impossible, for the *sought* is identical with the *searcher* from the very outset. In *At Swim-Two-Birds* the snake of fiction curls up and swallows its own tail.

If Flann O'Brien develops the critical legacy of Joyce and Beckett with regard to traditional narrative, he also inherits their iconoclastic attitude to the National Literary Revival. O'Brien's novels are generally set in deromanticized urban contexts and comically undermine the standard revivalist opposition between the country and the city: an opposition which idealized the rural landscape as a timeless and primeval idyll where the noble Irish peasant could live his life uncomplicated by the social and commercial relations of contemporary urban existence. O'Brien's satirical exposure of 'Gaelic Nationalist rural pieties' is perhaps nowhere more explicit than in *The Poor Mouth* where he explains, for example, how the inventors of the Revival Myth of the Irish countryside choose not to live there themselves because – '1. The tempest of the countryside was too tempestuous. 2. The putridity of the countryside was too putrid. 3. The poverty of the countryside was too poor. 4. The Gaelicism of the countryside was too Gaelic. 5. The tradition of the countryside was too traditional.'[2]

If *At Swim Two Birds* debunks the Anglo-Irish Ireland of Synge and the early Yeats, *The Poor Mouth/An Béal Bocht* parodies the romantic realism of writers like Tomás O Criotháin, Liam O'Flaherty and Frank O'Connor who drew inspiration from the Gaelic culture. Choosing a leitmotif from the elegiac conclusion to O Criomtháin's *An t-Oileánach/The Islandman* – 'I do not think that my like will ever be seen again' – O'Brien (writing under the pseudonym Myles na gCopaleen) mocks the plaintive style of such 'native' literature weighed down by a sentimentalism of grievance and loss. Composed originally in Gaelic, this novel is a hilarious language play of puzzles and puns which could be considered a sort of *wake* to the native tongue, an irreverent testimony to the fact that the Romantic Ireland of the Gael is dead and gone forever.

But O'Brien believed that the English language was quite as susceptible to 'communication breakdown' as the Gaelic. One of his characters defines the narrative as an attempt to 'unravel Babel' – an echo of Joyce's description of the *Wake* as a retelling of the story of Babel. All of O'Brien's novels from *At Swim two Birds* to *The Third Policeman*, *The Poor Mouth*, *The Hard Life* and *The Dalkey Archive* are replete with logical contradictions of sequence and sense, linguistic absurdities and ridiculous conversations conducted at cross purposes. As with Joyce and Beckett, the conventional temporality of linear narrative is 'dechronologised' (i.e. past, present and future are often confused or even reversed); and the quest-structure is frequently negated (as in the erratic wanderings of Sweeney in *At Swim-two-Birds* or the assassinated narrator's futile search for the black box in *The Third Policeman*). Moreover, the narratives themselves almost invariably take place *within* the narrator's own head and increasingly abandon any pretence to 'represent' some external action. In O'Brien's fiction, no single perspective or viewpoint is privileged. All things, as the epithet to *At Swim-two-Birds* announces, 'flee and yield place to each other'. The nameless solipsist of *The Third Policeman* sounds a characteristic Flann O'Brien anthem when he declares: 'I felt my brain cluttered with questions and blind perplexities . . . I felt completely alone'. Thus O'Brien debunks the grand illusion of realism with its attendant conventions of characterisation, sequential plot, naturalistic setting and fixed authorial viewpoint[2a].

O'Brien's writings also engage, finally, in a play of 'intertextuality' where cross-references are found not just within the framework of the author's own works (characters from one novel crop up in the next) but within the framework of Irish writing generally (e.g. the allusions to O'Criomtháin in *The Poor Mouth* or to Joyce who actually appears in person in *The Dalkey Archive*). Radical transgressions of novelistic conventions are witnessed in O'Brien's mixing of multiple styles and conflicting plots – in *At Swim-Two-Birds* he uses four separate narratives simultaneously –and his repudiation of the standard norms of psychological verisimilitude. O'Brien's texts might thus be described as anti-novels in Abrams' sense of narratives 'deliberately constructed in a negative fashion, relying . . . on annihilating traditional elements of the novel, and on playing against the expectations established in the reader by the novelistic methods of the past'[3]. This self-deconstructive logic reaches its extreme limit in the annihilation of the author himself (as in *At Swim-To-Birds*). Indeed this strategy is already evidenced in the author's use of different pseudonyms: Flann O'Brien, the Brother, Myles na gCopaleen. The 'real' author, Brian O'Nolan, vehemently denied any knowledge of his pseudonymous creations. In this respect, Roland Barthes' famous account of the 'death of the author' in modern literature provides an apt gloss on the writings of O'Brien and the other Irish modernists:

> Writing is that neutral, composite, oblique space where our subject slips away, the negative where all identity is lost, starting with the very identity of the body writing. . . . The image of literature to be found in ordinary culture is tyrannically centred on the author, his person, his life, his tastes, his passions. . . . The *explanation* of a work is always sought in the man or woman who produced it, as if it were always in the end, through the more or less transparent allegory of fiction, the voice of a single person, the *author* 'confiding' in us. . . . Linguistically the author is never more than the instance of writing. . . . His only power is to mix writings, to counter the ones with the others, in such a way as never to rest on any of them . . . a text is made up of multiple writings, drawn from many cultures and entering into mutual relations of dialogue, parody, contestation.[4]

II: Francis Stuart

The later Stuart belongs with Banville, Higgins and Jordan to the second generation of Irish novelists in the counter-tradition. Like the first generation, Stuart is centrally preoccupied with the dilemma of writing fiction after Joyce; but he tends to read the Joycean 'crisis of imagination' in a different way. Whereas Beckett and O'Brien struggled with the problem of how to get beyond imagination to the reality principle of historical memory, Stuart construes the problem of fiction as an attempt to escape from the oppressive reality of history into some new imaginative order. *A Hole in the Head*, published in the late seventies and perhaps Stuart's most experimental novel, is a self-reflexive narrative which deals both structurally and thematically with the specific problematic of creativity. Here the Joycean identification of imagination with reality is diagnosed as an excess of the reality principle which threatens to annihilate the possibility of fiction altogether. And so we find a reiteration of Stephen Dedalus' project to transform the imprisoning constraints of history into possibilities for imaginative renewal.

Stuart takes the title of *A Hole in the Head* from the legend of a certain primitive tribe who believed that by perforating the skull of young children they opened them to the influence of good and evil spirits, thus extending their range of knowledge. The hole in the head

is Stuart's metaphor for the imagination. The novel details the crisis
of the creative psyche of the writer in a contemporary Ireland let
loose upon the modern tide of mental and political derangement.

Terrorism and psychosis are for Stuart two fundamental
symptoms of a broken and estranged imagination. Barnaby Shane,
hero of the novel, is, significantly, a writer trying to come to terms
with both these forms of disorder. Shane is haunted by the failure to
write creatively, to translate the unruliness of his society into some
coherent fiction: 'If only I could think of anything but the one rather
hopeless subject – my failure to become the kind of writer I had
dreamed of being'. And yet despite the unwieldiness of his surrounding world, Shane refuses to relinquish his conviction that 'nothing of
any moment could happen outside of my own imagination'. He flatly
denies his psychiatrist's 'distinction between exterior and interior
reality'. But such a denial runs the risk of equating creative vision
and madness.

In general, Stuart seems to suggest that insanity occurs whenever
imagination becomes indistinguishable from reality, no longer
capable of discriminating between its own fantasies and fact. 'What
is dream-within-dream', the author asks at one point, 'what plain
dream, what drug-induced hallucination, and what the reality at the
heart of imagination?' Or again: 'Oh my contradictory yearnings, my
confusing fantasies! The mad shuffling between dream and reality'.
During the course of the novel, Shane has a relationship with his
muse, Emily Bronte, fellow legatee of the troubled Celtic psyche and
former inhabitant of the narrator's divided, schizophrenic Ulster
(much of the story unfolds in Belbury/Belfast). Stuart suggests that
Emily, like the writer-hero himself, was another perturbed imagination prone to violent and psychotic obsessions. On the basis of her
own past experience, Emily warns that unless the writer strives
patiently towards artistic order, his creative energy will degenerate
into hysteria: '"There's always just one more of anything that we're
obsessed and exhausted by". She too knew on a deeper level of
reality than my poor fancies, that the imagination, once aroused to
this intensity, wanted to roam further and further. "One day you'll
transform these passions into a legend, but meanwhile bear them in
patience and silence".' Shane frequently identifies with Heathcliff's
(Branwell's) *dementia*, and on key occasions argues that there is a
very thin dividing line between aesthetic and pathological fictions.
'"Hallucinations?", he asks, "optical, auditory illusions? The tilt of
an axis shifts and a new reality comes into focus".'

The main worry for Shane is that the creative mind often seems
inseparable from the insanity it intends to sublimate. The dilemma is
conveyed by the very instability and disjointedness of Stuart's own
narrative structures. The uneven, irregular quality of the novel's
style, its disruption of normal temporal and psychological patterns,
perfectly embodies the crisis of the novel's characters. Folly as
content echoes folly as form. But Stuart's whole effort is to show that

there is method in this madness, at both levels. Shane is surely speaking the mind of his author when he remarks that 'Drugs alone could not have induced in me a state in which the puzzle of Emily Bronte could have become clear. They played a part but it required an imaginative, not to say unbalanced temperament like mine, which at the same time felt very close to the subject, to barely solve it. A fiction writer with guilt and obsession of his own knows more about secret and shameful passions than the more sober research worker in the literary field'. Shane dismisses the mediocre conventions of 'medium-mix-fiction' precisely because it lacks all 'energy' and 'obsession'; and Shane's young lover, Claudia, claims that she has been committed to the Kye Sanitorium because like the writer, 'her imagination runs away with her too'. To the Reverend Mother's declaration that Claudia has a 'distorted imagination', Shane replies that the 'very valuable [are] driven to fantasy by their psychology'; and he well might have added, to *crime*. On this work, as in his earlier novel, *Blacklist – Section H*, Stuart is fascinated by what he calls the element of 'criminality in the immensely imaginative psyche' – that is, the potential for transgression and excess. But the difference between the criminal psychotic and the artist is that whereas the former confounds imagination and reality without knowing that he is doing so, the latter can do so while still being able to differentiate between them. As Shane puts it: 'Imaginative people can resolve inner tensions that keep less gifted ones behind asylum walls'.

Stuart's point seems to be that the imagination is a well-spring of creative energy which, if thwarted, expresses itself as mental derangement or terrorism: 'A flood of energy with nowhere to go except into fighting or clowning, apart from an occasional one of you who tries his hand at fiction or poesie . . . fulfilment denied results in violence, yes, but only when fulfilment is desired fiercely enough. Then you have the terrorist, or more rarely, the imaginative artist'. Stuart's writing is a plea for the aesthetic expression of imagination in a world dominated by the 'reality principle' of mediocre politicians. He regrets that 'even a fairly successful writer ranks well below even a minor politician in both parts of this island'; and he proceeds to advocate the need for a 'new mythology'. But for the author Shane, as for Stuart his author, there remains little hope for the creative principle of imagination. If it survives at all, it will only do so in the esoteric sanctum of a small minority of poetic seers: 'The new myths, if there be any, in order to redeem will deal with events of utter obscurity'. The relative obscurity of Stuart's own work is indicative of a certain despair before the despotism of contemporary history – a symptom perhaps of the modern Irish imagination?

Stuart would of course reply that the threat to the creative imagination is not some national disorder but a universal symptom of modernity. 'All over the globe', as the narrator of *A Hole in the Head* remarks, 'a tiny invisible fungus is annulling the nucleic acids which, as we know, are the basis of the imagination'. The contemporary society of Western materialism and consumerism is, for Stuart, so concerned with 'facts' that it produces a kind of collective banality. Under such a dictatorship of the 'reality principle' the only hope for imaginative life is to be found in the esoteric art of the individual. This is a typically modernist stance. But here, as elsewhere, Stuart is closer to the radical modernism of Beckett than to the revivalist modernism of Yeats. As he made plain in a *Crane Bag* interview in 1979, entitled 'Novelists on the Novel', the idea of a national literary movement offers no real salvation for the modern Irish writer:

> National literature is to my mind a meaningless term. Literature can't be national. Literature is individual. Nationality has nothing to do with it. We have here some outstanding writers. They happen to have been born in Ireland. I don't think they would have been interested in defining a national literature. Let us say there are some writers who are certainly worth discussing as individual writers[5].

Stuart is no doubt referring here to the Irish writers of the critical counter-tradition. The outstanding writer for Stuart is always outside of the mainstream. He or she is obsessed not with nations or traditions or collective memories but with the artistic processes of language, imagination and creativity. 'The nightmare of history' can only be redeemed, if at all, by the metaphysical magic of the solitary artist. Modernist fiction, Stuart believes, is 'being driven into a corner' by the contemporary craving of Western society 'for more and more facts'. Stuart considers the return of art to itself to be a good thing because the traditional realist novel 'became too spread out and tried to do all sorts of things, to describe and to comment and so on'. Modernist fiction, by contrast, is being 'forced to do the one thing it can do supremely well, better than science and better than any of the other art forms: to delve deeper and deeper into the self, into the human system'. Stuart concludes accordingly: 'I have an obsession with Art as one of the few hopes in a darkening world . . . I'm not interested in the normal work of fiction . . . the work that never sets out to do more than tell a story, entertain, give a twist, give facts'[6].

III: John Banville

Banville also shares the post-Joycean obsession with the possibility/impossibility of writing, and more particularly with the problematic rapport between narrative and history. His central role in the critical counter-tradition of Irish writing becomes quite explicit in his third novel, *Birchwood*, where he parodies the Big

House genre which had become the stock in trade of much traditional Anglo-Irish ficton. Agreeing with Stuart's indictment of the 'soft
centre' of mainstream Irish fiction as a sort of 'literary knitting'
Banville sets out in *Birchwood* to challenge the clichés of traditional
narrative. The novel opens with the narrator self-consciously arrang-
ing the materials for his story and proclaiming his intention faithfully
to record his memories in the form of fiction:

> I am therefore I think. That seems inescapable. In this lawless house I
> spend the nights pouring over my memories, fingering them, like an
> impotent Casanova his old love letters. . . . Some of these memories are
> in a language that I do not understand, the ones that could be headed the
> beginning of the old life. They tell the story that I intend to copy here, all
> of it, if not its meaning. . .

By inverting the fundamental maxim of Cartesian subjectivity, *I
think therefore I am*, Banville's narrator resolves to tell his story *as
it really was*. He asserts the priority of being (I am) over consciousness (I think), thereby subscribing to the claim of classical realism to
use fiction as a means of representing reality in a transparent and
unproblematic way. But the ensuing narrative confounds this
assertion and exposes the impotence of the narrator to go beyond his
own fictional reconstruction; the 'secrets' of being are withheld from
him. So that by the end of the novel the narrator is obliged to
concede that he cannot understand the world or the creatures who
inhabit it. 'Intimations abound, but they are felt only, and words fail
to transfix them'. The author concludes by citing the admission of
Wittgenstein – the modernist sceptic par excellence – in the
Tractatus: 'Whereof I cannot speak, thereof I will be silent'.

Banville's decision to begin and end the narrative of *Birchwood*
with allusions to two of the great philosophical practitioners of
modern European doubt – Descartes and Witttgenstein – displays
not only his preoccupation with the universal problems of modern
epistemology but also his determination to dispel the idea of a
national Irish literature limited to indigenous concerns. As he
explained elsewhere:

> I don't really think that specifically 'national' literatures are of terribly
> great significance. Perhaps for a country's self-esteem lip-service is paid
> to the national culture. We go on and on about our great writers but we
> have very few great writers, perhaps two. Two great writers or even ten
> great writers don't really make a literature. . . . The fact that Joyce and
> Beckett were born in Ireland or even wrote about Ireland is not really
> important. . . . There is an Irish *writing*, but there isn't an Irish
> *literature*. . . . We can't continue to write in the old way. Most of us do.
> Most of Irish writing is within a nineteenth-century tradition where the
> world is regarded as given. Everybody knows what the reality is and
> people sit down to write stories which occur in the known world with

known values. But the modern writer cannot take the world for granted any longer: take Rimbaud's derangement of the senses, take Nietzsche's transvaluation of all values ... I've never felt part of any (national) tradition, any culture even ... I feel a part of a purely personal culture gleaned from bits and pieces of European culture of four thousand years. It's purely something I have manufactured[7].

Not surprisingly, Banville's next three novels after *Birchwood* turned from Irish to European figures. In *Copernicus*, *Kepler* and *The Newton Letter* he explored the great scientific minds of modern Europe. Having deconstructed the worn-out narrative patterns of the Big House novel, unravelling its 'literary knitting' with pitiless irony, Banville investigates the highly problematic transition from the medieval to the modern understanding of reality. In these works, Banville rehearses the modernist obsession with the 'crisis of imagination' and its relationship to the 'facts' of the historical world.

* * *

Doctor Copernicus opens with the hero's first attempts to put names on things as the child Nicholas Copernicus begins to acquire the use of language. From the outset the central dilemma is posed: how can one know reality if the very words and concepts needed to understand it are themselves ways of creatively transforming reality. As he matures into a scholar of the universe, Nicholas comes to realise that 'the birth of a new science must be preceded by a radical act of creation'. But how is one to reconcile the classical desire to 'save the phenomena', to describe reality as it really is independently of human knowledge, with the discovery that all true knowledge requires an imaginative 'leap of creation'? Put in another way, if all theories are but names, but the world itself is a thing, as the Canon teaches Copericus, how can the scientist bridge the gap between name and thing? Copernicus gradually discovers that science is a form of 'ritual' or hypothetical 'play acting' which seeks to transmute 'into docile order the hideous clamour and chaos of the world itself'. But this endeavour to flee from the 'terrors of the world' into some miraculous tranquillity of imaginative order, brings with it a dilemma:

> He believed in action, in the absolute necessity for action. Yet action horrified him, tending as it did inevitably to become violence. Nothing was stable; politics became war, law become slavery, life itself became death, sooner or later. Always the ritual collapsed in the face of hideousness. The real world would not be gainsaid, being the true realm of action, but he must gainsay it, or despair. That was his problem.

Copernicus goes on to make his great discovery that the sun is the centre of the planetary universe and not the earth as had been previously taught by Ptolemaic science. But Copernicus is only able to make his 'leap of creation' by replacing the claim of traditional science to 'save the phenomena' with an act of imaginative faith which transcends the phenomena. In short, science cannot reach towards the truth of reality except through the prism of art. This was the great paradox confronting Copernicus. As Banville himself has observed: 'The phrase "to save the phenomena" is a very elegant way of lying. Pre-Copernican science and Copernicus himself were obsessed with saving the phenomena, with producing a theory which would agree with what one saw in the sky but which wasn't necessarily true. . . . The job of art is not to save the phenomena but to lose them, or to risk losing them'[8].

*   *   *

With *Kepler*, Banville pursues his fictional reconstruction of Europe's great scientific minds. This second novel of the sequence records the particular 'crisis of imagination' suffered by Johannes Kepler, born in Southern Germany in 1571, as he confirmed the Copernican revolution in astronomy by discovering that the orbit of Mars is not circular but elliptical. Banville's own elliptical narrative brilliantly juxtaposes Kepler's *inner* world of creative fantasy and *outer* world of everyday contingency. The fragmented narrative techniques, abrupt shifts between first and third person perspectives and reversible time sequences, illustrate the dramatic unpredictability and riskiness of Kepler's own quest for cosmic truth. It also serves to render problematic the traditional quest-structure of the novel genre. An early passage in the novel offers a masterful description of the clash between inner and outer worlds:

> Johannes Kepler, asleep in his ruff, has dreamed the solution to the cosmic mystery. He holds it cupped in his mind as he would a precious something of unearthly frailty and splendour. O do not wake! But he will. Mistress Barbara, with a grain of grim satisfaction, shook him by his ill-shod foot, and at once the fabulous egg burst, leaving only a bit of glair and a few coordinates of broken shell.
>   And 0.00429.
>   He was cramped and cold, with a vile gum of sleep in his mouth. Opening an eye he spied his wife reaching for his dangling foot again, and dealt her a tiny kick to the knuckles.

The formula '0.00429' salvaged from the wake of his dream is in fact a premonitory cypher for the relationship between the planetary ellipses and their distances from the sun. It is the germ of his great discovery; but it is granted to his waking consciousness merely as a fragment of broken shell. The remainder of the narrative records how Kepler struggles to reconstruct the total shell of his initial dream-intuition shattered by the 'disturbances' of the real universe around him. Kepler's task is to translate his *true fiction* into the

world of observable facts so that he may finally dispel the traditional illusion (or *false fiction*) of Ptolemaic astronomy which for
centuries had held that it was the sun, not the earth, which moves.
But Kepler's alchemical art of translation is constantly threatened
by the intrusions of the external world: 'these deformities, the
clamour and confusion of other lives, this familiar – O familiar! –
disorder. . . . If he managed, briefly, a little inward calm, then the
world without was sure to turn on him'.

And turn on him it does. The narrator's repeated efforts to
rehearse in a linear sequence the *essential* events of Kepler's
imaginative quest are perpetually frustrated by the *accidental*
interruptions of historical existence – the plagues, wars, political
upheavals and ecclesiastical intrigues of seventeenth century
Europe, the humiliating banalities of Kepler's domestic grind with
his mad witch-mother and fussing wife. These are the daily
irritations which the 'Imperial Mathematician and Court Astrono-
mer' labours to overcome in his pursuit of the magic formulae of
cosmic harmony. And of course there is a price to be paid. Having
completed his major life-work, the *Somnium*, in 1630, Kepler
prepares for death, still struggling to unlock the secret mysteries of
the universe and more painfully aware than ever that his dream of
intellect has been pursued at the expense of living fully in the 'real
world'. Kepler compares himself to a 'dying man searching too
late for the life that he had missed, that his work had robbed him
of.' Memory (the idiom of history) reinvades imagination (the idiom
of dream):

> When he finished the *Somnium* there had been another crisis, as he had
> known there would be. What was it, this wanton urge to destroy the work
> of his intellect and rush out on crazy voyages into the real world? It had
> seemed to him in Sagan that he was haunted, not by a ghost but some-
> thing like a memory so vivid that at times it seemed about to conjure itself
> into a physical presence. It was as if he had mislaid some precious small
> thing, and forgotten about it, and yet was tormented by the loss. . . .
> Everything is told us, but nothing explained. Yes. We must take it all on
> trust. That's the secret.

Banville's own fiction is obsessed with the collision between
historical memory and creative imagination. *Doctor Copernicus* and
Kepler are both strategically suspended between the claims of
historical and fictional narrative. And this problematic confusion of
genres is a singular mark of their originality. Francis Stuart has
accurately identified this central feature of Banville's project:

> Most writers who choose the historical novel as a means of
> communication do so for such reasons as: long narrative descriptions and
> scene-setting, a given plot for their story-telling, it suits their particular
> talents, or, again they may hope to gain popular success by dramatising

certain events from the past of the community from which their readers
come. . . . Few writers who have faith in their art as discovery and
exploration of areas that lie beyond fact, take it as their medium. Why
then are John Banville's last two novels set in the sixteenth and
seventeenth centuries? The question does not really arise, as Dr
Copernicus and Johannes Kepler are portrayed in that quest for reality
that pure scientists and imaginative artists pursue with passion – whether
in the past, today, or in the future, up to the final revelation or
destruction, as it turns out . . . Not the least of Kepler's discoveries was
that the solution was not to be found by peering into the heavens at night
(he had not a telescope until the end of his life), but in the mind, as
Einstein, three hundred years later, was also to prove: 'It seems to me
that the real answers to the cosmic mystery are to be found not in the sky,
but in that other, infinitely smaller though no less mysterious firmament
contained within the skull⁹.

                                *   *   *

In *The Newton Letter: An Interlude*, Banville does not try to tell a
story. He interrogates the very nature of story-telling in the double
sense of the narrative form of the writing and the imaginative powers
of the writer. The narrator is a contemporary historian who attempts
to make sense of the nervous collapse suffered by another 'scientific'
mind, Isaac Newton, at another point in history, 1693. The only
'factual' evidence he has to go on is an enigmatic letter sent to the
philosopher, John Locke, in which Newton intimates his crisis of
faith in the ability of the mind to explain the 'true' workings of the
external universe. Scientific facts, Newton seems to suggest, are
themselves fictions. The task of the contemporary historian-narrator
in the novel is to establish and interpret the 'facts' behind this
decisive 'interlude' in Newton's career. Not an auspicious project
by all accounts.

The narrator-historian rents a caretaker's cottage on an estate
called Fern Hill where he hopes to complete his seven year research
on Newton. The aristocratic estate, itself on the verge of collapse, is
anachronistic, an incongruity of history whose inhabitants prove
quite as mysterious and impenetrable as Newtown himself. While
resolved to remain detached and objective, the narrator becomes
increasingly obsessed by the inscrutable identities of his landlord
neighbours. As he does so he proceeds to construct elaborate
fictions in an effort to make some sense of the missing narrative links
– or 'interludes' – in their complex interrelationships. (One is
reminded of Beckett's Mr. Watt in Mr. Knott's house). Is Ottilie the
mother of the strange child? Or is it Charlotte? And who is the
father? Is the narrator in love with Ottilie or Charlotte? Or neither?
Or both? (At one moment, indeed, the narrator becomes so confused
by the mismatching of names and people that he declares his love for

'Charlottie.') Trapped in this labyrinth of indecisions and revisions, the narrator essays to resolve his doubts by resorting to fictional interpretations which invariably turn out to be mistaken. Even his love affair with Ottilie – his one 'real' experience – is, by his own admission, 'conducted through the intermediary of... a story, a memory History keeps revising, itself in the mind of the creator.'

This historian, not surprisingly, begins his narrative by conceding his own failure of imaginative nerve: 'Words fail me... I have abandoned my book... I don't really understand it myself... I've lost faith in the primacy of text.' The beginning of the novel thus bespeaks the ending; and the entire intervening narative is written retrospectively in the past tense; that is, in the form of a reminiscence which would explain the narrator's own failed quest for narrative coherence. In *The Newton Letter* the mind is its own prison and history the one possibility of salvation (what its narrator calls the possibility of 'the innocence of things, their non-complicity in our affairs'). But can the fiction-spinning mind ever dispense with its own interpretations? Can it ever hope to suspend its adulterating interference with the 'innocence of things?' Banville's narrator brings guidebooks on trees and birds with him only to discover that the 'illustrations would not match up with the real specimens.' In similar fashion, the human specimens of Fern House, and indeed the elusive Newton himself, stubbornly defy the historian's code of decipherment just as the truths of the universe defied Newton's scientific blueprints. History thus repeats itself in a timeless pattern of recurrence.

And so the narrator finds himself a prey to his own hermeneutic narratives. 'Look at me, writing history,' he self-mockingly jibes. Even the apparently reliable evidence of his perceptions capitulates to the seduction of ideas. At one point, for example, the narrator senses something scurrying in the grass: 'I thought it was a blackbird out foraging... but it was a rat. In fact it wasn't a rat. In fact in all my time at Ferns I never saw sign of a rat. It was only the idea.' The author cannot reach reality *in fact*. That is the cruel irony. Finally the narrator is compelled to liken his historical exegesis to the manoeuverings of an 'artist blissfully checking over the plan of a work' whose 'memory gathers its material, beady-eyed and voracious, like a demented photographer.' His entire stay at Ferns is itself transmuted by the act of recollection: 'It has all been lived already and we were merely tracing the patterns, as if not really living, but remembering... the past, immutable, crystalline and perfect.'

The narrator concludes accordingly that only the 'ordinary' and 'commonplace' could redeem him from his own myth-making consciousness. Like Newton before him, whose interlude represented a crisis of belief in the mind's ability to reach truth, the historian determines to abandon his writings in order to commit himself to silence (recalling the Wittgensteinian conclusion to *Birchwood*). The narrator explains his decision by alluding to a *second* letter to Locke in which Newton avowed his preference for a wordless communion with the common mortals of this world – 'the sellers and makers of things' – a non-fictional language 'in which commonplace things speak to me.'

Following Newton's precedent, Banville's historian also signs off with a second letter (the first being the 'confessional' novel itself) in which he celebrates a new-found, non-academic life with ordinary mortals in a mint mine in Iowa. In the same letter, he announces that Ottilie is pregnant by him and that the child's existence will ensure that his delusions ultimately yield to the reality of history. 'The future now has the same resonance that the past had, for me. I am pregnant myself, in a way. Supernumerous existence wells up in my heart.' The question as to whether he will return to Ferns and complete his work on Newton is, significantly, left open.

What then of Banville's narrative – the novel itself? What of the author's own narrative 'interlude' based on his narrator's 'interlude' based on Newton's 'interlude?' In an editorial note at the end of the novel, Banville informs us that the second Newton letter to Locke is in fact a fiction! And it requires no great leap of the imagination to realize that the narrator's own final letter is equally fictional. (A realization confirmed by the tell-tale facts that the narrator speaks of the future's resonance '*for me*'; that his own feeling of pregnancy is itself metaphorical; and that the reference to 'supernumerous existence' is a direct literary quote from Rilke's *Duino Elegies*.) The attempt to abandon fiction is thus exposed as fiction. Where Banville went from this, his story of interlude, was, of course, another story[10].

Conclusion

The representatives of the 'critical' counter-tradition in the Irish novel exemplify a common *crisis of imagination*. This crisis, as noted earlier, had been brought about by Joyce's and Beckett's debunking of the traditional model of narration – i.e. as a transparent representation in *language* of the way things are in *reality*. Traditional novel writing presupposed that these two poles of narration were somehow naturally given and distinct. Once this distinction between *word* and *thing* was deconstructed by Joyce and Beckett, the *distance* between the narrator's subjective consciousness and the historical world – which motivated the narrator's *quest* for meaning in the first place – was radically diminished. And so the crucial relationship between language and the real world, between fiction and history, between imagination and memory, itself became the self-relexive subject of novel writing. Instead of writing narratives *about* the world, in a straightforward representational manner, the disciples of Joyce and Beckett interrogated the very possibility, or impossibility, of such writing.

Most Irish novelists after Joyce and Beckett by-passed or ignored this crisis of narration. They continued producing traditional novels as if the classical realist model had never been put into question. A small number of Irish novelists did, as noted, respond to the challenge posed by Joyce and Beckett. Some of these experienced the crisis of fiction as a problematic attempt to recover the realities of historical memory from the solipsistic constructs of imagination; others experienced the crisis in the opposite sense as a struggle to salvage the creative powers of imagination from the oppressive facts of history. We have seen how three such 'critical' Irish novelists – Flann O'Brien, Francis Stuart and John Banville – registered the problem of narration in one or other, or both, of these ways. They are not, however, the only representatives of the post-Joycean counter-tradition. Neil Jordan's *The Past* grapples with similar themes as it recounts the narrator's efforts to reconstruct and resolve the mystery of his mother's *real* past through the *fictional* narratives of his mother's friends' reminiscences, only to discover that historical fact and aesthetic fantasy are inextricably linked. Similarly, Aidan Higgins' innovative novels, ranging from *Langrishe Go Down* and *Balcony of Europe* to *Scenes from a Receding Past* and *Bornholm Night-Ferry*, also focus in a self-reflexive way on the problematic rapport between writing and history. In *Balcony of Europe* we witness the narrator/artist labouring to wrest imagination free from the vortex of memory, from that circularity of a recurring past which Stephen Dedalus termed the 'nightmare of history'[11]. *Bornholm Night-Ferry* features an exchange of letters between an Irish novelist (with the mock-heroic name of Finn Fitzgerald) and his foreign lover (a Danish poetess, Elin), which seeks to conjure up an 'opposite land' of fictive refuge denied them in their daily reality, separated as they are by time, place and language.

What authors of the counter-movement in Irish fiction share is obsession with the *crisis of narrative*. Whether the authorial imagination at issue in their critical novels is seen as oppressor or oppressed, it is at all times fundamentally problematic for itself, an imagination which can no longer take writing for granted, but in true modernist fashion, makes it the very theme of writing.

It might be objected that the novelists of the Irish counter-tradition have generally been so preoccupied with the problem of narrative and its epistemological rapport with history, that they have tended to ignore the contemporary problems of their own history. The 'critical' novelists have been accused of indulging in an elitist escapism which opts for the international idioms of modernism over the demands of a national literature committed to matters of social and political relevance. Beckett, after all, is more interested in the literature of existentialist anguish than of nationalist revival; Banville writes about the life and times of Nicholas Copernicus not Michael Collins; Stuart invokes Emily Bronte as his muse not Kathleen Ni Houlihan; Higgins chooses the Baltic island of Bornholm as his ideal sanctuary not the lake isle of Inishfree. Whenever the 'critical' novelists do relate to an Irish context (as O'Brien in *At Swim Two Birds*, Stuart in *Hole in the Head* and *Blacklist Section–H* or Banville in *Birchwood*), it is usually with the purpose of parodying and demythologizing the pieties of national culture in the name of a sceptical individualism of revolt. It has been left therefore to those in the mainstream tradition of realist Irish fiction – in particular O'Faolain, Kiely, McGahern, McLaverty and Plunkett – to provide narratives of contemporary Ireland's social history. Joyce himself, it could be argued, avoided this alternative by combining an aesthetic commitment to modernist experimentalism with an historical commitment to the modern realities of Irish society. After Joyce, however, these respective commitments appear to have divided into two distinct movements of Irish fiction, the 'critical' and the 'realist'. The attempt it seems, has yet to be made to reunite these opposed commitments in a new post-Joycean synthesis.

Note: Since writing this essay, John Banville has published *Mefisto* (Secker and Warburg, 1986). It is seen by some as the fourth and final part of a tetralogy on the scientific imagination. Certainly there is a continuity of theme running from the Copernicus, Kepler, Newton series to *Mefisto*: viz. the complex rapport between memory and imagination, history and artifice. Gabriel Swan, the narrator-author, is, like his Proustian prototype, committed to the retelling of his life-history. The problem for Gabriel however is that 'times past' cannot actually be remembered except through the grid of fictional reinvention. Memory, as a faithful recorder of things as they really happened, is thus transformed into a form of narrative imagination which surpasses the plausible limits of history. When queried about the reality of what he recounts, Gabriel retorts: 'It's what I remember, what does it matter whether it's possible or not?' The act of fiction, as storytelling, repeatedly comments upon its own fictitiousness – as when having described a nun with a head-dress and ledger, the narrator self-consciously confesses: 'No, there was no nun. I invented her.' In *Mefisto*, as in his preceding triad of novels on the scientific imagination, Banville endeavours to deconstruct the accredited distinction between scientific fact and poetic invention. And yet he remains wholly aware of the vexed nature of such a deconstruction. If Mefisto is the guiding spirit of the modern Faustian project to invent a new order of creation, he is also an emblem of demonic destruction. Banville leaves the precise identity of his contemporary Mefisto suitably undecided.

5

HEANEY AND HOMECOMING

Seamus Heaney is often hailed as Ireland's greatest poet since Yeats. While such praise generally adverts to Heaney's remarkable sense of craft, his verbal and formal dexterity, it frequently betrays another kind of evaluation: one concerned less with Ireland's greatest *poet* than with *Ireland's* greatest poet. Here the emphasis falls on the typically and traditionally Irish quality of Heaney's writing. He is enlisted as the poet of the patria, a home bird, an excavator of the national landscape devoted to the recovery of natural pieties.

Heaney's primary inspiration, we are told, is one of place; his quintessentially Irish vocation, the sacramental naming of a homeland. Hence the preoccupation with images of mythology, archaeology and genealogy, of returning to forgotten origins. This revivalist reading conforms to the paradigm of the 'backward look' which, Frank O'Connor has argued, typifies Irish literature[1].

This orthodox view would have us believe that while other contemporary Irish poets embraced the more modernist idioms of existential *angst* or the crisis of language, Heaney remained faithful to the primacy of the provincial. He didn't need to take his tune from current trends in Continental or Anglo-American poetry; for he had discovered the cosmos, as it were, in his own backyard. Mahon, Montague, Longley and Kinsella engaged in metaphysical meditations about the problematic rapport between self, language and history. Durcan and Bolger composed biting satires about urban bourgeois hypocrisy and the ravages of advanced industrial capitalism. But Heaney stuck to the home patch. He resisted the modernist impulse and remained, inalienably, 'one of our own'. A true revivalist.

Some commentators have offered a more ideological interpretation of the nostalgia for lost traditions which is said to exemplify the 'native' strain of Irish literature. The harking back to an abandoned, or at least threatened, organic life-style still in harmony with all that is best in the national heritage, has been seen as an attempt to reconstruct a cultural unison which would overcome, by overlooking, the actual social divisions which torment modern Irish society. As one critic remarked: 'An emergent Catholic capitalist class espoused a myth of natural pious austerity in opposition to the profane forces of modernity, while the Anglo-Irish déracinés sought harmony with nature and a people characterised by wild, irrational, asocial energies'[2]. Viewed in such an ideological perspective, Heaney's poetic efforts to bring Irish culture 'home' to itself, might be dismissed as a conservative return to antiquated mythologies of 'tradition' and 'nature'.

By focussing on the central theme of 'homecoming' in Heaney I propose to show how it involves a complex conflict of sensibility which has little or nothing to do with insular notions of parochial *pietas*. I will analyse Heaney's preoccupation with 'homecoming' less in standard formal terms than in *philosophical* terms. My aim is to demonstrate that Heaney's treatment of 'homecoming' involves an unresolved dialectic between the opposing claims of home and homelessness. The revivalist reading of his work could do with some debunking. It is time to prise Heaney free from stereotypes.

*   *   *

First, it should be noted that Heaney's poems are not in fact primarily about place at all; they are about *transit*, that is, about transitions from one place to another. One need only look to the titles of some of his major works to see just how fundamental this notion of poetry as transitional act is: *Wintering Out, Door into the Dark, Field Work, Sweeney Astray, Station Island*. One of the central reasons for Heaney's preference for journey over sojourn, for exodus over abode, is, I suggest, a fidelity to the nature of *language* itself. Far from subscribing to the traditional view that language is a transparent means of representing some identity which precedes language – call it *self, nation, home* or whatever – Heaney's poetry espouses the view that it is language which perpetually constructs and deconstructs our given notions of identity. As such, poetic language is always on the move, vacillating between opposing viewpoints, looking in at least two directions at once.

Heaney has been criticized for refusing to adopt a clear political position, for not nailing his colours to the mast, particularly with regard to the 'national question' (i.e. his attitude to his native North). One Irish politician described him as an 'artful dodger' who displays 'all the skills of the crafty tightrope walker . . . sidestepping and skipping his slippery way out of trouble'[3]. Bemoaning the fact that his work is a 'job of literary journeywork', this same critic admonishes him to 'seek a less ambivalent position'. The point is, however, that Heaney is a poet, not a party politician. He does not deny that his work has political connotations – for that would be to deny that it is concerned with life as it is lived. But this does not mean that he is compelled to subscribe to a definitive ideological standpoint. His refusal to be fixed, to be *placed* in any single perspective is no more than a recognition that poetry's primary fidelity is to language as an interminable metamorphosis of conflicting identities. Heaney himself states his position on language as dual or multiple perspective in the following passage from *Preoccupations*: 'When I called my second book *Door into the Dark* I intended to gesture towards this idea of poetry as a point of entry into the buried life of the feelings or as a point of exit for it. Words themselves are doors: Janus is to a certain extent their deity, looking back to a ramification of the roots and associations and forward to a clarification of sense and meaning . . . In *Door into the Dark* there are a number of poems that arise out of the almost unnamable energies that, for me, hovered over certain bits of language. . . . '[4]. The poet's commitment to an aesthetic of endless migration is clear.

Heaney poetry seems to support the view that literature is essentially about language itself. Mallarmé and Rimbaud made this view the central plank of their modernist program; as did, in another context, Heaney's compatriots, Joyce and Beckett. This is not to suggest that Heaney approaches literature as some autonomous sphere; nor that his fascination with words degenerates into self-regarding formalism. It is simply to recognize that for Heaney reality as we perceive it is always profoundly informed by the words we use. And these words carry *several* meanings, for language is an endless creation of new worlds; possible worlds which remain irreducible to the univocal slide rule of a one to one correspondence between word and thing. That is why the double-faced Janus is the deity of Heaney's literary 'journey work'.

Heaney's commitment to the ambivalence of poetic language is, I believe, manifest in his exploration of the pivotal motif of 'homecoming'. Whereas in the early works, Heaney usually talks of home in terms of a personal quest for self-identity, in his later collections – and particularly *North* or *Station Island* – he begins to interpret homecoming more in terms of a linguistic search for historical identity. As he himself remarks in *Preoccupations*, words cease to be fingerprints recording the unique signature of the poet and become 'bearers of history'. But if Heaney insists that one of the tasks of the poet is to recover a sense of belonging to a shared past – 'an ancestry, a history, a culture' – he construes this task as a *project* rather than a *possession*, as an exploration of language rather than some triumphalist revival of a lost national identity.

Poetry, in short, comes to express the sense of 'home' less as a literal (i.e. geographical, political or personal) property than as a metaphorical preoccupation. Home is something that cannot be taken for granted as present. It must be sought after precisely because it is *absent*. For Heaney, homecoming is never the actuality of an event but the possibility of an advent.

*   *   *

At this point it may be useful to look at some poems in Heaney's collection *North* which deal explicitly with this theme. In a poem entitled 'Homecomings', Heaney would seem to be affirming the experience of home as a *positive* goal. He meditates upon the 'homing' manoeuverings of a sandmartin as it circles back to its nest:

> At the worn mouth of the hole
> Flight after flight after flight
> The swoop of its wings
> Gloved and kissed home.

The poet sees this instinctual, almost atavistic, homecoming of the sandmartin as an analogy for his own aspiration to return to an orginating womb of earth where he may regain a sense of prenatal silence, unity and belonging:

> A glottal stillness. An eardrum.
> Far in, featherbrains tucked in silence,
> A silence of water lipping the bank
>
> Mould my shoulders inward to you.
> Occlude me.
> Be damp clay pouting.
> Let me listen under your eaves.

This experience recalls the opening passage from *Preoccupations* where Heaney invokes the image of the omphalos as a hidden underground well of childhood memory. 'I would begin' he writes, with the Greek word, *omphalos*, meaning the navel, and hence the stone that marked the centre of the world, and repeat it, *omphalos*, *omphalos*, *omphalos*, until its blunt and falling music becomes the music of somebody pumping water at the pump outside our back door . . . the pump marked an original descent into earth, sand, gravel, water. It centred and staked the imagination, made its foundations the foundation of the *omphalos* itself'.[5]

These positive images of home are identified with nature, mother earth and childhood. They describe the experience of an edenesque dwelling in harmony with the natural environment. And, as such, they might be thought to invoke a time before time – before, that is, the arrival of language and self-consciousness. But we must not forget that Heaney's first collection of poems is entitled *Death of a Naturalist*. All of Heaney's writing is informed by an awareness that the poet as a resourceful dweller in language has replaced the naturalist as an innocent dweller in nature. So that if Heaney occasionally seeks to retrieve the experience of the 'naturalist', it is always as a 'post-naturalist': as someone who is, at best, hankering after something that he knows full well is irretrievably *lost*. Homecoming thus becomes a dialectical search for some forfeited or forbidden presence in and through the awareness of its *absence*. We should not be surprised therefore to find Heaney, in a poem called 'Kinship', referring to the *omphalos* as a grave; or to mother earth as the inevitable casualty of autumnal death and decay. Language has now, it seems, adulterated the pristine innocence of nature. The vowel of earth can do no more than 'dream' its root. Home can only be spoken of as some ground from which we have become irreparably uprooted.

In other poems in *North* (the title of this collection itself is a symbol amongst other things, for Heaney's own lost homeland or motherland), the theme of homecoming is submitted to self-questioning. The very attempt to return home is now equated by the poet with necrophiliac nostalgia; it assumes the character of a sacrificial death rite which provokes sentiments of recoil. In a poem called 'Stump', Heaney surmises that his homing instinct may well become a parasite of putrefaction as soon as it contrives to make of home a tribal aquisition. 'I am riding to plague again,' he rebukes himself. 'What do I say if they wheel out their dead?/I'm cauterized, a black stump of home'. In yet another poem, 'Roots', Heaney's suspicion of necrophiliac impulses reaches even more self-recriminatory proportions. Here he conceives of the tribal hankering after dispossessed origins or 'roots' as a sanguinary death cult bedevilling his Northern province and intruding upon private intimacies. Outside in the terraced streets the earth's 'fault is opening' as the gunshots of the sniper and the sirens of the army scream at each other. Inside in the bedroom, the poet tries to take refuge in love; but his dark bloodletting dreams, echoing the slaughter in the streets, contaminate the lovers' communion and deform it into the image of a mandrake (a poisonous plant whose root is thought to resemble a human form and to shriek when plucked):

> I'm soaked by moonlight in tidal blood
> A mandrake, lodged human fork,
> Earth sac, limb of the dark;
> And I wound its damp smelly loam
> And stop my ears against the scream.

*   *   *

Heaney's celebrated 'bog poems' provide arresting examples of the dialectic of homecoming and estrangement. For Heaney the northern bog is a sort of placeless place; it is a shifting palimpsest of endless layers and sublayers, an archival memory of lost cultures.

In one of the first of his bog poems – the last poem of *Wintering out* – Heaney describes how a great Elk and a morsel of butter were recovered from Irish bogs having been preserved for centuries in the dark and watery peat. The poem concludes with the following image of an interminable excavation for a vanished *omphalos*:

> Our pioneers keep striking
> Inwards and downwards,
>
> Every layer they strip
> Seems camped on before.
> The bogholes might be Atlantic seepage
> The wet centre is bottomless.

Heaney explains that while this bogland motif began as a germ of childhood association it gradually assumed the status of a cultural myth. 'We used to hear about bog-butter', writes Heaney of his early childhood, 'butter kept fresh for a great number of years under the peat. Then when I was at school the skeleton of an elk had been taken out of a bog nearby and a few of our neighbours had got their photographs in the paper, peering out across its antlers. So I began to get an idea of a bog as the memory of the landscape, or as a landscape that remembered everything that happened in and to it. In fact, if you go round the National Museum in Dublin, you will realize that a great proportion of the most cherished material heritage of Ireland was 'found in a bog'. Moreover, since memory was the faculty that supplied me with the first quickening of my own poetry, I had a tentative unrealized need to make a congruence between memory and bogland and, for want of a better word, our national consciousness'[6].

But if the bog becomes a symbol of national consciousness, it is not in the manner of an insular, self-righteous nationalism. Heaney is mindful of the fact that the lost homeland is less a territorial locality than an ontological locus whose universal dimensions forever elude the boundaries of a particular nation. The closer we get to home in this sense the more distant it becomes; its very construction is its deconstruction. 'The wet centre', as Heaney concedes, *is bottomless*. The bogholes of receding memory lead back to a fathomless ocean flow which transcends our contemporary grasp. Homecoming, poetically understood, means therefore that our literal or geographical home is actually de-centred. The very process of homecoming reminds us that we are now displaced, in exile, estranged (*unheimlich*). So that just as the fundamental question of Being, according to Heidegger, can only be retrieved from oblivion by 'de-structing' the pretension of Western metaphysics to represent some unbroken continuous tradition – so too with regard to the more exact question of cultural heritage. Or as another modern thinker, Michel Foucault, puts it: 'In attempting to uncover the deepest strata of western culture, I am restoring to our silent and apparently immobile soil, its rifts, its instability, its flaws; and it is the same ground that is once more stirring under our feet'[7].

But it would be a mistake to interpret this *defamiliarization* of the experience of tradition to mean that Heaney abandons all concern for the plight of his native Ulster. Heaney insists that his bog poems are also a reaching after 'images and symbols *adequate to our predicament*'. He explains that he felt it imperative to 'discover a field of force in which, without abandoning fidelity to the processes and experience of poetry . . . it would be possible to encompass the perspectives of a humane reason and at the same time to grant the religious intensity of the violence its deplorable authenticity and complexity'[8]. In other words, Heaney sees the contemporary conflict in Northern Ireland as, amongst other things, a symptom of a collision between the opposing claims of rationalistic order and religious atavism. He makes it quite clear, of course, that he is using the term *religious* not just in the more current sense of sectarian division between Catholic and Protestant, but in the anthropological sense of an ancient enmity between 'the cults and devotees of a god and a goddess'. There is, Heaney observes, 'an indigenous numen, a tutelar of the whole island, call her mother Ireland, Kathleen Ni Houlihan, the poor old woman, the Shan Van Vocht, whatever; and her sovereignty has been temporarily usurped or infringed by a new male cult whose founding fathers were Cromwell, William of Orange and Edward Carson, and whose godhead is incarnate in a rex or caesar resident in a palace in London. What we have here is the tail end of a struggle in a province between territorial piety and imperial power'[9]. By tracing the capillaries of our current political and social ideologies back to their roots in a hidden sublayer of mythologies, Heaney is attempting not to revive these mythologies but critically to explore and expose them.

Nor does Heaney confine himself to Celtic myth. Indeed, one of the most striking emblems of this dialectic between critical distance and mythic belonging is borrowed from the Greek myth of Antaeus and Hercules. Heaney casts Hercules in the role of triumphant reason, 'sky born and royal . . . his future hung with trophies'. Antaeus, by contrast, is portrayed as a mould-hugger, clinging to his unconscious terrestial past. By dispossessing Antaeus of his tribal fixation with ancestral origins, Hercules drags him–

> Out of his element
> Into a dream of loss
>
> And origins – the cradling dark,
> The river-veins, the secret gullies
> Of his strength,
> The hatching grounds
>
> Of cave and souterrain,
> He has bequeathed it all
> To elegists . . .

And so it is, in Heaney's own elegiac bog poems, that the homeless and vanquished Antaeus can only be recovered – if at all – in the suspended animation of his ancient slumber, brought home to us again as a 'sleeping giant/ Pap for the dispossessed'. Heaney comments on this key dialectic between rational consciousness and the mythico-religious unconscious as follows:

> Hercules represents the balanced rational light while Antaeus represents the pieties of illiterate fidelity. The poem drifts towards an assent to Hercules, though there was a sort of nostalgia for Antaeus . . . This is a see-saw, an advance-retire situation[10].

To reformulate this position in 'temporal' terms, we might say that the poetics of homecoming require us to juxtapose the *prospective* glance of Hercules and the *retrospective* glance of Antaeus. Otherwise put, it is the Herculean act of estranged detachment which enables us to remember the Antaean origin of 'cave and souterain'. To dispense with the distancing detour of elegy would be to diminish the possibility of homecoming as a liberating advent, cultivating it instead as a reactionary return to the past. For it is thanks to the critical challenge of the homeless Hercules that Antaeus' homing instinct may be transformed from tribal nostalgia into an authentic quest for a new cultural community. In this dialectical vacillation between the claims of Herculean reason and Antaean instinct, the *topos* of the past can come towards us as a *u-topia* of the future.

Heaney informs us in *Preoccupations* that one of the main sources of his 'bog' motif was Glob's *The Bog People* (a work he first read in translation in 1969, which was 'appositely, the year the killing started' in Ulster). Heaney is under no illusions about the potentially terrifying consequences of the 'quest for home' when this degenerates – as it so easily can – into tribal fanaticism. He offers the following account of how, on reading Glob's work, the various emblems of the 'northern' (Nordic) sacrificial practices came together with the contemporary realities of the 'northern' (Ulster) conflict:

> It was chiefly concerned with preserved bodies of men and women found in the bogs of Jutland, naked, strangled or with their throats cut, disposed under the peat since early Iron Age times. The author, P.V. Glob, argues convincingly that a number of these, and in particular the Tollund Man, whose head is now preserved near Aarhus in the museum at Silkeburg, were ritual sacrifices to the Mother Goddess, the Goddess of the ground who needed new bridegrooms each winter to bed with her in her sacred place, in the bog, to ensure the renewal and fertility of the territory in the spring. Taken in relation to the tradition of Irish political martyrdom for that cause whose icon is Kathleen Ni Houlihan, this is more than an archaic barbarous rite: it is an archetypal pattern. And the unforgettable photographs of these victims blended in my mind with photographs of atrocities, past and present, in the long rites of Irish political and religious struggles[11].

While recognizing the fecundity of this material for the poetic imagination, Heaney admits its dangers for political reality. The temptation to fudge the dividing line between a figurative and literal interpretation of this cult is strenuously resisted. Heaney states his critical reservations on this score when he comments on his attitude to 'The Tollund Man', another of his bog poems: 'When I wrote this poem, I had a completely new sensation, one of fear. It was a vow to go on a pilgrimage and I felt as it came to me . . . that unless I was deeply in earnest about what I was saying, I was simply invoking dangers for myself'[12]. This mention of fear is significant not only in its reference to the traditionally mystic attitude to the sublime or holy as *fascinans et tremendum*, but more directly still in its bearing on the experience of the *Unhomely* (see appendix). In 'Tollund Man', Heaney counterpoints the ritual act of returning home with a critical scruple of exile and distance. The poet describes an imaginary pilgrimage northwards to pay homage to an ancestor recovered from a bog still intact after thousands of years and attired in his sacrificial garb of cap, noose and girdle. But it is significant that the northern bog is not in fact in Ulster but in Jutland – and the ancestor in question is not an Irishman but a Tollund man. In other words, Heaney is returning to a home away from home: an *unheimlich* home.

The Tollund victim is described as a 'bridegroom to the goddess', the suggestion being that he has been sacrificed to the earth deity so that she might be sexually regenerated and he preserved in her 'cradling dark' for posterity. In this image of the sanctified scapegoat from the far north, Heaney finds an 'objective correlative', for the near north of his own homeland in Ulster. And the security which the sentiment of homecoming might normally confer is thus offset by a careful awareness of uncanny estrangement. 'Out there in Jutland', Heaney confesses, 'In the old man-killing parishes/ I feel lost,/ Unhappy and at home'.

Heaney does not ignore the disobliging implications of such death rites for his native North. In the 'Grauballe Man', he concedes that the perfected memory of the sacrificial bog-victim remains haunted by the present Ulster reality of 'each hooded victim/Slashed and dumped': the poet's response thus hangs in the 'scales with beauty and atrocity'. And elsewhere, in a poem called 'Funeral Rites', Heaney compares the 'slow triumph' of the funeral procession towards the mounds of the ancestral Boyne Valley (considered in Irish legend to be the mystical centre or *omphalos* of the earth)[13] to the ominous winding of a serpent. A similar note of caution is struck in the title poem of *North* which recounts how the poet had to travel to the 'unmagical' Nordic lands of Iceland and Greenland before he could hear again the voices of his own Viking ancestry in Ireland – 'Ocean deafened voices/Warning me, lifted again/ In violence and epiphany'. He imagines the swinging tongue of a Viking longship speaking to him 'buoyant with hindsight' of revenge, of 'hatreds and behind backs . . . memory incubating the spilled blood'. So that while beckoning the poet to 'lie down in the word-hoard' of his *literary* heritage, this ancestral voice simultaneously warns against a cyclical repetition of past atrocities at the *literal* level of political blood-letting[14].

Heaney remains mindful of the fact that a culture's 'great first sleep of homecoming' is also a death and a forgetting. The act of poetic remembering must always observe a delicate balance between the opposite risks of belonging to a home and being exiled from this home. To resolve this paradox by opting in absolute fashion for either extreme would be to betray the dual fidelity of his poetry.

It is altogether fitting, finally, that this paradox should find both historical and linguistic correlatives in Heaney's own predicament. Historically, Heaney is aware that the British plantation of Gaelic Ulster in the seventeenth century resulted in the displacement of the Irish language by English (an historical event which received more recent expression in this century with the drawing of a border across the map of Ireland). Part of Heaney's ambivalent predicament is due, consequently, to his maintenance of a notion of himself 'as Irish in a province that insists that it is British'[15]. And this double consciousness is operative at the level of his poetic language where two tongues engage in conflictual dialogue. As Heaney emblematically remarks: 'I think of the personal and Irish pieties as vowels, and the literary awareness nourished on English as consonants'[16]. The very words of Heaney's poems bear witness to this aesthetic of dual residence, to a poetic scruple of tireless migration.

Conclusion

This poetic paradox of 'homecoming' is powerfully sustained in Heaney's later work. In *Station Island* (1984), a collection which takes its name from the northern place of pilgrimage, Lough Derg, Heaney returns to an exploration of the homing instincts of religious and political reverence. Here, perhaps more explicitly than in any previous work, Heaney self-consciously interprets the fascination with 'home' as a need for tradition, community, memory, mythology, the collective unconscious. In the long title sequence, the poet is assailed by several accusing voices from his past – usually victims of the bloody carnage in his native Ulster. These 'ancestral' ghosts address him in dream or reverie as he rehearses the ritual stations of Lough Derg. Here is a privileged place and time for recollection, for coming to terms with what Joyce's Stephen Dedalus called the 'nightmare of history' – the revivalist claims of motherland and mother church. And here, more than anywhere, is the poet privy to the hauntings of his 'migrant solitude'.

The sequence opens with the poet's alter-ego, Sweeney, shouting at him to 'stay clear of all processions'. But the poet persists on the 'drugged path' of tribal ceremony; he embraces the 'murmur of the crowds', the pious solidarity of the living and the dead. The poet's visitor from beyond the grave is Carleton, another Irish writer who had experienced 'gun butts cracking on the door' and whose rejection of both 'hard-mouthed Ribbonmen and Orange bigots' (tribal northern gangs) had 'mucked the byre of their politics'. The poet confesses that he himself has 'no mettle for the angry role' of ancestral revenge; yet he is compelled by Carleton's counsel to 'remember everything and keep (his) head'.

For Heaney, however, as for Hugh in Friel's play *Translations*, 'to remember everything is a form of madness'. In the first instance, remembrance is racked with guilt – and particularly the poet's guilt about his lack of direct political involvement with the sufferings of his tribe. One visitation from an assassinated childhood friend provokes the poet to seek forgiveness for 'the way (he) has lived indifferent'. And another murder victim, a second cousin, chides the pilgrim for consorting with effete fellow-poets when he first heard the news of his death:

I accuse directly, but indirectly, you
Who now atone perhaps upon this bed
For the way you whitewashed ugliness. . .
And saccharined my death with morning dew.

Faced with this litany of ancestral accusations, the author drifts towards repentence. But he also realises that his primary commitment as a poet is to the exploration of the buried truths of *language* – which mediates, records and structures our experience – rather than to the immediate exigencies of political legislation or reprisal: 'As if the eddy could reform the pool'. The buried truths of language are revealed by poetry to the degree that 1) the poet takes the step back from our familiar use of words as means/end strategies and 2) listens in silence to what language is saying in and through us. The poem is in this way a response, before all else, to the silent voices of language itself. This is what modern thinkers such as Heidegger, Lévi-Strauss and Lacan have taught us. As the latter remarked: 'The subject is spoken rather than speaking . . . . It was certainly the Word that was in the beginning, and we live in its creation, but it is because the symbol has made him man'[17]. Heaney makes this point about his own work when he declares that 'the creative mind is astraddle silence'[18] – an echo perhaps of Beckett's pregnant statement that 'silence is our mother-tongue'.

The final visitation in the Lough Derg sequence of *Station Island* is Joyce's ghost. Joyce, like Carleton, serves as a *literary* conscience. But unlike Carleton's revivalist exhortation to remember everything, he recommends the modernist commitment to writing itself – to 'signatures' of the writer's own frequency. Joyce warns the poet that the obsession with collective guilt and tribal grievance is a mistake:

> That subject people stuff is a cod's game . . .
> You lose more of yourself than you redeem
> Doing the decent thing.
> Keep at a tangent.
> When they make the circle wide, its time to swim
> Out on your own and fill the element
> With signatures of your own frequency . . .
> Elver-gleams in the dark of the whole sea.

Significantly, the figure of Sweeney Astray – the exiled wandering bard of Irish legend and the subject of a verse translation by Heaney from the Gaelic *Buile Suibhne* – returns in the third section of the book as symbol of the dissenting and disinherited poet. Sweeney's migratory impulses confirm the Joycean plea. But one of the main strengths of *Station Island* is the refusal to choose between Heaney and Sweeney – between the guilt-ridden pilgrim of history and the carefree émigré of the imagination. As the Janus-faced author remarks early in the collection (citing Milosz):

> I was stretched
> between contemplation
> of a motionless point
> and the command to participate
> actively in history.[19]

Heaney's ultimate fidelity to the ambiguity of opposing demands, and to the inner manoeuverings of poetic language which sustain such demands, his refusal of any single place or position which would permit the illusion of a final solution, is proof of his tireless transiting between revivalism and modernism. Whether Heaney's continuing 'journeywork' will lead him closer to the radicalist modernism of Joyce or the revivalist modernism of Yeats remains an open question. Perhaps he will succeed in forging a post-modernist synthesis somewhere between the two – what we might call a poetics of perpetual detour?[20] As he observes in a poem called 'Terminus', (*The Haw Lantern*, 1987), dedicated to the god of boundaries and borders –

> Two buckets were easier carried than one.
> I grew up in between.

APPENDIX

Heaney, Heidegger and Freud – The Paradox of the Homely

Heaney's ambivalent attitude to homecoming – expressed as a double-movement of attraction and revulsion, intense questing and sceptical questioning – bears a certain resemblance to Martin Heidegger's notion of the poet's search for Being as a dialectical passage towards 'home' through the 'unhomely' (that is, our experience of the alien strangeness of death). And this attitude also corresponds, in several important respects, to Freud's identification of the unconscious with the 'homely/unhomely' paradox.

A comparison between Heaney and these two pioneers of modern thought could prove instructive, I believe, particularly with a view to indicating how Heaney's poetic concerns are not simply Irish but international, not simply parochial but universal. By proposing an anti-revivalist re-evaluation of his work, I hope to scotch the stereotype of Heaney as some latter-day piers ploughman from county Derry staving off the plague of modernity and guiding us back to a prelapsarian pastureland. The very mention of our supposedly homegrown, tradition-bound Heaney in the same breath as such 'alien' intellects may strike some as altogether inappropriate. But this is just another token of how pervasive the critical stereotyping of Heaney has become.

I

In a study entitled *Das Unheimliche* (translated as the 'unhomely' or 'uncanny'), Freud explores the paradox that the '*Unheimliche* is the name for everything that ought to have remained hidden and secret and has become visible'[21]. This study, which has become something of a *cause celèbre* for post-structuralist critics[22], reveals that while the term *unheimlich* refers ostensibly to what is unfamiliar or un-known, it also carries the opposite connotation of what is intimately familiar and homely (*heimlich*).

Analysing various extracts from Daniel Sanders' *Dictionary of German Speech*, Freud shows how in certain vernacular usages the *Unheimliche* is precisely that class of the strange which somehow re-evokes what is 'known of old and long familiar'. The etymological links between the terms *heimisch* (native), *Geheim* (secret) and *heimlich* (homely) are highly significant here. For they indicate how that which is *heimlich* can undergo a semantic slippage from its normal connotation of 'homely' (in the sense of being intimately familiar) into another related but ultimately reversed meaning – i.e. that which is so homely that it becomes secretive, 'concealed, kept from sight, so that others do not get to know of or about it, withheld from others'[23]. Hence one finds references to a *heimlich* love-affair (surreptitious, prohibited, sinful); a *heimlich* chamber (privy); or a *heimlich* activity (occult, hidden). *Heimlich* is thus revealed to be a highly ambivalent term which can allude *either* to what is congenially accessible *or* to what is so covertly occluded that it actually becomes occult, unspoken or forbidden. The following usage recorded by Sanders is instructive, particularly *à propos* of our consideration of Heaney's work: '*Heimlich* (is) like a buried spring or dried-up pond. One cannot walk over it without always having the feeling that water might come up there again. We call it *unheimlich*, you call it *heimlich* . . . something secret or untrustworthy'. In such wise, *heimlich* comes to mean that which is so intimate and private that it is suppressed from the everyday awareness of the public view. Grimm's dictionary reinforces these implications of semantic inversion by observing that *heimlich* finds its equivalents in the Latin *occultus*, *divinus*, *mysticus* and *veraculus*.

Freud contends that *heimlich* may be understood therefore as that which is so withdrawn from our common or conscious knowledge that it becomes, quite literally, *un*-conscious. The *heimlich* becomes an experience that we not only hide from others, but even from ourselves. And in this way, the term, *heimlich* 'comes to have the meaning actually ascribed to *unheimlich* . . . Thus *heimlich* is a word the meaning of which develops in the direction of ambivalence until it finally coincides with its opposite, *unheimlich*. *Unheimlich* is in some way or other a sub-species of *heimlich*'[24]. Identifying this dialectical relation of *heimlich* and *unheimlich* with that of the conscious and the unconscious, Freud goes on to suggest that our experience of the uncanny – especially when accentuated in works of imagination which blur the distinction between reality and fantasy – expresses itself as a doubling or division of the self. While the conscious self follows the sequential, narrative logic of our normal experience, our unconscious self remains haunted by the uncanny recurrence of the same things – 'the repetition of the same features or character traits or vicissitudes, of the same crimes, or even the same names through several consecutive generations'[25]. This splitting of the self into the conscious and unconscious is further explained by Freud in terms of a defence mechanism whereby the ego projects internal impulses and associations outward onto something foreign. 'When all is said and done', he surmises, 'the quality of uncanniness can only come from the fact of the 'double' being a creation dating back to a very early mental stage, long since surmounted – a stage, incidentally, at which it wore a more friendly aspect. The double has become a thing of terror, just as, after the collapse of their religion, the gods turned into demons'[26].

Considered in terms of the psychic development of the individual, the experience of the uncanny can be attributed to a 'harking-back to particular phases in the evolution of the self-regarding. feeling, a regression to a time when the ego had not marked itself off sharply from the external world and other people'. In other words, the uncanny may be seen, in part at least, as a sentiment that is triggered by the involuntary return of an original 'narcissistic' rapport with the world – in the womb or in early childhood – which has been *repressed*, and whose subsequent 'repetition' can strike us therefore as unsettling, estranging, even terrifying. The extension of the linguistic usage of *heimlich* into its opposite, *unheimlich*, is thus explained by the curious fact that the 'uncanny is in reality nothing new or alien, but something which is familiar and of old established in the mind and which has become alienated from it only through the process of repression'[27].

Freud observes that many people experience this feeling, in the highest degree, in relation to death and the return of the dead in ghostly or ghastly guise. Our experience of death strikes us as uncanny precisely because our primitive feelings and attitudes in this regard have also undergone a repression. 'All supposedly educated people', as Freud remarks, 'have ceased to believe officially that the dead can become visible as spirits, and have made any such appearances dependent on improbable and remote conditions; their emotional attitude towards their dead, moreover, once a highly ambiguous and ambivalent one, has been toned down in the higher strata of the mind into an unambiguous feeling of piety'[28].

Accordingly, the uncanny is held to be closely bound up with the return of unconscious feelings or primitive desires which were once secretly familiar (*heimlich-heimisch*) but were subsequently repressed. The prefix *un-* in *unheimlich* is to be understood less as a logical opposition than a dialectical repression-and-return. And this, in turn, explains why an uncanny effect is often most cogently produced in dream narratives, parapraxis (slips of the tongue), or the symbols and rhetorical tropes of literary works, where the distinction between reality (as a principle of repression) and imagination (as a principle of recall) has been effaced[29]. Indeed, the rapport between poetic language and the unconscious has been explored by several structuralist and post-structuralist critics – most notably, Lacan, Kristeva, Derrida and De Man. This approach is summed up in Lacan's famous maxim that 'the unconscious is structured like language'.

*   *   *

Freud's identification of the homely/unhomely paradox with the 'secretive' nature of unconscious experience, finds several echoes in Heaney's poetry. In the second of the Glanmore Sonnets, published in *Field Work*, Heaney describes the words of a poem as 'sensings, mountings from the hiding places/ . . . ferretting themselves out of their dark hutch'. This comparison of poetic energies with subterranean earth creatures emerging from hiddeness, extends into an allusion to the craft of sculpture. The stone, the poet tells us, connives with the artist's chisel, 'as if the grain remembered what the mallet tapped to know'. Such complicity of the materials of art (words for the poet/stone for the sculptor) with the productive activity of the artist (the poet's pen/the sculptor's hammer and chisel) is obliquely equated with the complicity between the unconscious and the conscious, between feeling and knowledge. Heaney concludes the poem by grafting these metaphors of underground and craft onto his own experience of Glanmore in Co. Wicklow as a 'hedgeschool' where he served his apprenticeship, catching his 'voice' from the environment. This is the 'middle voice' of circular reverie, of active passivity: *active* in so far as the poet's words unearth underground sources of feeling: *passive* in so far as this 'other' ground itself opens up hitherto unknown and unnamed dimensions of being: 'Vowels ploughed into other, opened ground,/ Each verse returning like the plough turned round'.

The link between the uncanny return of repressed memories and the 'mythical' or 'vernacular' practice of divination, observed by Freud, is also a key motif for Heaney. Moreover, in Heaney as in Freud, this motif is commonly associated with images of buried springs and wells. We have already adverted to the opening passage of Heaney's selected prose, *Preoccupations*, where he identified his memory of the well/ *omphalos* as a 'hankering after the underground side of things'. In this same passage, he goes on to describe this hankering as a desire to reactivate the unconscious energies of words which 'lie deep, like some spirit indelibly written into the nervous system'[30]. Indeed Heaney explicitly invokes the act of 'divination' to poetically retrace our familiar words back to their unfamiliar unconscious origins. 'Poetry as divination', writes Heaney, further expresses itself as 'revelation of the self to the self, as a restoration of a culture to itself'[31].

Developing this analogy, Heaney imagines the poet's pen to be a diviner's rod sounding out the 'hiding places' of suppressed experience. In Irish custom, the diviner is someone who uses a hazel plant to relocate the concealed water currents from which it was originally nourished. In a poem called 'The Diviner', Heaney writes as follows of the process of poetic recollection:

> Cut from the green hedge a forked hazel stick
> That he held tight by the arms of the V:
> Circling the terrain, hunting the pluck
> Of water, nervous, but professionally
>
> Unfussed. The pluck came sharp as a sting.
> The rod jerked down with precise convulsions,
> Spring water broadcasting
> Through a green aerial its secret stations.

This central image of the diviner – conjoining the classical allusion to the inspiration of the *vates* and the local allusion to the skill of detecting hidden waterflows – becomes Heaney's privileged metaphor for what he terms the 'technique' of poetic creation:

> If I were asked for a figure who represents pure technique, I would say a
> water diviner. You can't learn the craft of dowsing or divining – it is a gift
> for being in touch with what is there, hidden and real, a gift for mediating
> between the latent resource and the community that wants it current and
> released . . . Technique is what allows that first stirring of the mind round
> the word or an image or a memory, to grow towards articulation: articu-
> lation not necessarily in terms of argument or explication but in terms of
> its own potential for harmonious self-reproduction . . . Technique
> ensures that the first gleam attains its proper effulgence.[32]

While the operative terms of this passage – 'pure', 'divining',
'community', 'memory', 'harmonious', 'proper' – would seem to
subscribe to a romantic rather than a modernist aesthetic, the matter
is, as we shall see, not so simple. Although Heaney continues to use
the traditional terms of romanticism, his poems frequently display
an ironic and self-conscious detachment from the securities which
such terms afforded to his romantic predecessors. Thus whereas
Heaney is close to Wordsworth in many of his sentiments, his self-
scrutinizing approach to language gives a more modernist inflection
to his poetry. If Joyce was a modernist in revolt, Heaney might best
be described as a modernist *incognito*.

The images of divining and digging are also, by the poet's own
admission, 'sexual metaphors, emblems of initiation . . . analogies
for uncovering and touching the hidden thing'. Just as Freud located
the splitting of the self into conscious and unconscious in the half-
forgotten phase of infantile narcissism (where the ego first sees itself
mirrored and echoed in mother-nature or other symbols of primary
unity), so too in a poem entitled 'Personal Helicon', Heaney reiterates the childhood image of an out-of-bounds well whose very
prohibition prompts a return to the repressed:

> As a child, they could not keep me from wells . . .
> And old pumps with buckets and windlasses.
> I loved the dark drop, the trapped sky, the smells
> of waterweed, fungus and dank moss.

And in this same poem Heaney describes how his first intimation
of self-identity was occasioned by the narcissistic act of contemplating his own image in the dark waters of a well: 'a white face hovered
over the bottom' and gave back his own call 'with a clean new music
to it'. But while the poet acknowledges that his childhood propensity
to 'pry into roots, to finger slime,/ To stare, big-eyed Narcissus, into
some spring', is now 'beneath all adult dignity', he also recognizes
this phase of 'primary narcissism' (to use Freud's term for the child's
original feeling of oneness with the other-than-self) as an indispensable catalyst of self-identification. Without such narcissistic self-
discovery, it is possible that the poet would not now be in a position

to conclude from a perspective of poetic self-consciousness – 'I rhyme/ To see myself, to set the darkness echoing'[33]

In 'Anahorish' Heaney extends the implications of this retrieval of unconscious experience from individual to cultural self-remembrance. Here Heaney amplifies the notion of language as divination by describing how a meditation upon the lost etymological roots of this local name – 'Anahorish' meaning 'place of clear water' in Gaelic – prises open the congealed contours of the contemporary landscape and unleashes its secret linguistic origin:

> My 'place of clear water',
> The first hill in the world
> Where springs washed into
> The shiny grass
>
> And darkened cobbles
> In the bed of the lane.
> *Anahorish*, soft gradient
> Of consonant, vowel-meadow . . .
>
> Those mound-dwellers
> Go waist deep in mist
> To break the light ice
> At wells and dunghills.

But perhaps the most telling example of this paradoxical rediscovery of the unfamiliar (unhomely) in the familiar (homely), is witnessed in Heaney's reflections on the etymological sources of his own Ulster birthplace. 'Our farm was called Mossbawn' he writes. '*Moss*, a Scots word probably carried to Ulster by the planters, and *bawn* the name the English colonists gave to their fortified farmhouses. Mossbawn, the planters' house on the bog. Yet in spite of this Ordinance Survey spelling, we pronounced it Moss Bawn, and *bán* is the Gaelic word for white. So might not the thing mean the white moss, the moss of the bog-cotton? In the syllables of my home I see a metaphor of the split culture of Ulster'[34].

Such observations give some credence to the claim that Heaney is fundamentally preoccupied with a 'sense of place'. Landscape or local environment can assume the status of a certain 'sacramental' code – 'instinct with signs, implying a system of reality beyond the visible realities'[34a]. But such a reality is, for Heaney, fractured and foreclosed. Home is a word which can only be spoken – and desired – because one is *not* there. As Heaney remarks in his 'Open Letter' *Field Day* pamphlet with ironic solemnity:

> My *patria*, my deep design
> To be at home
> In my own place and dwell within
> Its proper name.[34b]

*   *   *

We have been concentrating on the more *positive* connotations of the dialectic of home and homelessness in the poetry of Heaney. But Heaney, no less than Freud, is painfully aware of the *negative* or 'uncanny' features of this dialectic. Already in his musings on the buried meanings of his native placename, Heaney offers a hint of the *impossibility* of returning 'home' and rediscovering there some harmonious unity. Mossbawn, as Heaney confides, itself contains a *split* meaning; it thus serves as a reminder of discontinuity, fragmentation and conflict. In his later work, and particularly the 'bog poems' sequence in *North*, Heaney self-consciously records his encounter with the darker worlds of violence and terror which the return to unconscious energies of the past can evoke. In such poems, as we have seen, Freud's references to the 'return of the repressed' in the guise of necrophiliac obsessions with demon gods or other 'terrifying, estanging and unsettling' phenomena, are graphically registered. We will finally take a brief look at Heidegger's treatment of the 'homely/unhomely' paradox; for the Heideggerian analysis adds another significant modernist perspective – existential *ontology* – to that of Freudian *metapsychology*.

II

Heidegger examines the phenomenon of the 'uncanny' not as a psychic experience of the unconscious, but as an existential experience of Being. In *Being and Time* – a seminal work for such contemporary philosophical movements as phenomenology, hermeneutics and deconstruction – Heidegger isolates the experience of 'uncanniness' as a distinguishing feature of modern man's sense of 'uprootedness' and 'estrangement'. Our being-in-the-world is authentic, writes Heidegger, to the extent that it faces up to the 'nothingness' which informs our contemporary relationship to Being. We are no longer at home in our world; we reside between two worlds, being 'too late for the gods and too early for Being'. The ancient experience of Being, in pre-socratic Greece for example, as a sacred presence in harmony with the cosmos, has been irretrievably lost. Moreover, any attempt to deny this loss, or to compensate for it by succumbing to the impersonal securities of ideological dogma (what Heidegger terms the 'they' or *Das Man*) is a form of inauthenticity. According to Heidegger, it is only when our existence (*Dasein*) encounters its own inherent anxiety that we are compelled to abandon the everyday illusion that we are 'at home' in the world and to thereby assume our true condition as alienated 'beings-towards-death':

In anxiety one feels 'uncanny' or 'unhomelike' (*unheimlich*). Here the peculiar indefiniteness of that which Dasein finds itself alongside in anxiety, comes proximally to expression: the 'nothing and nowhere'. But here 'uncanniness' also means 'not-being-at-home' (*das Nicht-zuhause-Sein*).[35]

By contrast, the average awareness of our existence flees from the 'uncanny'. It is thus characterized by the 'everyday publicness of the 'they' which brings tranquillized self-assurance – 'Being-at-home with all its obliviousness'[36]. By fleeing *into* the 'at home' shelteredness of our conventional stereotypes, we are in fact fleeing *from* the reality of not-being-at-home – that is, from the truth of our ontological relationship to the abyss of Being as it is exposed in the existential awareness of death. Anxiety, as the fundamental human response to the experience of not-being-at-home, brings us back from our absorption in the world of false familiarity.

In his later writings, Heidegger sees language, and particularly poetry, as the privileged mode of registering the home/homeless dialectic of contemporary existence. Poetry, Heidegger claims, unsettles our instrumental approach to everyday speech. By disclosing the inner nature of language itself, modern poetry reminds us that the genuine words for naming Being are *missing*. It thereby reveals that we can only begin to 'come home' to Being by first acknowledging its absence, by embracing our actual experience of homelessness. Poetry responds to the call of Being by its vigilant attentiveness to the lost *origin* of words. This origin of language is not some transcendental presence existing before or beyond history. It is a silence or gap in language from which words first emerge into human speech – what Heidegger calls the 'silent tolling of language' (*Das Geläute der Stille*). Poetry is described by Heidegger accordingly as a thinking back (*andenken*) to the forgotten sources of meaning; a thinking which serves in turn as a thanking (*danken*) and remembering (*Gedächtnis*) of that summons of Being which, in silence, first gives language. For Heidegger, it is not so much the poet who speaks language, but language which speaks the poet. In short, poetry 'defamiliarizes' our taken-for-granted attitude to language; it challenges the role of the human speaker as a controlling *cogito* who masters and manipulates words for his own pragmatic ends. To experience language poetically then is to take a 'step back' from our 'natural attitude' which sees Being as a literal possession or as a mere collection of facts to be passively mirrored and classified by our words[37].

In a detailed commentary on Hölderlin's elegy, 'Homecoming', Heidegger observes that this poem is less a celebration of returning to a 'home' than a tragic recognition that such a 'home' has disappeared. The poet's quest for an ontological home presupposes the absence of a literally existing one. And this experience of historical loss is attendant upon the awareness that 'the sacred names are lacking'. The modern world encounters homelessness because our quotidian language no longer names Being but is reduced instead to the technical and pragmatic transmission of information. 'For the poet', claims Heidegger, 'the assault of *techne* (as the wilful manipulation of language, and by extension of the world) is the happening whereby man ceases to be at home'. But he is careful to insist that it is only 'in his *exile* from home, that the home is first disclosed as such'[38]. Poetry is thus construed as an attempt to *prepare* for a home-coming by accepting the truth that we are no longer at home in our world.

'Homecoming', in other words, only becomes an ontological possibility when poets take upon themselves the *care* (*Sorge*) for the lost home, for the missing names. And it is by embodying this 'caring' in poetic language that *what is gone* may be transformed into *what is yet to come*. Consequently, poetic remembrance is not some revivalist nostalgia for an ancient patria, but the anticipation of new possibilities of home hitherto unimagined. Such remembrance evokes the *futurity* of homecoming rather than its *antiquity*. 'Homecoming is the return into the nearness of origin'[39]. But 'origin' is to be understood here not as a topographical fact but as an imaginary horizon that is still coming towards us. Poetry as home-coming transforms the poet and those who listen to his words, into a community of questers, and by implication, *questioners*. These questioners draw near to the origin because they project a beginning as opposed to simply repeating one. For the authentic 'home' is a non-present possibility which can never be revived or re-appropriated once and for all. The neighbourhood of the origin, into which poetry leads us, 'lets nearness be near and yet lets it be the sought-after, thus not near . . . It brings nearness near in that it keeps it away. The neighbourhood of origin is a mystery'[40]. The poetic project of 'homecoming' is, in short, invariably accompanied by the literal awareness of 'homelessness'[41].

Just as Freud believed that it was in the 'slip of the tongue' (parapraxis), when our conscious defences were momentarily left unguarded, that the suppressed truths of our unconscious spoke out, so too Heidegger believes that it is when our commonly taken-for-granted discourse is disrupted that the occluded Being of language reveals itself to us[41a]. Both agreed that it is the *inhabitual* language of poetry and dream which permits the uncanny or 'unhomely' (*unheimlich*) to come home to us. For poetry demonstrates that listening to the *estranging* call of language, and responding to it, is not a derived form of discourse but the original source of all everyday discourse (which has simply forgotten its origins): 'Authentic poetry is never merely a higher plane of ordinary language. Rather, on the contrary, everyday speech is a forgotten and worn-out, over-worked poem, out of which the call is scarcely audible anymore'[42].

The most urgent task of the poet in our 'destitute times', Heidegger concludes, is to make us aware of our destitution by reaching into the abyss of human existence – 'the dark of the world's night' – and showing us that the names for Being are no longer available. For Heidegger, as for Brecht, modernist art is characterised by its power of estrangement (*Verfremdung*). By disappropriating us from our conventional approach to words and images, it teaches us that our familiar reality is in fact something strange and alien. Consequently, the unrelenting effort of modernist poets like Trakl, Rilke and Celan to expose the concealed workings of language is in Heidegger's view not some idle self-regard but the self-scrutinizing conscience of our times. 'This is why poetic images', insists Heidegger, 'are imaginings in a distinctive sense: not mere fancies and illusions but imaginings that are visible inclusions of the alien in the sight of the familiar'[43].

As a footnote to Heidegger's exploration of the poetics of homecoming, it might be appropriate to mention the centrality of this theme in the work of another modernist German poet (considered by Heidegger to be one of the greatest of his generation), Paul Celan. Celan too described his poetry as a 'sort of homecoming'. The silences, dislocations and reversals of normal linguistic usage in his verse reflect the poet's paradoxical awareness – as both a displaced modern European and a post-holocaust Jew – of being an alien in the homeland of the German language. Celan admits the need to 'keep yes and no unsplit', to inhabit the frontiered limbo between light and darkness, because 'he speaks truly who speaks the shade'. He pursues this paradox exhorting himself as poet to 'call the shibboleth, call it out/ Into your alien home'. And in a poem called 'Homecoming' (*Heimkehr*), Celan realizes that the 'I' – the identity of the poet – can only be 'fetched home into its today' via the interminable detour of white distances 'along the sleigh track of the lost'. Vacillating in a transitional season between silence and speech, the poet hopes against hope that poetic remembrance might forge a daisy-chain between past and present where the claims of loss and presence, discontinuity and continuity, might 'almost' co-exist:

Dumb Autumn smells. The
Marguerite, unbroken, passed
between home and chasm through
your memory.

A strange lostness was
palpably present, almost
you would
have lived[44].

This poetics of homecoming – as outlined by a philosopher like Heidegger and, by extension, a poet like Celan – bears an obvious relevance to Heaney's preoccupation with home. By juxtaposing our analysis of Heaney with a summary of the Heideggerian poetics, I hope to have suggested the trans-national and singularly modern nature of his literary concerns.

6
THE LANGUAGE PLAYS OF BRIAN FRIEL

There has been much discussion in recent times about the *verbal* character of Irish theatre. Some argue that since the Irish are 'great talkers' off stage it is logical that their 'way with words' should be creatively explored on stage. Others claim that the Irish dramatist's preoccupation with language is a curse which hampers the genuine medium of theatre: the immediate, physical presence of actors performing in front of an audience. This criticism of Irish drama could be summed up in the protest – too much talk and not enough action! But what is the significance of this aesthetic opposition between talk and action? How, if at all, does it relate to the conventional wisdom that the Irish facility with words is the indispensable armour of the oppressed? Or how does it relate to Tom Paulin's suggestion that 'the history of a language is often the story of possession and dispossession, territorial struggle and the establishment or imposition of a culture'? ('A New Look at the Language Question', Field Day Pamphlet, 1984).

I propose to examine some of the implications of the verbal nature of Irish theatre with particular attention to what I call Friel's three 'language plays' – *Faith Healer*, *Translations* and *The Communication Cord*. In so doing, I wish to assess the modernist and revivalist implications of Friel's dramatic enterprise as an exploration of the twin modern crises of *identity* and *language*.

I

Brian Friel's plays in the eighties have become increasingly concerned with the problem of language. So much so that they constitute not just a theatre *of* language but a theatre *about* language. Words have become both the form *and* content of his dramas. And this replay of language within the plays themselves may well indicate a critical process of self-scrutiny wherein the native movement of verbal theatre is beginning to take stock of itself, to reassess its own assumptions.

Faith Healer (1980) is a story about the art of story-telling. It portrays the attempts made by three characters, a faith healer

(Frank), his wife (Grace) and his promotion agent (Teddy) to give order to their shared past by recollecting it in the present. But they cannot achieve a common version of events. Each character is separated by the subjective interpretation he/she brings to bear on his/her own experience of the past.

The play, however, is not so much about the characters themselves as the artistic performance in which they are engaged. Coleridge defined the power of 'poetic faith' to transform reality as a 'willing suspension of disbelief'. Friel calls it, simply, *faith*. Frank's 'performance' can only work when the healer and the healed come together in a ritual of magic communion – when they agree to play the language game of faith. The problem arises when the rules of the game are obfuscated or forgotten or interpreted in different ways by different players: in short, when the healing word no longer communicates a common message.

With *Translations* (1981) and *The Communication Cord* (1982), Friel's exploration of the transforming and deforming potencies of the word shifts from a personal to a communal perspective. *Translations* deals with the ways in which the consciousness of an entire culture is fractured by the transcription of one linguistic landscape (Gaelic and classical) into another (Anglo-Saxon and positivist). This loss of a communal continuity of language coincides significantly with the historical demise of the old Gaelic society in the famines of the 1830s and 40s. *The Communication Cord* features the sentimental efforts of the modern Irish bourgeoisie to purify the dialect of the tribe and reinstate the antique pieties of a lost culture.

* * *

Friel's obsession with the workings of words betrays more than an *aesthetic* interest in the instruments of his own profession. Though not wishing to miminize the aesthetic problem of language, Friel insists that he is also responding to the contemporary crisis of identity in Irish culture. 'The whole issue of language is very problematic for all of us on this island', he explains. 'I had parents who were native Irish speakers and also two of our four grandparents were illiterate. It is very close you know. I actually remember two of them. And to be so close to illiteracy and to a different language is a curious experience. In some ways I don't think we've resolved it on this island for ourselves. We flirt with the English language, but we haven't absorbed it and we haven't regurgitated it'[1].

Friel insists that the *aesthetic* and *cultural* dimensions of the language crisis entail a third and equally fundamental one – the *political*. He is refreshingly candid in his pronouncements on this aspect of his writing: 'It is back to the political problem – it is our proximity to England, how we have been pigmented in our theatre . . . with the use of the English language, the understanding of words, the whole cultural burden that every word in the English language carries is slightly different to our burden'[2]. Friel compares his own sentiment of linguistic difference and dissent to Stephen's declaration in *A Portrait* that he cannot, as an Irishman, write or speak the English language without 'unrest of spirit', without holding its words at bay. For the ruled the lexicon of the ruler remains an adopted one.

But Friel is not only an *Irish* writer; he is more specifically a *Northern* Irish writer. And this geographical distinction accentuates his sense of cultural, political and linguistic alienation. Though he repudiates the colonial identity of Britain, he also feels an outsider in the Republic. This sentiment of permanent dislocation carries with it both a liberty and an urgency to question the prevailing notions of cultural belongingness. 'If you have a sense of exile', Friel confesses, that brings with it 'some kind of alertness and some kind of eagerness, some kind of hunger. If you are in possession you can become placid about things'[3].

The festering wound of the North is a constant reminder for Friel that the body politic of the nation is deeply haemorrhaged. An amputated Ulster acts as a phantom limb haunting his work. Friel's residence is fundamentally dual, not only because he is an Irish dramatist working in the English language, but also because he is not fully at home either north or south of the Irish border. 'You cannot deposit fealty to a situation like that of the North which you don't believe in', he declares. 'Then you look south of the border and that enterprise is so distasteful in many respects. And yet both places are home in some way. It may be an inheritance from a political situation'[4]. Friel's *border mentality* epitomizes the dual personality of the Catholic minority in the North. And this duality is undoubtedly amplified by Friel's own formative memories of his childhood in Glenties, the Donegal border town which was to serve as the setting for his language plays (under the pseudonym of Baile Beag).

But while the diagnosis is to a large extent political, the prognosis for Friel is of a cultural order. The divisions within the four political provinces of Ireland may be overcome if and when a *fifth province* of the imagination has been created 'to which cultural and artistic loyalty can be offered'[5]. The creation of this fifth province calls for the provision of a new vocabulary, a new mode of communication which could acknowledge, and perhaps ultimately mediate between the sundered cultural identities of the island. A common sense of purpose, or at least the identification of a common problem, which is the *sine qua non* of any genuine community, may, he believes, be retrieved by discovering a common voice. The search for this common voice lies at the heart of Friel's dramatic obsession with words. His language plays are not confined to semantic matters. It is not by ignoring the four political provinces that the fifth province may be produced but by creatively reinterpreting the possibilities of the interrelationship. 'I think that the political problem of this island is going to be solved by language. . . . Not only the language of negotiation across the table, but the recognition of what language means for us on this island. . . . Because we are in fact talking about the marrying of two cultures here, which are ostensibly speaking the same language but which in fact are not'[6]. By recognizing the inadequacy and indeed redundancy of the shibboleths that have satisfied and separated us up to now, Friel's plays open up possibilities of finding a 'different voice' which might enable us to understand ourselves in a new way. This linguistic overhaul, he hopes, 'should lead to a cultural state, not a political one . . . out of that cultural state, the *possibility* of a political state follows'[7].

There is, however, yet a further dimension to Friel's dramatic engagement with language, a fourth dimension which grounds and underpins the other three – *aesthetic, political, cultural.* This fourth dimension might best be described as *ontological* for it concerns the very way in which language determines our innermost being-in-the-world. I employ this existentialist terminology advisedly, following Friel's own invocation of Heidegger's ontological definition of language in his prefatory program note to *Translations:* 'Man acts as if he were the master of language, while it is language which remains master of man. When this relation of domination is inverted, man succumbs to strange contrivances'. This citation is taken from an essay entitled, 'Poetically Man Dwells', published in Heidegger's major philosophical work on language, *Poetry, Language and Thought.* The passage from which Friel quotes proceeds as follows: 'It is language that speaks. Man begins speaking and man only speaks to the extent that he responds to and hears language addressing him, concurring with him. Language is the highest and foremost of those assents which we human beings can never articulate solely out of our own means'[8]. Heidegger argues here that man can only have a genuine rapport with the Being of the world if he obediently listens to *(ob-audire)* language, abandoning his habitual tendency to master it by reducing words to his own wilful contrivances. Man's being-in-the-world becomes authentic when he ceases to abuse language as a strategic instrument for the manipulation of people and things and responds to it instead as that which it truly is: the house of Being in which man may poetically dwell. Heidegger warns against the contemporary decadence of language evident in the prevailing habit of taking language for granted as a mere tool for conveying information and representing objects. This modern eclipse of the original vocation of language to reveal the poetic gift of Being has provoked a crisis of human alienation of unprecedented proportions. A conversion in man's historical or cultural being can never occur, Heidegger insists, without a prior conversion in that innermost region of our existence which is nothing less than our ontological rapport with the very essence of language itself. 'It is because language is the house of Being, that we reach what is by constantly going through this house. When wę go to the woods, we are already going through the word *woods*. When we go to the well, we are always already going through the word *well*. . . . All beings are, qua beings, in the precinct of language. This is why the return from the realm of objects and representation into the innermost region of the heart's space can be accomplished, if anywhere, only in this precinct'[9]. It is surely within this perspective that we should read Friel's caveat to those who seek to reduce his plays to political propaganda tracts. Of *Translations*, he writes: 'I don't want to write a play about Irish peasants being suppressed by English sappers. . . . The play has to do with language and only language'. And Friel adds that since he is determined that his drama should avoid being equated with 'public questions, issues for politicians', he will concentrate more on 'the exploration of the dark and private places of individual souls'[10].

Friel's trilogy of language plays – *Faith Healer*, *Translations* and *The Communication Cord* – constitute an impressively sustained attempt to bring about a conversion in our ontological attitude to language.

II: Faith Healer

In *Faith Healer*, Friel's probings of language focus primarily on its *aesthetic* power to recreate reality in fiction. His choice of the dramatic medium – a faith healer's performances – as the subject of the play, reflects Friel's critical concern with the *modus operandi* of his own professional activity as a playwright. The word-player is holding a mirror up to himself, examining his own conscience.

Friel does not shy away from these implications of the play. He freely concedes that *Faith Healer* is 'some kind of metaphor for the art, the craft of writing . . . and the great confusion we all have about it who are involved in it. How honourable and dishonourable it can be'[11]. Since writing is a pursuit that requires one to be introspective, it can lead to great selfishness. So that the natural impulse to pursue one's own creative talents is constantly invigilated by the 'third eye' of self-consciousness. But this in turn, Friel admits, can be a dangerous thing, because in some way 'it perverts whatever natural freedom you might have, and that natural freedom must find its expression in the written word. So there's an exploration of that element of the charlatan that exists in all creative work'[12].

In *Faith Healer* Friel's attitude to the creative work vacillates between the despondency of a sceptic and the ecstasy of a believer. The play teases out that subtle knot in which religious and aesthetic faith are intertwined. It is not so much a matter of rehearsing anthropological theories about the origins of drama in primitivistic ritual as a keen sounding of that deep psychic need for marvel and miracle to which both religion and theatre have always responded in their distinctive ways. *Faith Healer* has a perennial ring about it.

The play begins with Frank Hardy's incantation of an endless list of paltry towns and villages in which he has performed his art of healing: Aberarder, Aberayron etc. The names are reeled off like the litany of an ancient pilgrim mindlessly reciting his rosary beads of memory. The assonantal place-names are repeated, Frank tells us, for their purgative powers of 'mesmerism and sedation'. They serve as 'relics of abandoned rituals' in a secular age. Frank is the high-priest of his own imagination, recruiting the lingering pieties of senescent rural communities where mundane despair is beginning to replace orthodox religious belief. He is a hybrid creature possessing both the compassion of a messianic healer devoted to the infirm and the commericalism of a meretricious mountebank. He is an artist in straits, the evangelist of a message that has fallen into disrepute. Frank describes his own art of faithhealing accordingly as a 'craft without an apprenticeship, a ministry without responsibility, a vocation without a ministry'.

But while acknowledging that his art is obsolescent, Frank still clings to the conviction that it responds to an ineradicable need in himself and in his audience to be made 'whole and perfect', to be released from what they *are* into what they *might* be. People still hunger for the fiction of a life transformed. And so the show goes on. One half of Frank knows that he is a con man of many masks; but the other remains faithful to the suspicion that he is endowed with a unique and awesome gift which compels him to put it to the service of others. 'Was it chance? – or skill? – or illusion? – a delusion?', he asks himself bemusedly. 'Precisely what power did I possess? Could I summon it? When and how? Was I its servant? Did it reside in my ability to invest someone with faith in me or did I evoke from him a healing faith in himself? . . . Faith in faith?' Put in the terms of existential ontology, Frank's equivocations amount to the fundamental question: Am I the manipulative master or the obedient servant of the healing word?

Faith Healer is a play in four acts which records this crisis of faith as it is experienced by three characters – Frank the Irish miracle worker and his two English travelling companions: Grace his mistress and Teddy his stage-manager. All three deliver monologues in which they bear witness like modern day gospellers to the wandering, homecoming and sacrifice of the Fantastic Frank Hardy.

Grace recounts how Frank performed his art 'in such complete mastery that everything is harmonized for him . . . that anything is possible'. Her 'proud testament', as she significantly if half ironically terms it, pays reverence to his hypnotic play with words.– 'releasing them from his mouth in that special voice he used only then, as if blessing them or consecrating himself'. But Grace's testimony is also tinged with resentment. She is jealous of the way in which Frank's singleminded quest for artistic completion erased her from his orbit of concern as he withdrew into the sanctum of his 'private power'. This memory of exclusion prevents Grace from invoking the litany of placenames with the same impersonal devotion as Frank. She halts at the name Kinlochbervie. In this tiny sequestered village in Scotland their still-born child – a tangible symptom of their diseased life – was brought into the world and buried. Though she may grant to Kinlochbervie its ritual fitness in the aesthetic scheme of things – 'a nice name, a complete sound' – she cannot dispel the tragic reality which it connotes. This is where Grace's narration of the past parts company with Frank's. The gruesome memory of her child's death is refractory to the healing power of fiction. Frank's faith, by contrast, can only survive intact by obliterating this memory from his mind.

The bitter intrusion of the past causes Grace's faith to lapse. For a few brief moments she casts a cold eye on Frank's addiction to his own narrative. She recalls how Frank would humiliate her by constantly changing her name and rearranging the facts of her life (where she was born, how they met etc.) to suit his own scenario. His talent for healing others on stage was evenly matched by his 'talent for hurting' her in life. He had chosen, in Yeats's phrase, perfection of the work over perfection of the life. Not content to fictionalize only the characters of his performance, Frank dragged all of his family and friends (father, mother, wife, child, Teddy) into the quarrel between himself and his art. Each person became grist to his fictional mill.

Grace concedes this painful fact; but she cannot wholly consent to it. Indeed, her account of her tortuous wanderings with Frank gives us a good idea of how Synge's Pegeen Mike might have mused to herself had she left her homeland of Mayo and taken to the roads with her story-telling playboy: 'It wasn't that he was simply a liar – I never understood it – yes, I knew that he wanted to hurt me, but it was much more complex than that, it was some compulsion he had to adjust, to refashion, to re-create everything around him. Even the people who came to him . . . yes, they were real enough, but not real as persons, real as fictions, his fictions, extensions of himself that came into being only because of him. And if he cured a man, that man became for him a successful fiction and therefore actually real. . . . But if he didn't cure him, the man was forgotten immediately, allowed to dissolve and vanish as if he had never existed'.

Teddy is the third member of the performing trinity. He is described by Grace as a 'dedicated acolyte to the holy man'. But Teddy's apostolic posturings are tempered by his clowning humanity. The cockney comic in him keeps the religious votary in check: and if Teddy canonizes Frank it is not as a member of the ancient communion of saints but of the new communion of stage-

and-screen idols which includes Fred Astaire, Lillie Langtry, Laurence Olivier, Houdini, Chaplin and Gracie Fields. Teddy is the odd man out, an Englishman bemused by Frank's 'celtic temperament' and bewildered by his turbulent exchanges with Grace. As entrepreneurial mediator between Frank and his fictions, Teddy is determined to remain aloof and uninvolved, following his chosen thumb rule that friends is friends and work is work and never the twain shall meet. But Teddy's entire monologue belies his own rule and testifies to his incapacity to separate his professional commitment to Frank and Grace from his personal commitment to them as real people. Life and art are as inextricable for Teddy as for Frank and Grace.

Friel deftly underscores the discrepancies between the three narrators' accounts of their shared past. The conflict of evidence is particularly obvious in their different versions of the death and burial of the still-born child. We witness how fiction is deployed by each character as a strategy of psychological survival. Friel's juxtaposition of the three diverging testimonials reveals how each is caught up in a fictive re-enactment of the past, condemned to a stage performance. The monologue format is here ingeniously exploited by Friel as an exact correlative of their solitary confinement. They have ceased to communicate with each other; the confessional mode of private address has become the last resort of their language play.

By means of this play-within-a-play technique, Friel reiterates one of the cardinal themes of modernist theatre developed by Pirandello, Genet, Sartre, Beckett and others: the performer can never be released from his performance and his very existence as a player of roles depends on both author and audience keeping faith with his fiction. Theatre is an *interpretative* art whose very interpretation involves mediation. The final words of Grace's monologue are directed not solely to Frank but to Friel and the spectator as well – 'O my God, I'm one of his fictions too, but I need him to sustain me in that existence'. There is, as Sartre would say, *no exit*. . . .

Faith Healer terminates with Frank, in the last of the monological testaments, deliberating on his first and final performance of the 'miracle' in his native townland of Ballybeg in Donegal. Frank had intended his return from exile to be a glorious homecoming, the ultimate fulfilment of his promise – 'a restoration . . . an integration, a full blossoming'. Frank's valedictory speech is replete with mock-heroic allusions to the New Testament. He talks of those rare performances when he could have moved mountains; of how only one of the many that were cured came back to thank him; of Grace's father, the disbelieving Yorkshire Judge, dismissing his faithhealing as chicanery; of the trimphal homecoming to Ballybeg; the miracle of the healed finger performed with the wedding party in the pub; and the Gethsemane reckoning, with Grace and Teddy asleep, in the year when he prepared for his sacrifice, 'both awed and elated . . . as if he were entering a church'.

The apocalyptic overtones of Frank's portrayal of himself as a lamb being led to the slaughter are unmistakable. As he walks towards his faithless executioners, a prophet unrecognized in his own country, Frank speaks of being possessed of a strange intimation that 'the whole corporeal world – the cobbles, the trees, the sky, those four malign implements – somehow had shed their physical reality and had become mere imaginings, and that in all existence there was only myself and the wedding guests'. This intimation, he goes on, gave rise in turn to a still deeper sentiment that

> even we had ceased to be physical and existed only in spirit, only in the need we had for each other. And as I moved across that yard towards them and offered myself to them, then for the first time I had a simple and genuine sense of home-coming . . . and the maddening questions were silent.

This passage is a veritable *tour de force*, the pathos it evokes extending to the deepest reaches of symbolic association. Apart from its manifest biblical connotations, the speech also sends reverberations through the Irish literary subconscious. One thinks of Yeats's *Second Coming* or the enigmatic lines in *Ben Bulben* when he invokes the transfiguring potency of apocalyptic violence:

> Know that when all words are said
> And a man is fighting mad,
> Something drops from eyes long blind,
> He completes his partial mind,
> For an instant stands at ease,
> Laughs aloud, his heart at peace.
> Even the wisest man grows tense
> With some sort of violence
> Before he can accomplish fate . . .

One is also reminded of the 'terrible beauty' symbolism of the Irish nationalist ideology of martyrdom and blood-sacrifice (e.g. Pearse's appeal to bloodshed as a 'cleansing and sanctifying thing'). Viewed in this perspective, the complex relationship of conflict and complicity between Frank, Grace and Teddy might even be construed as a veiled allegory of Anglo-Irish relations. And it is perhaps useful – apropos of such a reading – to recall Friel's statement in 1972, that Irish theatre must be prepared to respond to the major crisis of faith in contemporary Irish politics and culture:

> The future of Irish drama . . . must depend on the slow development of the Irish mind, and it will shape and be shaped by political events. . . . I do not believe that art is a servant of any movement. But during the period of unrest I can foresee that allegiances that have bound the Irish

imagination – loyalty to the most authoritarian church in the world and
devotion to a romantic ideal we call Kathleen – will be radically altered.
Faith and Fatherland, new definitions will be forged, and then new
loyalties and then new social groupings. . . . The Irish imagination – that
vivid, slovenly, anarchic, petulant, alert to the eternal, impatient with the
here and now instrument – will have to set about shaping and interpreting the new structure in art forms[13].

Friel's casting of Frank as a hapless *salvator mundi* retains,
however, its primary function as a metaphor for the self-destructive
impulses of the creative artist overobsessed with his own art. The
story-teller who sacrifices life to fiction, Friel suggests, risks
becoming the victim of his own script, the dummy of his own ven-
triloquism. Placed in the context of the Irish dramatic tradition,
Faith Healer may be read accordingly as a cautionary tale in
response to the romantic optimism of Synge's *Playboy*. For if the
belief in the power of a lie made Christy into a likely gaffer in the end
of all, it makes Frank into a mutilated corpse.

And yet one cannot escape the feeling that Friel's verdict on his
own aesthetic profession is equivocal. A tentative plea of not guilty
is lodged somewhere between the final lines. We are left with a
sneaking admiration for these possessed players ready, quite
literally, to lay down their lives for their faith. Nor are we allowed to
easily forget that if nine times out of ten, Frank failed to perform the
miracle, one time in ten he *did* succeed in making the crippled
whole, the faithless faithful. In these exceptional moments of
dramatic magic, the healing touch worked. It is not as Beckett's Didi
commented of the two crucified thieves in *Godot* (one of whom was
saved) – 'a reasonable percentage'. But it is a percentage nonetheless. And one sufficient to sustain Friel's faith in his own writing
and the audience's faith in the power of his dramatic lie.

III: Translations

With *Translations* Friel's exploration of language play takes a
new turn. He moves beyond the critical examination of his own
aesthetic conjuring with words to the broader question of the socio-
cultural role of language in the historical evolution of a community.

Translations begins where *Faith Healer* ends – in the Donegal
town of Ballybeg. Only now it goes by its original Gaelic name of
Baile Beag. Friel has wound the clock back a century, recreating the
life and circumstances of this small Donegal community as it faced
into the social upheaval provoked by the Great Famine of the
1840's. The year is 1833 and the old Gaelic language and culture
are enjoying their last lease of life. The play relates the fortunes of a
hedge schoolmaster, Hugh – Frank Hardy's spiritual and tribal

ancestor – and his motley crew of scholarly disciples: the sixty year old 'infant prodigy', Jimmy Jack, fluent in Latin and Greek; Hugh's son and assistant, Manus; and the quasi-illiterate peasant pupils, Sarah, Máire and Doalty. The hedge school fosters a harmonious compound of Gaelic and Classical cultures. 'Our own culture and the classical tongue', boasts Hugh, 'make a happy conjugation'. Athene and Gráinne, Apollo and Cúchulainn rub shoulders here with unaffected ease. The poetic imagination still reigns supreme, roaming from Baile Beag to Athens and Rome in the breath span of a single verse.

But this cultural sanctuary is abruptly threatened by the arrival of a detachment of Royal Engineers from the British Army sent to make an Ordnance Survey map of the local landscape. This military mission is disguised as a benign exercise in geographical linguistics, its ostensible purpose being the transcription of Gaelic placenames into their English equivalents. Friel's play documents the consequences which this seemingly innocuous administrative project has upon the indigenous community. Special attention is given to the decisive role played by Owen, the school master's second son. Recently returned from the anglicized capital, Dublin, Owen enlists in the Survey project as translator and mediator between the two opposing languages, only to find himself spiritually spreadeagled in the collision of loyalties.

The play opens with two crippled beings struggling towards communication: Manus, the master's lame and loyal son, is trying to teach a local dumb girl, Sarah, to speak. After much encouragement, she succeeds in repeating the sentence – 'my - name - is - Sarah'. Manus hails this miraculous act of speech as the unlocking of a hidden landscape of consciousness. 'Marvellous', he expostulates, 'soon you'll be telling me all the secrets that have been in that head of yours all these years'. While Manus is shepherding Sarah into speech, Jimmy Jack is reciting, chorus-like, the Greek legend of the goddess Athene magically touching and transforming Ulysses with her wand. Friel provides us here with an Hellenic tale of faith-healing which subtly counterpoints the reciprocal act of communication whereby Manus and Sarah cure each other of the paralysis of solitude which their respective forms of crippledom embodied. Jimmy's facility with languages is a token of his attunement to the original harmony between word and world – what the Greek philosophers called the *harmonia* of the *logos*. We are told that for him the world of the gods and ancient myth is 'as real and as immediate as everyday life in the townland of Baile Beag'. Jimmy represents that declining old order where man still felt at one with the divine (he talks of gods and goddesses 'as if they lived down the road') and where language was still a cohesive rather than a divisive force. For Jimmy speech equals communication equals community.

The other characters in the opening act of the play are also defined in terms of their attitude to language. The first we hear of the master, Hugh, is that he is off at a christening, helping to choose a name for a baby. The choice of name is impatiently awaited by the community as a means of deciding the dubious identity of the child's father! Hugh is thus casually introduced as a minister of names and, by extension, a guarantor and guardian of the community's cultural identity. Moreover, by professionally imparting to his students the scholarly art of translating Gaelic words into Latin and Greek, Hugh permits the community to converse with cultures other than its own. It is of course significant that the classical tongues cultivated by the master represent *past* civilizations, now dead and gone: a hint of what is in store for his own Gaelic tongue and civilization. Hugh's vision is sighted on a vanishing kingdom. He is an inquisitor of origins and etymologies who speaks in the past tense. He is backward looking for the simple reason that the future holds no hope for his language.

When Hugh finally arrives on stage, he proudly announces the identity of the child disclosed at the 'ritual of naming' – or *caerimonia nominationis* as he hastens to add. He then proceeds to quiz his pupils on the Greek and Latin etymologies of the word baptize – *baptizein*, to dip; *baptisterium*, a bath etc. And when his pupils apprise him of the departure of one of his students from the school, he extends the importance of the naming motif with the humorous quip: 'Nora Dan can now write her name – Nora Dan's education is complete!'

But Nora Dan may well be one of the last graduates of Hugh's hedge school. English – the new colonial language of commerce and maps – is already making incursions into the old system of learning. Several of the young peasants greet the arrival of this tongue as holding out the promise of a new beginning. Máire is one such peasant pupil seduced by the allure of English words. She only knows three snatches which an aunt has taught her to recite by rote. Though still not having an idea what the words actually mean, she is prepared nonetheless to trade in her limited knowledge of the classics for more of the same: 'I don't want Greek. I don't want Latin. . . . Fit me better if I had that much English'. Máire belongs to the emerging generation of aspiring peasants tired of treading the mudtracks of oppressed Gaeldom. She dreams of finer things to come, citing the opinion of Dan O'Connell, the 'Liberator', that the sooner 'we all learn to speak English the better. . . . The old language is a barrier to progress'.

Máire has secured passage money to the New World and knows full well that the only *useful* language for her now is English. She sits on the hedge school floor excitedly scanning the map of America for the English placenames of her future abode. But the lens of her youthful fascination soon focuses on a more literal map nearer home. The British soldiers 'making the maps' for the Ordnance

Survey in the neighbouring fields have not escaped her attention. Máire's enthusiasm for the arrival of the Royal Engineers is, however, offset by two discreet allusions to the threat which their colonial culture represents to the native Gaelic-speaking community. First, we are casually informed that the hedge school is to be replaced by a progressive National school where every subject will be taught through English. And second, we learn of the imminent danger of a potato blight: 'just beyond where the soldiers are making the maps – the sweet smell was everywhere'.

The next character to make an appearance at the hedge school is the master's second son, Owen. He is something indeed of a prodigal son returning from his travels with a reputation of great business successes (Máire claims she heard stories that he owned 'ten big shops in Dublin'). Owen is accompanied by two English officers – Captain Lancey and Lieutenant Yolland – in whose employ he is presently engaged as a 'translator'.

(Hugh has already prepared us for the arrival of the English speakers. Having met with Captain Lancey on his return from the baptism, Hugh had pointed out to the Royal Engineer that his alien tongue 'couldn't really express us' and was only employed in the community on rare occasions for 'purposes of commerce' – a use, Hugh comments with jocular disrespect, to which the English language 'seemed particularly suited'. Hugh mischievously informs the officers that his people are not familiar with their literature: feeling 'closer to the warm Mediterranean. We tend to overlook your island'.)

Owen arrives first at the school – like an Indian scout preparing the way for the ensuing cavalry. He greets his father, brother and the local pupils with genuine affection and camaraderie. It is, after all, his first homecoming to Baile Beag. And it is no less festive than that of Frank Hardy a century later. Owen immediately enters his father's game of translating Irish into Latin and vice versa, thus reminding his people that he is still one of their own, still familiar with the rules of their language game. Owen is a master of what Patrick Kavanagh called 'the wink and elbow language of delight'. There follows a particularly poignant exchange between Owen and Sarah. Echoing the earlier act of communication between his brother (Manus) and the dumb girl, Owen asks her name. When she falteringly replies that it is Sarah Johnny Sally, he spontaneously adds: 'Of course! From Bun na hAbhann! I'm Owen Hugh Mor from Baile Beag'. Owen thus subscribes to the password of the tribe, uttering once again that communal dialect which identifies its members at birth according to their native origins – the name of their parents and local birthplace.

Owen does not try to hide the fact that he is on the pay roll of the Ordnance Survey expedition. On the contrary, he announces his brief as civilian interpreter with good-humoured candour: 'My job is to translate the quaint, archaic tongue you people persist in speaking, into the King's good English'. Owen then introduces the two officers who have been waiting in attendance. Captain Lancey is a hardnosed military expert with little or no culture. He mistakes Jimmy's Latin for Gaelic and is only interested in language in so far as it may prove a useful instrument in the colonial conquest of a landscape by means of a mechanistic mapping system. Lancey's attitude epitomizes the British Empiricist philosophy of language as a pragmatic reductionism of things to signs. 'A map is a representation on paper', he explains, subverting Hugh's pedagogical role. 'His Majesty's Government has ordered the first ever comprehensive survey of this entire country – a general triangulation which will embrace detailed hydrographic and topographic information and which will be executed to a scale of six inches to the English mile'. Nor does Lancey leave us in any doubt that this apparently inoffensive task of cartographical translation involves an ulterior purpose – the colonial and commercial exploitation of the native community as a whole. 'This enormous task', he blandly reveals, 'has been embarked on so that the military authorities will be equipped with up-to-date and accurate information on every corner of this part of the Empire . . . and also so that the entire basis of land valuation can be reassessed for reasons of more equitable taxation'. Lancey shows himself to be a patronizing hypocrite, however, when he presents the entire exercise as a token of British altruism, undertaken to 'advance the interests of Ireland'. The Irish people are privileged, he affirms, since no such survey will be undertaken in England! In short, Lancey's formal address exposes the devious uses to which his language is being put as an imperial ploy to patronize, deceive and conquer.

But Friel's depiction of the adversary resists the temptation of crude caricature. If Lancey is cast as a cheerless servant of the Crown, his subordinate officer, Yolland, impresses immediately as a sensitive and romantic youth. Yolland is a 'soldier by accident' whose birthplace was, significantly, only four miles away from that of William Wordsworth – a reliable signal, as it transpires, of his own spiritual identity. He takes his note from the temper of his native environment across the water: an imaginative disposition which enables him to empathize with this strange Gaelic culture into which he has been dispatched. Yolland is a self-proclaimed hibernophile enamoured of the local people and perturbed by his inability to understand their language. Struggling for words, in a manner reminiscent of Sarah's stammering towards speech, Yolland's opening address is in stark contrast to that of his military superior: 'I - I - I've nothing to say - really . . . I feel very foolish to - to - to be working here and not to speak your language. . . . I hope we're not too - too crude an intrusion on your lives'.

In all this, Owen plays a double language-game, commuting with apparent ease between the two parties. But the ease is no more than apparent. In reality, Owen's linguistic duality entails a fundamental duplicity. He mistranslates Lancey's message, winnowing off its mercenary implications in order to make it more palatable for the locals. Yet at the same time Owen is sufficiently circumspect to withhold his real name (and by extension, *identity*) from the English officers, operating under the pseudonym of Rolland. Owen is both a mistranslator and a misnomer, double-timing, as it were, in his efforts to keep in with both sides of the colonial schism. In response to his brother's objection that there is nothing incorrect about the existing Gaelic placenames, he declares – 'They're just going to be standardized . . . where there's ambiguity, they'll be anglicized'. Owen's description of this linguistic transposition is in fact a self-description, accurately foreshadowing his own fate. Friel touches here, with characteristic irony, on the crisis of cultural ambiguity which hallmarks the modern Irish psyche. *Tradition* can only survive by being 'handed over' *(tradere)* from one historical generation to the next; but this 'handing over' frequently requires a *translation* or 'carrying over' *(transferre-translatum)* which alters the original order of meaning even as it releases it into a new historical duration. The survival of tradition by means of translation from one language to another can thus be construed as 'a subversion or perversion of tradition conceived as *continuity*'[14]. Owen, the privileged *translator* who 'double-crosses' over and back between the old Gaelic idioms and the new English ones, is also a *traducer* who trades in one linguistic currency for another.

*   *   *

In the second act of the play, Friel provides us with two dramatic instances of translation. The first is a translation of labour (between Owen and Yolland); the second a translation of love (between Yolland and Máire).

The act opens with Yolland and Owen, bent over a Name Book and large map, embarked upon their task of transposing the Gaelic toponymy of Baile Beag into an English alternative. The translation of names also involves a translation of namers – the roles of colonizer and colonized are reversed, as Yolland and Owen undergo an exchange of identity.

While Owen is patently engrossed by the mapping process, Yolland is lost in a world of dreams, savouring each Gaelic word upon his tongue, reluctant to 'traduce' it into its Anglo-Saxon equivalent. So that when Owen offers the practical suggestion of rendering *Bun na hAbhann* (in Irish, mouth of the river) as *Burnfoot*, Yolland's reaction is one of protective deference towards the original: 'Let's leave it alone. There's no English equivalent for a sound like that'. But it is not just the sound that is at stake. It is the stored heritage of local history which each Gaelic name recollects and *secretes*. The translation of these placenames closes off rather than discloses their mnemonic secrets, distorts their former meaning.

Yolland describes his first encounter with the Gaelic language as a quasi-mystical revelation. The linguistic divide is experienced by him as a threshold demarcating fundamentally heterogeneous modes of consciousness. He speaks of discovering a new continent of feeling, one belonging to 'a totally different order. I had moved into a consciousness that wasn't striving nor agitated, but at its ease and with its own conviction and assurance'.

But the threshold is also a frontier. It cannot be crossed with impunity, as Yolland will discover to his cost. Already he has intimations of the impenetrable barrier of words which no translation, however well-intentioned, can traverse. 'Even if I did speak Irish', concedes Yolland, 'I'd always be an outsider here, wouldn't I? I may learn the password but the language of the tribe will always elude me, won't it? The private core will always be . . . hermetic, won't it?' Owen's reassuring rejoinder – 'you can learn to decode us' – has an ominous ring, its scarcely veiled sarcasm reflecting his private complicity with his own native tribe. In short the commercial collusion between Planter and Gael cannot be immunized against the cultural-linguistic conflict which opposes them.

If language unites people by permitting communication, it divides them by cultivating the possibility of separate tribal identities. This paradox is a heritage of the *felix culpa* of our first parents: their fall from the edenesque *Logos* which enabled God and man to speak with one voice. And this original sin of language – the sin of speaking in a multiplicity of conflicting tongues – finds its ultimate nemesis in the subsequent biblical account of the Tower of Babel.

(In *After Babel*, George Steiner writes of the literary history of translation as a series of attempts to build bridges between the disparate tongues of our fallen humanity. Friel has been deeply impressed by Steiner's disquisition and succeeds in *Translations* in dramatically extrapolating some of its scholarly insights. In an appendix to this study, we provide a short inventory of several key passages from *After Babel* which Friel has reworked in his own original idioms. What is of interest in this creative partnership of minds is the way in which Friel brilliantly contrives to refashion Steiner's academic research in a drama concretely situated in his own native cultural context. Friel's play serves in this respect as a fine example of how literary theory may be reclaimed by literature, of how criticism may be retranslated back into imaginative practice.)

Yolland cannot help recognizing that the whole business of toponymic translation constitutes an 'eviction of sorts': an 'erosion' of the traditional Gaelic pieties in the name of Imperial progress. But Yolland's disapproval is counterbalanced by his naive belief that there might exist an ideal system of translation where the obstacles thrown up by tribal dialects could be transcended. Yolland is hankering after a prelapsarian naming process, similar to that of Adam when he named the animals, capable of achieving an exact correspondence between word and thing. When Owen finally confesses to Yolland that his real name is not *Rolland* but *Owen* – or better still *Oland* by way of a perfect compromise between the nominal differences of Irish (Owen) and English (Yolland) – they celebrate their newfound confraternity of naming:

Owen: A christening! . . .
Yolland: A thousand baptisms! Welcome to Eden!
Owen: Eden's right! We name a thing and – bang! – it leaps into existence!
Yolland: Each name a perfect equation with its roots.
Owen: A perfect congruence with its reality. Take a drink.
Yolland: Poteen – beautiful.
Owen: Lying Anna's poteen.
Yolland: Anna na mBreag's poteen. . . . I'll decode it yet'.

Once again, Friel reminds us that the magical equation of word and world is achieved by the power of a lie! The fact that Owen and Yolland consecrate their new transliteral unity (as *Oland*) with Anna's illusionist brew is itself a hint of the disillusioning reality to follow.

*   *   *

Friel juxtaposes this 'translation of labour' sequence between Owen and Yolland with a scene featuring a 'translation of love' between Yolland and Máire. In this second exchange Friel highlights the impossibility of attaining an ideal system of language capable of decoding semantic differences into some common transcultural identity. Yolland and Máire meet at the local dance. Ever since Yolland arrived in the village they have been admiring each other from a distance. Now at last together they try to transcend this distance, stealing away to the fields so that they might communicate their mutual love. But if their love is mutual their dialect is not. Máire begins by speaking Latin which Yolland mistakes for Gaelic. Then she stammers forth the only three English words in her possession – water, fire, earth. But even though Yolland congratulates Máire on her 'perfect English', his lie of encouragement cannot alter the fact that they continually misunderstand each other's words. Finally they do appear to reach some level of communication by lovingly reciting to each other the litany of Gaelic placenames. The irony is of course that this source of semantic agreement is precisely the issue which so tragically divides their respective tribes. Their commonly uttered words still consign them to separate worlds as Friel himself indicates in a textual note: 'Each now speaks almost to himself/herself'. (One recalls Frank's and Grace's equally discrepant invocation of place-names in *Faith Healer*). As each name is intoned by one lover and antiphonally echoed by the other, they move closer together and embrace. This climactic touch serves as a sort of leitmotif reiterating the opening exchange between Manus and Sarah. The order is reversed, however, in so far as speech now becomes touch whereas in the former scene touch had become speech.

When Yolland and Máire finally kiss, their moment of loving silence is no more than a provisional reprieve from the decree of language. Sarah enters; and shocked by what she witnesses she rushes off calling out the name of Máire's suitor – 'Manus!'. Thus in a cruel twist of dramatic fortunes, Sarah's initial transition from silence to speech – her initiation into the naming process in the opening love scene between herself and Manus – becomes the condition for the betrayal of love.

According to the local code, Máire has been promised to Manus and this tacit tribal contract cannot be gainsaid or 'decoded' by an outsider – even in an act of love. As Jimmy Jack explains in his final speech, enunciating his own fictitious betrothal to the Goddess Athene: 'The word *exogamein* means to marry outside the tribe. And you don't cross those borders casually – both sides get very angry. Now, the problem is this: Is Athene sufficiently mortal or am I sufficiently godlike for the marriage to be acceptable to her people and to my people?'. Whatever about transgressing the mythological boundaries between the human and the divine, the real boundaries between one human code and another cannot be ignored with impunity. Yolland is assassinated by the Donnelly twins – renegade pupils from the hedge school; and Captain Lancey promises re-tribution on the whole community – he orders their livestock to be slaughtered and their abodes levelled.

Friel's irony excels itself at this point: Lancey's threat to destroy the very locality which his own Ordnance Survey was proposing to civilize and advance, renders the whole 'translation' process null and void. Nominal eviction has been replaced by its literal equivalent. This reversal of plot also extends to a reversal of character. Summoned before a local gathering, Owen is now compelled to give a literal translation of Lancey's punitive intentions, his compromising role as go-between now made embarrassingly plain. For the dubious benefit of his own tribe, Owen is forced to *retranslate* Lancey's English rendition of the names of the local villages to be destroyed back into their Gaelic originals. Owen's own labour of words has backfired; he is hoist with his own petard.

Máire also becomes a victim of this reverse play of language. Exposed in the abrupt polarization of the two rival tribes, she can no longer feel at home in her own community and yet has no other home to go to now that Yolland is dead. Employing again his dramatic technique of reverse repetition, Friel reinvokes the idiom of mapping to emphasize Máire's dilemma. Tracing out an imaginary map on that very spot on the hedge school floor where Owen's Ordnance Survey map had been spread, she lists off the placenames of Yolland's native Norfolk which he had taught her to recite during their love-duet the previous night – Winfarthing, Barton, Bendish, Saxingham etc. 'Nice sounds', she muses, as Yolland had done before her with reference to Gaelic names, 'just like Jimmy Jack reciting Homer'. But there is a fundamental difference between the recitation of Jimmy Jack and that of Máire and Yolland. Since the Greeks had no historic quarrel with the Gaels their two tongues could peacably conjugate in a way that English and Gaelic cannot. In one particularly striking moment, Máire recalls that Yolland's parting message to her was in fact a mistranslation: 'He tried to speak in Irish, he said – 'I'll see you yesterday' – he meant to say, 'I'll see you tomorrow'.' This mistranslation is a poignant signal of the fact that in the colonial conflict between England and Ireland the time was out of joint. In such a context, linguistic discrepancies are the inevitable consequence of historical ones.

These reversals of *plot*, *persona*, and *time*, are reinforced by a more generalized reversal of *perception*. The disarticulation of language brought about by the various abortive attempts at translation, also expresses itself at the level of the characters' distorted perception of the world about them. The last scene of the play is littered with misidentifications, on a par with the most convoluted comedies of Wilde or Shakespeare. Manus, who flees to Mayo, is mistaken for the assassins (the Donnellys); the fumes from the burning army tents are mistaken for the sweet smell of potato blight; Doalty is mistaken for the arsonist; a bacon-curing schoolmaster from Cork is mistaken for the village schoolmaster, Hugh – the National school replacing the old hedge school; and the anglicized Owen is mistaken for (in the sense of taking over from) his inveterately Gaelic brother, Manus, as faithful son to their father, Hugh.

All these instances of displacement consolidate Friel's message about the mis-taken substitution of Irish by English. But Friel, like Hugh, recognizes that this mistake is an irreversible, if regrettable, inevitability of history. 'We like to think we endure around truths immemorially posited', Hugh explains with rueful wisdom, 'but we remember that words are signals, counters. They are not immortal. And it can happen . . . that a civilization can be imprisoned in a linguistic contour which no longer matches the landscape of . . . fact'. The rich mytho-poeic resources of the Gaelic tongue, Hugh adds, were themselves a response to the painful historical circumstances which conditioned its development: 'Yes, it is a rich language . . . full of mythologies of fantasy and hope and self-deception – a syntax opulent with tomorrows. It is our response to mud cabins and a diet of potatoes; our only method of replying to . . . inevitabilities'. Thus in stoical acknowledgement that what is done cannot be undone, Hugh determines to make a virtue of necessity by creatively refashioning the English language so as to make sense of the new landscape of historical fact. At one point Owen tries to revoke the repercussions of translation, dismissing the whole sorry business as '*my* mistake – nothing to do with us'. But Hugh has had enough of self-deception. Pointing to the Name Book, he counsels his community to reclaim in and through the English language that which has been lost to it. 'We must learn those new names', he soberly challenges, 'we must learn to make them our own, we must make them our new home'.

*   *   *

If history has deprived the Irish of their native tongue, this will not prevent them from reinterpreting their identity in a new tongue. Speaking in his capacity as poet, Hugh bequeathes to his community a legacy of challenge, the challenge of an Irish literature written in English, the challenge to persist in an aesthetic reconquest of that cultural self-image vanquished by the *empirical* fact of colonization. We the audience recognize of course that the entire modern tradition of Irish writers of English – extending from Synge, Yeats and Joyce to Friel himself – has arisen as a response to just this challenge. We know that for the Irish writer this is his *heritage now*. The historical fatality of linguistic dispossession has not condemned the Irish imagination to dumb show. Our best writers have masterfully reworked their adopted language and also the images of their cultural past. Indeed *Translations* is itself a paramount example. Hugh outlines a blueprint for this poetic retrieval of lost ground when he appeals for an authentic discrimination between the separate laws of history and imagination, or if you wish between the laws of empirical necessity and cultural freedom. 'It is not', he insists, 'the *facts* of history, that shape us, but *images* of the past embodied in language. . . . We must never cease renewing those images; because once we do, we fossilize'. Jimmy Jack, the other-worldly poet of the old order, has fossilized precisely because he was unable to make that discrimination. The poets of the new order cannot afford the luxury of such indifference.

But Hugh's lesson in aesthetics also serves as a history lesson. Friel would seem to be cautioning us against the temptation of becoming political prisoners to historical fact. 'To remember everything is a form of madness', Hugh warns, implying a preference for a more discerning use of memory capable of distinguishing between the past that liquidates by a narrow obsession with revenge, and the past which liberates into new possibilities of self-recollection. Recalling the rebel Uprising of 1798 when himself and Jimmy went forth to battle, with pikes in their hands and Virgil in their pockets, Hugh humorously confesses that after several miles of marching they got drunk in a pub before staggering unheroically home. Hugh admits to the feeling of 'perception heightened . . . and consciousness accelerated' which the prospect of violence induced in them. But in a precise inversion of Frank's apocalyptic vision at the end of *Faith Healer*, Friel shows Hugh opting for an alternative version of home-coming, an option for a more domestic and poetic form of survival. 'Our *pietas* was for older, quieter things', Hugh recounts, 'the *desiderium nostrorum* – the need for our own'. If Frank suffers the capitulation of words to violence, Hugh averts violence in the name of the recreative power of words.

To rephrase this alternative in terms of a Yeatsian parallel, we might say that while *Faith Healer* mirrored the apocalyptic tones of *Ben Bulben*, *Translations* moves closer to the ancestral solace of *A Dialogue of Self and Soul:*

> Why should the imagination of a man
> Long past his prime remember things that are
> Emblematic of love and war?
> Think of ancestral night that can . . .
> Deliver from the crime of death and birth.

A cultural fidelity to the *images* of the past, Friel seems to suggest, is not necessarily reducible to the *facts* of the past. There may be other, more complicated ways of recovering what has been lost and settling one's score with history. One of these ways is the poetic possibility of forging a new language, of recreating a new home. Any attempt at such a cultural transition is, of course, fraught with risk and danger: the risk of losing everything, the danger of self-annihilation. But given the ominous alternatives, it may be a risk worth taking. Perhaps this is why Hugh agrees at the end of the play to teach Máire English. He concedes the necessity for change, telling Máire that the word 'always' is a silly one. But Hugh cannot guarantee that her acquisition of the art of translation will permit her to transport the secret heritage of the old culture into the new one. His parting verdict promises neither too little nor too much. 'I will provide you with the available words and the available grammar', he assures Máire, 'But will that help you to interpret between privacies? I have no idea'.

IV: The Communication Cord

The Communication Cord is in many respects the logical sequel to *Translations*. Friel has made quite plain his wish that the two plays be considered 'in tandem',[15] as consecutive forays into the border-lands of our language culture.

If *Translations* set out to chart the transition of a language from the mythological past to the pragmatic present, *The Communication Cord* operates in reverse order: it portrays the attempt to retrace language from its contemporary contingency back to its pristine ancestry. Both plays conspire to present us with a fascinating genealogy of the process of human speech, the ways in which we use words to progress or regress in history, to find or lose ourselves, to confuse or to converse. The fact that the former play is composed in *tragic* tones, while the latter is written as a *farce*, is in itself an indicator of Friel's tragic-comic realization that there is no going back on history; that the best that can be achieved is a playful deconstruction and reconstruction of words in the hope that new modes of communication may become possible.

Both plays situate the conflict of language models in the specific context of Irish culture. *Translations* deals with pre-famine Ireland bracing itself for the final transplantation of Gaelic into English. *The Communication Cord* takes up the story more than a century later. It shows us modern Ireland taking stock of its linguistic identity and attempting to recover the ancient pieties of its pre-famine heritage. While one play features the old language looking forward to its ominous future, the other features the new language looking back to its dispossessed origins.

The scene of the action in *The Communication Cord* – a 'restored' thatched cottage in Ballybeg – is an inverted replica of the 'condemned' school house of Baile Beag. In similar fashion, Tim Gallaher, the central character of the play – a university lecturer in linguistics preparing a Ph.D. on communication – serves as a mirror-image of his ancestral prototype, Hugh. Both are displaced scholars without tenure; both teach that the transmission of communal wisdom cannot be divorced from the ontological power of language. In fact, Tim is attempting to prove what was still self-evident for Hugh: that words which function as positivistic units or linguistic maps based on agreed codes are, at root, derived and often distorted forms of ontological 'response cries'. To put it in Heidegger's terms, Tim is resolved to return from the language of objects and represent-ation (Owen's modern legacy) to the ultimate origin of words in the interiority of the heart's space (Hugh's lost legacy).

The ersatz character of the refurbished cottage betokens the futility of any literal quest for the grail of a vanished past. Adorned with the antiquarian accoutrements of churn, creel, crook, hanging pot, thatched roof and open hearth, the cottage is described by Friel in a stage note as 'false . . . too pat . . *too* authentic'. It is, in short, an artificial reproduction, a holiday home of today counterfeiting the real home of yesterday. Moreover, Friel's scenario is no doubt also parodying the folksy rural romanticism of the Abbey tradition.

This play about communication begins, significantly, with a failure of communication. Tim is saying that the door to the cottage is open, while Jack McNeilis, his friend, misunderstands him to say that it is locked. From the outset their language is at cross purposes. If Owen was Manus's alter-ego in *Translations*, Jack is Tim's. Jack is a successful and self-assured barrister from Dublin. He possesses all those qualities of the modern Irish bourgeoisie which Tim lacks – efficiency, sexual confidence and above all (since language remains the key) a remarkable felicity with conversational repartee.

Jack's *nouveau-riche* family bought the cottage in Ballybeg and revamped its rustic charms in order to experience the 'soul and authenticity of the place'. Jack's description of this revivalist return to the land is presented as a saucy parody of Hugh's *pietas*. 'Everybody's grandmother was reared in a house like this', Jack quips, claiming it to be the 'ancestral seat of the McNeilis dynasty, restored with love and dedication, absolutely authentic in every last detail. . . . This is where we all come from. This is our first cathedral. This shaped our soul. This determined our first pieties. Yes. Have reverence for this place'. Jack's way of revering his 'father's house' is, ironically, to recite a tedious inventory or map of all the objects contained in the cottage (fireplace, pot-iron, tongs, etc.). He employs naming according to the model of utilitarian representation in order to classify each thing as a use-item. For Jack, language is not a house of being but a filing cabinet of objects.

But if Jack and Tim's ultimate concern is with words, their ostensible concern is with women. They have come to the cottage for the purpose of amorous exchange – Tim with the girl of his fancy, Susan; Jack with his latest catch, Ivette Giroux from the French Embassy in Dublin. When Tim tries to express genuine reservations about his feelings for Susan, Jack reassures him that it's a 'perfect match'. He means of course a perfect *commercial* match: 'you're ugly and penniless, she's pretty and rich'. One of the central themes of the play is thus discreetly announced – the conflict between Tim's view of communication as an ontological *response cry* and Jack's view of communication as a *commercial contract*.

Friel has Tim expound his linguistic thesis in the opening act of the play, thereby establishing the conceptual coordinates for the subsequent unfolding of the plot. Tim argues that language operates on two levels – as *information* and as *conversation*. At the first level, words function as messengers transmitting information from a speaker to a listener. Language becomes a process of encoding and decoding messages. Where a common code exists messages can be exchanged, where not there is misunderstanding. Echoing the terms of Lévi-Strauss, Tim explains that 'all social behaviour, the entire social order, depends on communicational structures, on words mutually agreed on and mutually understood. Without that agreement, without that shared code, you have chaos'. It is surely no coincidence that the example Tim chooses to illustrate his point is the absence of a common code of *translation* between two speakers of different languages.

At the second and more fundamental level, language transcends its pragmatic function as a formal transmission of information and seeks a more profound sharing of interpersonal experience: 'You desire to share my experience – and because of that desire our exchange is immediately lifted out of the realm of mere exchange of basic messages and aspires to something higher, something much more important – *conversation* . . . a response cry!' Response cries bespeak the existential interiority of the heart's space. They are by definition 'involuntary', Tim observes, in that they forgo all strategies of wilful manipulation or commerce. But the difficulty is how to discriminate between genuine response cries which speak straight from the heart and the mere pretence at such speech. How is language to escape from the insincerity of role-playing (or as Wittgenstein would put it, the ploys of 'language games')? Tim's inability to resolve this dilemma is not only the reason why he cannot complete his thesis or decide whom he truly loves; it is the very *raison d'être* for the play itself. It is the importance of being earnest all over again. Indeed Friel's debt to Wilde's comic genius is perhaps nowhere more evident than in *Communication Cord*.

*   *   *

The entire action of the play may be seen as an experimental testing of Tim's hypothesis of reconnecting the modern positivistic model of language to its ontological origins. The plot unfolds accordingly as a farcical rewind of *Translations*.

Tim is not only a recast of Hugh but also of Manus, the schoolmaster's sincere and penurious son. He is, as Jack jibes, 'worthy and penniless – all nobility and no nous'. Just as Manus remained implacably opposed to Owen's translation project, so too Tim denounces Jack's abuse of language as a transmission of financial and erotic messages as 'damned perfidious'. Like Owen, Jack is a dealer in identities, mediating between the cunning locals (he recognizes his neighbour Nora Dan to be a 'quintessential noble peasant –obsessed with curiousity, greed and envy') and the mercenary outsiders (Senator Donovan from Dublin and the German blow-in eager to purchase a property in the locality – Barney the Banks). Jack is at once adept in the communal game of *pietas* – as when, in mock-Heideggerean fashion, he goes to 'the well for a bucket of the purest of pure spring water' – and a master of modern pragmatism. The *map* of translation is replaced here by the *watch* of time-keeping: the new symbol of progress. Appropriately, Jack can mastermind the plot by virtue of the expert timing of his watch, whereas Tim, whose watch keeps stopping, has no control whatsoever over all the comings and goings.

Other characters in the play may also be seen as comic reincarnations of the *dramatis personae* in *Translations*. Claire,

Tim's former girlfriend and the true love to his heart, recalls both Sarah and Máire. She is described as 'open and humorous' and is bravely determined to communicate her love to Tim, come what may. The German prospector of property recalls the Royal Engineers. And Nora Dan recalls her eponymous forebear who left the hedge school as soon as she had learnt her name. The modern day Nora Dan, in a pastiche of the patrilinear nomenclature practised in *Translations*, explains her double name to Tim as follows: 'I get the Dan from my father – that's the queer way we have of naming people around here'. Nora Dan is a peasant who, Friel tells us, 'likes to present herself as a peasant'. She is a stage Irish-woman who has perfected her stagecraft.

Lastly, Senator Donovan is cast as a sort of modern antitype of Jimmy Jack. He is an 'amateur antiquarian', a self-made man full of his own importance as both doctor and politician, who extolls the 'absolute verity' of the cottage. Donovan is a caricature of all that is sentimental and sententious in the modern bourgeois Republic. He represents cultural revivalism at its worst. His speeches are reeled off like fatuous travesties of Hugh's and Jimmy's *desiderium nostrorum* – the sacramental longing for older, quieter things. Arriving in Ballybeg he pretentiously muses: 'This silence, this peace, the restorative power of the landscape . . . this speaks to me, this whispers to me. . . . and despite the market place, all the years of trafficking in politics and medicine, a small voice within me still knows the *responses*. . . . This is the touchstone . . . the apotheosis'.

Donovan's version of the response cry traduces Tim's own pre-dication of this term. And his interpretation of love play with pretty women as another means of moving from word representation to wordless response is a further falsification of Tim's real meaning. 'When you're as young and as beautiful as Madame Giroux', opines the lusty Senator, 'language doesn't matter does it? Words are superfluous aren't they?' The radical difference between Tim's and Donovan's respective attitudes to language becomes clear in their dramatic exchanges. While Donovan pursues his pseudo-cultural cant about getting back 'to the true centre' of spiritual renewal in the heart of rural Ireland, Tim confesses that he 'hates all it represents'. Similarly though Donovan tries to negotiate the sale of the cottage with Tim (mistaking him for the owner), Tim simply cannot make the cap of commercial proprietor fit. He cannot bring himself to con-form to the language-game of mercantile deceit.

Donovan's misidentification of Tim, a symptom of his misuse of language, is multiplied in the countless mistaken identities of the other characters: Claire is mistaken for Ivette; Donovan for Dr Bollacks; Barney the Banks for Jack and for a fictitious wife-beater; Nora Dan for a local scrambling champion, and so on. Friel seems to be suggesting that his confusion of each character with the other is a logical consequence of the historical translation, documented in

Translations, of the native Irish language and culture into the contemporary babel of the International European Community
(Donovan commutes between Dublin and Brussels as an E.E.C.
Senator). This mix-up of cultural and linguistic identities (Irish,
English, German, French) epitomizes the absence of a shared code
of communication which characterizes life in *Ballybeg* one hundred
and fifty years after its translation from *Baile Beag*.

While exploiting to the full the conveniences of modern multi-
national society, Donovan still clings to the illusion that nothing has
changed, that Romantic Ireland is alive and well in a restored
Donegal cottage waiting to be purchased by the highest bidder. In
other words, Donovan would have it both ways. He is hypocrisy incarnate, a symbol of the very *discontinuity* in Irish cultural history
which he refuses to acknowledge. But Donovan's charade of *pietas*
is finally scotched when, invoking the shibboleth of Ireland as the
'woman with two cows', he actually chains himself to an antique
cow harness in the cottage and is unable to extricate himself. The
myth becomes literal. As his rantings become more desperate, the
entire stage is plunged into darkness. All the characters lose their
bearings and stagger about in farcical mimicry of the cultural-
linguistic disorientation which has befallen them.

When the light returns the truth begins to dawn; the aliases are debunked and the artifices of the confounding language-games
exposed. This enlightenment of consciousness is nowhere more
evident than in the concluding love scene between Tim and Claire.
Their masks removed and their real feelings made plain, the lovers
move towards the most authentic form of language – the response
cry of silence. As Tim explains: 'Maybe the units of communication
don't matter that much. . . . We're conversing now but we're not
exchanging units. . . . I'm not too sure what I'm saying. . . . Maybe
the message doesn't matter at all then. . . . Maybe silence is the perfect language'. The positivist model of communication as the circulation of word-units in the symbolic form of *women* (Susan/Ivette/
Claire) or *commodities* (Donovan, Barney, Jack and Nora Dan are
all engaged in negotiations for the purchase of the cottage) is shown
to be hopelessly inadequate. The employment of language for the
exchange of women and property between the different individuals
or tribes in the play (Irish, German and French), does not produce
either communication or community (See Appendix III). The
ontological secrets of the heart's space cannot, Tim and Claire discover, be disclosed through the verbal exchange of informational
units, but only through 'reverberations' occasioned by a genuine
'response' of feeling. Responding to Claire's response cry – 'Kiss
me' – Tim embraces her. As he does so, the lovers lean against the
fragile upright beam of the cottage causing it to collapse around them
in a flurry of apocalyptic chaos. The local tower of babel is
demolished in one loving stroke. And even Jack, the wizard of word-
play, is compelled to resort to a response cry – 'O my God'.

Conclusion

What do Friel's plays say about language? More specifically, what do they tell us about their author's attitude or contribution to the native Irish tradition of verbal theatre? Are Friel's plays trojan horses in the citadel of this tradition, contesting its conventions of storytelling from within and pointing towards the possibility of more immediate, non-verbal modes of expression? Are the apocalyptic endings to his language plays symptoms of a crisis of faith in the power of words? Does Friel subscribe in the final analysis to a theatre of the Word or to a theatre of the Senses?

This formulation of the question is perhaps inadequate. Friel's work ultimately resists the facility of such an either/or alternativism. The conclusion to *The Communication Cord* is, for instance, disquietingly equivocal. The hint of some salvation through silence (recalling Heidegger's notion of a mystical 'tolling of silence' at the heart of language) is counteracted by the literal unleashing of darkness and destruction. While the abandonment of speech spells loving communion for Tim and Claire, it spells the collapse of the community as a whole. Silence is a double-edged sword heralding *both* the beginning of love and the end of society. While the departure from language may well lead to love, it may equally well lead to violence. So Friel's ontological optimism with regard to silence as the 'perfect language' appears to go hand in hand with a pessmistic, or at least sceptical, appraisal of its socio-historical implications. The term 'cord' itself conveys this double sense of a bond and an alarm signal.

Seen in conjunction with *Translations*, the ambiguity of Friel's conclusion becomes even more explicit. If *Translations* tended to mythologize language, *The Communication Cord* demythologizes it. While the former showed how language once operated in terms of a cultural rootedness and centredness, the latter de-centres all easy assumptions about the retrieval of lost origins. One displays the original fidelity of language to a timeless ontological piety of *nature;* the other affirms the irreversibility of *history* as an alienation from the natural pre-history of words: and this very affirmation exposes the impotence of language to save a community from the corrosive effects of time, from the mixed blessings of modern progress.

Seamus Deane, one of the directors of Friel's Field Day Theatre Company, states this dilemma in his preface to the *The Communication Cord*. 'Nostalgia for the lost native culture – so potent and plaintive in *Translations*', writes Deane, 'appears ludicrous and sham. . . . Real communication has begun to disappear the moment you begin to isolate it as a problem and give degrees in it. Friel has presented us here with the vacuous world of a dying culture. The roof is coming in on our heads. . . . There is little or no possibility of inwardness, of dwelling in rather than on history'. Situating this crisis of language in the more specific context of Irish cultural history, Deane adds: 'Irish discourse, especially literary discourse, is ready to invoke history but reluctant to come to terms with it. . . . So we manage to think of our great writers as explorers of *nature*, as people who successfully fled the historical nightmare and reintroduced us to the daily nature we all share, yet this feeling is itself historically determined. A colony always wants to escape from history. It longs for its own authenticity, the element it had before history came to disfigure it'.

By refusing to flee from history and from its complex rapport with language, Friel's drama is political; but in a sense radically opposed to political propaganda. Friel's drama is political in the manner in which it protests against the abuse of language by covert political ideologies. Moreover, Friel's insistence that *Translations* and *The Communication Cord* be considered 'in tandem', suggests that the respective claims of mythologization and demythologization, of the old Gaelic-classical culture and the emerging Hiberno-English culture, are *both* valid. The tension between their different approaches to language is in itself creative. (It has certainly proved conducive to some of Friel's finest dramatic work.) It is perhaps in this context that we should read Hugh's remark that 'confusion is not an ignoble condition!'

But the implications of this dialectic extend even further, calling into question the received notions of what 'culture' actually means. Friel refuses to accept the conventional policy of treating the cultural and the socio-historical as entirely separate spheres of discourse. His language plays represent a powerful evocation of the ways in which our cultural use of words determines our society and is determined by it in turn. Friel regards culture, in F.S.L. Lyons's phrase, as 'everything from the furniture in men's kitchens to the furniture in their minds'. Hence Field Day's determination to foster a new dialectical rapport between language and history. Such a dialectic, if successful, might not only project new possibilities for the future development of Irish culture, but might also liberate the dramatic tradition of story-telling from its more encrusted orthodox moulds. The fact that the six directors of Field Day include both poets (Seamus Deane, Seamus Heaney, Tom Paulin) and non-poets (Stephen Rea, a performer, and David Hammond, a musician) may well be an indication of Friel's own desire, as dramatist, to combine both the verbal and non-verbal resources of his art. As the prefatory note to *The Communication Cord* intimates: 'if a congealed idea of theatre can be broken then the audience which experience this break would be the more open to the modification of other established forms. Almost everything which we believe to be natural or native is in fact historical; more precisely, is an historical fiction. If Field Day can breed a new fiction of theatre, or of any other area, which is sufficiently successful to be believed in as though it were natural and an outgrowth of the past, then it will have succeeded. At the moment, it is six characters in search of a story that can be believed.'

Friel, like Christy Mahon in *The Playboy*, is asking his audience to make his fiction true. He is asking that the promise of Field Day be made real by the power of a lie. Unlike Christy, however, and the Irish dramatic movement which produced him, Friel holds out the possibility of a new kind of storytelling, one more cognizant of history and more attentive to those forms of expression which reach beyond the word.

Appendix I: The Native Tradition of Verbal Theatre

In addition to our analysis of Friel's language plays it might be useful i) to rehearse the main lines of argument concerning the 'verbal' character of traditional Irish drama and ii) to enumerate, in this light, some major objections to Friel's language plays on the grounds that his supposedly 'nationalist' bias distorts the relationship between historical fact and dramatic fiction.

The indigenous movement of verbal theatre boasts an august lineage extending from Goldsmith, Wilde, Shaw, Synge, Yeats and O'Casey to such contemporary dramatists as Murphy, Kilroy, Leonard and Friel. All of these authors share a common concern with the play of language; they have created plays where words tend to predetermine character, action and plot. Oscar Wilde stated his own commitment to language when he wrote:

> It is very much more difficult to talk about a thing than to do it. There is no mode of action, no form of emotion that we do not share with the lower animals. It is only by language that we rise above them . . . (Action) is the last recourse of those who know not how to dream[16].

Synge confirmed this predilection for words when he argued that 'in a good play every speech should be as fully flavoured as a nut or an apple'. The *Playboy* proves his point. This drama is a powerful example of native language resources brought to full fruition in the speeches of its characters. But it is a language play in another sense also. The *Playboy* is a drama about the power of words to transform oneself and one's world. 'By the power of a lie' – that is, by his fantastic story of fictional parricide – Christy Mahon ceases to be a 'stupid lout' subservient to his tyrannical father and becomes instead the 'only playboy of the western world'. Deploying words in an imaginative way Christy persuades himself and others to believe in his fiction; and the fiction recreates reality according to its own image. By playing out his fantasy of heroic rebel, Christy actually *becomes* a great lover and a great athlete. When his father eventually intrudes upon the scene, the verbal fiction is momentarily shattered. Christy is accused by Pegeen Mike of being a fake who in reality possesses 'no savagery or fine words in him at all'. The accusation is highly significant for it epitomizes Pegeen's own failure of imaginative nerve before the discrepancy between narrative word and real world. 'A strange man is a marvel with his mighty talk', says Pegeen, 'but there's a great gap between a gallous story and a dirty deed'.

Christy resists such scepticism however. His fall from grace is no more than provisional. Tenaciously reaffirming the triumph of fiction over fact, he proclaims himself a hero in spite of Pegeen's rebuke. 'You've turned me into a likely gaffer in the end of all', he retorts. Father and son set off on the roads to have 'great times . . . *telling stories* of the villany of Mayo and the fools is here'. The marvel of 'mighty talk' vanquishes the daily treadmill of mediocrity. And Pegeen is compelled to acknowledge that what she has lost is not the 'small, low fellow, dark and dirty' that Christy *was*, but the playboy of the western world he has *become* through the power of a lie.

Synge's portrayal of the transfiguring power of the word is representative of the mainstream of the Irish dramatic movement. In a study entitled 'Anglo-Irish Playwrights and the Comic Tradition', Tom Kilroy, another Irish dramatist of the verbal school, argues that the indigenous fascination with the play of language is a direct response to the Anglo-Irish experience of a displaced or de-centred cultural identity. Writing of Goldsmith, one of the inaugurators of the native dramatic tradition, Kilroy remarks that his works are informed by an interplay between two contrasting *styles* of language: a 'low' style imbued with natural integrity and imaginative feeling and a 'high' style marked by pretentiousness, hypocrisy and snobbery. The tension between these opposing cultures of language provides his plays with their singular verbal intensity. Goldsmith, he concludes, 'had an acute ear for the way in which language betrays a distortion of personality and a benevolent discernment of how metropolitan culture produces such artificiality. The perspective from which he perceived this is that of a figure off-centre, personally awkward in a society which measured correct bearing with calibrated accuracy, feckless in a society dedicated to thrift and efficiency'.[17]

In recent years there have been several attempts to challenge the primacy of verbal theatre in Ireland. Tom MacIntyre's experiments with mime, dance and gesture in *Doobally/Blackway*, *The Great Hunger*, *The Bearded Lady*, *Rise up lovely Sweeney* and *Dance for Your Daddy*, are, in large part, motivated by the conviction that the Irish preoccupation with verbal theatre has neglected the more fundamental aspects of dramatic art – namely the rituality of performance and the carnal immediacy of movement. MacIntyre believes that these latter qualities provide better means of expressing the root dimensions of human emotion – the subterranean 'black way' of our preverbal and preconscious experience. He describes his theatre as 'collaborative, pictorial and gestural' in defiance of the verbal tradition. 'We are not interested', states MacIntyre apropos of *Rise up Lovely Sweeney*, 'in the theatre of discourse but in the theatre of experience. We're not putting arguments to the viewer but events that are highly charged and which we ask viewers to receive on terms that they themselves largely create'[17a].

This plea for a more *embodied* form of drama has gained considerable momentum in Ireland with the emergence of performance art and such experimental theatre groups as Red Rex, Operating Theatre and The Dublin Mime Company. Such groups are committed to a drama of the senses. As Roger Doyle explained with respect to the work of Operating Theatre: 'Theatre is freeing itself from the bondage of the word. . . . The communication is now in the actors not in the words they speak. The idea is to bring visual life back into the theatre. Theatre does not have to be a written medium. Too often the word is mistaken for the actor. This creates a block in the audience's perception of the performance. There has been too much emphasis on declaiming lines and not enough on the rhythym of word sounds'. Olwen Fouere, another member of this group, explains their innovatory project as follows: 'Words may even distract from the inner life of the show. . . . They are such a limited way of communicating. They reach an audience only through the intellect. The body and the voice *without any words* have much more potency on stage'[18]. It is surely significant that this alternative model advanced by the Operating Theatre group draws from the combined resources of a visual artist (Coleman), an actress (Fouere) and a musician (Doyle).

This challenge to the hegemony of verbal theatre in Ireland is perhaps most cogently formulated by David McKenna, the director and critic, in a recent manifesto entitled *The Word and the Flesh – A New View of Theatre as Performance*. He opens with this salvo: 'Irish theatre began with the word, the word, unfortunately, of a Great Poet (W.B. Yeats) and it has been dominated by the word ever since'[19]. McKenna decries the fact that in Ireland the writer has invariably been considered the 'unique starting point of the process' of drama. This prejudice, he submits, has been the major cause of the 'lack of attention paid to the performer in Irish theatre, an oversight which has produced a stagnant and repetitive relationship between actor and audience'. Adverting to the ways in which theatre has been developing internationally in terms of experimental performance – largely due to the pioneering work of Stanislavsky, Artaud, Piscator, Brecht and Brook – the author regrets that 'in Ireland we have been *telling stories*'. McKenna attributes much of the blame to Yeats's underestimation of the pre-verbal 'dionysian spirit' and 'sensual exchange' which he believes are the very flesh and blood of powerful drama. As one of the most decisive and formative influences on modern Irish theatre, Yeats 'left the field to the story-tellers. These people produced charming tales, mostly of rural life, ranging from the whimsical and commercial to the magical and superstitious. The Abbey Theatre was their hearth. . . ." The manifesto concludes by indicting the Abbey's legacy of 'processing well-spoken automatons . . . shrouded, hobbed, muffled; and untrained in those 'gestures which create a tangible dramatic world'. (To be fair to Yeats, however, it must also be remembered that he was not only a poet of words but an experimental playwright whose Noh plays introduced dance, ritual, music and gesture into Irish drama).

While Friel's language plays are not explicitly identified by these critics, they are exemplary instances of verbal theatre – albeit in a highly self-questioning mode.

Appendix II: Friel and Nationalism

Considerable controversy has surrounded the political implications of Friel's concern with cultural identity. This is well illustrated in the following description by the critic, Brian McEvera, of *Translations:* 'I find *Translations* (and to a certain extent the stance of Field Day) deeply worrying. . . . By the time the play had ended I was having doubts. I felt manipulated. Obviously, I sensed that the play was lop-sided, that traditional nationalist myths were being given credence. I was uneasy at the whole notion of the shift from Irish to English as a form of cultural suppression. . . . The play actually shores up a dangerous myth – that of cultural dispossession by the British – rather than what I take to be the historical actuality, the abandonment of the language (by the Irish people themselves). . . . Friel's work is directly political in its implications; and its 'awareness' is one-sided. The 'shape' observed is a nationalist one – and a limited partial view of nationalism at that'. McEvera ends his critique by declaring his hope that either 'the more overt political element will disappear from (Friel's) work', or else that he will 'confront directly in his work those aspects of nationalist violence which have so far been submerged'[20]. Edna Longley makes a similar point when she accuses Friel and his Field Day group of repeddling nationalist myths of a pre-lapsarian past destroyed by British colonialism. 'Does *Translations* itself renew 'images of the past', or does it recycle a familiar perspective?' she asks. Her answer is plain: 'The play does not so much examine myths of dispossession and oppression as repeat them'[21]. Citing the particular moment in *Translations* when the soldier/survey officers use unhistorical bayonets after Lieutenant Yolland is murdered, Longley argues that Friel's real, though unacknowledged, subject is 'the behaviour of British troops in the Catholic ghettoes of Belfast and Derry during the nineteen-seventies'. And she goes on to observe that at the end of the play Owen, who has 'collaborated' with the Survey, reverts to potentially violent tribal loyalty. Rather than confronting the contemporary realities of Northern Irish politics, Friel and Field Day are charged with chasing the dream of a political impossibility: the return to 'a mythic landscape of beauty and plenitude that is pre-Partition, pre-Civil War, pre-famine, pre-plantation and pre-Tudor'[22]. Longley concludes that Friel's drama has become fossilised because 'he explores the ethos of a particular community exclusively in relation to British dominion over the native Irish. No perspective discriminates between past and present, nineteenth-century Ireland and twentieth-century Northern Ireland. There is simply equation. . . . *Translations* refurbishes an old myth'[23].

These objections to the political content of Friel's plays are frequently related to the charge that he abuses the criteria of historical truth and fails, for ideological reasons, to observe the way things really were – the *facts*. In a *Crane Bag* exchange between Friel and Professor J.H. Andrews, author of a scholarly book on the Ordnance Survey of Ireland, entitled *A Paper Landscape* (which by Friel's own admission was a major source of inspiration for *Translations*), Andrews isolates some empirical inaccuracies in the play. These range from Friel's anachronistic reading of the nineteenth century Ordnance Survey in terms of a Cromwellian policy of plantation, to more particular details such as the Survey Officers prodding the ground with bayonets which they were not in fact allowed to possess[24].

These objections to Friel's drama are, I believe, largely beside the point. The charges of political nationalism and historical inaccuracy mistake the primary intent of Friel's work by reading it as a sociological tract. The author's primary intent, as I hope to have shown, is to dramatically interrogate the *crisis of language* as a medium of *communication* and *identity* – a crisis which is an indispensable ingredient of contemporary Irish culture. Moreover, Friel's preoccupation with language does not simply conform to the mainstream Irish tradition of verbal 'story-telling' (See Appendix I), but puts this very tradition into question by highlighting the *problematic* functioning of language itself.

Appendix III: The Conflict of Language Models (Ontology Versus Positivism).

Friel's work operates with two basic linguistic models – one ontological, the other positivistic. The former treats language as a house of Being; the latter treats it as a mechanical apparatus for the representation of objects.

As we had occasion to remark above, Friel's ontological approach to language is, philosophically speaking, akin to that of Heidegger. Here language is celebrated as a way to truth in the Greek sense of the term, *A-letheia*, meaning un-forgetfulness, un-concealing, disclosure. Language tells us the truth by virtue of its capacity to unlock the secret privacies of our historical Being (the 'interiority of the heart's space'). In *Translations* Friel identifies this ontological vocation of the Word with the Gaelic and Classical languages. It manifests itself in the local community's use of naming to release the secret of their psychic and historical landscape or in Hugh's excavations of Latin and Greek etymologies. Friel's play illustrates Heidegger's claim that language is the house of Being not only in so far as it permits us to dwell poetically in our world but also in that it grants us the power to recollect our past, to divine our forgotten origins. (It is perhaps not insignificant that Friel's collection of stories published just two years after *Translations* is called *The Diviner)*. Language houses Being by recalling things from their past oblivion, thus attuning us once again to our lost identities, enabling us to re-member *(an-denken)* our alienated, dismembered selves. Poetic words are not, Heidegger teaches us, as also does Hugh, 'copies and imitations'; they are 'imaginings that are visible inclusions of the alien in the sign of the familiar'[25].

Friel opposes this *ontological* model of language to the *positivist* use of words as agents of pragmatic progress. This alternative positivist model is perhaps most closely associated with the philosophy of British Empiricism, which served in recent centuries as the ideological mainstay of British colonialism; though it has found a more contemporary ally in the scientific structuralism of Lévi-Strauss and others. Positivism maintains that words are mechanically given *(positum)* – objects in a world of similar objects. They are eminently unmysterious entities to be used as instruments for the representation, mapping or classification of reality. And the reductionist goal of positivism is to produce an exact decoding of the world by establishing a one-to-one correlation between *words* and the *facts* of empirical experience. Language is thus reduced to a utilitarian weapon for the colonization of Being. It murders to dissect.

John Locke was one of the most notable proponents of British Empiricism. He believed that only such a philosophy of perception and language could prevent our thoughts from straying 'into the vast ocean of being', could remove the metaphysical 'rubbish from the way of knowledge'. A keen defender of the right of proprietors – which he saw as an inalienable right of man and an essential prerogative of any gentleman's son – Locke construed language according to an equally proprietorial epistemology. He promoted the ideal of a perfectly transparent language resulting from the accurate mapping of words onto empirical sensations. The domestication of reality by means of this rigid conformity of words to sensory objects would lead, he believed, to a rigorously scientific knowledge. Naturally there was to be no quarter given to poetic or ontological language in this scheme of things. And in *Thoughts Concerning Education*, Locke advises parents who were unfortunate enough to have children born with a poetic propensity, to 'labour to have it stifled and suppressed as much as may be'. This empiricist view of language is caricatured by Friel in *Translations* as the reduction of a living ontological landscape to the practical proportions of a six-inch map. The following comment from Lord Salisbury which Friel places alongside his quotation from Heidegger in the prefatory notes to the play, clearly reveals the author's satiric intentions: 'The most disagreeable part of the three kingdoms is Ireland; and therefore Ireland has a splendid map'. Once exposed to the linguistic lens of empiricism, the landscape ceases to *be* and becomes merely *useful:* language as *evocation* is replaced by language as *information*[26].

Another (more flexible) positivist model of language to have gained widespread currency in recent years is linguistic structuralism. The two most influential exponents of this model are Ferdinand de Saussure and Claude Lévi-Strauss. The structuralists may be classed as 'positivistic' to the extent that they attempt to reduce language to a mechanistic system of formal substitutions, to a skeletal logistics of signs. 'Language is a *form* not a *substance*', ran Saussure's celebrated maxim. And it was on the basis of this maxim that structuralist linguists could argue that the entire complex of language be considered as an impersonal system of coded relations between its constituent units (semantic or phonetic), with no on-tological rapport whatsoever with nature, history or the human subject. Words are thus treated as neutral objectified units of ex-change in an abstract network of coded messages. The ontological question of the *authenticity* of language as a disclosure of personal and historical meaning no longer arises. The flesh of *subjectivity* – the 'interiority of the heart's space' – has been stripped away to leave the clean bare bones of *structure*.

Lévi-Strauss' original contribution to structuralism lay in his equation of the codes of the language system (as an exchange of structural units) with the codes of kinship systems (as an exogamous exchange of women – or by extension, other consumer commodities – between different tribes). This primitive model of kinship as a mechanism of utilitarian and commercial substitution is, Lévi-Strauss believes, the determining structure of all languages. In a passage remarkably apposite for a reading of Friel's language plays, Lévi-Strauss claims that we should regard 'marriage regulations and kinship systems as a kind of language, a set of processes permitting the establishment, between individuals and groups, of a certain type of communication. That the mediating factor, in this case, should be the *women* of the group, who are circulated between classes, lineages, or families, in place of the words of the group, which are circulated between individuals, does not at all change the fact that the essential aspect of the phenomenon is identical in both cases' *(Structural Anthropology)*[27]. This structuralist model of language bears particular relevance to Friel's third language play, *The Communication Cord.*

Appendix IV: Friel and Steiner

The following is a list of key passages from George Steiner's essay 'Understanding and Translations' (contained in *After Babel: Aspects of Language and Translation*, Oxford University Press, 1975, pp 1–50) which served as a major critical and philosophical source for Friel's language plays.

1. 'In certain civilizations there come epochs in which syntax suffers, in which the available resources of live perception and restatement wither. Words seem to go dead under the weight of sanctified usage: the frequence and sclerotic forces of clichés, of unexamined similes, or worn tropes increases. Instead of acting as a living membrane, grammar and vocabulary become a barrier to new feeling. A civilization is imprisoned in a linguistic contour which no longer matches, or matches only at certain ritual, arbitrary points, the changing landscape of fact' (p. 21).

2. 'We have histories of massacre and deception, but none of metaphor. . . . Such figures (i.e. metaphors) are new mappings of the world, they reorganize our habitation of reality' (p. 23).

3. 'No semantic form is timeless. When using a word we wake into resonance, as it were, its entire previous history. A text is embedded in specific historical time: it has what linguists call a diachronic structure. To read fully is to restore all that one can of the immediacies of value and intent in which speech actually occurs' (p. 24).

4. 'The schematic model of translation is one in which a message from a source-language passes into a receptor-language via a transformational process. The barrier is the obvious fact that one language differs from the other, that an interpretative transfer sometimes, albeit misleadingly, described as encoding and decoding, must occur so that the message 'gets through'. Exactly the same model – and this is what is rarely stressed – is operative *within a single language'* (p. 28).

5. 'What material reality has history outside language, outside our interpretative belief in essentially linguistic records (silence knows no history)? Where worms, fires of London, or totalitatian regimes obliterate such records, our consciousness of past being comes on a blank space. We have no total history, no history which could be defined as objectively real because it contained the literal sum of past life. To remember everything is a condition of madness. We remember culturally, as we do individually, by conventions of emphasis, foreshadowing, omission. The landscape composed by the past tense, the semantic organization of remembrance, is stylized and differently coded by different cultures' (p. 29).

6. 'The metaphysics of the instant, this slamming of the doors on the long galleries of historical consciousness, is under-

standable. It has a fierce innocence. . . . But it is an innocence as destructive of civilization as it is, by concomitant logic, destructive of literate speech. Without the true fiction of history, without the unbroken animation of a chosen past, we become flat shadows. Literature, whose genius stems from what Eluard called *le dur désir de durer*, has no chance of life outside constant translation within its own language. . . . In short, the existence of art and literature, the reality of felt history in a community, depend on a never-ending, though very often unconscious, act of internal translation' (p. 30).

7. 'Languages conceal and internalize more, perhaps, than they convey outwardly. Social classes, racial ghettoes speak at rather than to each other' (p. 32).

8. 'When anti-thetical meanings are forced upon the same word (Orwell's newspeak), when the conceptual reach and valuation of a word can be uttered by political decree, language loses credibility' (p. 34).

9. 'At any given time in a community and in the history of language, speech modulates across generations' (p. 34).

10. 'Eros and language mesh at every point. Intercourse and discourse, copula and copulation, are sub-classes of the dominant fact of communication. They arise from the life-need of the ego to reach out and comprehend, in the two vital senses of 'understanding' and 'containment', another human being. Sex is a profoundly semantic act. Like language, it is subject to the shaping force of social convention, rules of proceeding, and accumulated precedent' (p. 38).

11. 'Hence the argument of modern anthropology and the incest taboo, which appears to be primal to the organization of communal life, is inseparable from linguistic evolution. We can only prohibit that which we can name. Kinship systems, which are the coding and classification of sex for purposes of social survival, are analogous with syntax. The seminal and semantic functions (is there, ultimately, an etymological link?) determine the genetic and social structure of human experience. Together they construe the grammar of being' (p. 39).

12. 'Under extreme stress, men and women declare their absolute being to each other, only to discover that their respective experience of eros and language has set them desperately apart' (p. 45).

13. 'Lévi-Strauss's contention is that women and words are analogous media of exchange in the grammar of social life' (p. 45).

14. 'It is not as "translators" that women novelists and poets excel, but as declaimers of their own, long-stifled tongue' (p. 45).

15. 'Any model of communication is at the same time a model of trans-lation, of a vertical or horizontal transfer of significance.

No two historical epochs, no two social classes, no two localities use words and syntax to signify exactly the same things, to send identical signals of valuation and inference. Neither do two human beings. Each person draws, deliberately or in immediate habit, on two sources of linguistic supply: the current vulgate corresponding to his level of literacy, and a private thesaurus. The latter is inextricably a part of his sub-conscious, of his memories so far as they may be verbalized, and of the singular, irreducibly specific ensemble of his somatic and psychological identity. Part of the answer to the notorious logical conundrum as to whether or not there can be a 'private language' is that aspects of every language-act are unique and individual. . . . The concept of a normal or standard idiom is a statistically-based fiction (though it may have real existence in machine-translation). The language of a community, however uniform its social contour, is an inexhaustibly multiple agg-regate of speech-atoms, of finally irreducible personal meanings. . . . We speak to communicate. But also to conceal, to leave unspoken. The ability of human beings to misinform modulates through every wavelength from outright lying to silence' (p. 46).

16. 'Thus a human being performs an act of translation, in the full sense of the word, when receiving a speech-message from any other human being. Time, distance, disparities in outlook or assumed reference, make this act more or less difficult. Where the difficulty is great enough, the process passes from reflex to conscious technique. Intimacy, on the other hand, be it of hatred or of love, can be defined as confident, quasi-immediate trans-lation. . . . With intimacy the external vulgate and the private mass of language grow more and more concordant. Soon the private dimension penetrates and takes over the customary forms of public exchange. . . . In old age the impulse towards translation wanes and the pointers of reference turn inward. The old listen less or principally to themselves. Their dictionary is, increasingly, one of private remembrance' (p. 47).

17. 'Interlingual translation is . . . an access to an inquiry into language itself. "Translation", properly understood, is a special case of the arc of communication which every successful speech-act closes within a given language. . . . The model "sender to receiver" which represents any semiological and semantic process is ontologically equivalent to the model "source-language to receptor-language" used in the theory of translation. . . . In short, *inside or between languages, human communication equals translation*. A study of translation is a study of language' (p. 47).

7
TOM MURPHY'S LONG NIGHT'S JOURNEY
INTO NIGHT

Tom Murphy's *The Gigli Concert*, premiered at the 1983 Dublin Theatre Festival, confirmed his reputation as an innovative force in modern Irish drama[1]. The *Irish Literary Supplement* hailed it as 'one of the finest Irish plays of the decade', while *Theatre Ireland* declared it to be 'the most significant event in European theatre since the première of *Waiting for Godot* in Paris in 1953'. In this chapter, we will analyse how this play represents a dramatic challenge to the mainstream tradition of Irish theatre rooted in the Irish literary revival.

While Brian Friel's Field Day company has come to represent a particularly Northern movement of critical response to the fundamental problems of tradition, history, language and identity confronting contemporary Irish culture[2], Murphy's recent work with the Druid and Abbey theatre companies has now established him as perhaps the most significant Southern counterpart to such a critical movement. The Field Day Theatre company has been perceived, in general, as an exploration of the more *historical* dimension of cultural displacement (particularly as it has found explicit expression in the conflict of Northern Ireland where Field Day originates). Murphy's work, by contrast, has focused on the *existential* malady of inner displacement and division to which, he believes, the inhabitants of the southern, ostensibly more 'settled', provinces are singularly prone.

Murphy has probed the dark recesses of modern Irish experience with unrelenting obsessiveness. In a Murphy drama, the border that truncates and polarizes is *within*: it marks more of a metaphysical rupture between self and self than a geographical/historical partition between one community and another (Northern/Southern, Irish/ British etc.). The metaphor of the 'wall' which recurs throughout Murphy's plays signals a confinement to our solitary, divided selves. As Malachy puts it in *On the Inside* (1976): 'Self-contempt is the metaphysical key. How can you, I ask myself, love someone, if first, you do not love yourself?' 'My spirit is unwell too', declares Harry in *The Sanctuary Lamp* (1976), as he wrestles with the angel of his own 'holy loneliness', keeping demonic vigil over his deceased loved one (Teresa) and his deceased God (the play takes place within a church: Nietzsche's 'madman' was also carrying a 'sanctuary lamp' when he announced the 'death of God').

In all of his plays, Murphy seems to be saying that we are still, always, *on the outside* (the title of his first play, 1959) even, and most agonizingly, when we are *on the inside*: that is, even when we contrive to escape the alienating circumstances of modern existence by seeking asylum in the sanctuary of our own inner selves. It is perhaps Michael, in *A Whistle in The Dark* (1970), who most poignantly sums up this condition of existential dis-ease when he utters his cry of self-contradiction: 'I want to get out of this kind of life. I want . . . I want us all to be – I don't want to be what I am. . . . But I can't get out of all this. . . . What's wrong with me?'

This metaphysical experience of the dark abyss of self-division (most of Murphy's plays take place at night), confessionally registered yet comically resolved, is the abiding motif of Murphy's *oeuvre* which includes over fifteen plays. It suggests that his work shares less with the native *folk* concerns of Synge, Yeats or Molloy, than with the existentialist explorations of such dramatists as Ionesco, Sartre or Beckett. As Christopher Murray has observed: 'All of Tom Murphy's work is a "whistle in the dark", an exultant cry of triumph over the facts of death and history. The subject matter can be serious, but the struggle to establish a self, a personality free from the subtle determinants of society, is presented with comic vigour, with what Nietzsche . . . called metaphysical delight'[3].

Murphy's drama departs from the indigenous tradition of the well-made folk-drama and embraces, with Friel and Beckett, the modernist obsession with the crisis of human communication and identity. While his plays ostensibly conform to the Irish norm of 'verbal' theatre, they substantially modify this norm concentrating more on the *mood* or *tone* of feeling created by language than on the narrative plot or storyline as such. Murphy's characters tend to tell stories about themselves rather than simply play out a role in a story told about them (by the author). The action develops in the actors rather than the actors in the action. Brian Friel has described Murphy as the 'most distinctive, restless and obsessive imagination working in the Irish theatre today'. There is little doubt that Murphy's many experiments with form and dialogue (especially in the surreal and stylized later plays) testify to a sense of dramatic *navigatio*, of tirelessly attempting to articulate the inarticulate, to sound the unconscious, or as Beckett once put it, to 'eff the ineffable'.

I

Murphy may be said to belong to a counter-tradition in Irish drama to the extent that he poses a direct challenge to both the naturalism and folksy romanticism of the mainstream theatre of the

Literary Revival. While this Revival was largely created in a metropolitan context for a metropolitan audience it promoted an idealized image of rural Ireland which corresponded to the emergent culture of Irish nationalism. In drama, the Revivalist movement was particularly associated with the work of the Abbey Theatre. In their 1906 manifesto entitled *Irish plays*, Yeats and Lady Gregory equated the best in Irish life with the rural peasants and their legendary landscape. These dramatists maintained that they had 'taken their types and scenes direct from Irish life itself'. This life, they added, 'is rich in dramatic materials, while the Irish peasantry of the hills and coast speak an exuberant language and have a primitive grace and wildness due to the wild country they live in, which gives their most ordinary life a vividness and colour unknown in more civilised places'4. This revivalist identification of national life with rural life led to a theatre often dominated by the pull of the past where a displaced modern individual sought to recover an identifiable place in a traditional community usually associated with his or her peasant ancestry.5

The plays of Tom Murphy explode the myths of revivalist drama. *On the Outside*, *Famine*, *A Whistle in the Dark*, *Conversations on a Homecoming* and *Bailegangaire* expose the pieties and pretences of rural folklore. Moreover, Murphy's deromanticization of the established canons of folk drama corresponds, at the level of form, to his increasing use of *non-naturalistic* scenery, characterization and dialogue, exemplified in the almost surrealist idioms of *Morning After Optimism* and *The Gigli Concert*. Indeed, in the latter, Murphy has succeeded in reversing the revivalist transposition of urban to rural, introducing the disillusioned rural 'Irishman' directly into the modern metropolis of social and existential crisis.

II

The Gigli Concert works at several levels. It highlights the dramatic collision between tradition and modernity, between rural and urban values, between the cultures of the Gael and the Planter. But it does so in a way that circumvents political stereotypes. The two main characters of the play are an anonymous self-made 'Irishman' whose ambition it is to sing like the great Italian opera singer Beniamino Gigli, and the English-born J.P.W. King who postures as a native psychotherapist capable of resolving our most turbulent desires. The allusion to the old chestnut of Anglo-Irish relations is obvious – and there is even a northern mistress called Mona to make up the triangle. But one of the singular strengths of Murphy's writing is to avoid cliché and confound predictable expectations. Murphy goes straight for the jugular of psychic confrontation. He presents his drama as an existential psychodrama where the claims of historical fact and subjective fantasy overlap with mischievous ease. The key to the whole problem, he suggests, is in the intimate relation between language and illusion. He compels us to recognise how we use words to lie to ourselves, to invent myths, to conceal what we are and create what we might be.

The Gigli Concert is – along with Friel's 'language plays' – verbal theatre in its most accomplished and critical form. Rarely has an Irish dramatist so convincingly exposed the role that *language* plays in the unconscious world of our fears and aspirations. Several of the play's dialogues are unrelenting. But Murphy refuses to compromise. He compels his characters to work with language until its surface meanings collapse either into silence (the impossibility of communication) or music (the epitome of communication). Either way, *The Gigli Concert* reminds us that we cannot take words for granted; that they are never innocent and rarely mean what they *appear* to mean. Murphy suggests that by feeding the heart on fantasies, words can become as loaded and destructive as time bombs. Appropriately, J.P.W. describes his philosophy as 'dynamatology' – a double reference to explosives and to the Greek term for the hidden world of 'possibility' *(dunamis)* opened up by the imaginative resources of language. Dynamatology, in its author's words, promises 'to project you beyond the boundaries that are presently limiting you'. If this is 'political' theatre, it is so not in any explicit ideological sense, but in the sense indicated by Seamus Heaney when he says that 'the *imagined* place is what politics is all about. Politicians deal in images'[6]. It is in fact by exposing the imaginative underworld of our political stereotypes and clichés, turning them inside out and tracing their origin back to the buried fears and aspirations of the human psyche, that Murphy shows how the worlds of public and private experience feed off each other. In this way, Murphy grafts a 'drama of society' onto a 'drama of character', as Patrick Mason, the director of the Abbey première of *The Gigli Concert*, observes:

> Murphy's theme is the brokenness of spirit and the strange demons that lie in the Irish psyche. The hero in this play who is the magician and poet is an Englishman. The Irishman is the corrupt, self-made building contractor who has sold his soul. It's an interesting antagonism, a reversal of the traditional stereotypes, which makes the play absolutely fascinating. Murphy is not a writer who deals in a naked political dialectic. The play also has a universal theme of what use is beauty. In a world that is increasingly corrupt and factual, what do you do about those inner urges that just won't go away and every now and then burst out into some kind of expression? Obviously the whole business of wanting to sing like Gigli is an extreme but extraordinary expression of that creative need[7].

III

The Gigli Concert is not so much a play within a play as a psychodrama within a psychodrama. It stages a turbulent exchange between its two central characters. One is from the 'outside', J.P.W. King, the middle-aged Englishman masquerading as a 'resident' psychotherapist (he claims he had a Tipperary grandmother) with messianic pretentions to help men realize their secret dreams. The other is from the 'inside', an 'Irishman' (as the script describes him) with no name, address or telephone number, posturing as a musically gifted cobbler's son from the Italian town of Recaniti who wants to sing like the great opera singer, Beniamino Gigli. The drama unfolds as a sort of life and death struggle between these *frères ennemis*, whose complicity of mutual misunderstanding suggests at times that they are more similar than they pretend, perhaps even alter-egos of each other (as James and Edmund in Murphy's earlier play, *The Morning after Optimism*, 1973). J.P.W. and the Irishman are psychic doubles of a divided self seeking the completion of a possible unity. As such, they might be viewed as dramatic approximations of Seamus Heaney's poetic dialectic between the two extremes of the Irish imagination in his 'Hercules and Antaeus' poem in *North*. Of this dialectical opposition, Heaney wrote: 'Hercules represents the balanced rational light while Antaeus represents the pieties of illiterate fidelity. The poem drifts towards an assent to Hercules though there was a sort of nostalgia for Antaeus.... This is a see-saw, an advance-retire situation. There is always the question in everybody's mind whether the rational and humanist domain which produced what we call civilization in the West, should be allowed full command in our psyche, speech and utterance....'[8].

But what is the precise nature of the opposition between Murphy's protagonists? J.P.W. represents the intellectually 'progressive' future-oriented ethos of English and European Enlightenment; he claims to be a 'dynamatologist' sent over to Ireland by the movement's founding-father in order to propagate a new method for helping people to realize their 'potential' (*dunamis*). By contrast the 'Irishman', or Beniamino as J.P.W. insists on calling him, ostensibly represents the native West-of-Ireland ethos of cunning instinct, memory and tradition; he has experienced this ethos as fundamentally repressive and has sought to escape from it, first by becoming a *nouveau-riche* 'operator' in the building trade, and finally by seeking a form of perfection beyond the materialist idols of power and wealth – the sublimity of music. Though he prides himself on being a no-nonsense self-made-man who knows far more about life than any professional philosopher, Beniamino feels compelled nonetheless to procure the therapeutic 'self-realizing' services of an 'intellectual' such as J.P.W.

Beniamino is an Irishman thoroughly disabused with the cult of bourgeois opportunism and careerism of which he is a victim. (This cult was brought about, in part, by the modern transition from De Valera's idyllic ideology of pastoral piety to Lemass's hardnosed ideology of commercial 'rising tides' and Taca – political fundraising – development schemes). Thus while he may invoke the authority of facts and figures, Beniamino ultimately wishes to escape from the constraints of such empirical necessities into the 'possible and possibilizing' world of pure art. He wants to trade-in fact for fiction, his self-made-man success story having degenerated into a nightmare of despair. Delinquent itinerants, he complains, have overrun his domestic 'territory'; and instead of communicating with his wife and nine year old son, he can now only utter a 'roar of obscenity'. The centre can no longer hold. And so Beniamino wants to transmute the dark energies of that roar within him into music. He wants, quite simply, to sing like Gigli.

As the play unfolds we gradually learn that the differences between the two characters are more apparent than real. If the Italianate Beniamino is no more than a pseudonym for the nameless Irishman, the messianic-sounding name dynamatologist is itself no more than a pseudonym for the hapless, narcotic-and-vodka crazed mess of broken dreams that J.P.W. really is. (Both characters admit at different times that they 'do not know how (they) will get through the day'). Far from being able to 'make all things possible', as his professional title and philosophy profess, J.P.W. King is no *salvator mundi*; and while he chides Beniamino for believing that the 'Romantic Kingdom is of this world', it transpires that he himself is neither king of this world nor of any other. In short, the analyst is just as screwed up as the analysand.

J.P.W. claims that his dynamatological theory will replace the oppressive 'I am who I am' model of divine power (the *Yahweh* God who cast Adam and Eve out of Eden into *angst* because they ate of the forbidden fruit of imagination, i.e. acquired the Creator's Knowledge of good and evil) with a new 'I Am Who May Be' model capable of realizing the divine potentialities of each human being. But J.P.W. has *in fact* been no more successful in realizing his own possibilities than his deceiving and self-deceiving client. He has squandered his potential for love in unrequited infatuation for an intangible 'Helen' who finally dismisses him as little more than an 'obscene telephone caller'. And his proud story of domestic happiness – an idyllic wife and house with clematis growing round the doorway – is itself exposed as just another self-incarcerating fantasy. In reality, the one woman who *truly* loves him, the down-to-earth, plainspeaking, physical Mona, is taken for granted until it is too late. (The moment J.P.W. comes to realize that Mona had longed all these years to have a child with him – a *real* potentiality for life which J.P.W. had entirely ignored – is the same moment that he learns that she is dying from cancer). The time is out of joint for this modern day prince of Kierkegaardian Denmark; and no amount of fanciful subterfuge can, it seems, put it right.

The final bombshell to explode J.P.W.'s dynamatological illusions, comes ironically in the shape of Beniamino himself. He returns in the last act to announce that his desire to sing like Gigli was not in fact some life-long ambition to transcend misery, as he had pretended, but a desperate obsession provoked by one of his many recurring depressions. In other words, J.P.W.'s own Faustian dream of enabling others to realize *their* dreams founders on the rocks of factuality. In one fell swoop both he and his client are exposed as frauds. Thus while presented as polar opposites in the early scenes, the roles of the two protagonists are now exchanged – a transitional operation enacted on stage as the analyst behind the desk swops with the analysand and begins to pour out his own story of childhood trauma. In this overlapping process, both are seen to inhabit the same inner circle of darkness and despair which as J.P.W. prophetically spoofs is 'where the battle must be fought', and to share the same unrealizable desire to translate their self-destructive obsessions into the creative art of a Gigli song. Beniamino's initial claim that the 'only way to communicate is to sing' has now become J.P.W.'s own credo. Gigli's operatic scores have invaded not only his office/apartment (where Beniamino has installed a hi-fi system) but also his very soul ('Gigli is a devil' who possesses one's entire being, Beniamino had warned). And as Beniamino finally returns to 'normality', a sort of Dorian Gray reversal occurs whereby it becomes J.P.W.'s turn to rave and rant and reach out for the impossible possibility of a perfected music.

Impotent to realize the quasi-mystical promise of what he terms the 'quiet power of the possible' (a phrase used by the existentialist philosopher, Martin Heidegger, in *The Letter on Humanism*, to define the hidden play of Being)[9], J.P.W.'s belief in the creative potential of dynamatology appears to degenerate into a caricature of itself (with all the destructive connotations implied by the allusion to dynamite). The final explosion is not that from the barrel of Beniamino's putative pocket-gun, which it transpires was merely another strategy, but from the break-up of J.P.W.'s own professional illusions. 'Mama, do not leave me in the dark', cries the dynamatologist from the depths of his Faustian dream. (Indeed the Faustian theme is also echoed in J.P.W.'s relation with the Gretchen-like Mona and the use of Boito's *Faust* as one of the scores in the play). His ultimate cry into the dark falls somewhere between the sigh of Goethe and the howl of Ginsberg.

And yet from the apocalyptic darkness a hint of redemption emerges. For a few brief moments, it seems that J.P.W. does in fact sing like Gigli. It is no more than a glimpse, a possibility. It might be just another illusion, one last psychic play of self-deception resulting from an overdose of alcohol. But then again, it might not. There is at least a suggestion that the very tenacity of J.P.W.'s new-found 'act of faith' to sing like Gigli, has maybe yielded not just another artifice, but genuine art. It is no more than a *maybe*. But that is as much as can be expected from the heretical God of the Possible – the I Am Who May Be who has supplanted the I Am Who Am (i.e. the old paternalistic God hostile to the Adamic presumption that the human imagination is capable of projecting possibilities of a new creation).

Thus it transpires that Beniamino's imposture has, ironically, infused J.P.W.'s hitherto 'spiritless being' not only with the audacity of despair but also and more importantly, with the 'longing to soar': the audacity to believe in his own belief, to transform his obsessive fantasies into creative fiction, to realize the impossible possibility of pure Being. In a conclusion reminiscent of the final scene in Synge's *Playboy* when Christy departs triumphantly from the stage having become 'a man by the power of a lie' (the fiction of parricide), J.P.W. packs his bags and exits – exultant in the belief that his dream has been, or at least *may be*, realized; and leaving behind him a society of dreamless resentful pragmatists who, as Beniamino has warned, would 'kill him if he stayed'. Perhaps after all, in the shadow of the deceased Father-God, a son has been born.

IV

One of the most conspicuous features of Murphy's work is its ability to transcend, while reflecting, its local setting and thus assume a stature of international proportions. For while at one level the exchanges between J.P.W. and Beniamino can be interpreted as emblems of the age-old conflict between England and Ireland – with the Northern Mona as a sort of neglected go-between: the woman victimized by the male-dominated struggle for power – they also and more immediately represent the problematic opposition between two universal value systems: the future-orientated Enlightenment versus past-oriented traditionalism; humanist intellect versus native instinct; utopian idealism versus pragmatic materialism.

Murphy's capacity to amplify the parochial into the universal by going beyond the established conventions of folk-poetic Irishry is a hallmark of his drama. In *The Gigli Concert* we witness an author grappling with native concerns yet fully cognizant of the profound fascination which modern European culture – from Gigli to the existentialists – exerts upon 'the native mind'. To take just one comparative example, it is interesting to observe the parallels between Beniamino's desire to sing like Gigli in order to escape the mess of everyday existence and Roquentin's desire, in Sartre's *Nausea*, to reach the condition of pure Being symbolized by the song of a negress:

It does exist . . . if I were to get up, if I were to snatch that record from the turn-table which is holding it and if I were to break it in two, I wouldn't reach *it*. It is beyond – always beyond something, beyond a voice, beyond a violin note. Through layers and layers of existence, it unveils itself, slim and firm, and when you try to seize it you meet nothing but existents, you run up against existents devoid of meaning. It is behind them: I can't even hear it. I hear sounds, vibrations in the air which unveil it. It does not exist, since it has nothing superfluous in relation to it. It *is*. And I too have wanted to *be*. Indeed I have never wanted anything else.

Sartre contends that the greatest power of the song is that it projects an aesthetic world of pure possibility 'cleansed of the sin of existing'. Murphy's view of things is in this respect strangely akin to that of the existentialists. Life, for both, is absurd, chaotic, insane; it can only be redeemed, if at all, by a stoical belief in the transforming power of imagination. All truth is an artefact, taught Nietzsche, but one which we could not survive without. The only way to combat the absurdity of existence is, therefore, to keep on believing in meaning in spite of everything, like Sisyphus rolling his rock to the top of the hill in the belief that he will eventually reach the summit; and that even if he doesn't the struggle itself – the act of faith in the possible – justifies the effort. Or as Beckett's 'unnamable' narrator put it, if 'I can't go on, I'll go on'. Indeed, Murphy's misfits bear a striking resemblance to Beckett's in that both succeed in representing the modernist/universalist dimensions of 'existentialist man' in recognizable localized settings. Perhaps Beckett's move to Paris and Murphy's ten year sojourn in London (where he worked at *The Royal Court* and *Old Vic*, and wrote and staged his first plays) helped both to bring universal 'outside' perpectives to bear on their formative indigenous experience.

V

If one examines the implications of this universalist existentialism in the Irish context of most of Murphy's plays a slightly unsettling assumption emerges. The common message that Murphy's angst-ridden characters convey is that the mainstream traditions of Irish society are moribund. In *On the Outside*, set at the doorway of an Irish rural dancehall, it is the small-town provincialism of moral *resentment* and begrudgery which the author exposes. In *Whistle in the Dark*, it is the psychic paralysis produced by introverted family competitiveness. In *On the Inside* and *The Sanctuary Lamp*, Murphy turns his satirical attention to the life-denying oppressive-ness of Irish Jansenism. 'Holy medals and genitalia in mortal combat with each other', as Malachy remarks in the former, 'is not sex at all'. Murphy caricatures this jansenistic God of selfmortificatory devotionalism in *The Sanctuary Lamp* as a necrophiliac 'metaphysical monster' whose supposedly 'real presence' of consolation (symbolized by the lamp) is little more than a mask for the 'violence-mongering furies' of a moribund deity. Abandoned to their own self-destructive solitude, Murphy's godless but god-obsessed 'orphans' resort to the last possible refuge – the sanctuary of insanity: 'Do you think madness must at least be warm', muses Harry, 'I don't mind admitting I keep it as standby in case all else fails'. In the *Famine* and *The Blue Macushla*, Murphy indicts the chauvinistic and pseudo-patriotic hypocrisy which, he believes, has so contaminated political life in Ireland. The latter play is a trenchant send-up of narrow Irish nationalism, from the highest of government ministers to the lowest of paramilitary fanatics (the *Erin go Brágh* splinter group of a splinter group!); it recounts how such forces conspire to rob one Eddie O'Hara of his 'person' (his sense of self as biographically detailed in the opening soliloquy of the play) and ultimately of his life. 'Wearing patriotism on your sleeve like gold cufflinks', Murphy suggests, is more conducive to the spread of a contagious national disease than to one's sense of personal integrity. Lastly, in *The Gigli Concert* Murphy unleashes his iconoclastic ire on the consumerist Irish bourgeoisie who resent any deviant flight of creativity, force many of their artists into exile, and, as Beniamino admonishes (and he should know as he was once one of them), try to destroy those who remain.

This angry, at times apocalyptic, attitude to contemporary Irish society has made, in Murphy's case, for a highly charged drama. The exuberance of dramatic form and language – sometimes straining at the seams – which Murphy's uncompromising *non serviam* has produced cannot be underestimated. And yet one is tempted to ask if his global repudiation of Ireland's social, religious and political institutions does not run the risk of excessive caricature, even falling back, at times, into the romantic cliché of the *poète maudit:* the solitary wounded artist guarding the last flame of vision within his breast against the benighted hostility of the community at large. Kierkegaard dismissed the anonymous masses that threatened the creative individual as the 'Crowd', Nietzsche as the 'Herd', and Sartre as 'les salauds'. Murphy's heroes do not usually give an explicit identity to this social collectivity; it has contaminated the very air they breathe; it is witnessed in the visible scars of their failure; it is quite simply that faceless omnipresent 'they' invoked by Beniamino when he warns J.P.W. that there's kindness in the world but *'they'll* kill you if you stay over here'. Murphy's response to this threat of the irrational collective is invariably one of fierce individualism, recalling Swift's savage indignation at the 'yahoo' mentality.

In Murphy's world, the individual is the agent of liberation; the collectivity – and its related idioms of history, tradition, authority, politics, nationalism etc. – the agency of coercion. Nearly all of his plays are centred around an isolated individual's struggle for self-realization over against the oppressive constraints of his/her social environment. Whether it be Eddie O'Hara in *The Blue Macushla*, John Connor in *Famine* or J.P.W. in *The Gigli Concert*, in each case the line of demarcation between spiritual salvation and social insanity is perilously thin. Ireland remains Murphy's first and only love, where genius and lunacy go hand in glove.[10]

Murphy's plays declare war on the paralysing forces in our society, compelling us to sound out our most hidden frustrations and fears and encouraging us, where possible, to transcend them in humour and faith. For these above all are the characteristic virtues of Murphy's dramatic enterprise – the laughter that emancipates and the leap of faith towards new *possibilities* of experience, more perfect, more creative, more human. Murphy will not stop writing until we are all singing like Gigli.[11]

Stills from *Angel* (top) and *Maeve*. By kind permission.

8
NATIONALISM AND IRISH CINEMA

The use of Irish films to tell stories of national heroism began early. Certain stereotypes recur which exemplify the cause of cultural nationalism. From its beginnings in the early decades of this century, Irish cinema has been dominated by a number of inter-connected motifs: the idealization of the past, the lure of a primitive landscape, the compelling power of violence and its quasi-mystical rapport with feminine sexuality or Catholic spirituality, and finally an unflagging fidelity to motherland, tribe and family[1]. So pervasive has this cluster of motifs been in the cinematic representation of Ireland, that any new attempt by Irish film makers to examine these themes in a critical manner runs the risk of being co-opted back into the very tradition which it is opposing[2]. Neil Jordan's *Angel* (1983) and Pat Murphy's *Maeve* (1981) are two recent Irish films which make such an attempt. But before analysing these works in detail it may be useful to look at some of the films which actively promoted the traditional stereotypes.

I

In 1911 Sidney Olcott made *Rory O'More*, one of the first films to be shot in Ireland explicitly dealing with the historic national struggle. Set during the Fenian Rebellion of 1798, the film recounts the ordeals of the eponymous rebel as he is hunted and imprisoned by the British before being rescued from the gallows by the good offices of his devoted mother, heroic fiancée (appropriately named Kathleen) and the family priest. Luke Gibbons offers this resumé of a typical sequence from the film: 'Rory is warned of his impending arrest by his faithful girlfriend Kathleen and takes to the hills – which coincidentally happen to be in the vicinity of Killarney! This provides the pretext for a series of picturesque set-pieces in which Rory and Kathleen are framed dramatically against the wild, rugged landscape, each change of scenery being preceded by appropriate titles in case we miss the whole point of the exercise: 'The Gap of Dunloe', 'The Lakes of Killarney' and so on'[3].

In 1934, Frank O'Connor's *Guests of the Nation*, treating of the

I.R.A.'s execution of two British soldiers in 1921, was made into a silent movie. O'Connor was so impressed by the merits of the film directed in theatrical fashion by Denis Johnston, that he advised the government to provide the necessary money to have the picture refilmed. It would, he argued, add to the prestige of the Irish abroad, 'showing the great spirit of the War of Independence and the spirit of comradeship that existed between the opposing forces, as well as the devotion to duty of the men who fought'[4]. Needless to say, O'Connor's appeal for government financing fell on deaf ears. Perhaps one of the reasons being that no one – besides O'Connor and a few well-wishers – really believed that a 'spirit of comradeship' did exist between the I.R.A. and the British Army during that internecine war.

In 1935, *Dawn*, produced and directed in Ireland by Dan Cooper, was released. This film also dealt with the War of Independence, but in a more militaristic spirit. *Dawn* portrayed the brutal atrocities of the Black and Tan Brigades and celebrated the heroic resistance of one Brian Malone, who deserted from the Royal Irish Constabulary to join the I.R.A. It concluded with a dawn funeral procession by the I.R.A. and a call for 'the struggle to continue'.

Each of these films interpreted political violence according to the yardstick of a dominant national ideology. Regardless of whether this ideology conformed more to the Free State version of Anglo-Irish cooperation (*Guests of the Nation*) or to the militant Republican version of armed resistance (*Rory O'More* and *Dawn*), the common purpose of these films was to propagate a romantic vision of Ireland which would 'add to the prestige of the Irish abroad'. And a similarly romanticized portrait has been promoted by the great majority of subsequent films dealing with the national question, from *The Gentle Gunman* (1952) and *The Rising of the Moon* (1957) to *Ryan's Daughter* (1970). In view of this pervasive tradition, it is not surprising to find one contemporary Irish critic issuing the following negative verdict:

> One of the depressing consequences of an Irish film industry has always been the likely re-enforcement of stereotypes of Irish character, history and landscape: the cinematic versions of women in red shawls, upright yet drunken men, sentimental nationalism, the sheepdog in the lane, the heifer in calf, the schoolteacher in trouble, the pastoral western retreats from social and political conflict. *Ryan's Daughter* has had too many fathers and too many sons. And it is clear that the native productions, insofar as there have been any in our cinema history, have offended no less than the international productions[5].

I believe that there have been some notable exceptions to this general tendency, in particular Neil Jordan's *Angel* and Pat Murphy's *Maeve*, both of which work against the romantic grain of traditional Irish cinema and propose alternative models of narrative which challenge the viewer to reassess the dominant myths of national culture.

II: Angel

Angel debunks the orthodox portrayal of Irish political violence and deromanticizes several of its stock motifs – most notably that of the national hero at arms. Rather than conforming to any specific ideology, this film exposes the hidden unconscious forces which animate ideological violence, irrespective of its Republican, Loyalist or British Imperialist hue. Jordan's cinematic exploration of the psychic roots of violence permits him to cut through ideological conventions and disclose that fantasy world of inner obsession which, he believes, is the source of both our political and poetic myths.

T.S. Eliot defined the genuine artist as someone with an educated nervous system. According to this definition, *Angel* is an instance of genuine art, functioning as it does to educate the viewer's inner sensibility, to enable us aesthetically to experience the unconscious drives which inform our everyday actions and perceptions. As Jordan himself explains: 'What I get the greatest pleasure out of is trying to make manifest how . . . a perceiving eye can see and feel the world. I suppose really that fiction or any art is like sensual thinking. It's like thinking through one's senses . . . [which] is deeper, more valuable than abstract thinking.'[6] In this respect, Jordan has learned much from his mentor, John Boorman, with whom he worked as creative consultant during the making of *Excalibur*. Jordan shares Boorman's determination to investigate the pre-rational powers of collective, national or personal mythology which continue to motivate much of human existence. Boorman has defined his own cinematic preoccupation with myth in terms of Jungian psychology: 'I read Jung and began to feel that . . . myths contained all that was important about a race, not only about its past, but also intimations of its future'[7]. While Jordan would seem to subscribe to the conviction that myths play a central role in the formation of a national consciousness, he is equally aware that they can contribute to its deformation. Moreover, he explores the mythical not in terms of ancient legend but in terms of contemporary experience. His approach is critical in that it brings ethical scruples to bear on the exploration of the mythic unconscious, disclosing how it can as easily. lead to destructive fanaticism as to creative renewal.

*   *   *

Angel tells the story of a saxophone player, Danny, who encounters paramilitary violence and eventually becomes seduced by its allure. It is set, significantly, in Northern Ireland and opens with a dance band playing in a rural ballroom. The initial sequence introduces three women into Danny's orbit of performance: Deirdre or D, the beautiful lead singer in the band; a deaf-mute teenager named Annie; and a young bride in white who asks Danny to dance but is quickly snatched away by her jealous husband. Danny is drawn to each in turn. But it is with the mute Annie that he makes love after the dance in a shelter outside the ballroom. Though their encounter is casual, almost accidental, it is far from manipulative. In a love scene accompanied by the elegiac score of Verdi's requiem, the spectator glimpses a tale of fleeting innocence. From their shelter, Annie and Danny see a car drive up to the ballroom. Four masked men exit and proceed to murder the manager of the showband because they believe he has paid protection money to a rival paramilitary group (which remains unidentified). When the unsuspecting Annie leaves the shelter to approach the killers they shoot her also. The gang escapes just before the ballroom, which they have mined with explosives, erupts into flames. Thus begins Danny's first encounter with the horror which will lead him to the heart of darkness. Romantic Ireland is irrevocably dead and gone.

This episode of violence unfolds with an arresting rapidity, each image of mounting brutality cutting in upon the next. But amidst this traumatic sequence of terror Danny fastens upon the stark image of a raised orthopaedic shoe, like a cloven hoof, worn by one of the killers. This frame is to become an indelible memory for Danny, repeated in successive flashbacks as he plummets towards an ever-deepening obsession with revenge. (A montage technique also used by Boorman to good effect in such films as *Point Blank* and *The Exorcist II*).

Recovering from shock in a Belfast hospital, Danny is visited by two police detectives (presumably R.U.C. or Anti-Terrorist Squad) called Bloom and Bonner. He tells them less than he knows and says nothing of the central clue – the orthopaedic shoe. The violence has become so internalized for Danny that he is determined to investigate it for himself. Danny chooses to explore this evil at a metaphysical level beyond the legal logic of politics and police. But his refusal to co-operate with the forces of Law and Order is portrayed as a sort of complicity with the criminal act itself; he is slowly becoming entranced by the malignity he seeks to destroy. Danny's inordinately personalized quest for revenge eventually assumes the proportions of an impersonal madness.

*   *   *

And so begins Danny's gradual substitution of violence for art. This transition from an 'angelic' to a 'demonic' *persona*, is epitomized by Danny's departure from the band and his musical/love partner, Deirdre, as he removes his saxophone from its case and replaces it with an armalite. Indeed Deirdre's plaintive singing of the heroic Irish ballad *Danny Boy* has become, ironically and despite her intentions, a mock-heroic call to arms! The exchange of musical instrument and gun is a decisive scene. It occurs in Danny's childhood bedroom at his Aunty Mae's house. Employing sombre, dreamlike images, Jordan shows Danny undergoing here what psychoanalysis has rather clinically described as a 'transfer of unconscious desires', as he switches from one 'transitional object' (the sax) to another (the machine gun). The transfer is patently a regressive one, conveyed in a trancelike sequence without the use of words or abstract theorizing.

Jordan offers the following account of this crucial psychic transition from artistic creativity to violent destruction:

> When you begin to work artistically you throw yourself to, a certain extent into chaos, into the area of your mind and experiences which is very volatile, even in some cases dangerous. The attraction of art, and perhaps the beauty of it, is that it can encapsulate all the beauty of sensual experience and at the same time allow you to meet this chaos and the darker side of your personality in, perhaps, the most meaningful way. Now violence to me – the attraction of violence – is the polar opposite to that. It does throw one into contact with chaos, with the darker side of human experience, with evil, and it does so, obviously, in the most brutal way imaginable.[8]

But while stressing the difference between art and violence as two ways of responding to the 'dark side' of the psyche, Jordan is equally aware, as is clear in *Angel*, of the uncanny similarities they possess:

> I think the lure of art for people is that very often it will give their lives a pitch of intensity they don't normally have. The lure of violence is quite similar, because it gives them this pitch of excitement, this visceral drive, and results in the decay of the human person. . . . In Danny, I wanted to posit a very innocent character who plays the saxophone and is obsessed with his instrument the way any musician is. It's interesting, by the way, that a lot of musicians call their instruments their axe. It's a strangely violent image. But there's a mechanic-of-the-arts thing about him; he's at home with his instrument, he knows how the key works, he could mend it himself even, and the first time he sees the gun, the appalling paradox of it is that on that basic mechanical level – a child's fascination with how the thing works – it has the same draw for him as the saxophone[9].

One of the strengths of *Angel* is its precise ability to focus on this 'basic mechanical level' of reflex attraction and recoil, symptomatic of the workings of the subconscious. In this way Jordan investigates that fundamental nexus between aesthetic creativity and violence which has become one of the most frequented stamping grounds of contemporary art. One thinks of Yeats's *Ben Bulben*, Heaney's *North*, D.M. Thomas's *The White Hotel*, Visconti's *The Damned*, and perhaps most of all, Thomas Mann's *Dr. Faustus*. This last work examines the complex relationship between invention (the atonal symphonies of Schoenberg) and political barbarism (Nazism), concluding with an impassioned plea for the recognition of the artist's ethical responsibility: 'One does wrong to see in aesthetics a separate and narrow field of the human. It is more than

that, it is at bottom everything; it is what attracts and repels. . .
Aesthetic release or the lack of it is a matter of one's fate, dealing out
happiness and unhappiness, companionship or helpless if proud
isolation on earth.'[10] Mann's conclusion could well serve as an
epilogue to *Angel*. Unable to find aesthetic release through his
music, due to his psychic paralysis after Annie's murder, Danny
resorts to the alternative 'play' of destruction (i.e. that which
ironically occasioned his paralysis in the first place). Though
initially motivated by the desire to avenge his lover, he soon finds
himself embroiled in an inexorable spiral of blood-letting.

*   *   *

After he leaves hospital, Danny succeeds in tracking down one of
the killers, thanks to the cleft-foot clue and a chance encounter (as
'chance' indeed as the original encounter with the angelic Annie).
He executes the 'terrorist' executor with the same mechanical ease
with which he formerly played his instrument; and from then on it's
simply a question of tracking down the other three members of the
gang. As Danny progresses in his new vocation of avenging angel
(and in avenging his angel – Annie – he himself becomes an avenging
'fallen' angel), he discovers that the assassins he has pledged to
assassinate have private lives just like himself. This theme of the
'double' or *Doppelgänger* is heightened by the fact that each
revenge-shooting is preceded by a scene where Danny confronts his
paramilitary opponent in the intimacy of the latter's domestic
existence. The first two assassins are confronted by Danny in the
secluded privacy of their homes, the third in his sequestered forest
love-nest. And the fourth gang-leader – who in a surprise denoue-
ment turns out to be the police inspector, Bonner – is finally tracked
down in his birthplace: Bonner dies, gripping Danny in a desperate
love/hate embrace, with the words – 'Stay with me. I grew up around
here'. Moreover this same phrase, 'stay with me', was also uttered
by the second assassin after he had been shot by Danny, thereby
functioning as a refrain to reinforce the sinister collusion between
Danny and the killers. Before each execution, Danny feels
compelled to enter the inner circle of the victim's life, to find out his
name, to understand his secret loves and hates. 'I want to know
everything he ever did', Danny says of one of the killers. It is this
ironic mode of interplay between the public outerworld of the thriller
plot and the private innerworld of psychic motivation which
hallmarks *Angel* as an original exploration of Irish (and non-Irish)
political violence.

Deirdre makes relentless efforts to enter Danny's inner world and
thereby retrieve him from the engulfing void of evil. But she fails to
convince him to replace the armalite with the saxophone; and in
their final encounter in the magic-lantern marquee she ultimately

recoils from his contaminated nothingness. 'You're dead,' she cries, 'you make me feel unclean.' And it is at this point that Deirdre explicitly affirms one of the major themes of the film – that the impersonalizing spell of violence makes all men, whatever their political persuasion, the *same*. She announces that detective Bonner is hunting for Danny: 'They're looking for you, *they're like you* only they have uniforms on.' *Angel* thus suggests how violence deprives humans of their individual identity and makes them into 'nobodaddies' of death. 'I am nobody,' admits one of the killers to Danny, announcing their common identity (the same phrase is casually repeated by Danny later in the film). Or as the police inspector, Bloom, puts it: 'It's deep, it's everywhere, it's nowhere . . . *Nothing* can get hold of you . . . Nowadays, here, everybody's guilty.' It is surely significant that for most of the film Jordan leaves the spectator in doubt with regard to the exact political identity of the various agents of violence. As the plot unfolds, there are some hints that the protection-racket gang are Republican/Catholic and that the four assassins (including the police agent, Bonner) are Loyalist/Protestant. But Jordan seems to be saying that the particular *ideology* of bloodshed is largely irrelevant. What the film really seeks to detect is the psychological and metaphysical motivation which can transform the hero, Danny Boy, from an angel into a psychopath (a point echoed by the young bride of the dancehall scene who warns Danny that 'men start out as angels but end up as brutes').

* * *

To this end, Jordan juxtaposes the *surface-structure* of the 'detective' narrative, full of fast-moving suspense, with a *deep-structure* of psychic probing. This latter structure penetrates to the underworld of unconscious obsession which preconditions the narrative action of the 'political' plot (i.e. the gang's assassination of Annie, Danny's assassination of the gang, and the police hunt for both the gang and Danny). The psychic deep-structure of the film lies beneath the 'police story' – as the detective, Bloom, says to Danny: 'You can go places where I can't go' – and operates according to a radically different temporality. Borrowing the structuralist terms of Saussure and Barthes, we might say that while the deep-structure unfolds 'synchronically' by repeating key visual and sound motifs, the surface-structure progresses 'diachronically' according to the standard conventions of a sequential plot[11]. It is the deeper synchronic structure that expresses the poetic, ethical and psychological dimensions which most interest Jordan:

> 'Given that the film is a thriller,' (says Jordan) 'and given that I wanted to speak about morality and questions of good and evil and the soul, I didn't want to make it with the speed, and the glitter, and the *distractions* with

which action films are normally made. I wanted to do precisely the opposite of that. When someone is holding a gun on somebody else I wanted him to be actually asking the question of what they're like. I wanted all the time to polarise and contrast the act of violence with the actual poetic dimensions of people's lives.'[12]

Having traced the broad outlines of the surface plot, we now briefly examine some of the recurring cross-reference motifs of the film's deep-structure: a structure which operates at a *vertical* (counter-narrative) rather than *horizontal* (narrative) level.

Firstly, there is the *dance motif*: Annie, the bride, Deirdre and Aunty Mae all invite Danny to dance with them at different points in the film. Secondly, there is the *music motif*: Danny's most intimate moments of communion are signalled by music or song – D's singing of *Danny Boy*, Aunt Mae's improvisation of a music-hall ditty, the Verdi chant which accompanies the love scene with Annie and recurs at key junctures throughout the film, and the musical performance in the asylum where the inmates waltz in a ghost-like trance. Another telling piece of music in the film is 'Strange Fruit', Billie Holiday's anti-violence song of the thirties. 'You could almost transpose the whole lyrics over to Ireland,' comments Jordan, 'there you're speaking about a situation where human beings killed people they didn't know for reasons which had nothing to do with any kind of human emotion whatever. It had just to do with racial differences; and it's a similar kind of situation that I was talking about in the film.'[13] A third vertical motif is the *laying on of hands*; this healing 'angelic' act recurs throughout the film as Danny is embraced by Annie, Deirdre, Aunty Mae and Mary. The accumulative significance of the act is crowned when the child faithhealer lays his hands on Danny's bleeding arm in the closing sequence of the film.

Danny's spiritual *navigatio* has come full circle. He meets the faith-healer in a caravan shrine constructed on the very site where he had originally been embraced by Annie outside the country dance hall. Surrounded by burning candles, which recall the fairy lights of the opening sequence, Danny kneels to receive the purgative touch of another angel-child. (A scene somewhat reminiscent of Rilke's plea to the metaphysical angel in *The Duino Elegies* when he asks, 'who, if I cried, would hear me from the order of angels' and save us from 'the dark turn of the world', from 'the guilty river god of the blood'.) Exiting from the caravan Danny encounters the fourth killer, Bonner, in the burnt-out hall; but he escapes death when Bloom arrives on the scene to shoot Bonner. The film ends with an apocalyptic wind sweeping through the gutted ballroom.

A fourth and arguably most effective use of synchronic deep-structure is Jordan's deployment of *framing images*. These images introduce a mood of meditative stillness and timelessness, which cuts across and suspends the highspeed action of the surface-plot. Some conspicuous examples of such framing scenes are: the haunt-

Stills from *Angel*. By kind permission.

Stills from *Maeve*. By kind permission.

ing and strangely unreal montage of the asylum sequence which precedes the second execution, brilliantly counterpointing the worlds of 'sanity' and 'madness'; the elegiac scene with the Salvation Army band on the waterfront which follows the second assassination; the mountain landscape of uncanny silence which punctuates Danny's execution of the third killer in his car; and the final faithhealing rite between Danny and the child which precedes the execution of Bonner.

These framing episodes are *synchronic* to the extent that their stylized unreality interrupts the linear melodrama of the narrative, turning our attention to a deeper level of awareness. This deeper level is what Roland Barthes calls the *'third meaning'* – a supplementary or surplus meaning which elicits a disruptive logic of the unconscious in defiance of the two conscious meanings of standard referential narrative: the *informational* and the *ideological* (see Appendix on *Barthes' Third Meaning*). With this 'alienation' device, Jordan's vertical images serve to freeze the flow of the action, *defamiliarizing* our common expectations and heightening our critical perception. Jordan's abrupt juxtaposition of synchronic and diachronic structures makes the viewer reflexively aware of his/ her own responses. By disrupting the realist conventions of cinematic representation, he exposes the way in which the very process of fictional narrative operates.

This technique enables the viewer to delve beneath the ideological clichés of political violence to its unconscious hidden dimension. Indeed we might say of Jordan's *Angel* what Pauline Kael said of Bertolucci's *The Conformist* (another contemporary film which explores the depth psychology of violence): 'you don't think in terms of entering a story being acted out, because (the film itself) provides a consciousness of what's going on behind the scenes.'[14]

One of the most important consequences of this disruption of linear narrative in *Angel* is the film's refusal to allow the spectator to passively identify with the avenging hero. The legendary national stereotype of Danny boy (which incidentally served as title for the film on its release in America) is debunked both formally and thematically. *Angel* may be considered accordingly as a radical deromanticisation of the cult of heroic violence which has fueled sentimental nationalism in many of its traditional and contemporary guises.

III: Maeve

If Neil Jordan's *Angel* disputes the cinematic stereotype of the national hero in arms, Pat Murphy's *Maeve* dismantles the corresponding stereotype of the national heroine in alms. This latter stereotype has dominated film portrayals of Irish women not only in the early cinema of the cultural revival but also in much contemporary cinema. In a study entitled 'Aspects of Representation of Women in Irish Film', Barbara O'Connor states the problem thus:

> Among the most powerful tools of women's ideological oppression, is their media representation. These images of women have contributed in no small way to a patriarchial hegemony in which the real class and gender relations of women in society have been replaced by myths. Cinema, as one of the mainstream media, has been instrumental in the repression of a woman's discourse. . . . Film production in the early decades of the new Irish State was characterised by a choice of theme whose aim was the consolidation of this state (exemplified by strict censorship). The consequences of this for the representation of women was that they were either absent from a screen which was concerned with the epic deeds of the male heroes of Irish history or cast in the role of mother or sweetheart of these same heroes. Turning from a celebration of Irish customs and traditions to a critique of many aspects of our way of life, the 'New Wave' of film makers opened up some space for women to re-emerge into history[15].

Perhaps the most important figure in this New Wave of critical film makers to challenge the mythic representations of Irish women is Pat Murphy. *Maeve* is a film which rescues the mythological Queen Maeve from her ideological distortion in the official revivalist version of Irish history and restores her, 'demythologized' as it were, to the contemporary social context of war-torn Ulster. Murphy achieves this rewriting of orthodox myth by advancing an avant-garde feminist cinema whose object is 'the deconstruction of the forms of dominant cinema, which are seen as essentially patriarchal, and their replacement with new "feminine" forms.'[16]

The forms of dominant cinema are, however, pervasive. Apart altogether from such internationally produced melodramas as *Rory O'More* or *Ryan's Daughter*, there have also been a large number of 'home produced' films which continue to cast Irish women in the stock roles of passive romantic heroine or helpless victim. Wynne-Simmons' *Outcasts* recounts how an innocent mute girl becomes the scapegoat of an intolerant community in rural Ireland but survives her sacrificial plight to serve as an immortal spirit haunting the community and reminding it of its evil deeds. *Cal*, a film version of Bernard McLaverty's novel directed by Pat O'Connor, provides another representation of woman as an innocent casualty of political violence: not only is the heroine's UDR husband shot by the IRA but she then has the tragic misfortune to fall in love with her husband's assassin. Caught between the pincer-jaws of sectarian tribalism, the heroine emerges as a sacrificial victim whose heavenly wisdom alone offers hope for the future. Other recent examples of what we might call the 'Deirdre of the Sorrows' myth (in contrast to the 'Maeve' anti-myth) are to be found in the portrayal of women in such films as Kieran Hickey's *Attracta* and Edward Bennett's *Ascendancy*, both of which cast their heroines as hapless spiritual casualties of the Ulster crisis. Most of these films not only conform to the traditional typecasting of Irish women; they also subscribe to the cinematic conventions of naturalistic narrative.[16a]

*   *   *

Pat Murphy's *Maeve* runs directly counter to this mainstream. Made by an Irish woman to champion the cause of women's liberation in Ireland, this film is also set in modern Ulster and takes as its central heroine a Belfast girl suffering from the tribal conflicts of male aggression. (Maeve and her family are abused by the British army and her boyfriend is a member of the Provos). But Pat Murphy radically shifts the emphasis of her portrayal so that her heroine moves from the passivity of paralysis to the activity of protest. She departs from the orthodox mythology of Deirdre of the Sorrows in order to embrace the opposing and unorthodox mythology of Maeve as a figure of resistance and revolt. Maeve not only suffers but acts. To the military and patriarchal ideology of men she opposes the liberation struggle of the female body. The war of the sexes replaces the war of the tribes. As Luke Gibbons has remarked: 'Sexuality . . . as represented by powerful female figures such as Maeve, had to be written out of Irish history, a task for which a heightened narrative impelled by violent action was eminently suitable. It is hardly surprising then that the return of another Maeve to Ulster should bring about a direct confrontation with this mythic version of the past. The only difference is that now the drama is taking place on the streets.'[17].

The process of writing powerful women out of Irish history had already begun with Standish O'Grady, one of the major influences on the national cultural revival. In order to provide appropriate heroic narratives of 'gods and fighting men', O'Grady felt compelled to alter certain parts of the *Táin Bó Cuailgne* saga where Ulster is invaded by the warrior Queen of Connaught, Maeve. Maeve's rebellious spirit and 'loose morality' of sexual liaison, were so out of keeping with O'Grady's romantic ideology that he felt compelled to exclude them. As Philip Marcus observes in his book on O'Grady: 'The treatment of Maeve was perhaps most at variance with the source materials. O'Grady tried to make her seem more "feminine", to endow her with some of the personality traits traditionally associated with the "weaker sex", and at times the proud amazon of the sources seems more like the delicate fainting heroines of the nineteenth-century novel.'[18]

Maeve decomposes not only the national stereotype of romantic heroine but also the traditional relationship in Irish cinema between mythic landscape, male heroism and linear narrative. The romantic tradition of Irish cinema used rural landscape as a reminder of the lost heroic age, of what O'Grady called the 'early Irish tales that cling around the mounds and cromlechs'. This reduction of historical time to a kind of eternal landscape was, in O'Grady's words, able to evoke legends 'believed in as history, never consciously invented . . . and drawing (their) life from the soil *like a natural growth*.'[19]

Murphy (like Jordan) uses flashback techniques to dispel the *natural* appearance of linear narrative. Several of these intercuts show us the young child, Maeve Sweeney, accompanying her father from their home in urban Belfast on visits to the ancient stone monuments of the surrounding rural landscape. Her father, like O'Grady and other exponents of the Revival, sees the ruins of the past as bearers of national myths which he has come to believe in as realities. The landscape thus serves to identify political history with the magical power of nature. As they contemplate the legendary countryside, Maeve's father narrates the great tales of the nationalist Revival. But Murphy strategically dislocates the normal flow of naturalistic narrative by decentering the traditional relationship between male (as controlling centre) and female (as passive background). Using various distancing devices, Murphy compels us to recognize that the images before us on the screen – no less than the 'stories in stones' that Maeve's father recounts – are *constructs*. This negates the desire of the paternal author to *mask* his own dominant role in the narrative by presenting it as if it were as *natural* as the stones in the landscape. In *Maeve* we are never allowed to forget that the inherited versions of history – as narrated by Maeve's father and boyfriend for example – are governed by a male vision of things. Gibbons details certain key scenes in which the controlling narrative of the father is exposed:

> In the opening scene of the film, Martin Sweeney, Maeve's father, escapes from the oppressive reality of a bombscare outside the front window of their house, and retreats to the safety of the back kitchen. Entering what is conventionally designated as female space, he removes various obstacles such as washing and clothing, and proceeds to write a letter to Maeve which we hear in voice over – at which point Maeve herself first appears on the screen. Throughout the film, Martin's intrusions and storytelling attempt to occupy woman's space, usurping and pre-empting alternative female versions of reality. In one scene he interrupts an anecdote about a neighbour which Eileen, Maeve's mother, is recounting, and converts it into a rambling narrative of his own. The extent to which this continual appropriation of history removes women to the periphery is suggested in one striking later sequence in which Martin loses himself in an even more drawn out narrative than usual, while the young Maeve hovers in the background, edging herself along the circular walls of a ring-fort. As she reaches the centre of the frame, directly behind Martin, she alights from the stone wall of the fort thereby parting company with the dominant conception of history. Martin's authority has

been displaced, a fact which is expressed cinematically in both of the storytelling sequences in question by the manner in which he is prevented from assuming the role of an invisible, omniscient narrator, and is forced instead to relate history in the form of a direct address to camera. By drawing attention to the authorial presence of the camera, and reminding the audience that they are in fact looking at a visual construction of reality, one of the main conditions of classical illusionistic narrative is undermined. . . .[20]

*   *   *

We witness a similar deconstruction of naturalistic narrative in a later sequence where Maeve engages her Republican boyfriend, Liam, in a long political argument about the use of violence in contemporary Ulster. During this exchange, which takes place on a hill overlooking Belfast, Liam's controlling *ideological* narrative is gradually subverted by Maeve's interpolation of fragmented word-associations which disrupt the illusion of linear realist dialogue. By means of this Brechtian estrangement technique, Liam's ideology is exposed as a patriarchal myth masquerading as reality. 'Whatever way you look at it,' as Pat Murphy explained in an interview in *Iris*, 'the language of Republicanism is patriarchal.'[21] (And the film also features scenes, it must be noted, which expose the equally patriarchal character of the Loyalist and British colonialist ideologies). Brushing the realist conventions of visual and verbal narrative against the grain, Pat Murphy discloses how ideological myths – of whatever political persuasion – are fabrications of the mind, not facts of nature (as they pretend to be). Her shift of emphasis from the *content* of the storyline to the *form* of cinematic storytelling serves to remind the viewer that our political culture – like the film *Maeve* itself – is a *construct* not a *given*. The film and the character of Maeve are, therefore, also myths of a kind. But they are *self-critical* myths which expose the very process whereby myths are made and unmade. Unlike ideologies which lie to hide the truth, they are, as Maeve reminds Liam, 'lies which tell the truth'. This self-exposure of the devices of cinematic representation is witnessed not only in the self-conscious use of direct address to camera, of protracted non-naturalistic monologue and of flashback sequences which interrupt the forward flow of the story, but also in a number of pointed allusions to the television medium as a means of insulating people from their surrounding social environment. Here again Luke Gibbons provides a perceptive commentary:

> Television acts as a metaphor for the way in which images and representations often function as protective measures against the encroachments of an intolerable reality. In the opening scenes of the film television violence competes for attention with the real life threat of the bomb-scare outside the front window, allowing Martin to retreat to the

back-kitchen to compose the letter to Maeve which initiates the action of the film. The feelings of security generated by representations, which place the spectator at one remove from reality are shattered, however, in a subsequent scene (a flashback to the past) in which Maeve's family, watching July 12th celebrations on television, are abruptly brought back to earth by a brick coming through the window of their front room. In a later episode, the use of television as a security monitor in a Republican pub shows how representations no longer merely simulate but actively participate in the violence they portray, the image becoming an accomplice in, rather than a refuge from, the propaganda of the deed. In a similar manner, it is suggested, Martin's stories and fictions no longer serve to prevent his immersion in reality, a point illustrated to stark effect in one strange, almost surreal sequence, in which he is forced by a squad of British troops to unload a consignment of televisions from the back of his van onto the street, their screens silent, blank and ineffectual[22].

*   *   *

By traditional standards, Maeve is very much an anti-heroine. She refuses the romantic roles of sentimental girlfriend, domestic daughter and long-suffering victim. The rebel Maeve defies both the female stereotype of the sorrowing Deirdre and the male stereotype of the armed warrior. Yet while she critically dissociates herself from the romantic myth of national heroine devoted to her military hero or tribal landscape, Maeve never resorts to indifference. She remains aware of the immense social and moral responsibility resulting from the discovery that national myths are historical constructions. But this sense of responsibility leads her to commit herself not to a patriarchal movement of resistance through ideology, but to an opposing female movement of resistance through the body. 'When you're denied power,' as she explains to Liam during their final exchange, 'the only form of struggle is through your body.'

Maeve seems to suggest that one of the most effective ways of divesting history of the ideological myths of the dead past is to affirm the positive powers of desire and sexuality. Over and against the sectarian violence of Ulster, dominated as Maeve puts it by the ideology of 'purity and death', the solution lies not in some escapist return to the haven of family domesticity – for this would simply be to reinforce the traditional gender stereotypes which oppose the public world of male action to the private world of female passivity – but in the assertion of the body as a site of political struggle where private and public coincide. Rescuing the female body from the dominant representations of romantic nationalism, Maeve resolves to liberate Republicanism from its male-dominated mythology. So doing, she transcends tribal factionalism in the name of a universal solidarity between all those oppressed by patriarchal ideologies. This new found solidarity is illustrated in the hospital scene where the Catholic Maeve finds herself side by side with an old Protestant woman who sings 'Abide with me'. The concluding scenes of the film offer a vivid summary of the central implications of Maeve's revolt: 'Many of the film's key concerns – landscape and memory, history and narrative, male discourse and female solidarity – converge in the penultimate scene set in the Giant's Causeway, one of the most important antiquarian sites in Ireland. The total disintegration of the male controlling voice is evident in the figure of the ranting orator, hurtling the rhetoric of the Ulster covenant at the sea while Maeve, Roisin and Eileen find refuge behind the rocks, sharing jokes and confidences and experiencing a new collective identity.' In the last scene, we see Martin alone in darkness, talking to himself about his interrogation by the RUC, a casualty of his own self-deception: 'I used to think that these things would never happen to me, even when they did. 'Cos you see, that's the only way to go on. . . . In the end, it is not Maeve but Martin who is the *outsider*.'[23]

Conclusion

Angel and *Maeve* are both innovative films which debunk some of the stereotypes which have dominated not only mainstream Irish cinema but the national cultural revival as a whole. Both films are set in deromanticised urban contexts and deal with themes of contemporary relevance: the recent violence in Ulster; the modern popular culture of dancehall, pub gigs and television; and the sexual and psychological relations between men and women. Both films also succeed, at a formal level, in deconstructing the uniform narratives of classical realism which encourage the viewer to passively identify with heroic characters in an unbroken linear plot. Such narratives are easy to follow, using techniques which ensure unbroken continuity of action, so that with the final 'closure' of the plot the viewer is also 'closed', i.e. satisfied and unquestioning[24]. The consequences of such narrative orthodoxy for the representation of social relations are that 'it can produce only the natural world of the dominant ideology. . . . Contradictions are masked by the construction of myths such as the unchangeable human (and one might add "national") condition.'[25]

Neil Jordan and Pat Murphy are two young directors who have been deeply marked by the formal experimentalism of the radical New Wave of modern European . cinema and have responded accordingly by dismantling many of the old narrative conventions which in Irish cinema so faithfully served the ideology of revivalism. Their respective critiques of the orthodox typecasting of national hero and heroine have not just focussed on *what* is portrayed but also and more importantly on *how* it is portrayed. In short, the shift in *content* has been accompanied by a corresponding shift in *form*[26]. Jordan and Murphy are not content with merely telling stories; they critically expose the way in which stories are constructed by means of camera work, cinematic narrative, framing devices and flashbacks, thereby reminding the viewer that highly complex structural devices are at work in the visual telling of a story, or at a broader level, in the making of a myth.

It has been argued that an overemphasis on formal breaks with dominant visual representation has often resulted in the production of avant-garde work whose codes are understood only by a film élite (who could be charged with both cultural arrogance and political naiveté[27]). This accusation might be made by some against *Angel* and *Maeve*, works whose formal radicalism has no doubt been partially responsible for their relative lack of commercial success or widespread diffusion. Neither film has received the kind of popular acclaim enjoyed by such romantic/realist epics as *Ryan's Daughter* or *Cal*. But one cannot deny that *Angel* and *Maeve* have, despite all the odds, made a remarkable impact on Irish film-making and film-viewing – an impact which extends well beyond an elitist art house following. Jordan and Murphy have set radical precedents for future experimental projects in Irish cinema and proved that it is possible to penetrate beneath the surface of official ideologies and expose the hidden processes whereby national myths and stereotypes are constructed.

Appendix: Barthes' 'Third Meaning'

Roland Barthes' analyses – both structuralist and post-structuralist – of the rhetoric of cinematic images provide a useful framework for a critical appreciation of Neil Jordan's use of synchronic (i.e. counter-narrative) images in *Angel*.

Barthes is aware of the paradox that the cinema, while being one of the most advanced forms of fictional representaton, is no less 'realist' in its dominant forms of narrative than the older art forms of the novel or drama. 'The more technology develops the diffusion of information (and notably of images),' writes Barthes, 'the more it provides the means of masking the constructed meaning under the appearance of a given meaning' ('Rhetoric of the Image' in *Image-Music-Text*, Fontana, 1977, p. 46). But Barthes acknowledges the possibility of cinematic images producing another kind of meaning which is properly 'filmic' in his analysis of Eisenstein's use of synchronic montage techniques. Barthes calls this a *third meaning* which disrupts and transcends the conventional meanings of cinematic realism ('The Third Meaning' in *Image-Music-Text*, *op. cit.*, pp. 52–69). The First Meaning of the cinematic image works at an *informational* level (i.e. it communicates descriptive information about the surface-structure of setting, plot, characterization etc.). The Second Meaning works at a *symbolic* level (i.e. it points to the political, economic or ideological message signified by the images of a film). The Third Meaning, however, breaks with the linear sequence of narrative information and reference and opens up what Barthes calls the 'metonymic logic of the unconscious' ('The Struggle with the Angel' in *Image-Music-Text, op. cit.*, p. 141). This metonymic logic operates by virtue of vertical displacement and repetition rather than by the normal means of sequential repre-sentation. It estranges us from the predictable expectations of 'realist' narrative allowing for 'surprises of meaning'. Barthes offers the following suggestive account of this Third Meaning:

> I receive a third meaning – erratic, obstinate. I do not know what its signified (reference) is, at least I am unable to give it a name, but I can see clearly the traits, the signifying accidents of which this – consequently incomplete – sign is composed. . . . Here the image cannot be conflated with the simple existence of the scene, it exceeds the copy of the referential motif, it compels an interrogative reading . . . a 'poetical grasp' (. . .) The third meaning is one 'too many', the supplement that my intellection cannot succeed in absorbing, at once persistent and fleeting, smooth and elusive . . . it seems to open the field of meaning totally, that is, infinitely (. . .) It is discontinuous, indifferent to the story and to the obvious meaning (as signification of the story). This dissociation has a de-naturing or at least distancing effect with regard to the referent (to 'reality' as nature, the realist instance). Eisenstein would probably have acknowledged this incongruity, this im-pertinence of the signifier (image). . . . It is clear that this obtuse meaning is the epitome of a counter-narrative, disseminated, reversible, set to its own temporality; it inevitably determines a quite different analytic segmentation to that in (narrative) shots and sequences – an extraordinary segmentation: counter-logical and yet true. . . . This meaning can only come and go, appearing – disappearing ('The Third Meaning', *op. cit.*, pp. 54–5, 62–3).

The Third Meaning which emerges from the synchronic use of images is characterized accordingly by an uncanny experience of discontinuity, abruptness and timelessness: a certain feeling of disorientation which momentarily allows the signifier (image) to float free from its signified (reference-message). If we cling to our conventional realist modes of reading a film we fail to grasp this Third Meaning or else dismiss it as superfluous or even absurd. What takes place here is 'from the referential (reality) point of view, literally *nothing*; what happens is language alone, the adventure of language, the unceasing celebration of its *jouissance*' ('Structural Analysis of Narratives' in *Image-Music-Text, op. cit.*, p. 124). To properly savour the Third Meaning is to resist the naturalist tempta-tion to 'reduce the text to a *signified*', by holding 'its *signifiance* fully open' ('Struggle with the Angel', *op. cit.*, p. 141). This crucial 'pregnant moment', at once totally concrete and totally abstract, is for Barthes the great achievement of Eisenstein's use of counter-narrative images ('Diderot, Brecht, Eisenstein' in *Image-Music-*

Text, op. cit., p. 73). As such, it calls for a reading that is at once instantaneous and vertical, prising open the linear time of the surface plot to reveal an 'other text': a second deeper text which in Eisenstein's words 'cannot be seen and heard but must be listened to attentively. . . . The center of gravity is no longer "between shots" – the shock – but the element "inside the shot" – the accentuation within the fragment.' It is precisely the absence of any continuous link between one such fragment and the next which permits the open-text of disjunction to issue in a Third Meaning. The audience's ability to adequately respond to this properly *filmic* dimension of meaning, arising from the fragments of a second text which never excedes these fragments, depends on a 'veritable mutation of reading and its object, text or film', which in Barthes' view 'is a crucial problem of our time' ('The Third Meaning', *op. cit.* p. 68).

9

AN ART OF OTHERNESS:
A STUDY OF LOUIS LE BROCQUY

Le Brocquy's journey as a painter has been marked by two overriding and interrelated obsessions – the phenomenon of whiteness and the image of the head. What appears most to fascinate the painter about these two subjects is their basic refusal to be represented in terms of a single perspective. They are for le Brocquy an invitation, above all else, to an irreducible *otherness of perception.*

I

The colour white has been a frequent obsession of artists. Malevitch, the revolutionary Russian painter, made his controversial tableau *White on White* (1917) the centerpiece of the avantgarde Suprematist movement. Whiteness was the ultimate statement of Suprematism as a search, through the material of paint, for the 'infinite intangible' – the matrix where the visible intersects with the invisible. It was for similar reasons that Herman Melville, the American novelist, chose the elusive whiteness of the whale as a central theme in *Moby Dick* describing it as 'not so much a colour as the visible absence of colour, and at the same time the concrete of all colours . . . a dumb blankness, full of meaning . . . a colourless all-colour.' From *The Blue Door,* one of his earliest works painted in 1932, to his *Presences* sequence in the fifties and sixties, to his more recent studies of heads emerging from white backgrounds, le Brocquy has pursued his exploration of the essential *ambivalence* of whiteness as colourless all-colour. In all of these paintings, white serves as the hidden dimension from which forms emerge and recede, an absence which presences, an interplay of light and shadow in which substance – devoid of circumstance – dissolves. John Russell, the American critic, has described le Brocquy accordingly as a painter who 'lays siege to whiteness'.

In his series of head images, begun in the mid-seventies, le Brocquy makes a partly white face both emerge from a white background and at the same time recede back into it: 'It is the play between the different areas of white which makes the paintings go taut with energy. The face which looms up leads us to sense the presence of the person in the white surrounds. Yet these surrounds elicit at the same time a feeling of absence, of a void. This void enters the face through the white areas of the latter. We look again and again at this face which leads us once more into the white background. And so a circulation of glances (or energies) is set up and it is this circulation which produces the characteristic ambivalence (presence/absence, passing/timelessness, animation/coldness) of the portraits, their 'spiritual' energy.'[1]

Le Brocquy's preoccupation with the face or head image appears to have, appropriately enough, a double focus. On the one hand, it draws its inspiration from the ancient practice of stone headcarving which dates back to the very origins of Western art. 'The heads themselves in the high-relief sculpture of Celto-Ligurian Entremont,' writes le Brocquy, 'and the heads within the "plummet-measured face" of Romanesque Clonfert (are) at once persons and stone bosses, both durable and timeless, forever emerging and receding.'[2] Le Brocquy maintains that what most interests him about these ancient heads is their ability to signify 'a profound parodox – a succession of presents spread out before us, without beginning or end.'[3] On the other hand, le Brocquy's fascination with the head image has resulted in a series of portrait studies of modernist artists – both Irish (Joyce, Beckett, Yeats) and non-Irish (Strindberg, Bacon, Lorca). These portraits seek to represent the artists' spiritual consciousness through the material medium of paint. And this attempt to give palpable expression to the modernist consciousness through the primitivist idiom of the head image involves le Brocquy in a fundamentally ambivalent probing of different and often conflicting planes of time and space. The result is an endless series of inconclusive representations which bear witness to the essential *otherness* of human experience, that is, its refusal to be represented in a single image of identity.

Le Brocquy's 120 Studies towards an Image of Joyce are a good case in point. This series eptiomises the painter's commitment to the multi-faceted nature of perception. The quality of open-endedness ensures that no one image can be isolated from the sequence and accorded a privileged status. Like Joyce's own disclosure of the multiple meanings of words in *Finnegans Wake*, le Brocquy's multiple representations of the Joyce head reveal that the goal of a definitive identity forever eludes us. The potentially interminable character of the series as 'studies *towards* an image . . . ' may be seen as a sort of visual palimpsest, a painter's witness to the impossibility of freezing creative consciousness in a fixed perspective. The recognized Joyce is thus rendered unrecognizable, his familiar identity defamiliarized. And in this respect, we might say that le Brocquy is being faithful to one of the most basic impulses of modernist art: the disclosure of the pluri-dimensional character of human consciousness. His work may be viewed accordingly in terms of Cézanne's resolve to *éclater la perspective*, Rimbaud's call for a *dérèglement systématique des sens*, or indeed Joyce's discovery that language is a 'bringer of plurabilities'. Le Brocquy provides us with the best guide to the understanding of his own work in the following description of what he calls the 'multiple identity' of the Joyce heads:

> Ever since I rediscovered for myself the image of the head, I have painted studies of James Joyce . . . Thus almost 120 studies towards an image of James Joyce have emerged in one medium or another. It remains an *unending task*. For to attempt today a portrait, a single static image of a great artist like Joyce seems to me futile as well as impertinent. Long conditioned by photography, the cinema and psychology, we now perceive the human individual as faceted, kinetic. And so I have tried as objectively as possible to draw from the depths of paper or canvas changing and even contradictory traces of James Joyce . . . I myself see these studies rather as an indefinite series without beginning or end and thus perhaps in tendency counter-Renaissance, as in a sense was also Joyce himself.[4]

Modernism, as we have noted in preceding chapters, revolted against the Renaissance convention of classical realism which promoted the illusion of a single controlling perspective. Joyce's dismantling of classical (linear) narrative and le Brocquy's refusal of classical (perspectival) representation both attest to their counter-Renaissance impulse. Le Brocquy's head series shatters the illusion of orthodox realist portraiture and introduces an arresting sense of *otherness*. One of the consequences of this formal experimentalism in his studies of the canonized figures of Irish national literature – Yeats, Joyce, Beckett – is to oblige the spectator to view these familiar faces in an unfamiliar way, revealing a disturbingly *alien* quality which forbids the security of immediate appropriation.

Roland Barthes, the French philosopher, speaks of the inability of bourgeois realism to 'imagine the other'. Once the bourgeois realist is confronted with the other, 'he blinds himself, ignores and denies him, or else transforms him into himself. In the petit-bourgeois universe . . . any otherness is reduced to sameness.'[5] Le Brocquy's paintings are, in this sense, a rebuke to the norms of bourgeois realism. By resisting our uniform modes of perception, they refuse to reduce the other to the same. We thus witness the images of the great modernist artists self-destruct before our eyes, exposing the art product as an endless production of meaning. We, the spectators of these images, are denied any dominant position from which to tally the representation with some supposed 'original'. Le Brocquy's portraits of the artists implicate the onlooker in the artistic process itself. As a perpetual dissemination of traces they cannot be retraced to some 'real' model existing outside of the series of representations. Thus le Brocquy's images of Joyce reveal that Joyce's identity as an artist is as elusive as the art which he created and in which, in his own words, 'the forms multiply themselves indefinitely'[6]. Unable to possess the image we are compelled to imagine it, and indeed ourselves, as other. For as le Brocquy explains, 'art is neither an instrument, nor a convenience, but a secret logic of the imagination. It is *another* way of seeing, the whole sense and value of which lies in its autonomy, its distance from actuality, its *otherness*'[7].

II

Some might view this modernist preoccupation with the otherness of art as a symptom of elitism or even obscurantism. But the matter is not so simple. There are many modern artists and critics who would argue the opposite, viewing the aesthetic of otherness as a form of radical, even revolutionary, consciousness. Thus we find the Marxist playwright, Bertholt Brecht, championing the alienation or estrangement (*Verfremdung*) effects of modernist theatre. Brecht's own experimental drama renounced the tendency of bourgeois audiences to passively identify with the language, plot or characters on stage through an uncritical process of psychological realism. Brecht affirmed that the major task of art was to challenge our preconceived assumptions and enable us to see the world in a new way. 'A work which does not exhibit its sovereignty vis à vis reality,' Brecht wrote, 'and which does not bestow sovereignty upon the public vis à vis reality is not a work of art.' And Joyce, it might be recalled, made a similar point when he explained that he wrote the nighttime language of *Finnegans Wake* 'because a great part of every human existence is passed in a state which cannot be rendered sensible by the use of wide awake language.'[8]

In his last published work, *The Aesthetic Dimension* (1979), the German philosopher, Herbert Marcuse defends the radical potential of art's 'distance from actuality'. Challenging all forms of aesthetic realism (be it the Socialist Realism of orthodox Marxism or the Classical Realism of bourgeois conformism), Marcuse argues for a recognition of the arresting strangeness of art: 'The radical qualities of art, that is to say, its indictment of the established reality and its invocation of the beautiful image (*schöner Schein*) of liberation are grounded precisely in the dimension where art *transcends* its social determination and emancipates itself from the given universe of discourse and behaviour. . . . The world formed by art is recognised as a reality which is suppressed and distorted in the given reality. This experience culminates in extreme situations (of love and death, guilt and failure, but also joy, happiness and fulfillment) which explode the given reality in the name of truths normally denied or even unheard. The inner logic of the work of art terminates in the emergence of another reason, another sensibility, which defies the rationality and sensibility incorporated in the dominant social institutions.'[9]

What Marcuse refers to here as the inner logic of the aesthetic dimension is what le Brocquy called the secret logic of imagination. This logic subverts actual worlds in the name of possible worlds; it refuses to subscribe to the everyday exigencies of social pragmatism in order to disclose hitherto occluded dimensions of meaning. Le Brocquy insists upon the necessity of such aesthetic transcendence with uncompromising candour: 'In the context of our everyday lives, painting must be regarded as an entirely *different* form of awareness, for an essential quality of art is its *alienation, its otherness*. In art at its most profound levels, actuality – exterior reality – is seen to be relevant, parallel, but remote or curiously dislocated.'[10] In other words, art must keep the established reality – be it social or perceptual – at arm's length. For only by thus alienating itself from reality can it liberate the alienated dimensions of reality. Le Brocquy's work is, by his own admission, an attempt to give '*possible* form to that which is impalpable and interiorized' by revealing that 'reality is that which is possible, conceivable and not merely what is actual and phenomenal.'[11]

This is not, of course, to consign modernist painting to a reactionary creed of art-for-art's sake. The alienation of art should not be misconstrued as an *indifference* to social well-being. On the contrary, as Marcuse reminds us, the autonomy of art contains the categorical imperative – *things must change.*[12] It is precisely the aesthetic dimension of transcendence which keeps us perpetually dissatisfied with the established order of things. The *difference* of art reminds us that the world too can be *different*, that there is always something *more*. So that if le Brocquy's images are not immediately familiar to orthodox one-dimensional consciousness, this is not an argument against these images but against the existing orthodoxy.

The modernist aesthetic of otherness has therefore radical social implications. By refusing to conform to the officially accepted paradigms of perception, art revolts against the social order which it is supposed submissively to represent. Modernist art protests against the suppression, however subtle, of *alternative* ways of viewing our world; it explodes the norms of conventional communication and response. 'Art has its own language and illuminates reality only through this *other* language.'[13]

III

There have, of course, been several attempts to undermine the otherness of art. Both the Agit prop and Performance Art movements in the West and the Socialist Realist movement in the East have, in their different ways, sought to subordinate art to the existing social reality. Performance art, for example, breaks down the barriers separating the aesthetic and the everyday by presenting art as an immediately consumable commodity. The Performance artist works to demolish the distance between the art object and its audience, as for example during the 1980 ROSC exhibition in Dublin when street bystanders were invited to devour a Joyce-Tower made of locally baked brown bread. The purpose of this *happening* was clearly to annihilate the notion of art as some autonomous activity displayed in galleries or museums. But it could be argued that by collapsing the divide between the otherness of art and the sameness of our consumer society, the Performer divests his work of its radically estranging and therefore emancipating power. Once art entirely abandons its distinctly aesthetic dimension does it not endorse the formless reality which it presumably wishes to indict? Such exercises in anti-art as this Rosc Performance or Andy Warhol's famous line of Campbell's soup tins may well be self-defeating to the extent that they succumb to the everyday world of consumer exploitation which radical art intends to subvert. As Brecht warned, the total repudiation of aesthetic form and distance leads all too often to a regressive banalization of experience.

While le Brocquy's paintings alter aesthetic form, they do not abandon it. They remain essentially liberating in so far as they disassemble outworn forms of representation, not in order to sanction formlessless, but in order to reconstruct *different* forms. Le Brocquy's art reinterprets our everyday way of seeing, transforming meaning as it has *already been expressed* into meanings *yet to be expressed.* In this sense, it is an uncompromising indictment of the perceptual, and by implication social, *status quo.* For once our inner vision changes we realize that the outer world can also change. Aesthetic transformation may thus serve as a prelude to social transformation; but it can only do so by insisting on the *difference* between the worlds of art and reality, that is, by refusing to become a weapon of propaganda or a commodity of consumerism. In short, it is precisely the otherness of art which reminds us that the world as it is can be made *other* than it is.

If we look towards the East, we find the official aesthetic of Socialist Realism obliging artists to compose works which faithfully reflect the 'genuine social reality'. The irony is that it is the party propagandist, not the poet or painter, who ultimately decides what is 'genuine', what is 'social' and what is 'reality'. As Leonid Brezhnev remarked in his address to the 1981 Soviet Party Congress: 'The Party encourages. . . . art's active intervention in the solution of our society's problems. . . . The heroes of works of art should not withdraw into trivial affairs but live with the concerns of their country at heart.' Brezhnev goes on to champion a literature devoted to the heroic life of the socially committed worker, be it 'a building team leader, a collective farm chairman, a railway worker or army officer' etc. Nor does he make any bones about affirming the Party's duty to monitor the 'ideological orientation of art' and to ensure it remains 'active in the building of communism'. But is there not a patronizing benevolence in this glorification of the factory-floor in the name of the collective good? Does it not amount to saying that the toil, suffering and exploitation of the worker (East or West) is an aesthetic model of experience (which it patently is not)?

Le Brocquy's art could certainly not be described, by any stretch of the imagination, as an 'active intervention in the solution of society's problems'. But his unflagging commitment to the exploration of visual *inwardness* may be seen as a disclosure of an aesthetic dimension which refuses the misery of exploitation and manipulation. By sustaining an irreducible distance, one might even say antagonism, between the interiority of art and the exteriority of the social universe, le Brocquy's work testifies to the fact that the present world of domination can never fully eliminate the potential world of freedom. The basic thesis that art must be a factor in changing the world, as Marcuse has observed, 'can easily turn into its opposite if the tension between art and radical praxis is flattened out so that art loses its own dimension for change. . . . The flight into inwardness may well serve as a bulwalk against a society which administers all dimensions of human existence. Inwardness and subjectivity may well become the inner and outer space for the subversion of experience, for the emergence of another universe.'[14]

Le Brocquy maintains that there is a deep connection between the aesthetic dimensions of *inwardness* and *otherness*. As he explained in an interview with Harriet Cooke: 'I often think of painting as being a kind of personal archaeology. I feel one is digging for things and suddenly something turns up which seems to be remarkable; something apparently *outside* oneself, which one has found in fact *inside* oneself.'[15] By means of palpable paint, le Brocquy is groping towards an impalpable interiority of meaning, what he calls 'the inner reality of the human presence beyond its merely external appearance'[16]. But when le Brocquy speaks thus of the primacy of subjective inwardness he is not for a moment advancing the romantic supremacy of the individual will or cogito (which typifies both Cartesian subjectivism and bourgeois individualism). Le Brocquy has repeatedly affirmed that his painting is not primarily self-expression, but the exploration of an interior dimension of otherness which explodes our assured personal identity and suspends our controlling will. (It is what Beckett, in his Proust essay, called the revelation of involuntary imagination). Le Brocquy defines subjectivity accordingly as 'an interior invisible world', an 'autonomous disseminated consciousness surpassing individual personality.'[17] He believes that the painter must await the emergence of the image without imposing his own voluntary projections: 'When painting I try not to impose myself. Discoveries are made – such as they are – while painting. The painting itself dictates and although the resultant image may seem rhetorical to some, it appears to me to be almost autonomous, having emerged under one's hands not because of them. . . . *Invention* for me is *discovery*.'[18] By embracing the polyvalent stream of inwardness, the artist strives to overcome his centralizing cogito in order to 'discover, uncover and reveal.'[19] Seamus Heaney, has written perceptively of this aspect of le Brocquy's archaeology of painting as an emergence of the *other* through the inner dissolution of the mastering *self*: 'Yet that hand does not seek to express its own personality. It is obedient rather than dominant, subdued into process as it awaits a discovery. What it comes up with will sometimes feel like something come upon, a recognition. Like a turfcutter's spade coming upon the body in the bog, the head of the Tollund Man, ghostly yet palpable, familiar and other, a historical creature grown ahistorical, an image that has seized hold of the eye and will not let it go.'[20]

IV

How, if at all, does le Brocquy relate to his own culture or to those other Irish authors and artists whose work we have been examining in the preceding chapters? True to the paradox of the artistic consciousness as a dialectic between sameness and otherness, le Brocquy maintains that, like Joyce before him, it was only after his departure from Ireland and subsequent encounter with 'foreign' cultures that he became deeply interested in his native culture.

'Although I was born in Dublin in the year of the Rebellion,' he writes, 'and brought up entirely in Ireland, I do not remember being conscious of being particularly Irish. . . . None seemed to me less mainfestly Irish than that small family whose name I bore. Then one day in my 21st year, I precipitously sailed from Dublin into a new life as a painter studying in the museums of London, Paris, Venice and Geneva. . . . Alone among the great artists of the past, in these strange related cities, I became vividly aware for the first time of my Irish identity to which I have remained attached all my life.'[21]. But le Brocquy strenuously resists the dangers of what he terms 'self-conscious nationalism'. He believes that art betrays itself as soon as it subscribes to cultural insularism. While admitting that the 'flowering of our imagination is nourished by roots hidden in our native soil', le Brocquy opposes the manipulative uses of a self-righteous national identity.

The art critic, Dorothy Walker maintains that le Brocquy's preoccupation with head images and cyclical structures is a distinct borrowing from the Celtic heritage[22]. This debt to Celtic visual motifs combines with le Brocquy's modernist commitment to innovative forms of representation which run counter to the Renaissance conventions of classical realism and centralized linear perspective. Le Brocquy himself has argued that we are currently witnessing a revolutionary transition from an essentially *perceptual* and outward-looking art to a new de-centralized art which rediscovers the source of meaning 'within the mind and within those *conceptual*, interiorised images of a world transformed.' While the perceptual era, devoted to exterior surface phenomena, held sway from the Renaissance up to the turn of this century, in recent decades 'the painter has been insistently aware of those renewed conceptual tendencies characteristic of painting in our time.'[23]. Le Brocquy suggests that it was Joyce's enthusiasm for this counter-Renaissance tendency that accounts for his profound interest in the Medieval and Celtic universes of nighttime consciousness (a suggestion confirmed by Arthur Power who was told by Joyce that 'the Renaissance and its return to classicism was a return to intellectual boyhood')[24]. We thus find le Brocquy surmising that the plural identity of his own images of Joyce 'may represent a more medieval or Celtic viewpoint, cyclic rather than linear, repetitive yet simultaneous and, above all, inconclusive.'[25]

In his fragmented and polymorphous images of Joyce, le Brocquy succeeds in evoking the fundamental ambivalences of time, space and emotion which so typify the world of *Ulysses* and *Finnegans Wake.* The pluralizing interiority of consciousness tends to produce, le Brocquy notes, 'an ambiguity involving a dislocation of our individual conception of time (within which coming and going, beginning and end, are normally regarded) and confronts this *normal* view with an alternative, contrary sense of simultaneity or timelessness, switching the linear conceptions of time to which we are accustomed to a circular concept returning upon itself, as in *Finnegans Wake*'. And le Brocquy adds his conviction that this alternative mode of vision can be reproduced in a certain paratemporal dimension of painting, a dimension which manifests itself in a double role 'involving a transmogrification of the paint itself into the image and vice versa.'[26] 'In my own small world of painting' he writes 'I myself have learned from the canvas that emergence and immergence – twin phenomena of time – are ambivalent: that one implies the other and that the state or matrix within which they co-exist apparently dissolves the normal sense of time, producing a characteristic *stillness*.'[27] This is certainly an accurate description of that enigmatic confluence of presencing and absencing which le Brocquy's studies of the head image embody. Indeed le Brocquy explicitly relates the visual paradoxes of his own paintings to the verbal paralogisms of Joyce's writing, simultaneously day-consciousness and night-consciousness, 'like Ulysses and Finnegan, or like a living human head, image of the whole in the part, the old synecdochism of the Celt'.[28]

Is this, le Brocquy asks finally, 'the underlying ambivalence which we in Ireland tend to stress . . . the indivisibility of birth and funeral, spanning the apparent chasm between past and present, between consciousness and fact?'[29] It may well be. But if it is, such a Celtic prototype offers le Brocquy and Joyce not the solidarity of some antiquarian repossession but the solitude of modern dispossession: less a Celtic Twilight than a Celtic darkness, an encounter with an inwardness that remains so irretrievably other that it abrogates any triumphalist tenure within a continuous tradition[30]. When Stephen Dedalus talked of forging the conscience of his race he significantly reminded us that it was still *uncreated*. Cultural identity, like national identity, is not something presupposed; it remains an open-ended task, an endless narrative to be reinterpreted by each artist in his own way. The time-space ambivalence of consciousness which manifests itself in le Brocquy's art is so different from our given modes of perception that it shatters rather than substantiates any centrist notion of identity. As another contemporary painter Patrick Collins remarked, one of the most consistent features of Irish art has been its propensity to erase any suspicion of a stable or unchanging tradition. In the best works of modern Irish art, Collins claims, the poet or painter brings himself 'to the point where he eliminates himself' and, by extension, the orthodox tradition from which he derives[31]. So that if the Irish hero Finn becomes Finn-again in Joyce's writings, or the Irish writer Joyce becomes Joyce again in le Brocquy's paintings, it is only in both cases by becoming radically *other*.

Le Brocquy's dual fidelity to the *otherness* of both ancient Celtic and modern experimental art suggests that his work may be appropriately located in the tension between the revivalist and modernist impulses of contemporary Irish culture.

Appendix: le Brocquy and Ballagh –
A Postmodern Dimension?

Le Brocquy's work may be usefully compared and contrasted with that of another contemporary Irish painter who seeks to negotiate a passage between tradition and modernity – Robert Ballagh.

Whereas le Brocquy's work seems to celebrate the otherness of art, Ballagh is more concerned to demystify it. He likes the idea of his art being *used*. Hence his decision to make stamps for the Irish postal system, posters for the trade unions, colour screens for the student cafeteria in University College Dublin and pop portraits for such patrons of the nation as Brendan Smith and Charlie Haughey. Ballagh is proud of the possibility that in years to come his stamps may be considered more important than his paintings. He refuses the view that socially useful or commissioned works are a betrayal of art. And he has little time for the view expressed by Clement Greenberg, the high priest of modernist abstraction, that painting has nothing to do with anything other than itself. Even those who defend the autonomy of art cannot escape, says Ballagh, the

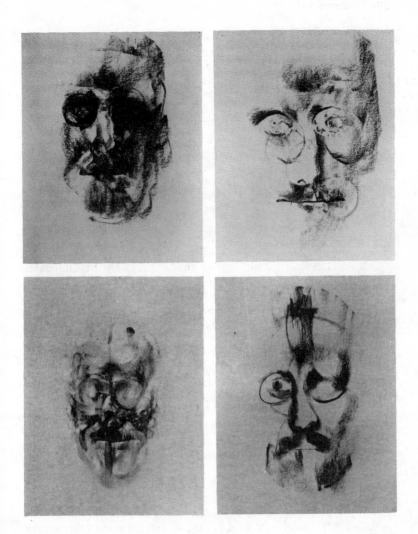

Studies towards an image of James Joyce. By kind permission of the artist, Louis Le Brocquy.

Above: No. 53, Winter in Ronda, (1979) and below, The Conversation (1977). By kind permission of the artist, Robert Ballagh.

investment speculations of the gallery-dealer system.

Art has always been linked to commercialism and developments in technology, Ballagh points out in reply to those who dispute his use of techniques drawn from popular culture and the mass media. There has, he insists, never been anything immaculate about the conception of art: 'Artists are fooling themselves and everyone else if they fuss about at the edge of society saying "I'm pure, I'm a virgin, I won't sully my hands." '(quoted in *Robert Ballagh*, by Ciaran Carty, *Magill*, Dublin, 1986). For Ballagh, the artist is just as conditioned by the society in which he/she lives as any other kind of worker; and painting, like every other mode of production, is the expression of a specific place and time in history. A child of the contemporary age of comic strips, movies and rock music, Ballagh approves of the collapse of the old dichotomy between High Art and popular culture. He sees his New Realist portraits as pop posters designed to speak to the many rather than the few – their purpose being communication rather than contemplation.

Ballagh considers this set of preferences as an option for the more populist impulse of postmodernism over the elitist formalism of modernism. In this respect, as in many others, he would appear to be radically different from le Brocquy. But the matter is not so simple. Le Brocquy and Ballagh have more in common than first meets the eye. Both would share the postmodern credo (announced by architect Philip Johnson) that 'you cannot *not* know history'. Both believe that the consciousness of the artist is deeply informed by a particular set of cultures and traditions. And both reject the modernist cult of the Briefly New – the illusion that every art movement must be a Giant Leap Forward for Mankind, a total break with everything which preceded it – preferring to 're-connect' (Ballagh's phrase) with the discarded traditions of Western art. Moreover, this postmodern desire to 're-connect' has for Ballagh, as for le Brocquy, nothing to do with a revivalist program of reactionary restoration. In contradistinction to the conservative habit of *imitation*, the postmodern tendency in Ballagh and le Brocquy functions according to the radical method of *quotation* –the belief that art opens onto the future by quoting its own past, rewriting and reinventing itself in a paradoxical and often even parodic fashion. Postmodernism sees history less as *continuity* than as *collage*. The modern aesthetic of inevitable novelty and progress is replaced by a postmodern mixing of multiple styles and images drawn from past and present.

Le Brocquy's head series might be described as postmodern in this sense. They represent a curious blending of the old and the new, the ancient and the modern. At one level, they depict the great minds of modern art – Yeats, Joyce, Beckett, Bacon, Lorca. Yet at another, they look back (as le Brocquy informs us) to the ancient sculpted heads of Celto-Ligurian Entremont and of Romanesque Clonfert.

The end of Western art is thus superimposed on its beginning. Linear chronology is deconstructed into an ambiguous co-existence of different time-frames. This double vision, this temporal ambivalence, is not something invented *ex nihilo* by le Brocquy. It is discovered within the very consciousness of those he portrays. In Beckett's work, for example, he discovers that 'going is confounded with coming, backwards with forwards'. And in Joyce he discovers the convergence of dayconsciousness and nightconsciousness, of the modern-day Finnegan and the mythological Fionn MacCumhaill – 'spanning the apparent chasm between past and present'.

Ballagh also espouses the postmodern view of art as a collage of quotations drawn from the diverse traditions of the past. 'Art cannot escape the past and the traditions that are ingrained in our consciousness,' observes Ballagh. 'We have to see where we come from. We have to recognize that we go further back than the modernist experience' (quoted in *Robert Ballagh, op. cit.*). But where le Brocquy used quotation as *paradox*, Ballagh uses it as *parody*. We could cite here, for example, his series of contemporary pastiches of classic masterpieces by Goya, Delacroix and David, or his mocking allusions to Velasquez and Vermeer in his own deconstructive self-portraits *Winter in Ronda* and *The Conversation*.

Another postmodern feature which le Brocquy and Ballagh share – despite the significant differences of their aesthetic practices – is a determination to dismantle the Renaissance and Romantic cult of the 'unique image'. This postmodern determination is exemplified in several contemporary works (e.g. the philosophies of Derrida and the deconstructionists, the writings of Calvino and Pynchon, the films of Lynch or the later Fellini, etc.), works which undermine their own status as original, isolated or finished objects. This is generally achieved by setting an open series of images into motion which expose their own lack of originality or uniqueness by perpetually alluding to other images or texts which have preceded them and preconditioned their meaning in some manner. Ballagh's parodies of the classical and Renaissance art-images and his use of pop poster reproduction techniques do this in an obvious way. But le Brocquy's work also testifies to a postmodern desire to debunk the fetish of the *unique image*. As we have noted, the multi-faceted character of his head images refuses the Renaissance cult of an original and centralizing image. The multiplication of the image into an indefinite series of traces without beginning or end is essentially counter-Renaissance for le Brocquy, allowing for a mode of vision that is recursive rather than unique, and inconclusive rather than fixed. But, by le Brocquy's own insistence, this counter-Renaissance tendency is not just a re-connection with pre-modern paradigms of Celtic and medieval art; it is also, and fundamentally, a reflection of the fact that we belong to a postmodern era of technical reproduction. 'Long conditioned by photography and the cinema,' le Brocquy affirms, 'we now perceive the human individual as faceted, kinetic.'

The works of le Brocquy and Ballagh compel us – in very different ways – to question the conventional rapport between images and their originals. By reproducing an almost endless series of reproducible images, they disinherit our received assumptions about representation. They undermine the modern cult of the authentic original and render the relationship between image and reality, copy and model, radically undecidable. In this postmodern gesture, le Brocquy and Ballagh find common ground.

Traditions & Myth ,a Introduction
Predict... to

    Militant Nationalist and

    Says that a Suffering Prison
mentality — inherit

relates modern Mythology (Catholic
Catholicism — with its promise
of ... absolution and resurrection
in the same mythical framework
the IRA and Sinn Fein exploited
to 'Transcend' the current political Extrem
with the Sacrifice Martyrdom as victory
idea

10
MYTH AND MARTYRDOM I:

SOME FOUNDATIONAL SYMBOLS IN IRISH REPUBLICANISM

In an essay entitled 'Universal Civilization and National Cultures', the French philosopher Paul Ricoeur suggests that nationalist movements are almost invariably motivated, at some deep and often preconceptual level, by a 'mythical-nucleus'. If one wishes to analyse this ideological deep-structure, Ricoeur argues, one has to cut through to that 'layer of images and symbols which make up the basic ideals of a nation or national group'[1]. Is such a 'mythical-nucleus' detectable in the extreme nationalist ideology of the Provisional I.R.A.? To what extent can this ideology be said to represent, however indirectly, the 'basic ideals of a national group'? And where are we to discover the mythical paradigms and symbols which might serve as guidelines for such an analysis? The following study is an attempt to provide a partial answer to these questions.

I: The Militant Nationalist Tradition

With the emergence of leaders like Gerry Adams and Danny Morrison in the late seventies and early eighties, the Provisional I.R.A. was said to have taken a turn to the left. This appeared to signify a movement beyond the 'traditional Republicanism' of Daithí Ó Conaill, Ruardhí Ó Brádaigh and Seamus Twomey toward a more 'radical Republicanism' which combined nationalism with revolutionary socialism. It could be argued that these two ideologies had always co-existed to some degree in the militant Republican tradition; but it was clearly the rhetoric of extreme political nationalism which dominated the Provisional movement when it first emerged in the late sixties.

In January, 1970, the Kevin St. headquarters of the Provisional I.R.A. issued a statement entitled *Where Sinn Féin Stands*. Here they outlined their aims, policies and major points of difference from other 'parliamentary' radical groups (in particular Official Sinn Féin and the Irish Communist Party). In this publication the Provisionals declared: 'Ours is a socialism based on *the native Irish tradition* of Comhar na gComharsan, which is founded on . . . our Irish and Christian values'. To this they added the all important qualification

– *'we take our inspiration and experience from the past'*. But what precisely do the Provisionals mean when they claim to take their inspiration from the 'past'? Although the Provisionals call themselves socialists, at their annual conference in Dublin, October 1971, they explicitly proscribed all 'members of the communist party *or any other radical group'*. They also took this opportunity to denounce the efforts of the left-wing Officials (later to become The Workers Party) to seek a parliamentary socialist solution to the northern problem by concentrating on i) the democratic election of a working-class party, and ii) the Two-Nations theory (i.e. the renunciation of the nationalist ideal of a United Ireland). The Provisionals' dissociation from the anti-nationalist Marxism of the Officials is unequivocal: 'We call on them to cease describing themselves as Sinn Féin. That honoured name has never belonged in Westminster, Stormont or Leinster House. Let them join with their new-found friends in their "Liberation Front" or whatever they wish to call it and leave the Republican Movement alone.'[2] A Commander in Chief of the Provisional I.R.A. in the seventies, Seamus Twomey, confirmed this preoccupation with traditional nationalist aims when he stated: 'At heart I am a socialist . . . but at the same time a right-winger . . . our prime and main objective is the unification of our country . . . and our definition of nationalism implies *the militant Republican tradition.'*[3]

What exactly is this native Republican 'tradition' which the Provisionals invoked to sanction their military campaign? What is this 'past' from which they claimed to 'take their experience and inspiration'? In short, where are we to seek out the ideological origins of the Provisionals' rhetoric, and by extension, action? The most obvious pointer would seem to lie in the very appellation of the movement itself – 'Provisional'. This title is borrowed from the 1916 Proclamation of the 'Provisional Government of the Irish Republic'. What is more, the most cursory perusal of any page of the Provisional I.R.A.'s publication *An Phoblacht* (itself derived from the titular address of the same 1916 Proclamation – 'Poblacht na hEireann') will confirm the Provisionals' deep identification with the heroes of Easter Week.

Taking this as a clue to the locus of the 'past' which the Provisionals invoke, let us try to decipher the *mythical-nucleus* latent in the symbols of the 1916 Proclamation itself. The opening phrases of this foundational document of traditional Irish nationalism are highly instructive: 'Irishmen and Irishwomen: In the name of God and of the dead generations from which she receives her old tradition of nationhood, Ireland, through us, summons her children to her flag and strikes for freedom.' The appeal to Irishmen and women is not made by the signatories themselves, but only *through* them by Ireland. Ireland is addressed here as a maternal and mythical personification of the Nation who addresses her children in the name of God and those *dead generations* who have sacrificed themselves for her nationhood.

It would seem, therefore, that just as the Provisionals conceive of themselves as the legatees of the 'past' generation of 1916 (a conception which most Irish nationalists would, of course, dispute), this generation in turn has acted on behalf of an even older heritage of 'dead generations'. This extended genealogical invocation would have linked the 1916 heroes not only with their founding Fenian forebears of the preceding century, but also with former Irish patriots such as O'Donnell and O'Neill, and ultimately with the legendary heroes of mythological Erin i.e. Oisín, Cúchulainn, Mannanán, Caitlín Ní Houlihán and most importantly Fionn MacCumhaill and his warrior band, the Fianna. It is essential to recall that it was from this mythological Fianna that the whole Fenian movement leading up to 1916 took its name and 'inspiration'. And as we shall shortly have occasion to remark, the *symbols* of the Rising stem largely from the Fenian revival of ancient mythological lore.

The suggestion here is that the *rationale* of the 1916 Republican movement – and by implication the Provisional Republican movement which lays claim to its heritage – may have as much to do with the mythic resuscitation of some sacred national 'tradition' as with revolutionary socialist scruples (although Connolly would seem to be an exception here). Is it possible that the guiding motivation of militant Republicanism was, and still is to some extent, less the appropriation of the socio-economic means of production, than an exigency of sacrifice to a mythological Ireland: an ancestral deity who would respond to the martyrdom of her sons by rising from her ancient slumber to avenge them? Is this possibility not strongly suggested by the fact that the operative terms of 1916 have always been 'sacrifice' and 'rising' – originally scheduled, let us not forget, for Easter Sunday! – rather than 'proletarian revolt' or 'class war'?[4] The concluding sentences of the Proclamation would seem to furnish additional evidence for such an hypothesis: 'In this supreme hour the Irish Nation must, by its valour and discipline and by the readiness of its children to sacrifice themselves for the common good prove itself worthy of the august destiny to which it is called.' On Easter Monday, 1916, amidst much confusion and alarm the General Post Office in Dublin was occupied by Pearse's troops and the Rising began.

But the ultimate triumph of the Rising was really secured when Pearse and his fellow signatories were executed by the British in Kilmainham Jail. The very rebels who had been spat upon by the Dublin people as they were led as prisoners from the General Post Office became national heroes, almost overnight, as soon as their lives had been sacrificed. As Bernard Shaw observed: 'those who were executed became ... martyrs whose blood was the seed of the Irish Free State.'

The mythological interpretation of militant republicanism is not entirely unprecedented. Augustine Martin in 'Reflections on the Poetry of 1916' and Ruth Dudley-Edwards in her biography of Pearse, have each alluded to the link between Irish nationalism and the mythic ideology of sacrificial blood-letting, martyrdom and the ancestor cult. And the seasoned Civil Rights campaigner, Eamon MacCann, writes as follows of the redemptorist martyr cult of Irish nationalism in his *War and An Irish Town*: 'One learned, quite literally at one's mother's knee, that Christ died for the human race, and Patrick Pearse for the Irish section of it. . . . Nationalist candidates were not selected, they were anointed. Religion and politics were bound up together, were regarded, indeed, as being in many ways the same thing.'[5] But while these and other commentators have succeeded in identifying this mythic dimension they have not proceeded to interrogate its origins or presuppositions *qua myth*. The analysis undertaken here attempts such an interrogation. By isolating the mythological essence of the foundational symbols of the 'militant republican tradition' we hope some light may be shed on the Provisionals' claim to take therefrom both their 'experience' and 'inspiration'.

II: The Myth of a Recurring Past

We have come to the holiest place in Ireland; holier to us even than the place where Patrick sleeps in Down. Patrick brought us life, but this man died for us . . .
(Patrick Pearse at the graveside of Wolfe Tone).

Our reading of the textual symbols of the Easter Proclamation identified the primary motif of sacrifice in the name of the deities and dead generations of the 'past'. This motif is fundamentally mythological as Mircea Eliade points out in his *Myths, Dreams and Mysteries:* 'Myth is thought to express the absolute truth because it narrates a *sacred history;* that is, a trans-human revelation which took place at the dawn of the Great Time, in the holy time of the beginning. . . . The myth becomes exemplary and consequently *repeatable*, and thus serves as a model and justification for all human actions. . . . By *imitating* the exemplary acts of mythic deities and heroes man detaches himself from profane time and magically re-enters the Great Time, the Sacred Time.'[6]

By means of a mythological repetition of the 'past', the nationalist leaders, it may be argued, sought to redeem Ireland. Incarcerated in a history of colonial oppression, the evangelists of the Provisional Republic appealed to a prehistorical mythic power whereby their present paralysis might be miraculously transcended. By *repeating* the names and deeds of the ancient heroes and martyrs of Erin they sought to revive her sacred destiny. The only way to redeem the nation seemed to be the negation of present history in favour of some Holy Beginning, some eternally recurring Past. And this recurrence of the primordial Spirit of Erin would be brought about, following the laws of myth, by blood-sacrifice. This is certainly the *mythos* to which Pearse subscribed when he claimed that 'bloodshed is a cleansing and a sanctifying thing'. In brief, sacrifice obeys the laws of myth not politics: it operates on the assumption that victory can only spring from defeat, and total rejuvenation of the community from the oblation of a chosen hero or heroic elite. But while myth seeks to transcend the logic of pragmatic political action, it can nonetheless influence the political consciousness of a people in a significant manner. In *States of Mind: A study of Anglo-Irish Conflict, 1780–1980*, Oliver McDonagh argues that the pervasive optimism of Ireland's political *myths* is the logical counterpart of the pessimism of its political *history*: ' . . . a past seen in terms of subjection and struggle, seen as a pageant or tournament of heroic defeat, is one of the roads towards fundamental distrust of or even disbelief in achievement . . . it is true that the characteristic Irish time-frame inclines Irishmen to a repetitive view of history and that such a view inclines them – perhaps in defensive wariness and from fear of failure – to prize the moral as against the actual, and the bearing of witness as against success.'[7]

The predominant symbols of the 1916 leader's own rhetoric would appear to corroborate this seemingly extravagant reading. Pearse was perhaps the most articulate spokesman of this mythic consciousness. In a farewell letter to his mother written from his cell in Kilmainham prison shortly before his execution, he bade her 'not to grieve for all this but to think of it as a sacrifice'. He included a poem entitled 'A Mother Speaks' in which he identifies himself with the sacrificed Christ 'who had gone forth to die for men' and compares his mother's faith in his powers of renewal with Mary's faith in the resurrection: 'Dear Mary, I have shared thy sorrow and soon shall share thy Joy'. This motif of blood sacrifice is even more explicitly evinced in the final lines of Pearse's play *The Singer* when the hero McDara exclaims: 'I will stand up before the Gaul as Christ hung naked before men on a tree.' But the *mythos* of sacrifice was not merely a private fantasy. In the months following the Rising numerous posters with the caption 'All is Changed' were to be seen in Dublin depicting the martyred Pearse in a *pieta* position supported by the mythic figure of Mother Erin (brandishing a tricolour)[8].

It was this same Pearse who had, just twelve months previously, reverently solicited the authority of the dead generations in his panegyric over O'Donovan Rossa's grave. In this address, steeped throughout in mythological idioms of seasonal and generational renewal by blood, Pearse claimed that the 'new generations' that had been 'rebaptized in the Fenian faith' would shortly come of age as a 'miraculous ripening seed.' He concluded with the now immortal lines: 'life springs from death and from the graves of patriot men and women spring living waters. . . . The fools, the fools, the fools, they have left us our Fenian dead and while Ireland holds these graves Ireland unfree shall never be at peace.' But Pearse's most un-equivocal rendering of the sacrifice myth is perhaps to be found in *The Coming Revolution* where he writes: 'we may make mistakes in the beginning and shoot the wrong people; but bloodshed is a cleansing and sanctifying thing, and the nation which regards it as the final horror has lost its manhood.'

Thomas MacDonagh was another of the signatories instrumental in the propagation of the myth of sacrificial renewal. In his *Literature in Ireland* he described the revival of the national spirit as the 'supreme song of victory on the dying lips of martyrs' and elsewhere declared his own death to be but a 'little phase of an Eternal Song'. The allusion here to Pearse's symbol of the 'singer' is not accidental. Both of these leaders were poets who conceived of the Rising in fundamentally mytho-poetic terms. Both envisaged their imminent martyrdom as a sort of leitmotif recapitulating the Eternal Song of sacrifice-and-rebirth which harmonized all those 'dead generations' of Irish heroes. While a purely political revolution could provide only a temporary – because 'temporal' – solution, a *mythic* Rising reaching back to the roots of the national spirit could ensure an 'eternal' victory. These leaders realized from the outset that their heroic stand would constitute no more than a *symbolic* Rising with little or no hope of practical political success. But their conviction seems to have been that by their temporal defeat an Eternal Nation might be induced to *recur* and reinstate itself. This attitude is epitomized by Pearse's surrender-statement that though the Irish had lost their victory in life 'they would win it in death.' It was on similar grounds that MacDonagh defended the proclamation at his trial: 'You think it a dead and buried letter, but it lives, it lives; from minds alight with Ireland's vivid intellect it sprang; in hearts aflame with Ireland's mighty love it was conceived. Such documents do not die.'

Mary Ryan, one of the last acquaintances to visit MacDonagh before his death, reported that his last words aside from prayers were 'God save Ireland'; and added, betraying a nuance she herself could scarcely have suspected: 'At four o'clock when the shooting was done a gentle rain began to fall – the tears of Dark Rosaleen.' Dark Rosaleen was, of course, one of the several mythic personi-fications of Ireland. She had been immortalized in a Thomas Mangan poem and had served as a common motif in the Fenian rhetoric of the preceding century. Indeed, the mythological symbol of the Red Rose – emblem of Ireland's eternally self-renewing Spirit – played a central role in both the Fenian and 1916 poetics. In the nineteenth century such poets as Mangan, Davis, Ferguson and De

Vere had richly exploited the sacrificial resonances of the Rose symbol (renewal through blood, dawn, spring, crucifixion.) in their evocation of a 'hidden' mythological Ireland[9]. The primary images of this mythologized Erin had, in turn, been handed down from the previous generations of Spalpín poets: Ó Rathaille, Ó Suilleabháin and Ó Longáin. These Gaelic bards had personified the sufferings of the native community in the form of visionary evocations (*aisling* or *spéir-bhruinneal*) of ancient Celtic heroes and deities. Thus, for example, MacDonagh's appeal to the 'passionate proud woes of Roisín Dubh' is an adaptation of Mangan's poem *Roisín Dubh*, which is itself a borrowing from the earlier Gaelic poetics of devotion to this mythic goddess. Similarly, Joseph Plunkett –another of the 1916 leaders – wrote a poem entitled *The Little Black Rose Shall be Red at Last* in which he rewords De Vere's lyric of the same title. Plunkett dedicates this poem to the mythic figure, Caitlín Ní hÚllacháin, and prays in the final lines that by sacrificing himself to inevitable 'doom', the 'dark rose shall redden into bloom.' The reference to 'doom' at this key point in the poem is significant for it confirms our suggestion that the *mythic* recourse to miraculous powers of transmutation is primarily motivated by the closing off of all normal channels for effecting political change *in* history. A certain *fatalism* is inherent in most invocations of the mythic past.

The translation at the turn of the century of the Celtic mythological sagas (the Táin, Ossian, Finn cycles etc.) by O'Grady and O'Shaughnessy was, no doubt, a further source of inspiration for the ancestral myths of 1916. These translations helped in particular to focus the minds of the Anglo-Irish members of the National Revival on the mythological heritage of what Daniel Corkery called the 'hidden Ireland of the Gaels' which had survived in the poetic symbols of the native Gaelic tradition. This Hidden Ireland was perhaps most powerfully represented by the eighteenth century Gaelic poetry of 'dispossession' known as *an duanaire*. In these poems the recognition of tragic failure and defeat in the political *present* was compensated for by the recollection of a mythic *past* (or the anticipation of a mythic *future*) where the fatalities of history could be redeemed. The Gaelic poets of *an duanaire* frequently invoked such ancestral myths in order to resuscitate the morale of a people bent low by famine, colonization and religious apartheid. As Corkery points out in his study of this period, the poetry was more racial and national than personal in character[10].

This subordination of individual utterance to the archetypes of national experience is typical of mythic forms of expression. In this spirit, Ó Rathaille described Ireland as 'some fair daughter of celestial powers' (*do geineadh ar gheineamhain/di-se an tír uachtaraigh*), and declares that he will suffer 'amid a ruffian hoarde' until the ancient heroes return from over the sea of death (*go bhfuillid na leoghain tar tuinn*). In another poem one finds an even more explicit appeal to the ancestral genealogy which unites the poet with his deceased forebears: 'Since the heroes of the Lame of Leni and of the Lee have been laid low/I will follow the beloved among/ heroes to the grave/those princes under whom were/my ancestors before the/death of Christ'. In the nineteenth century these same preoccupations with some Holy Time of the Great Beginning were evidenced in the Fenian poets. The following opening lines from Darcy Magee's poem *The Celts* are exemplary: 'Long, long ago, beyond the misty space/of twice a thousand years/in Erin old there dwelt a mighty race'.

Contemporary commentators of the 1916 Rising seemed to grasp the significant role of sacrifice more readily than the more empirically-minded critics of our own day. Chesterton immediately recognized this mythic dimension: 'Pearse and his colleagues died to be in the Greek and literal sense martyrs; they wished not so much to win as to witness. They thought that nothing but their own dead bodies could prove that Ireland was not dead.'[11] Indeed we need only recall the incredible transformation which their martyrdom effected to realise just how deeply-rooted in the Irish national psyche is this mythological cult of sacrifice. As Lennox Robinson remarked as early as 1918: 'Everything in Ireland has either taken place *before Easter Week* or *after Easter Week*. Right down to the heart of Irish nationality it cut, and the generations to come will continue to feel the piercing terror of the sword thrust.'[12] James Stephens also adverts to the sacrificial motif in his *Insurrection in Dublin* written several months after the Rising: 'The day before the rising was Easter Sunday and they were crying joyfully in the churches "Christ has Risen". On the following day they were saying in the streets "Ireland has risen". ' In a poem entitled *Spring 1916* Stephens elaborates on this theme, substituting the Celtic hero, Mannanan, for Christ.

> Be green upon their graves, O happy Spring . . .
> Now are we born again and now are we
> – Wintered so long beneath an icy hand –
> New-risen into life and liberty,
> Because the Spring is come into our land . . .
> Be with us Mannanan[12a]

III: Yeats and the Symbolism of Sacrifice

It is in Yeats's poetic testimony of the Irish nationalist uprising, however, that the whole *mythos* of sacrifice finds its most eloquent formulation. In his much quoted poem, *Easter 1916*, Yeats confesses astonishment at how such ordinary men as MacDonagh, Connolly and Pearse had been totally transformed by sacrifice –

'Now and in time to come/wherever green is worn/(they) are changed, changed utterly/A terrible beauty is born'.

Two themes of major importance emerge here. Firstly the theme – central to mythic logic – that 'beauty' is the offspring of 'terror'. In other words (though we are reading freely here between Yeats's lines) the terror inspired by the Easter Sacrifice served as some sort of magic passport ferrying the martyrs from their local time to a sacred time where they might secure the Beatific power of renewal. Yeats, of course, made no secret of his admiration for ancient mystery-rites and even fostered a project of establishing a mystical Celtic order of such practices in the Castle on the Rock at Lough Kay. His perpetual yearning for a Unity of Culture capable of trans-muting the Irish people into an 'enduring Nation' and his belief in the existence of a 'supernatural racial Memory' also testify to his mystic temperament. 'Was not a nation', Yeats ponders in *The Trembling of the Veil*, 'as distinguished from a crowd of chance comers, bound together by that Unity of Image which I sought in national literature!' And would not such a Unity of Culture and Image be impossible without some apocalyptic terror? Talking of the great cultural martyrs, who sought in the past to forge such a unity, he writes: 'We gaze at such men in awe, because we gaze not at a work of art but at the re-creation of the man through that art, the birth of a new species of man, and it may even seem that the hairs of our heads stand up, because that birth, that recreation, is from *terror*[13].' Yeats adds, appropriately, that 'these things are true also of nations', and 'though the gate-keepers who drive the nation to war or anarchy, that it may find its image, are different from those who drive individual men, . . . they work together'. It requires no great feat of imagination to identify these gate-keepers as those 'dead generations' invoked by the 1916 martyrs.

The second theme of key importance in Yeats's *Easter 1916* is the cultic immortalization of an act. The mediocre men who are so utter-ly changed by their 'terrible' deed are not only changed 'now' but also 'in times to come'. The significance of their deed is not buried with their bones but flows eternally from their graves and nourishes all those subsequent generations of martyrs who sacrifice them-selves for an 'enduring nation'. The 'terrible beauty' is not, strictly speaking, something 'born' but something perpetually 're-born' in periodic rites of terror. Yeats leaves us in no doubt as to his inten-ded meaning when, in another poem *Song*, he reminds us that 'Padraig Pearse had said/That in every generation/Must Ireland's blood be shed'. Only by means of such sacrificial commemoration can the Sacred Time of the nation return. 'When supernatural events begin,' writes Yeats, 'a man first doubts his own testimony, but when they repeat themselves again and again, he doubts all *human* testimony.'[14] To illustrate this point, Yeats cites the example of the ancient priests who received their supernatural power through repeated contemplation of the image of Apollo, and closer to home, the case of Gemma Galgaris who, in 1889, was said to have caused deep wounds to appear in her body by contemplating her crucifix. Similarly, by reiterating the sacrificial deeds of 'dead generations', the national martyr reactivates the primordial spirit of his sacred ancestors. This is what Yeats has in mind when he concludes his poem *The Statues* with the rhetorical question: 'When Pearse summoned Cuchulain to his side/What stalked through the Post Office?'[15]

In several other poems, Yeats develops the central Fenian symbol of Ireland as a Rose. Thus in the *Rose Upon the Rood of Time* he celebrates the mythic spirit of Erin as the mystical Rose of sacrifice and rebirth: 'I would . . . sing of old Erin of the ancient ways/Red rose, proud rose, sad rose of all my days.' And in *The Rose Tree*, Yeats features an imaginary dialogue where Pearse laments to Connolly that the Rose Tree of Ireland is withered. The latter replies that it needs to be watered if the 'green' is to re-emerge and the garden to blossom again. The last verse provides us with one of the most succinct expressions of the whole mythic cult of sacrifice:

> But where can we draw water
> Said Pearse to Connolly
> When all the walls are parched away?
> O plain as plain can be
> There's nothing but our own red blood
> Can make a right Rose Tree.

Another mythic symbol of nationalist sentiment which Yeats rehearsed and refined was that of *Cathleen Ní Houlihan*. In a note dated 1903 and addressed to Lady Gregory, Yeats describes this figure as 'Ireland herself . . . for whom so many songs had been sung and for whom so many had gone to their death'. His famous play, called after this mythological goddess, was set during the 1798 rebellion and enacts the myth of Erin being revived by the blood of her heroes. Cathleen summons Michael Darcy, a young peasant about to be married, to revolt, counselling blood-sacrifice as the only means to redeem the nation. In return for such sacrifice, she promises that the heroes 'shall be remembered for ever'. The play aroused deep reverberations in the Irish nationalist consciousness when it first appeared in 1902. Stephen Gwynn declared that the effect was such 'that I went home asking myself if such plays should be produced unless one was prepared for people to go out and to shoot and be shot'. P.S. Hegarty, a Republican rebel, referred to it as a 'sort of sacrament'; and Constance Markievicz hailed it from her execution cell in 1916 as a 'gospel'. What is more, Pearse himself enthusiastically acclaimed the play; and Plunkett was inspired to dedicate his nationalist poem, *The Little Black Rose*, to this same Celtic goddess. Yeats was by no means unmindful of this extensive influence and asked himself remorsefully, in later years, whether his play in fact 'sent out/Certain men the English shot?'[16]

*   *   *

But it is perhaps in Sean O'Faoláin's autobiography *Vive Moi* that we find the most lucid acknowledgement of the mythico-cultic preoccupations – sacrificial and ancestral – that enlivened the Republican ideology. O'Faoláin himself had fought in the Irish Republican Army before becoming a writer and reveals here an intimate understanding of the mythic spirit which informed the whole nationalist movement: 'And so blinded and dazzled as we were by our Icons, caught in the labyrinth of our dearest symbols – our Ancient Past, our Broken Chains, our Seven Centuries of Slavery, the Silenced Harp, the Glorious Dead, the tears of Dark Rosaleen, the Miseries of the Poor Old Woman, the Sunburst of Freedom that we had almost always believed would end our night and solve all our problems with the descent of a heavenly human order which we would immediately recognize as the reality of our never articulated dream. . . . I had nothing to guide me but those flickering lights before the golden Icons of the past . . . the simplest pieties of Old Ireland.' Thus exposing the underlying *mythos* of the post-1916 Republican movement, O'Faoláin goes on to explain the split of the Irregular I.R.A. from the Regular I.R.A. (i.e. Free State Army) in 1922 in terms of a profound conviction that they alone – the Irregulars – 'represented the Symbolical Living Republic first declared during the 1916 Rebellion and set up as a *de jure* . . . underground government during the troubles.'[17]

This statement of O'Faoláin's demonstrates that the mythic pietism of the 1916 Rising continued as a motivating ideology in the subsequent Republican struggle against the British (War of Independence) and Free State government (Civil War). It is not difficult to trace the line of continuity from this 'old' Republicanism to the 'new' Republicanism of the Provisional I.R.A. The Provisionals' present campaign may be said to constitute, to some extent at least, a repetition of Pearse's attempt to 'rebaptize' the nation in the 'Fenian Faith'. Now, as before with Pearse, and before him again with the Fenian fathers and their ancestors, it is a baptism by blood. In this mythological perspective there seems but a thin dividing line between Pearse's statement that bloodshed is a sanctifying thing and Seamus Twomey's suggestion in his *Crane Bag* interview, that a lasting peace in Ulster can only come from the terror of apocalyptic violence: 'From all wars peace has sprung. Peace has never been built out of anything else but violence.'[18]

The point here, however, is not that the old I.R.A. would acknowledge a link between their faith in a Symbolical Underground Republic and the faith of the Provisionals in an identical ideal. (Indeed, it is almost certain that most of them would not.) The point is that the Provisionals *do* insist on such a link – the all-important difference being, of course, that they believe this Symbolical Living Republic to be *still* 'underground'. This faith constitutes the

Provisionals' loyalty to a 'native tradition of Irish Christian values' in opposition to the established Republic of the twenty-six counties. It is moreover to this former Symbolical Republic – with its *mythos* of renewal through sacrifice – that the Provisionals refer when they speak of 'taking their inspiration and experience from the past'.

IV: On the Sacrifice Myth

The sacrifice myth which animated the 1916 ideology sprang as much from the pagan *mythos* of seasonal rejuvenation and blood-letting rites as from the Christian message of salvation. This is an essential point ignored by many critics who explain the 1916 ideology of sacrifice in terms of a standard Christian devotionalism, thereby disregarding the fundamentally *mythological* nature of this ideology. As several contemporary theologians, among them Bultmann and Moltmann, have claimed, the common interpretation of Christ as a propitiatory sacrifice in which man could subsequently share by means of ritual repetition, arises from the superimposition of a pagan *mythos* of cult-sacrifice (based largely on Hellenic mystery rites) onto the original biblical and *anti-cultic* understanding of Christ as Messiah. Whereas the Gospels saw Christ's death and resurrection in the eschatological light of a future Second Coming, the derived Hellenized notion conceived the Christian event in terms of a mythological remembrance of a past cosmic sacrifice along the model of the mystery-cults of Attis, Osiris and Dionysius. The basic conviction of these pagan mystery-cults was that by ritually rehearsing the violent sacrifice of the cult-hero or *Kyrios*, one could likewise participate in his renewal. As Jürgen Moltmann observes in *The Theology of Hope*:

'The influence of cultic piety shows itself not only as a formal event in the self-presentation of Christianity on Hellenistic soil, but quite certainly extends also to the understanding of the event of Christ. The Christ event is here understood as an epiphany of the eternal (past) in the form of a dying and rising Kyrios of the *cultus*. . . . Initiation into the death and resurrection of Christ then means that the goal of redemption is already determined for in this baptism eternity is sacramentally present . . . the cross becomes a timeless sacrament of martyrdom which perfects the martyr and unites him with the heavenly Christ'[19].

Whether one accepts that the mythic strain in Christianity stems from a derivative Hellenic (rather than original Hebraic) influence, the fact remains that the *sacrificial* component of much traditional Christianity *is* mythic and must be recognized as such. We are thus reminded that the basic religious notions of martyrdom, apocalypse and ritualistic commemoration, which exerted such a profound influence on Pearse and his colleagues, stand – at least in part – in the lineage of sacrificial cultism which dates back to the ancient mythological cycles of renewal and rebirth.

But what are the philosophical and anthropological explanations for the extraordinary perdurance of sacrificial myths? Myth has frequently been used to translate the impotence of man's historical existence into the omnipotence of a prehistory. As Eliade has shown in his analysis of the structures of primitive myth, the power *(Mana)* of ancestral deities was considered capable of magically intervening in this world to vanquish an oppressive enemy, produce a double-harvest or overcome pestilence. When all the practical possibilities of dealing with suffering seemed exhausted, this Sacred Power of the Beginning could be prevailed upon. But in order to reactivate this primordial power man first had to sacrifice himself to the mythological deities and heroes of the tribe[20].

From its origins, myth frequently assumed the form of a *cult* based on the violent practices of mutilation and blood-letting (as its Latin etymology indicates – *cultivare*: to cut, till or worship by cutting). In many instances, blood was an indispensable ingredient, the coveted ambrosia of the gods. Eugen Fink, the German philosopher, has defined the mythic cult accordingly: 'The cult is integrally related to the consecration of a victim or scapegoat; it is a great ritual gesture which reaches out towards a Totum or Whole. The cult participant allows himself to be magically "possessed" by this power which the cult symbolizes. . . . The Totum thus reinvests one of its parts (the sacrificial victim) and transports this wordly fragment beyond this world absorbing it back into its Total Self. . . . The cult may therefore be defined as that point of confluence between the human and the divine run through with terror.'[21]

This identification of myth as the nexus of exchange between supernatural power and sacrificial terror is all important. Blood sacrifice is the ransom exacted by the mythic deities in return for the privilege of miraculous intervention. But the cult sacrifice never constitutes more than a *provisional* purchase of power. Man never succeeds in securing this power once and for all; for he is, at all times, a creature bound to historical time. He must return, therefore, to the sacrificial cult at certain regular intervals. He must periodically open his (and his community's) veins to the flow of divine power in order to renew himself and his community. By means of such periodic blood-letting, the cult enables man to pre-empt history. It empowers him to give the lie to the intractable world of fact, sanctioning his accession to another world of consciousness where different laws apply and where he may be relieved of all the onerous inconveniences which bear him down. If only man is prepared to submit his world to the terror of a purging apocalypse, the mythological deities will permit him to feel free, unfettered and divine – that is, of course, *for a time*. One of the main purposes of initiatory and sacrificial rites, is to bring historical time to a standstill and revivify those mythic paradigms which have survived as the *depositum* of ancestral experience. To re-enact these paradigms is to participate once again in the Golden Age of the ancestral *Majores*. In other words, by participating in an original sacred time that represents all times, men cease to be men and become *Man*. Under the penumbra of myth, experience escapes its contingent singularity and is transformed into a recurring Archetype. Through cultic identification with the archetypal figure of the hero, the individual seeks to recapitulate the Archetype in his own self and to subsume this self into the Archetype.[22]

The sacrificial cult thus promises to grant the community a victory over history by permitting it to return to its prehistoric origin, where it might be contemporaneous with its heroic founders. We may say then that myth is fundamentally 'ecstatic' in so far as it endorses man's magical participation in the immemorial past. That is to say, through myth man stands outside *(ex-stasis)* the futile flow of profane history which no longer seems to offer any prospect of rational reform or progress. He has recourse to the mythic law of the 'eternal recurrence of the same' (i.e. the recurrence of the same ancestral heroes, of the same paradigms of destruction and renewal, of the same time of the Holy Beginning). Since no solution to his alienation is to be found in the present, man submits himself to a transforming myth, thereby reactivating the original sacred power which exists before and beyond history.

The experience of renewal through bloodshed central to sacrificial myths, is perhaps most plausibly explained in terms of a community's experience of despair before a cruel history. This experience gives rise to feelings of revenge and resentment which ultimately express themselves in acts of violence. Just as this 'cruel history' was the cosmic evil of famine and disease for primitive man, and the political evil of the Roman Empire for the early Christians, it was and is British Rule for many Irish Republicans. Max Scheler's analysis of the violence arising from such an experience of impotence is most suggestive: 'Revenge tends to be transformed into resentment the more it is directed against lasting situations which are felt to be injurious but beyond one's "control" – in other words, the more the injury is experienced as a destiny. This will be most pronounced when a person or group feels that the very fact and quality of its existence is a matter which calls for revenge. . . . When the repression is complete, the result is a general negativism – a sudden, violent, seemingly indiscriminate and unfounded reprisal on things, situations or persons whose loose connections with the original cause of the hatred can only be discovered by a complicated analysis.'[23]

Jean-Paul Sartre offers another interesting perspective on the human recourse to mythic modes of behaviour in his *Sketch for a Theory of the Emotions*[24]. The mythical consciousness, Sartre argues, is not some lawless disorder but 'an ordered pattern of means directed towards an end'. Myth, in other words, is a strategic mode of consciousness whereby we seek to negate a real world that has grown intolerable in order to transform it into an imaginary world which we can tolerate. This may occur whenever our normal avenues of behaviour – what Sartre calls our 'hodological maps' (Greek, *hodos*, path or way) – no longer seem functional or simply prove too difficult to pursue in a conventional manner. Thus confronted with what appear to be 'impossible situations', we depart from the pragmatic patterns of so-called *rational* behaviour and have recourse instead to *magical* behaviour. But this magical behaviour is just as intentionally structured as the rational behaviour it replaces. Put in another way, once the real world proves 'non-utilisable' or 'unmanageable', we deploy emotion to transpose this world into an unreal one where the normal laws of experience no longer operate. In short, we negate the world in order to better cope with what appears to be an intractable problem. Far from being a 'passing disorder of the organism', therefore, myth is revealed as a highly ordered strategy which 'transforms the determinist world in which we live into a magical world'. Of course, strictly speaking, what myth transforms is not the world itself – which remains as unmanageable as before – but the *manner in which we intend the world*. By altering our *attitude* to the world, myth provides imaginary solutions to real conflicts. Hence the enormous appeal of mythological paradigms of belief for the consciousness of an oppressed or colonized people.

All of these philosophical commentators of mythic consciousness agree that myth is not some innocuous museum piece of the antique past. Because the very structure of myth lays claim to a certain timeless and repeatable experience which promises to redeem human history, it can be said to have as much stake in the present as in the past. In this sense, myth is not without relevance to the ideologies and actions of contemporary man. 'While myth relates to events that happened at the beginning of time,' as Paul Ricoeur remarks, 'it also has the purpose of providing grounds for the ritual actions of men today.'[25] It is our conviction that it was with just such a purpose in mind that Provisional Sinn Féin claimed in their 1970 manifesto to take their 'inspiration' from the tradition of the 'past'.

This is not, of course, to deny that other factors of a more pragmatic social, economic and military nature have fundamentally motivated the actions and strategies of extreme Republicanism. Indeed, these factors constitute the official rhetoric of the movement. Our analysis of some of the foundational symbols of Irish Republicanism simply intends to recall that there also exists a hidden *mythic* dimension, ignored by most contemporary commentators, which has played a formative role in what might be described as the 'ideological unconscious' of the militant nationalist tradition in Ireland.

11

MYTH AND MARTYRDOM II: LONG KESH
AND THE PRISON TRADITION

On the 9th of April 1981, Bobby Sands, a Republican hunger-striker in the H-Block of Long Kesh prison in Belfast, was elected with a massive 30,000 vote to the Westminster Parliament. On the 5th of May, Sands died and was buried with full military regalia in Milltown Cemetery in Belfast. He had become a national martyr.

In the months that followed, nine other Republican hunger-strikers in Long Kesh followed Sands to the grave in pursuit of a 'political status' which the British Government refused to grant. The death of Sands and his fellow hungerstrikers bore the unmistakable stamp of sacrificial martyrdom and captured the sympathy not only of a vast number of Irish nationalists but also of a considerable body of international opinion. During his fast, Sands wrote a diary in his cell using biro refills and sheets of toilet paper. His final entry testifies to the sacrificial character of his 'endurance campaign' – his firm belief that victory could only be attained through death:

> 'It had been a hard day but wasn't every day the same and God only knew what tomorrow would bring. Who would be the unlucky unfortunates tomorrow, supplying the battered bloody bodies for the punishment block? Who would be hosed down, beaten up or torn apart during a wing shift? Tomorrow would only bring more pain and torture and suffering, boredom and fear and God knows how many humiliations, inhumanities and horrors. Darkness and intense cold, an empty stomach and the four screaming walls of a filthy nightmare-filled tomb to remind me of my plight, that's what lay ahead tomorrow for hundreds of naked Republican Political Prisoners-of-War, but just as the morrow would be filled with torture so would we carry on and remain unbroken. It was hard, it was very, very hard, I thought, lying down upon my damp mattress and pulling the blankets around me. But some day victory would be ours and never again would another Irish man or woman rot in an English hell-hole. . . . That's another day nearer to victory, I thought, feeling very hungry. I was a skeleton compared to what I used to be but it didn't matter. . . . They have nothing in their entire imperial arsenal to break the spirit of one single Republican Political Prisoner-of-War who refuses to be broken, I thought, and that was very true. They can not or never will break our spirit. *"Tiocfaidh ár lá,"* I said to myself.

"*Tiocfaidh ár lá*" (our day will come).'[1]

The election of Bobby Sands as a Westminster MP marked a watershed in the Republican movement in the North. On the 20th of August, 1981, several months after Sand's death, Owen Carron, his election agent, won the vacated seat as *Provisional Sinn Féin* candidate for Fermanagh-South Tyrone. And on the 9th of June, 1983, Gerry Adams, the leader of *Provisional Sinn Féin*, was elected as Westminster MP for West Belfast, thereby confirming the significant rise of electoral support for non-constitutional nationalism in Northern Ireland in the wake of the H-Block campaign.

In this study I want to examine the 'sacrificial' dimension of this campaign in the light of the Republican prison tradition and its relation to the nationalist ideology of martyrdom analysed in the preceding study.

I

Sean MacBride, a leading Dublin jurist, recipient of the Nobel Peace Prize and a founder member of Amnesty International, wrote a lengthy introduction to Bobby Sand's prison diary when it was published after his death[2]. MacBride begins with a quotation from a poem by the 1916 martyr, Padraig Pearse, evoking the sacrificial status of the hungerstrike campaign:

What if the dream come true?
And if the millions unborn shall dwell
In the house that I shaped in my heart,
The noble house of my thought?. . .
Was it folly or grace?
No man shall judge me but God.

The implication here is that Bobby Sands and his fellow hunger-strikers have, through their sacrifice, earned a sacred place in the 'noble house' of Pearse's nationalist dream, defying the official laws of human judgment (which dismisses their death as 'folly') in an appeal to a Divine judgment (which bestows upon them the 'grace' of martyrdom). Pearse, as we noted in the previous study, conceived of his own death as a sacrifice for the motherland, explicitly identifying with the crucified Christ 'who had gone forth to die for men' in his eve-of-execution poem, 'A Mother Speaks'. The Catholic concept of the Mass as a 'real sacrifice' has been a central symbol for the Republican tradition of martyrdom; and the H-Block hungerstrikers, going to their death over sixty years after Pearse, acknowledged that daily Mass in the prison was one of the main sources of their strength[3]. Nor was this sacrificial identification with Christ lost on the H-Block sympathizers. Many of the placards carried in the hungerstrike support marches portrayed Sands and his colleagues in crucified postures (recalling the 1916 posters of the pietà-like Pearse), the barbed wire of Long Kesh transformed into a crown of thorns, the H-Block blanket into a burial shroud. Indeed, during several such marches, the prisoners' families themselves wore blankets and wire crowns to symbolically express their conviction that the hungerstrikers who were sharing in Christ's martyrdom would one day rise up victorious from their ashes. One H-Block document even showed a drawing of the Pope blessing the kneeling prisoners under the title, *Pope John Paul II and Human Rights*, and quoted the Pope's pointed statement during his Drogheda address in September, 1979, that 'the Law of God stands in judgment over all reasons of state.'[4] (This same document associates the prisoners fasting protest with the historic suffering of the Irish Catholic people during the terrible famine of the nineteenth century.)

It was Pearse's dream above all that informed the traditional ideals of Gaelic Catholic nationalism. And while it is probably true that Sands and his fellow inmates would have given only passing allegiance to these ideals before their imprisonment, once confined to Long Kesh, deprived of 'political status' and subjected to degrading treatment, the Catholic religion and the Gaelic language became (as Sands' diary testifies) symbols of primary significance. In prison, to be Gaelic and Catholic was almost synonymous with being nationalist; for all three categories of identification served to remind the Republican inmates of their forefathers' long history of persecution. The Pearsean dream, in short, was more relevant to the *sacrificial* ideology of the Republicans' prison campaign than to the *revolutionary* ideology of their military campaign.

MacBride describes Sands' prison testimony as a 'tale of faith' and 'triumph of endurance' which became a 'morale booster' for a cause that depended 'more on integrity and courage than on what politicians and lawyers term reason and common sense'. He goes on to observe that the death of Sands and his fellow hungerstrikers was 'to the bulk of the Irish people a tragedy that tore asunder the strings of their hearts and their consciences'. Only a small minority of the nation still suffering from a 'slave mentality' which hankers after the 'trappings of British influence in Ireland' were, he argues, hostile to the hungerstrikers' aim of a United Ireland (however much they might, like MacBride himself, abhor the IRA's use of violence). MacBride is probably representative of majority nationalist opinion when he claims that the hungerstrike phenomenon must be understood in terms of the Irish people's *historical memory* of British colonial misrule. In reply to those, particularly in Britain, who complain that 'our memories are too long and that we should forget the past', MacBride declares that it is only by *remembering* the colonial heritage of partition, imprisonment and 'every conceivable form of coercive and repressive legislation', that we may begin to comprehend the real implications of the H-Block campaign. The hungerstrike, MacBride concludes, is not some isolated political happening of our time but a deep symptom of a historically recurring persecution: 'a fall-out resulting from the cruel interference by Britain in the affairs of the Irish nation.' MacBride's *Introduction* to the Bobby Sand's Diary thus identifies the basic *rationale* of the Republican prison campaign in terms of the memory of the nationalist people's historical suffering, a memory of heroic martyrdom invoked not only in MacBride's opening quotation from Pearse but also in his final quotation from W.B. Yeats:

> Some had no thought of victory
> But had gone out to die
> That Ireland's mind be greater
> Her Heart mount up on high;
> And yet who knows what's yet to come? . . .

MacBride's quotation does not include the remaining lines of Yeats' stanza, but the sentiment is already clear, and the reader can supply it for himself –

> . . . For Padraig Pearse has said
> That in every generation
> Must Irish blood be shed.

II

It might be useful at this point to examine in more detail the Republican prison tradition which so powerfully informed the response of the nationalist population to the H-Block hungerstrike. This tradition corresponds to what Tim Pat Coogan, editor of *The Irish Press* and author of a best-selling book on the H-Block campaign, called the 'endurance' strategy of the Republican Movement[5]. The national heroes of this endurance tradition are legion, but it was perhaps Terence McSwiney, the Sinn Féin Lord Mayor of Cork who died on hungerstrike in an English prison in 1920, who most concisely articulated this ideology of suffering. In his inaugural speech as Lord Mayor he stated: 'The contest on our side is not one of rivalry or vengeance but of endurance. It is not those who can inflict the most but those who can suffer the most who will conquer. . . . It is conceivable that the army of occupation could stop us functioning for a time. Then it becomes simply a question of endurance. Those whose faith is strong will endure to the end in triumph.'[6] Coogan has argued that McSwiney's was a 'particularly Irish form of self-sacrifice' which caught 'the imagination of the world at the time, and of the IRA ever since'[7]. He also makes the interesting observation that during the time of the native Brehon laws which governed Ireland prior to the Anglo-Norman invasion, one of the most effective ways of retaliating against a wrongdoer was for the offended party to starve himself outside the guilty person's house!

The Republican tradition of prison endurance is certainly long-standing. It has found many adherents throughout this century. Tom Clarke's prison experience earned him the honour of heading the 1916 Proclamation of the Irish Republic. Joseph McGuinness, while still in Lewes Jail, won the first seat for Sinn Féin, largely due to his popular appeal as an 'endurance' candidate. Other instructive examples include the release of IRA leader Patrick McGrath from prison in 1939 as a result of the massive public outcry caused by his 43-day hunger strike, and the similar release of another Republican hunger striker, Davy Fleming, from an Ulster prison in 1946. Furthermore, the significant lobbying power of Sean McBride's *Clann na Poblachta* party in 1948 was no doubt in large part due to its spectacular 'release the prisoners' campaign. And the popular prestige of such provisional leaders as Daithí Ó Conaill, Ruardhí Ó Brádaigh and Gerry Adams, would appear to be related to the fact that each served his time as a prison 'martyr'. (Indeed, the relegation of a leader such as MacStiofáin was surely not unrelated to his last minute decision to call off his much publicised hunger strike in Portlaoise prison). It is, moreover, a fact that most democratically elected political leaders in the Republic also owe part of their status in the community to the fact that they themselves, or their fathers before them, suffered imprisonment or death at the hands of the colonial oppressor. Obvious names here would include De Valera, MacBride, Fitzgerald, Cosgrave, Boland, etc. (And it is arguable, ironically, that the humiliating public trial of Charles Haughey, on charges of gun-running while a government minister in 1970 did more, in retrospect, to help than to hinder his popular standing in the South, and even his eventual election as Taoiseach of the Irish Republic)[8].

It is against the background of this long Republican tradition of prison endurance that we may best understand the extraordinary impact of the H-Block campaign. This campaign began as far back as 1976 when the British government removed the 'special category' status for political prisoners in Long Kesh. Ciaran Nugent was the first to go 'on the blanket' on the 15th of September of that year and was soon followed by some 370 Long Kesh internees who immediately grasped the national and international impact of his protest. By declining to grant the prisoners' demands the British hastened the deterioration of events. The Republican prisoners reacted by disobeying prison regulations and were soon living in excrement-covered cells which Cardinal Ó Fiaich, Primate of the Irish Catholic church, described as 'unfit for animals'. After his visit to Long Kesh on 19 July 1978, the Cardinal issued this controversial statement:

> In the circumstances I was surprised that the morale of the prisoners was high. From talking to them it is evident that they intend to continue their protest indefinitely and it seems they prefer to face death rather than submit to being classed as criminals. Anyone with the least knowledge of Irish history knows how deeply rooted this attitude is in our country's past. In isolation and perpetual boredom they maintain their sanity by studying Irish. It was an indication of the triumph of the human spirit over adverse material surroundings to notice Irish words, phrases and songs being shouted from cell to cell and then written on each cell wall with the remnants of toothpaste tubes[9].

The Cardinal went even further to explicitly defend the prisoners' demand to be recognized as special prisoners, pointing out that the rapid jump in the prison population of Ulster from 500 to 3,000 was inexplicable unless a new type of political prisoner had emerged[10].

Other prominent Catholic churchmen expressed similar sympathy with the prisoners' plight, thereby considerably increasing public awareness of the situation. Bishop Cahal B. Daly of Ardagh and Clonmacnoise was quick to take up the cause while adverting to the implications of IRA propaganda in this regard. In his address for the World Peace Day on 1 January 1979, Bishop Daly was the first to acknowledge that the IRA 'are exploiting the H-Block situation with disquieting success'; to such an extent indeed that in the United States where the funds campaign had been virtually neutralized there had been 'a new upsurge of financial support on behalf of this organisation.' But while denouncing the IRA's 'unscrupulous manipulation of the Human Rights aspect' of H-Block, Bishop Daly felt obliged to point out the British government's share in the blame:

> These conditions are objectively in conflict with all recognized codes governing the environment in which prisoners are allowed to live. The Provisional IRA have, however, by a strange paradox, received great help from an unexpected source – the mistakes of the British administration and security chiefs, mistakes in which they have persisted with remarkable obstinacy in the face of the lesson of all Anglo-Irish history and all experience. The IRA was practically a spent and discredited force until they were handed the H-Block situation as a propaganda gift. This, and the unnecessary army harassment of innocent people, especially young people, among the 'men of no property', are now virtually the only source of vestigial sympathy or of recruitment for the IRA.[11]

While the sacrificial propaganda of the H-Block campaign was most immediately recognized by the alarmed leaders of the Catholic community in the North, they were not the only ones to raise a voice of warning. Several Protestant churchmen – most notably

Dr. Coggan, the Archbishop of Canterbury and Dr. John Austin Baker, chaplain to the speaker of the House of Commons – clearly acknowledged the historical connotations of the H-Block campaign and appealed (in vain) to the British government for concessions.[12] Many constitutional nationalist leaders, both north and south, together with prominant Irish-American senators in Washington (like Kennedy, Cary, Moynihan and O'Neill) also made repeated efforts to convince Mrs. Thatcher to compromise on the issue. The Irish media were highly conscious of the explosive nature of the H-Block protest, with an *Irish Press* editorial describing it as a 'major obstacle along the road to eventual peace'[13] and a distinguished columnist in *The Cork Examiner* speaking indignantly of the British governments' 'Nazi-like behaviour in Long Kesh.'[14]

Witnessing the massive impact which their campaign was having on public opinion at home and abroad, the Long Kesh inmates must have surely been tempted to believe that William McKee, a former IRA leader in Belfast, was right when he claimed that 'this war will be won in the prisons'. Standing in their 'filthy cold tombs', their blankets cloaked about them as they chanted Gaelic phrases and prayers from cell to cell, like some chorus in an ancient tragedy, the H-Block prisoners must have seen themselves – at moments at least – as sacrificial victims of a fallen and divided nation which could only be redeemed by their deaths, rising up miraculously from their excrement and ashes. The prisoners' ultimate decision to perish of hunger was, no doubt, for them and for many of their sympathizers, the final seal on the coffin of martyrdom.

III

Whereas the constitutional politicians object that violence can only beget violence, the IRA reply that theirs is a violence to end all violence. This latter attitude to violence is sacrificial in that it sees suffering and bloodshed as prerequisite to the ultimate attainment of justice, freedom and peace[15]. But the violence of the IRA is also sacrificial, as we have seen, to the extent that it is as much a violence suffered as a violence inflicted. From the point of view of the age-old nationalist tradition of martyrdom, violence 'endured' has often proved to be the most effective way to gain widespread community support. The Republican militants in Ulster today continue to invoke the authority of the executed founders of the Republic. In 1978 a spokesman for Provisional Sinn Féin proudly stated that the 'IRA is not ten years old but over sixty years old'[16]; and for many Republicans the frequent invocation of the 1916 and Fenian martyrs at IRA funeral orations or in the daily columns of the Provisionals' newspaper, *An Phoblacht*, invests their campaign of 'resistance and suffering' with the sanctity of an ancestral rite. The following extract from the popular Republican Ballad *Who is Ireland's Enemy*, provides a typical example of the traditional ideology of sacrifice which conceives the history of Fenian martyrdom as a 'sacred debt' which remains to be paid in the present:

Who shattered many a Fenian mind in dungeons o'er the foam
And broke the loyal Fenian hearts that pined for them at home.
Who shot down Clark and Connolly and Pearse at dawn of day,
And Plunkett and McDermott and all who died as they . . .
Who robbed us of McSwiney brave, who murdered Mellows too,
Sent Barry to a felon's grave and slaughtered Cathal Brugha?
'Twas England robbed our Motherland,
'Twas England laid her low,
Rise up, oh dead of Ireland, and rouse our living men,
The chance has come to us at last to win our own again . . .
And in your name, oh holy dead,
Our Sacred Debt to pay.

The sacrificial victim must undergo his passion and demise before arising to liberate his community from its historical bondage. By commemorating the sufferings of their Fenian forebears, the IRA seem to be operating on the conviction that they can fulfil the redemptive promise of their martyrdom[17].

That the military odds are stacked high against an IRA military victory is indubitable. By the early eighties they counted no more than two hundred active members against 20,000 British troops, 7,000 armed police and twice that number of Loyalist paramilitaries, not to mention the Irish army and police force south of the border. But for the IRA, strength is not in numbers. The power they wield in the Republican community, both north and south of the border, springs largely from their outnumbered status. It is only when they step back into the shadow of their persecuted ancestors, as the H-Block protests and hungerstrikes showed, that they succeed in reanimating the hidden and often unconscious sympathies of the Irish people. Their suffering (*pathos*) is the surest way of soliciting sympathy (*sym-pathein:* to suffer with). Without it, Sands, Carron or Adams might never have been elected Westminster MPs.

It is because the IRA campaign *cannot* achieve military victory (and is at times even suicidal) that it *can* assume a sacrificial mystique. The Provisionals might well reply to the threats and entreaties of the politicians from Westminster and Dublin what the 1916 insurgents in Bolands Mills replied to the offer of surrender: 'We came here to die, not to win.' This is, moreover, why the boasts of successive British Secretaries in Northern Ireland that the IRA is finally defeated merely serve to augment the stigmata prestige of this tiny sect. Political impotence at the constitutional or parliamentary level (and it must be recalled that no *Provisional Sinn Féin* M.P. ever took his seat at Westminister), is the *sine qua non* of their sacrificial potency.

As observed in our preceding study, it is whenever the official channels of constitutional change appear inoperative that the Irish Republican movement has had most effective recourse to the strategy of seeking a national renewal through martyrdom. The IRA are only too well aware that the most important step towards the founding of the Irish Republic in the South was not the half-baked revolt of a few badly armed patriots in 1916, but the subsequent execution of these patriots by the British. Connolly on a wheelchair before a British firing squad gained far more than Connolly with a gun. The IRA know that the most useful Republican for the propaganda cause is a dead one. Deep in their memory is inscribed Pearse's motto that 'from the graves of patriot men and women spring living nations.'

By playing the role of sacrificial executioner, the British Empire contributed greatly to its loss of the south of Ireland. By ensuring that the British continue to play this role in Ulster today, the IRA believe they hold the key to a United Ireland. In their exclusive concentration on the security and economic dimensions of the Ulster crisis and their general ignorance of the persuasive sacrificial factor, the British have unwittingly perpetuated violence in Northern Ireland. They have repeatedly assumed the role of the magistrate Creon before the Republican Antigone. The self-righteous intransigence of the British Northern Secretary, Roy Jenkins, for example, before the requests of the imprisoned and hunger-striking Price sisters in 1974, reset the scene for the timeless defence of the tragic heroine: 'I do not heed your mortal edicts which cannot invalidate the unwritten laws of the gods . . . laws which are not of today or yesterday, but of all times.' And Margaret Thatcher's adamant refusal to grant 'political status' or alter concessions regarding visits and clothing to the Long Kesh hungerstrikers in October 1980, and again in March 1981, further confirmed the British government's misjudgment of nationalist reaction. Thus 'Ireland's enemy' became an indispensable accomplice to the rites of sacrifice.

By committing acts of violence, the IRA draw upon themselves the retaliatory wrath of the ruling authorities. It almost seems at times that one of the reasons for the IRA's offensive is to invite a reaction. Though it is important to point out here that this sacrificial motivation is merely one side of the coin (i.e. the largely unconscious ideological identification with the Fenian tradition of martyrdom). The IRA's *explicit* aim remains that of military attack and victory as illustrated in a recent statement by an IRA army council spokesman: 'The British know we are not a spent force and that we will continue.'[18]

The IRA can be sacrificially effective only when the oppressor conspires to oppress, when the executor agrees to execute, in short when they stir up national and international sympathies by being interned without trial, tortured, and denied other basic human rights. In fact, it is probably accurate to say that, apart from the death of the ten H-Block hungerstrikers in the Spring of 1981, the IRA have never *in recent years* received more support throughout the entire Irish nation (or elsewhere) than the day thirteen innocent civilians were shot dead by the British army in Derry in 1972. The IRA subsequently christened the event *Bloody Sunday*, exploiting to the full the sacrificial connotations of Bloody Sunday in 1920 (when British agents indiscriminately murdered members of the crowd at a Gaelic football match in Croke Park in Dublin). This symbolic appelation soon gained currency throughout the four provinces. Three days after the Derry massacre, 30,000 people marched on the British Embassy in Dublin and watched it burn to the ground. 20,000 attended the funerals in Derry and a national day of mourning was declared. Years later, thousands still commemorate Bloody Sunday on January 30th. The commemoration march is, not surprisingly, organised by the IRA. Sean McBride has accurately identified the consequence of the Bloody Sunday massacre for the IRA's cause: 'This act of oppression by the British forces influenced the young people to turn more and more towards the IRA and physical force. The IRA availed of the situation to become the defenders of the Catholic population against the attacks of the police and the British military forces.'[19]

The British mishandling of the Republican endurance campaign led to other sacrificial victories for the IRA. One thinks of the British government's introduction of internment without trial on 9 August 1971. 300 suspected 'terrorists' were arrested in their beds during a series of dawn raids by the British army; 6,000 refugees fled southwards to the Republic, generating widespread public concern. On 16 August a strike was staged to denounce internment and on 12 September 10,000 people held a follow up protest meeting in Casement Park in Belfast, the first of a long series. The IRA had once again succeeded in recharging their dwindling support.

More grist to the sacrificial mill came with the moves to censure media broadcasts or publications supportive of the Republican campaign or even featuring members of *Provisional Sinn Féin*. On 18 October 1976, Conor Cruise O'Brien, then Minister for Posts and Telegraphs in the Republic, introduced measures to this effect causing an immediate public outcry. The British government's decision on 4 June 1980 to censor an ITV programme dealing with the Amnesty report on British Army torture in Northern Ireland met with similar disapproval and once again highlighted the IRA as a 'victimized' body. But the most blatant act of media censorship which provided the IRA with a massive propaganda victory was the decision taken in August 1985, by the BBC Board of Governers in response to British Government pressure, to ban an interview with the *Provisional Sinn Féin* spokesman, Martin McGuinness. This decision resulted in mounting support for the censored party not only in Ireland but also in the British Broadcasting service which called a nationwide one day strike, sparking off what one member of the BBC Governing Board described as the 'worst crisis in the station's history'. In her attempt to 'starve the terrorists of the oxygen of publicity', Mrs. Thatcher succeeded, ironically, where McGuinness himself would have surely failed (had the interview *not* been censored) – that is, in providing *Provisional Sinn Féin* with one of their most significant propaganda triumphs to date.

This image of *victimization* has been reinforced down through the years by the British Army's infliction of 'cruel, inhuman and degrading treatment' on IRA prisoners (as condemned by the European Commission of Human Rights in Strasbourg, August 1976). And the employment of Sensory Deprivation torture methods on 12 Republican detainees in 1971, both in Castlereagh barracks in Belfast and in certain army bases in England, gave rise to a series of influential protest publications (in particular *The Guinea Pigs* by John McGuffin, *Le Laboratoire Irlandais* by Roger Faligot and the information bulletins of Denis Faul and Raymond Murray sent to all major international associations for the defense of human rights). The controversial use in Ulster of Diplock Courts (trial without jury) or of rubber bullets which killed several women and children, and more recently of a shoot-to-kill policy and controversial conviction of suspects of IRA bombing in Britain, might also be mentioned here[20]. Furthermore, the extensively publicised hunger strikes staged by the Price sisters and Francis Stagg and the beatings meted out to 32 Republican women prisoners in Armagh prison in February, 1980, furnished additional evidence of the 'oppressive' role of the British authorities – a role which reached its most conspicuous manifestation in the mishandling of the H-Block Campaigns.

The reason for this inventory of injustices is to demonstrate how the IRA win public sympathy not when they perpetrate violence but when they draw it upon themselves. At the level of tacit popular support, their 'patriot game' (to cite another Republican ballad) is more likely to be won when it is conducted according to the rules of sacrifice rather than of military aggression; they play to capacity audiences when they are vanquished, not when they vanquish. This may account, indeed, for the curious fact that IRA activists can be denounced for their campaign of bombing and killing by the majority of the nationalist community and yet acclaimed as martyrs by this same community once they are harassed by the British security forces, censored, tortured, imprisoned or assassinated. It is certainly this sacrificial logic of martyrdom which operated in the minds of the nationalist community when Bobby Sands and his nine fellow hungerstrikers were transformed, in the popular perception, from 'delinquent criminals' into 'national heroes'.

Conclusion

Our analysis of the strategy of sacrifice has confined itself to the Catholic and Nationalist community in Northern Ireland. That members of the Protestant community have also endured hardship and injustice is undeniable (particularly in the border areas); and it must not be forgotten that Loyalist paramilitaries were also interned, tortured and deprived of Special Category status. (Though the Loyalist number of 800 prisoners in 1980 was considerably less than the Republican one of over 2,000). Loyalists too are victims of the Ulster troubles. But while the Unionist/Loyalist community has had its share of suffering, it does not identify with this suffering as a fundamental symbol of its own specific tradition or ideology[21]. Suffering for them is not transformed into sacrifice and martyrdom; it is not commemorated but feared rather as a threat to their very existence as a distinct community. Hence while the Republicans revere the graves of their martyred heroes (be it the 1916 leaders in Dublin, Wolfe Tone in Bodenstown, the Bloody Sunday victims in Derry or the hungerstrikers in H-Block), the Loyalists tend more to identify with the triumphalist emblems of their historical victories: King Billy and Carson. The Apprentice Boys parade and the Orange Day marches celebrate political and military success, not failure. And when the Loyalists stage an annual ritualistic burning of the Lundy simulacrum (Lundy was the 'traitor' who attempted to open the gates of Derry to the besieging army of King James), it is not to sanctify the sacrificial victim but to pour scorn upon him[22]. The Loyalist ideology is perhaps best summed up in the catchcry of Randolph Churchill, who first played the Orange Card in 1886 against Gladstone's Home Rule Bill: 'Ulster will fight and Ulster will be right'. This is in stark contrast to the sacrificial ideology of Republicanism which finds typical expression, as we saw, in McSwiney's credo that 'it is not those who inflict the most but those who suffer the most who will conquer'. This credo, invoking the deep rooted Catholic Fenian tradition of martyrdom, has been reinvoked again and again throughout the last 60 years of the Republican 'endurance' campaign. A recent but by no means exceptional example was to be found on the wall of an Ulster prison cell where a Republican inmate had written the following confiteor: 'I am one of many who die for my country . . . If death is the only way I am prepared to die. To be free is all I want and many like me think the same.' Our study has tried to adduce some evidence to suggest that not a few people inside and outside the prison walls of Ulster did, and perhaps still do, rightly or wrongly, consciously or unconsciously, think the same.

* * *

The Republican myths of martyrdom are, of course, no less

susceptible to moral judgement than the Loyalist myths of triumph. A French commentator of the hungerstrike campaign, Manuel de Diéguez, observed that it is 'frightening to think that the call to sacrifice and salvation through martyrdom is a source of motivation for a devoted population to obediently die in order to receive the rewards of their sacrifice. This mechanism appears indiscrimate: one can die in this fashion as easily for Hitler, Napoleon, Caesar or Alexander as by the side of Demosthenes for the liberty of Greece.'[23] Whatever about the justice of de Diéguez's remarks in relation to the H-Block campaign, they do raise an important philosophical issue – that of the ethical discrimnation between different ideological interpretations of national myths (sacrificial or otherwise). This question will be considered in our concluding study, 'Myth and the Critique of Ideology'.

12
FAITH AND FATHERLAND

Many people in Ireland still consider their identity to be linked in some vague but deep sense with their religion. In the North, for example, it has become commonplace to use the label 'Catholic' to identify the nationalist community and the label 'Protestant' to identify the loyalist community. While this mix of national and religious identities is not as obvious or sectarian in the South, it remains implicit; and in times of internal conflict – as recent debates on constitutional changes with regard to public and private morality have showed – many of the citizens of the Republic still consider a challenge to their confessional convictions as a threat to their unique sense of 'Irishness'.

I

Outsiders often tend to view this continuing equation of political and religious identities as a symptom of eccentric backwardness or heroic conservatism. I suspect, however, that in the face of such 'outside' opinion, many Irish citizens would respond: 'but you foreigners don't really understand us; you don't appreciate that the conflict in Northern Ireland, for instance, is not in fact a religious war at all – the I.R.A. or the U.D.A. don't care about the theological doctrines of their religious traditions – the violence is *really* about opposed tribal fidelities or economic class interests,' and so on.

Similarly, in response to the suggestion that the South displays a conservative religious outlook in its laws on divorce, contraception or homosexuality, many might wish to distinguish between the conservative *ought* of the official legislation and the more liberal *is* of people's everyday lives. After all, were there not thousands attending family planning clinics and flouting the anti-contraception laws of the Republic up to 1985 (laws which one leading politician referred to as an 'Irish solution to an Irish problem')? Some might claim accordingly that we are not really as backward as we appear to be, and that when the time is ripe we will be prepared to make all kinds of generous concessions to a more pluralist society. Or to juggle with Saint Augustine: 'Lord, make us pluralist, but not yet!'

Some might well go on to cite the fact that a large proportion of our people can tune into the 'permissive' B.B.C., and that even our own R.T.E. has itself done much in recent times to open the windows to the outside world and ventilate controversial matters hitherto confined to the confessional.

But what is at issue here? Are we in the Republic not in fact saying that we want to have our cake and eat it? That we want our *ideals* to reflect one set of values (often synonymous in the South with the anti-materialist teachings of the Church) and in *real* life to enjoy quite another set of values, i.e. the benefits of advanced technological affluence, Anglo-American liberalism and E.E.C. consumerism? In short, are we not saying that we are prepared to give the nod to the old isolationist rhetoric of a rural Holy Ireland with comely maidens dancing at the crossroads, while practising a cosmopolitan code of modern materialism?

This double-think has been reflected in a variety of contradictory practices. We believed it our national duty to buy Irish but bought British whenever the opportunity arose (as the Newry busroute amply testified). We ritually deplored the spread of alien permissiveness but switched from home produced programmes like *Folio* or *Féach* to the Hollywood soap-operas of *Dallas* or *Dynasty* without the slightest hesitation. In other words, political corruption and narcotic-erotic highjinks could be vicariously consumed in Californian other-worlds, yet we preferred to deny that they might exist on our own Holy Ground here in Ireland. Further instances of our double-think were, arguably, evidenced in the debate on the constitutional amendment on abortion in 1984. Here many appeared willing to run with the secular hare and hunt with the sacred hounds; that is, do everything to amend our Constitution to reinforce the existing legal prohibition on abortion, while continuing to do little to amend our punitive attitudes to those unmarried mothers who had chosen *not* to abort that life which, once born, our society would stigmatize as 'illegitimate' for the rest of its days. I mention this to illustrate a contradiction in our moral attitude; a contradiction which, from the point of view of some unmarried pregnant girls of our society amounts to this: the constitutional *law* of our land proclaims 'do not abort', while the social *practice* of our land often whispers the very opposite – 'if you do not abort then do not expect to keep your job, or your good name or the potential status of legitimacy for your child'. Translated into plain language this means: in Ireland it is constitutionally illegitimate to abort and socially illegitimate not to.

Southern Catholics might well ask themselves why they have such little confidence in the teachings of their majority Church that they need the Constitution of the State to copperfasten these teachings in law? Or why they have so little confidence in their national identity that they somehow feel that any further attempt to separate the laws of the majority Church from those of the State, would result in a diminution of their sense of 'Irishness', opening the gates to an irresistible immoralism which would swamp us all?

I am not implying that a nation should dispense with its religious traditions or cultural ideals. Each nation needs to preserve a set of values by means of which it can provide itself with a sense of rootedness and self-identity, thereby differentiating itself from other national identities. Nobody wants an anonymous world-state in which all the customs and characteristics of the various peoples would be annihilated. But while every self-respecting society requires a set of 'oughts' to motivate the 'is' of its everyday life, is there not a danger of allowing those 'oughts' to become so abstract or removed from our real experience that they cease to positively inform it? If this happens our ideal of ourselves will congeal into a lifeless cliché. What is required therefore is not a total renunciation of our most cherished ideals, but a critical discrimination between those ideals which keep us imprisoned in a dead past and those which liberate us into a living future.

It is arguable that just as we in Ireland have allowed a purely rhetorical aspiration for a United Ireland to replace any policy for achieving it in reality, so too we may have so elevated certain of our religious aspirations that we now risk depriving much in our everyday experience of its genuinely religious dimensions. If what we believe we *ought* to be becomes totally disconnected from what we know in our hearts we *are*, then the relationship between the ideal and the real ceases to be a creative dialogue: it becomes instead a schizophrenic split between an authoritarian master-mentality and a resentful slave-mentality.

To prevent such a schizophrenia from taking hold we might well compare some of our idealized religious self-portraits with the harsh facts of contemporary reality: we might ask why religious vocations and church observances have been falling so drastically in recent years; why anti-clericalism has become so rampant in the younger generation; why many of those struggling for women's or minority rights feel hard done by the Irish Church; why violence and heroin addiction have become endemic in our urban communities North and South; or why the Irish Church, once famed throughout Europe for its learning and missionary enlightenment, and capable of producing an innovative philosopher of the calibre of John Scotus Eriugena, should now be more renowned – at least at home – for its anti-intellectualism[1].

And why is it, lastly, that the same Catholic church which throughout the centuries was such a powerful agency of liberation and education for the dispossessed Irish – providing them with a basic sense of human dignity and self-respect – has become in more recent times the very opposite: that is, an agency so preoccupied with a conservative defence of 'faith and morals' (which all too frequently means blind faith and sexual morals), that a considerable number of young Irish citizens today regard it as a reactionary apologist, rather than a radical challenger of the status quo? Such questions are not intended to condemn Irish religion *per se* but, on the contrary, to identify some of the difficulties which have to be faced if religion is to be taken seriously by the young generations growing up in Ireland today.

II

The problems outlined above have a complex history which in some respects is particular to the Irish problem of *identity*. We cannot properly understand our present crisis of value without paying some attention to the cultural and ideological background which has shaped many of our religious assumptions. In attempting here to analyse the origin of some of these assumptions our method will be less that of the historian concerned with 'hard facts' than that of the philosopher concerned with a specific *interpretation* of these facts: that is, with the emergence of a *national consciousness* governed by a chosen set of ideals and ideologies. In short, we will focus on the ways in which we as a nation have chosen to *represent* ourselves, and examine the central role played by religion, and particularly Catholicism, in the creation of this national self-image.

One of the first clear instances of an overlap between religious and national identities in Ireland was witnessed when the colonial fanaticism of the Cromwellian plantation forged the self-protective alliance of 'faith and fatherland' in the minds of the colonized natives. As one Protestant planter put it as early as 1625: 'the very ground the Irish tread, the air they breathe, the climate they share, the very sky above them, all seem to draw them to the religion of Rome.' The Cromwellian Act of Settlement of 1652 in effect divided the inhabitants of Ireland into 'English Protestants' and 'Irish Papists'[2].

This division was to re-emerge with the campaign for the emancipation of Catholics in the nineteenth century: a campaign which challenged the fusion of Protestant and Imperial interests exemplified in the rise of the Orange Order after the 1830s. The ranks were now drawn up along confessional lines with the largely Catholic Nationalists promoting a Home Rule for Ireland Bill and the Protestant Unionist party opposing and ultimately defeating it. It was out of such protracted antagonism between the ideological interests of Nationalism and Unionism that there arose the Orange catchcry that Home Rule is Rome Rule, and the answering reply that Protestant Rule is British Imperial Rule.

The resulting equation of Catholic with nationalist and Protestant with anti-nationalist was thus less a question of theology than of ideology: a political rhetoric whereby the two communities reinforc-

ed their opposing identities. This equation, in other words, served as
an ideological strategy deployed by both the Unionist and Nationalist parties to simplify reality by 'fastening the loyalty of their
members on central symbols'[3]. Catholic and Gaelic became
symbols used by many nationalists as a way of achieving separation
from Britain. And the reverse was equally true: Protestant and
British became symbols used by Unionists as a means of preserving
the union with the United Kingdom.

So what role did the ideal of 'Holy Ireland' play in all this? And
how did this ideal relate to the confessional difference between Irish
Catholicism and Irish Protestantism? In 1906, Douglas Hyde,
founder of the Gaelic League and future first President of Ireland,
offered the following quaint description of Irish religion:

> A pious race is the Gaelic race. The Irish Gael is pious by nature. He
> sees the hand of god in every place, in every time and in every thing. . . .
> The things of the Spirit . . . affect him more powerfully than the things of
> the body. . . . What is invisible for other people is visible for him.
> *(Religious Songs of Connaught)*.

Here Hyde was speaking as a Protestant cultural nationalist about
a national Catholic culture. He knew that it was considered far more
'natural' for a Catholic to subscribe to the terms *Gaelic* and
nationalist than for a Protestant to do so. Thus his rather uncritical
appraisal of the piety of the Gael may have been somewhat motivated by his eagerness to accommodate himself, as a Protestant, to the
desired definition of a Gaelic nationalist. Hyde's eulogy of the pious
Gael is what might be described as a Protestant's ideal of Gaelic
Catholicism dressed up in a romanticised peasant garb.

Hyde was by no means an isolated example of this attitude. Yeats,
Lady Gregory, AE and other Protestants of the literary revival, subscribed to a similarly sacralized view of the Irish Catholic peasant –
particularly up to Independence when the Catholic culture was seen
(and rightly) as the victim of colonial persecution. Yeats, for
example, would conclude his poem, *Under Ben Bulben*, by
championing the Gaelic-Catholic peasantry over and above the
Anglo-Irish Ascendancy: 'Sing the peasantry, and then/Hard-riding
country gentlemen/'. In other words, even Yeats would have horse-
trotting 'Prods' play second fiddle to bog-trotting 'Papists' . . . in
literature at any rate.

But what prompted Irish Protestant nationalists such as Hyde and
Yeats to sponsor an idealised portrait of the Catholic peasantry?
There may well have been a touch of residual colonial guilt in such
idealization: a secret regret almost that they, as Protestants, were
born into the winning side and so bore a special responsibility to
undo not only the *political*, but also the *cultural* wrongs of colonial
history.

But this Protestant nationalist view of Catholicism was to change

somewhat *after* Independence when the Catholic nationalist culture
was restored to power. While the Constitution of 1937, for example,
pledged to honour all religious denominations on the island, it was
clear that it privileged a Catholic ethos in certain aspects of legislation. So that instead of the sectarian wrongs of colonial history being
righted (by establishing laws equally acceptable to both traditions),
there was a feeling among many Irish Protestants that they were
simply being reversed, i.e. that a new form of discrimination was
creeping in.

Such accusations of complicity between Catholic Church and
Southern State were not, however, confined to Protestants. In fact
they assumed far more aggressive expression in the writings of such
Catholic authors as Joyce, O'Faolain and O'Flaherty: writers who
felt that Catholicism, having ceased to be the colonial victim of
oppression, had now become a post-colonial oppressor in its own
right. As Sean O'Faolain remarked: 'Here in the Republic . . . we
have two parliaments: A parliament at Maynooth and a Parliament
at Dublin. . . . The Dail proposes; Maynooth disposes.'[4] Such
writers implied that Irish Catholicism had somehow *internalized* its
colonial master in its historical memory; so that liberated at last, it
sought subtly to emulate him. Perhaps Hyde had something similar
in mind when he claimed that the English are the old masters whom
'we love to hate yet never cease to imitate'.

III

But the stereotype of the 'pious gael' was also cultivated by the
Catholic community, and particularly by the Church.

It was quite logical in a sense for the Catholic Church to lay claim
to an idealized view of its own religion; for the Gaelic Catholic
peasantry had been deprived of legitimate power for centuries (particularly during the period of the Penal Laws). And over these same
centuries the Church had survived as not only the protector of its
persecuted flock but also as a *sanctuary of its dreams.*

The notion of 'Holy Ireland' was a popular example of such a
dream, in so far as it referred *back* to an idealised past of saints and
scholars *before* the arrival of the Protestant planters; or else *forward*
to an idealised future *after* Ireland became an independent Catholic
nation once again. In short, as long as colonial oppression reigned,
the name of Holy Catholic Ireland could remain unblemished for the
simple reason that a *religion of aspiration* remains precisely a
utopian ideal and not a concrete reality. And perhaps this tendency
to idealise had something to do with the *symbolizing process of
sublimation* – a process whereby what we lack in history we compensate for in our dreams. The more colonially suppressed the
Catholic identity, the more sublime the myth of a 'Holy Ireland'.

Lévi-Strauss has described this aspect of religious mythologizing as 'the fantasy production of a society seeking passionately to give symbolic expression to the institutions it *might* have had in reality' (had the historical circumstances of that society been more conducive to the actualization of its projects). But since the 'remedies were lacking', the society finds itself unable to fulfill its desired goals and so begins 'to dream them, to project them into the imaginary'[5]. In short, for a colonially oppressed people religion can readily serve the ideological purpose of inventing *mythic solutions* to problems which remain unsolvable at the socio-political level.

But what would happen once Ireland achieved Independence? What would happen once we were provided with the possibility of translating our sublimated ideals into reality? For centuries the Catholic religion identified with its colonized flock against the colonial foreigner – to such an extent indeed that Cardinal Cullen was able to affirm in the 19th century that Irish 'nationality simply meant the Catholic Church'. After Independence, however, and particularly during the Civil War, the Church found itself divided against a significant portion of what she considered to be her own people. With the alien oppressor gone from the scene, the violence that exploded in the Civil War between Irishman and Irishman could no longer be attributed to an *external* cause (i.e. the colonial British occupation). It had to be acknowledged as 'our own', that is, as a rupture *within* the Catholic nationalist community itself. So that with the setting up of the Irish Free State after the treaty of 1921, the Church found itself in the ambiguous position of being at once the representative of the ideals of the Catholic nationalist population and at the same time of siding with one 'legimate' portion of that population (the Free State) against another 'illegitimate' portion (those Republicans who rejected the treaty in the name of the still unrealized ideal of a United Ireland).

In 1922, the Irish Hierarchy declared that they thought the wisest course for Ireland was to accept the Treaty and make the most of the freedom it brought – 'freedom for the first time in seven hundred years'. The Republicans who violently opposed the Free State were held to be guilty of a far greater crime than their Fenian predecessors, for these Republicans were threatening to undermine the good name of Holy Independent Ireland itself. Accordingly, we find the Hierarchy throwing their lot in with the Provisional Government, denouncing the Republicans as 'parricides, not patriots'. As one veteran I.R.A. campaigner, Connie Neenan, acerbically commented: 'Before we were Saints and heroes – now we were burglars and bank robbers. . . . The ecclesiastical powers were against us, and they were very vocal. . . . They just wanted the *Status Quo* back in any shape or form.'[6]

Of course the Hierarchy saw their condemnation of the Republicans – which in some instances included excommunication and the denial of the sacraments – as a genuinely *nationalist* stance. They saw themselves as protecting the moral integrity of Ireland against those who had chosen 'to attack their own motherland . . . *as if she were a foreign power'*. They even went so far as to declare that the I.R.A.'s campaign of violence against the Free State had done 'more damage in 3 months than could be laid to the charge of British rule in 30 decades'! Because the Republican dissenters were tearing at the sacred vestment of Catholic nationalist unity, the Church endeavoured to win them from their 'evil ways'. What was at stake, insisted the Hierarchy, was nothing less than 'our *Christian heritage* and our *name as a nation'*.[7].

But this civil war opposition between the Hierarchy and the Republicans was not to last long. In time, De Valera's men returned to the fold of Dáil Eireann under the name of Fianna Fáil. And by the same stroke, the prodigal sons were embraced by Mother Church.

The spirit of family reunion was evidenced in De Valera's Constitution of 1937 which inserted articles acknowledging the special position of the Catholic Church and banning divorce. In the minds of some – not least members of the Protestant minority – De Valera had produced a Catholic Constitution for a Catholic people. But whatever interpretation one chose, it was clear that the Church, having recovered from its insecure and embattled role during the Civil War, now found its teachings reflected in the constitutional law of the land for the first time in Irish history. Archbishop McQuaid was happy; so was De Valera, who had no hesitation in declaring, during a broadcast to the United States, that 'We are a Catholic Nation'. A curious echo this, some might say, of the claim by Craigavon, N.I.'s first Prime Minister, that he wanted a 'Protestant parliament for a Protestant people'. The confessional lines of partition thus seemed reinforced.

IV

But the relationship between Church and State did not end there. Once the quarrels between De Valera and the Hierarchy had been patched up, it was still obvious that the dream of Holy Ireland was not yet a reality. There was a lingering suspicion that something remained a little malodorous, not to say rotten, in the state of Erin. The independent Southern State was still a far cry from the promised land. But how was this continuing discrepancy between the ideal 'ought' and the actual 'is' of Irish national life to be accounted for? With the English gone, the majority of the I.R.A. turned respectable, and the Protestant minority in the South as good as gold (since they had been relieved of their colonial status), what would now explain why the ideal of Holy Ireland had not yet been convincingly realised?

Several commentators have argued – among them the historian Margaret O'Callaghan – that between the twenties and the fifties, 'sexual immorality' became something of an ideological scapegoat in this regard[8]. In other words, the former *political* threat to our national integrity was now replaced by a *moral* threat. And since it was continually asserted in these rather insular years, that this threat to our 'Faith and Morals' came principally from 'abroad' (that is from the liberal licentiousness of 'foreign' countries), the presumption could be sustained that the root cause of our evils came once again from *without*.

Let me take some examples. In a statement in 1924, Cardinal Logue set the tone for subsequent clerical attacks on the immoral nature of foreign dress, dance, cinema and evil literature which threatened to corrupt our chaste youth. Despite the fact that 'men are now engaged in a laudable effort to repair the rack and ruin of the past', wrote Logue, 'there are moral abuses which require to be condemned. The dress, or rather the want of dress of women at the present day is a crying scandal'. He affirmed the Hierarchy's commitment to 'make Ireland what she *ought* to be, a good, solid, Catholic nation', by denouncing the 'regular mania' for dancing which is the 'outcrop of the corruption of the age'.

'It is no small recommendation of Irish dances,' wrote the Maynooth Bishops in 1925, 'that they cannot be danced for long ·hours. . . . They may not be the fashion in London or Paris. They should be the fashion in Ireland.' '*Irish* dances,' they concluded, 'do not make for degenerates.' (Ironically, it was this same Irish dancing, particularly at crossroads, which had been condemned by the clergy in the preceding century).

But dance and dress were not considered the most pernicious of alien influences. 'Evil literature' emanating from foreign lands was decried by Archbishop O'Donnell as an even more corruptive carrier of immorality. And to immunize the national body against such disease, the Archbishop appealed to the Church's educational system to interest the young 'in the beauties of the native tongue'. 'The spirit of Irish classes,' the argued, 'is dead against this trash.'

Nor did other media such as cinema (or later television) escape the censorious scrutiny of the Hierarchy. Bishop McNamee of Ardagh berated the 'powerful *anti-nationalism*' of films, which, he asserted, served to bring 'vivid representations of foreign ideals' before the vulnerable minds of the people; and he added his conviction that only the 'Gaelic movement provided a powerful antidote to the pleasure-seeking spirit of the times'.

Thus we find the revival of Gaelic culture being used – some would say abused – for the ideological purpose of innoculating the Irish people against the traffic of alien, immoral culture. And one can only assume that Merriman's *Midnight Court* or *The Love Songs of Connaught* were not the staple diet in those 'Irish classes'

prescribed by the Bishops. One may also assume that many nationalists had forgotten that the Church which now so fervently espoused
the Gaelic cause was the same institution which, in its support for
the Act of Union in 1800 and in its rulings from Maynooth in the
nineteenth century, had done much to aid and abet the anglicization
of Ireland.

The Church's defence of national Faith and Morals against alien
practices did not fall on deaf ears. The State responded with filial
obedience introducing a series of laws which embodied the Catholic
moral code. To mention the most obvious examples, there was the
Censorship of Publications Act of 1929; the Censorship of Films
Act of 1923; the legislation prohibiting divorce in 1925; the
legislation requiring the licensing of dance halls and banning contra-
ceptives in the 1930's; Article 42 of the Constitution, safeguarding
the privileged role of the Church in education; the Constitutional
underwriting of the special position of the Catholic Church enshrined in Art. 44 (repealed in 1972); the Church's controversial role in
the Mother-and-Child-scheme crisis in 1951; and more recently the
passing of a constitutional amendment in 1983, the wording of
which was unacceptable to the minority Churches and to a considerable number of the majority Church, and the defeat of the divorce
referendum in 1986.

I rehearse this litany of Church-influenced legislation not to
engage in Unionist apologetics (for quite clearly the Stormont
regime was far more confessionally biased in almost every respect),
but to demonstrate that the ideological equation of Catholic Church
and Irish Nation was in fact reinforced after Independence rather
than the reverse.

Margaret O'Callaghan is correct in interpreting the Church's
desire, after Independence, to influence the laws of the State as a
symptom of growing insecurity before the influx of a cosmopolitan
liberalism; a liberalism which, it was felt, might further endanger the
Church's historic role as the protector of the ideals of a threatened
people. O'Callaghan concludes that the clergy's puritanical zeal
during this period should be viewed 'not merely as an intensification
of a Jansenist streak in Irish Catholicism, but as a reaction to the
demands that they believed Independence made upon the people's
moral calibre'[9]. In short, their almost obsessive concern to preserve
the Holy name of Ireland within a narrow sphere of Faith and
Morals may perhaps best be understood in the historical context of a
Church which had formerly served as the 'only institutional voice of
a wronged Ireland and now found itself, in the absence of a colonial
enemy, with the same crusading spirit that the former centuries had
made a part of its being'[10]. Moreover, since the very ideal of national
self-identity had developed historically in *reaction* to the colonial
outsider, it was not entirely surprising that once Independence was
achieved, the Church's protectionist reaction against alien
materialism could now be seen as a means of preserving this ideal of
national identity. In other words, a new post-colonial outsider had

been identified – the permissive pagan foreigner – whom we would love to hate yet never cease to imitate. Once again, we witness an *interiorization* of the colonial model.

V

Let me try to sum up the argument. It would seem that the Church's repeated attempts after Independence to promote an idealized version of Gaelic Catholic nationalism was motivated, in part at least, by a desire to preserve its traditional role as protector of the Irish people; and that it sought to fulfill this vocation by purging the nation of extraneous immoral influences: that is, by keeping it *pure*. Thus *sexual purity* became synonymous in an almost symbolic way with the ideal of *national purity*. In the process, the root cause of our national impurities could once again be attributed to the old master: pagan Britain. The central difference was, of course, that this alien culture was now exerting its nefarious influence on our moral as opposed to our political being.

To be fair, the Hierarch generally refrained from explicitly identifying the terms 'foreign' and 'pagan' with 'English' and 'Protestant'; but it must have been obvious to most concerned that the evil literature and cinema which so threatened the purity of Irish youth was unlikely to be scripted in Italian or Russian. Certainly, D.P. Moran's racist pleas for the protection of 'Irish Ireland' from all non-Catholic and non-Gaelic cultures, in *The Rosary* and *The Catholic Bulletin*, left his readers in little doubt as to his intentions. This influential author even went so far as to denounce Yeats's winning of the Nobel prize in 1923, declaring that 'the line of recipients of the Nobel prize shows that a reputaton for paganism in thought and deed is of very considerable advantage. . . . ' Indeed, so incensed was AE by Moran's xenophobic stance and in particular by his assertion that 'the Gael must be the element that absorbs' lest 'pagan, alien and un-Irish philosophies' corrupt our national being, that he riposted as follows: 'We do not want uniformity in our culture, but the balancing of our diversities in a wide tolerance. The moment we had complete uniformity our national life would be stagnant.'[11]

AE was simply confirming here Parnell's generous hope that all the children of the Nation be cherished equally, regardless of the purity or impurity of their racial genes or their religion. And by the same token, he was, of course, reiterating the interdenominational project not only of the United Irishmen movement (which invoked a common heritage of Protestant, Catholic and Dissenter) but also, let it not be forgotten, of many of the 1916 leaders who stressed the need for non-sectarian institutions in a new independent Ireland. (Connolly was quite clear on this point and Pearse also in his pleas for interdenominational third level education in *An Claidheamh Soluis)*[12].

Those rightly proud of the Nationalist, Gaelic and Catholic traditions which have contributed to Irish culture over the centuries would, I suggest, best serve those traditions by dismantling the tribal ideology which has divided the different communities on this island and betrayed the 'common name of Irishman'. This need not entail a jettisoning of all inherited ideals, only a critical discrimination between those ideals which discourage and those which encourage a more open understanding of our national identity. The ideological tendency, particularly since Independence, to identify Irish nationalism with stereotyped versions of Catholicism and Gaelicism has resulted in an exclusivist cliché: one, indeed, which has done a fundamental disservice to the unique qualities of each of these cultural heritages (that is, the Nationalist, the Catholic and the Gaelic). In the process, religion has suffered, our sense of national identity has suffered and the Irish language has suffered. This ideological tendency has only exacerbated the partitionist mentality both north and south of the border, and done little to advance the cause of either Irish or Christian reconciliation. It has insured, rather, that the border has been drawn not just on the outer geographical map but on the inner soul of our nation. Is it not time to disentangle the convoluted web of ideological hegemony and restore to each ideal – Gaelic, Catholic, Nationalist – its distinctive promise?[13].

Let me conclude this analysis of the ideological relationship between Faith and Fatherland by putting some questions to our two major religious denominations, Protestant and Catholic: questions which require radical responses, if future generations on this island are to cultivate a genuine sense of the sacred and thus belie the Swiftean foreboding that we Irish 'have just enough religion to make us hate but not enough to make us love'.

Of Ireland's Protestant Churches it might be asked: Are you prepared to repudiate the colonial stereotype of Irish Protestantism as inherently superior to Irish Catholicism? Are you prepared to live instead by the liberating heritage bequeathed by such Irish Protestants as Berkeley, Tone, Davis, Mitchel, Ferguson, Parnell, Hyde, Yeats, MacNeice, Hewitt and others? Are you prepared to foster the enlightening role of Protestantism as guarantor of 'civil and religious liberties', by *protesting* against all forms of discrimination, South *and* North? (I am thinking in particular of the collusion between certain Protestant leaders and paramilitary violence in the North). In short, are you prepared to heed the words of a former Protestant Dean of St. Patricks that here in Ireland 'we have had too much religion and not enough Christianity'.

Of Ireland's majority Catholic Church it might be asked: Are you prepared to disavow the stereotype of Irish Catholicism as sole protector of the 'Holy Name of Ireland'? Are you willing, accordingly, to accept that the doctrinal convictions of one Church should not be enshrined in the laws of the State to the exclusion of the aspirations of minority religions or, indeed, of those citizens who have chosen to have no religion? In other words, are you prepared to acknowledge that one cannot credibly denounce majority confessional rule in the North while defending it in the South? Did Vactican II really mean 'no change' as Archbishop McQuaid of Dublin once remarked?; or did not its rethinking of traditional Catholicism require, for example, a transformation of our institutions of education so that the generations now growing up learn a message of tolerance, critical questioning and social commitment to the outcast members of our society, rather than a message of authoritarian puritanism or blind obedience? As one Irish Bishop put it, the Church must become less obsessed with the sexual morality of the bedroom and more concerned with the social morality of the boardroom.

The Irish churches might do well to abandon their holier-than-thou isolationism, admitting that while they have indeed produced their share of saints and scholars and withstood centuries of persecution, they are today no less nor no more holy than most other religious communities on this globe. Far from warranting the abandonment of our 'common religious heritage', such an admission would encourage the development of this heritage in the direction of a genuine pluralism. The provision or fortification of legal dykes, such as the Constitutional ban on divorce in the Republic or the legislation against Sunday recreation in Ulster, are not viable methods of ensuring the preservation of religious values. The Irish Council of Churches was correct when it recommended in 1985 that the 'Churches will have to look to the faith of their members and the nurture of it'[14]. The laws of Church and State have been confused for too long in both parts of this island. This confusion is understandable, as our analysis has suggested, in the light of the protracted colonial (and post-colonial) conflict whereby Catholicism provided the symbols around which the sense of Irish nationalist identity was sustained, and Protestantism provided the symbols for the maintenance of the Unionist identity as guaranteed by the link with Britain. But this confusion of ethnic and religious identities is no longer tenable. The historical overidentification of Protestantism with the Unionist ideology of siege and of Catholicism with the Nationalist ideology of grievance has nowhere to go, but backwards. A pluralist Ireland would be one in which the distinctive religious traditions could be respected without any one tradition being allowed to dominate the value system of the state – North or South or both – at the expense of the minority religious communities. Any Christian Church which lays claim to hegemonic status ceases to be Christian. The religious triumphalism of 'majority rule', based on the crude calculation of sectarian headcounts has, one would hope, had its day.

13

BETWEEN POLITICS AND LITERATURE:
THE IRISH CULTURAL JOURNAL

It has become common in Ireland today to suppose that politics and literature should be kept separate. Any attempt to deviate from such a strategy of mutual exclusion can only lead, in Conor Cruise O'Brien's memorable formula, to an 'unhealthy intersection'. I wish to challenge this assumption, pointing out that some of this country's most inventive thinking and writing over the last one hundred and fifty years was produced in cultural journals such as *The Nation, The United Irishman, The Irish Statesman, An Claidheamh Soluis, The Bell* and others – journals which refused the polarization of literature and politics into opposed discourses and believed that the struggle for a new national identity was best served by combining imaginative creativity with a keen sense of social commitment.

I: The Historical Genesis of Journals in Ireland

(a) The Propagandist Journal

The journal began to play an important role in Irish life in the early decades of the nineteenth century. Between the Act of Union in 1800 and the Rising of 1848, over 150 periodicals were launched in Ireland.[1] Only a tiny portion of these managed to last more than five years; and those that did, did so, it appears, because they succeeded in aligning themselves with a specific ideological identity. One of the most conspicuous features of Irish society between 1800 and 1850 was that it was bitterly divided, so that the journals published during this period were for the most part of a polemical, and frequently sectarian, character. One finds an extensive list of journals dividing rather predictably along confessional and political lines. On the one hand, there were the periodicals that subscribed to the Catholic-Whig-Anti-Union grouping; on the other, those that represented the Protestant-Tory-Pro-Union grouping. On many occasions, indeed, a journal of one persuasion arose as a direct response to a journal of the opposite persuasion. For example, there was the *Protestant Penny Magazine* and the *Catholic Penny*

Magazine; the *Union Magazine* and the *Anti-Union Magazine* and so on.

One cannot fail to remark how the majority of journals published between 1800 and 1830 were propagandist responses to the Colonial Act of Union.[2] The Unionist journals agressively defended the Union as the indispensable guarantee to their otherwise threatened identity as a non-Gaelic and Protestant community in Ireland. While the Nationalist journals attacked the Union as the major threat to their native, Gaelic, Catholic identity as a community. The following passage from an editorial in the *Irish Magazine and Monthly National Advocate* (1822) is representative in this regard: 'We feel that the Union is not only the greatest evil with which the country is affected but that it is in reality the prolific source of many of the other evils under which we labour. . . . For this there is only one course to be taken, let every independent man in Ireland stand up for a Repeal of the Union. . . . If they wish the salvation of their country they will not delay. . . . The Orange idolaters of Ireland are too vicious to learn truth and too prejudicial to be convinced.'

It is significant that both Nationalist and Unionist journals were written, published and read in the name of defending a specific communal identity against another which menaced it. The tribal conflicts which in preceding centuries had been fought out on the battle fields were now largely fought out in print. Ideas replaced arms as the weaponry of colonial confrontation. Thus, for example, the motto of the *Irish Catholic Magazine* (1829) reads 'Happy homes and altars free', while that of the *Irish Protestant* was 'Fear God, Honour the King'. This admixture of political and religious idioms to bolster up one community at the expense of another was a typical feature of early nineteenth century journals. The anti-Unionist *New Irish Magazine* carried pot-boiling pieces entitled 'The Hydra of Methodism' or 'Shameful Conduct of the Methodists: Addressed to Ladies who circulated Bibles'; while the pro-Unionist *Church of Ireland Magazine* was full of equally acrimonious rhetoric. Founded to combat 'Romish ignorance, superstition and idolatry', the *Church of Ireland Magazine* reminded its readers that 'popery, however painted, and however masked, remains always the same, the enemy of reform, the advocate of inquisitorial tyranny and the patroness of persecution.' This sectarian journal lasted an amazing 44 years from 1825 to 1849. Indeed the more provocative the editorial policy the longer the magazine was likely to be produced. These journals created a sense of communal solidarity by trading on the widespread feeling of tribal division. The sense of community in question was *intra-communal* rather than *cross-communal,* reactive rather than explorative: it resulted from the consolidation of the besieged planters in one corner and the colonized natives in the other.[3]

(b) The Literary Journal

It was not really until the 1820s and 1830s that another, less sectarian kind of journal began to emerge in Ireland – the literary journal. The literary journal focused on the world of *belles-lettres* and attempted to discover a common spiritual heritage which might surmount the sectarianism of the religious and political quarrels. Thus, for instance, *The Belfast Magazine and Literary Journal,* which appeared in 1825, declared its express determination to 'avoid controversial theology and party politics' in favour of the 'peaceful pursuit of literature'. In similar fashion, *The Dublin Magazine or General Repertory of Philosophy, Belles-Lettres and Miscellaneous Information* proclaimed its editorial policy to be *above* party politics i.e. 'to arrest the decay of literature which has been generally considered the certain herald of declining greatness, in every age and nation'. The aristocratic journal, *Ancient Ireland* (1835), also promoted an ideal of aesthetic harmony and reconciliation, affirming itself to be 'solely and altogether a literary publication: Politics and polemics are totally excluded from these pages'.

While several of the sectarian magazines enjoyed life-spans of up to fifty years, none of the major literary magazines mentioned lasted for more than eleven months. *The Irish Monthly Magazine*, a sectarian periodical of the anti-Unionist variety, explained the speedy demise of the literary *Dublin Magazine* as follows: 'In the first volume of this periodical we did not meet with a single political article. What a publication for a country suffering under political disabilities! The poor slave was either contented with servitude, or afraid to complain; and amused himself by playing with flowers of literature, which soon withered and died in his hands.' The implication here is that journals without a political commitment or *parti-pris* are journals without guts – irrelevant, elitist, ephemeral. As a disenchanted editor of one of the many failed literary journals remarked in 1931: 'A thing impossible at the present moment, in the present state of affairs in this country, to establish a literary periodical, conducted in a fair, temperate, gentlemanly way . . . '

This is not to suggest, of course, that the propaganda journals omitted all reference to literary or cultural matters. But when such non-political material was included, it served the purpose of either providing picturesque relief – e.g. twee travelogue articles such as 'Three Weeks in Donegal', 'A Connaught Ramble' – *or* of surreptitiously shoring up a sectarian viewpoint. When the Rev. Otway, for example, decided to publish some of William Carleton's early stories of Irish peasantry in his *Church of Ireland Magazine*, he did so under such slanted editorial headings as 'Popular Romish Legends' or 'Irish Superstitions'. In some respects, this condescending nod to a native literature of peasant lore also corresponded to the fashionable anthropological interest of educated British opinion, typified in Arnold's vision of the quaint, dreamy, entertaining Celt.

And it is no accident that Arnold's benign portrait of the antiquated Celt went hand in glove with his total opposition to the Home Rule for Ireland Bill. As Seamus Deane has remarked, this Arnoldian attitude to the Irish expressed itself in the attitude: 'the Celts can stay quaint and stay put'.[4]

The anti-Unionist journals also had their token literary article; but here again the literature was considered less in terms of its artistic merit than in terms of its political implications for the 'cause'. A telling instance of this can be found in the *Irish Catholic Magazine* (1829) which included comments on the 'gloomy timidity of evange-lical prudery' alongside essays on the upsurge of a new and rebellious generation of Catholic readers. 'We who remember Ireland for the last fifty years,' reads one contribution, 'view with astonishment the progress of education in this country. There is at length, a popular mind in Ireland enlightened and organised. We are becoming a reading and thinking nation. . . . ' But the emergence of such a new educated generation also spelt the possibility of a new kind of journal, one which would combine genuine literary interests with more broadly political ideas of inter-denominational concern, ideals which could cut across the tribal conflict between Planter and Gael and seek a broad cultural consensus for a new Ireland. Thus we witness the gradual burgeoning of non-sectarian cultural journals which transcend the format of the propaganda pamphlet. These strove to rise above the narrow divisiveness of party politics without being apolitical in the manner of the effete literary journals.

(c) The Cultural Journal

The new cultural journal sought to provide a common forum for Catholic and Protestant authors on *both* literary *and* socio-political matters. One of the earliest examples of such a non-sectarian periodical was the *National Magazine*, founded in 1830, which after the bitter polemics occasioned by the Act of Union, looked forward to the possibility of a more inclusive national identity, a new vision of united 'Irishness' which might give common cause to Protestant, Catholic and Dissenter. The *National Magazine* featured many articles on Irish literature, legends and cultural life, declaring at the same time an active interest in political and social affairs. 'We propose to make politics a frequent subject of discussion in our pages,' ran one editorial, 'though as the political world now stands, we belong to no party.' In other words, if the old political framework militated against a genuine sense of national partnership, a new framework would have to be invented. Such journals ceased to be merely *reactive* (in the sense of polemical responses to the latest sectarian squabble) and became *creative* (in the sense of projecting novel visions of Irish culture and society).[5]

It should be mentioned, however, that the initial spate of non-sectarian cultural journals encountered numerous obstacles and only few survived for any considerable time. First, the established reading public were accustomed to partisan journals and found any departure from this format unsettling. Second, the hoped-for generation of new readers, rising up from the darkness of down-trodden peasantry, were still only semi-literate (particularly in English, which was the language used in the large circulation journals) and were often without sufficient money to purchase a quality magazine. Several penny magazines arose towards the middle of the nineteenth century to cater for this emerging mass readership, but these tended to slip back, once again, into the sure-bet saleability of sectarian *cliché*. The *Catholic Penny Magazine* equated Irish nationalism with Catholicism, while its Protestant Penny counterpart equated civilisation with Protestantism (and included fanatical attacks on the doctrine of transubstantiation, the Virgin Mary, nuns and the Pope, with headings such as 'Jew horror-struck at the host assuming the form of a crucifix'!) The non-sectarian journals thus found themselves in something of a vicious circle: they invoked the support of the new generation of enlightened readers whom they set out to enlighten.

But there was yet another reason for the initial resistance to non-sectarian cultural journals in Ireland: namely, the deeply-rooted prejudice, shared by both Protestant Ascendancy and Catholic middle-class, that anything Irish was necessarily inferior to anything English and ultimately doomed to failure. As Barbara Hayley has observed: 'The ascendancy and would-be ascendancy, the trades-people and "comfortable" Irish ... were resistant to Irish periodicals for snobbish reasons. Time and again one reads of their reluctance to take magazines of "local manufacture"; for them *Blackwoods, Frasers,* and *The Gentleman's Magazine* (periodicals of English provenance) had a more cosmopolitan appeal, displayed on their literary tables.'[6] To add to the difficulties, the majority of Irish booksellers served as agents for the British periodicals and had no great desire to jeopardise this established market by supporting Irish rivals.

The various responses to this colonial mentality were instructive. Some Irish editors adopted a defensive or defeatist rhetoric, decrying their fellow countrymen for making Ireland a failed cultureless land by absconding to England or by subscribing to the latest cults of London fashion. Other Irish editors did a little double-think and continued to have their periodicals *published* in London so that Irish material could be seen to carry the seal of Imperial approval. Moreover, this lamb-in-lions-clothing solution was practised not only by Protestant journals but also by Catholic ones such as the *Dublin Review* (which lasted for a remarkable 133 years from 1836 to 1969) and whose main contributors hailed from the

Catholic Seminary of Maynooth. A third response by Irish editors was to dig their heels in, refuse to pander to defeatist pessimism or colonial snobbery, insisting that non-sectarian journals *could* be written, published, sold and read in Ireland despite the odds. It was, arguably, this third defiant response to the colonial inferiority complex which ultimately provided the best kind of cultural journal, combining high-quality political and literary commentary. First and foremost of such defiant cultural journals was *The Nation*.

The Nation, whose first number appeared on October 15, 1842, was in many respects the great breakthrough. Published weekly, it promoted both literary excellence and socio-political reform. In other words, it refused the security of being exclusively political or exclusively literary. While committed to specific political objectives, such as the improvement of the land tenure system and the repeal of the Act of Union, it believed such reforms to be but half measures unless accompanied by a new vision of the Irish national community. This required a re-definition of our cultural identity beyond the conventional moulds of sect and party. Davis, himself a Protestant, resolved to break for good with the sectarian equation of religious confession and political purpose, declaring the creation of a common national identity to be the work of Catholic, Protestant and Dissenter. Davis recognised the indispensable role of the cultural journal for this work and as editor of *The Nation* persuaded countless Irish writers to stay in Ireland and write for their people so that as many as possible might participate in open debate on the national question.

The Nation did not pander to the masses, as did the Penny magazines, nor did it scorn or snub them like the elitist, London-based, literary periodicals. And unlike the legion of sectarian journals that preceded it, *The Nation* refused to be content with preaching to the converted – be they Catholic or Protestant. It determined to interrogate ideas of cultural tradition and heritage not so as to sentimentalise the past or escape into its archaic irrelevancies, but so as to regain that sense of self-respect necessary to construct an alternative national literature and politics. This was the invaluable legacy of Mangan, Davis, Ferguson, Gavan Guffy and the other contributors to *The Nation*. Finally, *The Nation* recognised that the work of shaping a new cultural identity could be greatly assisted by reviewing the age-old, locked-in conflict between Ireland and England in the comparative light of other national struggles; and so we find numerous studies comparing Ireland's plight with that of America, France and the other European nations. In this respect, *The Nation* proved the point that a genuine national awareness presupposes an international awareness if it is not to stagnate into self-regarding insularity; that to understand ourselves we must also understand how other peoples in other countries think, feel, work, struggle and aspire.

II: In Search of a New Nation

The Nation was to serve as a positive blueprint for Irish cultural journals for the next century and more, championing as it did the twin virtues of literary adventurousness and socio-political commitment. Amongst such journals we could mention *The United Irishman* edited by John Mitchell and Arthur Griffith, *An Claidheamh Soluis* edited by Patrick Pearse, *The Workers Republic* edited by James Connolly, *The Irish Statesman* and *The Irish Homestead* edited by George Russell and Horace Plunkett and *The Bell* edited by Sean O'Faolain and Peader O'Donnell. Indeed it is interesting to note how this catalogue of editors reads like a list of honour of some of Ireland's finest literary and political minds. How strange to think that Griffith, Davis, Mitchell, Connolly and Pearse – minds that helped to shape the identity of the energing Irish Nation – all began as editors of journals. (A sad reminder also of the present uninfluential role of journals in Ireland).

Let us take a closer look at the significance of some of these journals which emerged during what might be termed the Golden Age of Irish cultural debate.

Griffith's *United Irishman* flourished during the latter part of the nineteenth century. One of its major objectives was the ending of colonial landlordism and the attainment of land for the people in a new Young Ireland. Much of *Sinn Féin's* ideological programme was thrashed out in these columns. As F.S.L. Lyons remarked in *Ireland since the Famine: 'The United Irishman* was to become for Griffith's contemporaries as potent a force as *The Nation* had become for the contemporaries of Thomas Davis.'[7] Griffith opened his columns to wideranging discussion on various types of new organisation which might link together 'the scattered literary and political societies and produce a practical programme for the future'.[8] His principal hope for the journal was to develop what he called a 'disciplining of the mind', which he saw as a prerequisite to the practical political transformation of the nation. With *The United Irishman*, and later with its political offshoot, *Cumann na nGaedheal,* Griffith endeavoured to advance the struggle for Irish independence by 'cultivating a fraternal spirit among Irishmen' – in other words, by cultivating a new sense of community.

Another journal which contributed from a different angle to the promotion of a national community was Pearse's *An Claidheamh Soluis.* This journal drew from a variety of talented Gaelic scholars, both Catholic and Protestant, who saw it as essential to incorporate Ireland's Gaelic heritage in the shaping of a post-colonial Irish society. Responding to Douglas Hyde's plea for a de-anglicization of Ireland which might liberate the nation from colonial servility, *An Claidheamh Soluis* included a number of spirited contributions from Eoin MacNeill, The O'Rahilly and, of course, Pearse himself:

all central figures in the founding of the Irish Republican Brother-hood. It was, moreover, MacNeill's essay 'The North Began', published in November 1913, which placed this journal at the hub of intellectual debate in the country and, as F.S.L. Lyons remarked, opened 'a whole new chapter of Irish history'. MacNeill appealed for an internal Irish settlement. 'It is evident,' he wrote, 'that the only solution now possible is for the Empire to make terms with Ireland or let Ireland go her own way. In any case, it is manifest that all Irish people, Unionist as well as Nationalist, are determined to have their own way in Ireland.'

An Claidheamh Soluis was founded with a view to intellectually furthering this ideal of national self-determination. Though unashamedly nationalist in its convictions, this journal, like the best of its kind in the early years of this century, advocated a generous and inclusive nationalism. 'We never meant to be gaelic leaguers and nothing more than gaelic leaguers,' wrote Pearse. Indeed, it makes for chastening reading even today to see how Pearse used his journal as a platform to advance the idea of a non-sectarian National University system with Trinity as one of its central pivots (an idea which was strenuously opposed by both a Protestant 'Save Trinity' campaign and a Catholic 'Save the Catholic Universities' campaign). In this respect, Pearse parted company with an editor like D.P. Moran, whose journal *The Leader* (1900) advocated a xenophobic programme of sectarian nationalism and whose racialist motto ran as follows: 'The foundation of Ireland is the Gael and the Gael must be the element that absorbs.' It was Moran's editorials which furnished much of the ideological ammunition for that move-ment of cultural protectionism which joined forces with equally bigoted journals like the *Irish Rosary* and *The Catholic Bulletin* to champion the censorship laws of the twenties and thirties. One of the most notorious results of this was the establishment of the Commission on Evil Literature in 1926 which berated many of Ireland's finest writers for encouraging pagan, alien and un-Irish philosophies. One realises just how grievous a loss to Ireland was Pearse and his journal when one considers the way in which his originally high-minded equation of a nation 'gaelic and free' was travestied by D.P. Moran and his blinkered, racist colleagues.

A third important cultural-political journal to contribute to the formative debate on the Irish National question was James Connolly's *The Workers Republic*. This journal argued, in an unpre-cedented manner, for a reconciliation of the aims of international socialism and national independence, a combination which Connolly believed to be an effective response to the particularity of the Irish situation. 'The struggle for Irish freedom has two aspects', wrote Connolly, 'it is national and social. The national ideal can never be realised until Ireland stands forth before the world as a nation, free and independent. It is social and economic because no matter what the form of government may be, as long as one class owns as private property the land and instrument of labour from which mankind derive their subsistence, that class will always have it in their power to enslave the remainder of their fellow creatures'. Connolly's journal, like Pearse's and Griffith's, also had its attendant political expression: the Citizen Army and trade union movements. These were journals which managed to keep their heads above the clouds *and* their feet firmly planted on the ground.

A fourth influential journal which assisted greatly in the provision of innovative debate on the national question was George Russell's *Irish Statesman*.[9] Russell's journal – which he began editing in 1923 at the request of Horace Plunkett – has been described by Terence Brown in *Ireland: A Social and Cultural History,* as 'one of the most remarkable cultural organs modern Ireland has known – humane, politically engaged and broadly literate'. This journal was nationalist in yet another sense, what might be termed Anglo-Irish nationalist. Russell waged a vigorous campaign against the Censorship bill and its ideological assumption that the only legitimate definition of Irishness was 'Catholic' and 'Gaelic'. While acknowledging the rich and indispensable resources of the Gaelic, Catholic heritage, *The Irish Statesman* persistently brought home to its readers that the Irish national community was a pluralistic one which also contained a richly deserving Anglo-Irish component. 'The moment we had complete uniformity our national life would be stagnant.' Russell announced, 'We are glad to think that we shall never achieve that uniformity which is the dream of commonplace minds. . . . ' In opposition to D.P. Moran's vision of a single, Gaelic hegemony, Russell sponsored a doctrine of national synthesis in which each cultural and ethnic group would have its legitimate place. 'We wish', he wrote, 'the Irish mind to develop to the utmost of which it is capable and we have always believed that the people now inhabiting Ireland, a new race, made up of Gael, Dane, Norman and Saxon, has infinitely greater intellectual possibilities in it than the old race which existed before the stranger came. The union of races has brought a more complex mentality. We can no more get rid of these new elements in our blood than we can get rid of the Gaelic blood'. Foregrounding the significant achievements of the Anglo-Irish literary revival, Russell concluded that Ireland had not only 'the unique Gaelic tradition, but has given birth, if it accepts all its children, to many men who have influenced European culture and science, Berkeley, Swift, Goldsmith, Burke, Sheridan, Moore, Hamilton, Kelvin, Tyndall, Shaw, Yeats, Synge and many others. If we repudiate the Anglo-Irish tradition, if we say these are aliens, how poor does our life become'[10].

The Irish Statesman – like its companion journal, *The Irish Homestead*, which Russell also edited for a time – was determined to keep Ireland free from self-righteous nationalism by keeping it open to cultural diversity at home and abroad. Hence one finds in these pages articles on Irish culture and politics juxtaposed with studies comparing these national concerns with those of other European nations confronting the challenge of modernity. Writing in 1923 on the question of National Culture, Russell stated his own position accordingly: 'We say we cannot merely out of Irish traditions find solutions to all our modern problems. . . . We shall find much inspiration and beauty in our own past but we have to ransack world literature, world history, world science and study our national contemporaries and graft what we learn into our own national tradition, if we are not to fade out of the list of civilised nations.'[11] It is significant that Russell's resolve to conflate the Gaelic and Anglo-Irish traditions with international ideas from abroad led not only to a theory of pluralist culture, but also to a decentralised cooperative movement which he set up with Horace Plunkett.

Thus we see how some of Ireland's most formative cultural journals served to inaugurate critical discussion on four of the central ideological standpoints which conjoined in the early decades of this century to found the national philosophy of modern Ireland: 1) progressive nationalism *(The United Irishman)*; 2) Gaelic revivalism *(An Claideamh Soluis)*; 3) socialist republicanism *(Workers Republic)*; 4) Anglo-Irish liberalism *(The Irish Statesman)*.

III: The Bell

Before concluding I would like to refer to one other publication which merits inclusion in the golden age of Irish cultural journals which lasted approximately from 1850 to 1950 – *The Bell*. This magazine was founded in 1940 by Sean O'Faolain and Peadar O'Donnell, two intellectuals actively engaged in the political struggle for Irish Independence as well as being amongst the most talented creative writers of their generation. *The Bell*, like the best of its predecessors, succeeded in combining an urgent commitment to social questions with a keen concern for literary excellence. It lasted for fourteen years, appearing monthly (with certain lapses) until 1954.

Unlike so many of its contemporaries in Britain, such as *Scrutiny* or *Penguin New Writing*, *The Bell* refused to be an exclusively literary review. It included many fascinating sociological studies on the transitional crises of Irish society in the forties and early fifties. Like *The Irish Statesman* before it, *The Bell* argued that Ireland was not some homogeneous cultural unit but a complex teeming synthesis of differing views and life styles. On the question of language, for example, O'Faolain spoke of the need to acknowledge that 'the sum of our local history is that long before 1900 we had become part and parcel of the general world-process with a distinct English pigmentation'; and this meant, for the editors of *The Bell*, that 'our object is not unilingualism, but that we should speak, according to our moods and needs, both Gaelic and English'. It also implied that *The Bell* should celebrate the fact that 'Irishmen writing in English have won distinctiveness for an Irish literature which stands apart from, and even challenges, the achievements of contemporary writers elsewhere.'

And so *The Bell* set about providing a reflective exploration of contemporary Irish life which would illustrate its national and cultural diversity. In 1941, for instance, the editors organised a symposium on Irish culture in which the Gaelic, classical, Norman and Anglo-Irish traditions were represented by a wide variety of contributors. Indeed this project of pluralistic, non-sectarian debate, inviting Irish readers of different traditions to participate in the creation of a new cultural community, is powerfully evidenced in O'Faolain's first editorial entitled *This is Your Magazine*. It is worth quoting this editorial in some detail.

'*The Bell*', writes O'Faolain, 'has, in the usual sense of the word, no policy. . . . This magazine will grow into character and meaning. By the time you have read three issues you will be familiar with its character. . . . That would not happen with every magazine, but this is not so much a magazine as a bit of life itself, and we believe in life, and leave life to shape us after her own image and likeness.' It is no longer necessary for a journal to invoke the old shibboleths of ancient Gaeldom or Anglo-Irish Ascendancy, O'Faolain affirms, for such symbols belong to the time when, as he puts it, 'we growled in defeat and dreamt of the future.' All our symbols, O'Faolain goes on, 'have to be created afresh and the only way to create a living symbol is to take a naked thing and clothe it with new life, new association, new meaning, with all the vigour in the life we live in the Here and Now. We refused to use the word Irish, or Ireland, in the title. We said, "It will plainly be that by being alive". Our only job was to encourage life to speak. When she speaks, then *The Bell* will itself become a symbol, and its "policy" will be self-evident.' Addressing the reader directly, O'Faolain then declares: 'You possess a precious store of (Life). If you will share it with all of us you will make this bell peal out a living message. *The Bell* will ring a note this way and a note that way. The wind will move it and a faint sigh come from the top of the tower. Some traveller will finger the rope and send out his cry. Some man who knows how to ring a proper peal will make the clapper shout. People will hear these chance notes to the north and people will hear them to the south . . . a linking, widening circle of notes, a very peal of bells, murmuring over the land.' This journal, concludes its editors, will aim to create a genuinely participatory community of minds by making the collective order of practical facts answerable to the 'individual veracity' of imagination and vice versa: '*The Bell* is quite clear about certain practical things and will, from time to time, deal with them – the language, partition, education and so forth . . . we are living experimentally. Day after day we are all groping for reality, and many of our adventures must be a record of error and defeat. . . . In recording them all, the defeats and the victories, the squalors and the enchantment, how can we have any "policy" other than to stir ourselves to a vivid awareness of what we are doing, what we are becoming, what we are? That is why this is your magazine.'

We quote these passages from *The Bell's* first editorial at such length because they succinctly convey the preoccupations of this pioneering journal. Now that Ireland had reached its long-fought-for national Independence, the editors felt it possible to open Irish minds to life as it was lived in the present, that is, unencumbered by nostalgic abstractions from the past or millenial abstractions about the future. Ireland had come of age. The moment for critical stock-taking had arrived. Thus O'Faolain's Nietzschean appeal to life with a capital L and democratic appeal to the reader, with a capital R, presupposes the possibility of a communal consensus which could reconcile the diverse elements, native and non-native, that make up contemporary Irish life. Terence Brown supplies an apposite assessment of *The Bell's* contribution in this regard: 'O'Faolain and his contributors' through attending in an empirical, investigative manner to Irish realities opened windows in *The Bell* to show how much Irish life was not some absolute state of national being but an expression of man's life in a particular place, bound up with European history, geography, economics and social forces of all kinds. *The Bell* was therefore a vital organ of empirical, humanistic self-consciousness at a moment when the new state was entering on a period of profound challenge. As such it probably helped to make more generally available ideals of rational reflection and social analysis without which the country could not have responded to the post-war crisis as capably as it did. . . . Perhaps *The Bell* helped to prepare the ground in the wider community for a period when social analysis was to become a crucial partner in a process of modernization with economic development.'[12]

Brown's verdict is undoubtedly just; but it only takes account of half of the evidence – the positive half. It is true that *The Bell* was one of Ireland's most successful and influential journals, being able to boast, in its heyday, of a print-run of 3,000 copies. It is also true that it secured the collaboration of some of Ireland's finest literary and critical minds – amongst them John Hewitt, Patrick Kavanagh, Brendan Behan, Denis Johnston, Anthony Cronin, Louis MacNiece, Austin Clarke and many more. But it is equally true that *The Bell* was to be the last journal of its kind for a considerable time to come. This sense of an ending was recognised by O'Faolain himself in his

ultimate 'signing-off' editorial. It is instructive to contrast the almost
prophetic optimism of *The Bell's* first editorial with the pessimism of
its final one. In this valedictory address, O'Faolain sounds a note of
rueful disaffection in sharp contrast with his earlier messianism: 'I
have, I confess, grown a little weary of abusing our bourgeoisie,
Little Irelanders, chauvinists, puritans, stuffed-shirts, pietists,
Tartuffes, Anglophobes, Celtophiles . . . I am surprised to find
myself suddenly grown detached and impersonal about them . . . and
when all is said and done, what I am left with is a certain amount of
regret that we were born into this thorny time when our task has been
less that of cultivating our garden than of clearing away the
brambles.'

Thus we observe that the positive organic metaphor of Life,
fructifying and expanding in all sorts of creative directions (which
informed the first editorial), has been replaced here by the negative
organic metaphor of a rank and overgrown garden. Cultivating
exotic gardens was, it seems, the leisured luxury of the vanishing
Ascendancy class; the intellectuals of the New Ireland had been
condemned to the more menial chore of distributing the weed-killer.
The transition from the excited innocence of *The Bell's* initial
project to the sobering experience of reality is symptomatic of the
editors' general disillusionment.

Similarly we find that the salvific connotations of the metaphor of
the bell itself – e.g. annunication, liberation, resurrection, revelation
and so on – have ultimately fallen on unheeding ears. After eleven
volumes O'Faolain looks back disenchantedly at his earlier boast
that Life would create new symbols of consensus by creating in and
through *The Bell* a new community. Far from congratulating himself
on the establishment of a new community – as Davis, Griffith, or
Pearse might have done – O'Faolain bemoans the fact that he, and
by implication, the writers and readers of *The Bell,* are still as
isolated as ever. He refers to himself with humorous self-mockery as
an old campanologist, a lonely unheeded bell-ringer having more in
common with Yeats's sixty-year-old smiling public man than the
Nietzschean Yea-Sayer of a life-enhancing culture. Life with a
capital L had, it appeared, become as vacuous an abstraction as
those hackneyed symbols of ancient Ireland – Roisín Dubh and
Caithlín Ní Houlihán etc. – whose propensity to 'growl in defeat'
and 'dream of a future' he had so sanguinely repudiated in his
opening editorial. Now it is O'Faolain's turn to growl in defeat and
dream of a future. We have seen, in the passage cited above, how he
growled about thorns and brambles; his futuristic dreaming,
however, is equally telling. O'Faolain conjures up some glimmer of
hope by driving a wedge between politics and literature. If *The Bell*
failed it had failed, notes O'Faolain, because 'politics and social
problems had intruded' onto its pages; and so O'Faolain imagines a
future time when it may be that 'poetic truth, which lives remote

from the battle, is more to be sought for than political truth.' Forsaking the earlier claim of communal consensus, he now has recourse to the individualist model of the romantic solitary nursing his genius far from the madding crowd: 'It may be, and one hopes so, that somewhere, some young poet, scornful of us and our controversies, has been tending in his secret heart a lamp which will, in the end, light far more than we can ever do. . . . It is one thing to have a noble vision of life to come and another to have to handle what does come.'

In other words, O'Faolain is subordinating the quest for communal debate to the quest of each individual artist – 'the heart's search for the heart', as he puts it, 'that he may sooner or later come to himself'. He affirms the existence of an insurmountable gulf separating the public realm of political commitment and the private sanctuary of aesthetic purity. Denouncing present politicians and 'our censorious people' as tiresome 'haters of life', O'Faolain vows to hand over the intellectual reins to those apolitical artists who will 'purify the source of art i.e. themselves.'

O'Faolain's acceptance of the impossibility of creating, or at least continuing, a non-sectarian cultural journal which might conscript the dual vehicles of political and literary debate into the service of a new communal identity was, doubtless, a response in large part to the Ireland of his time. Settled into a comfortable partitionist view of itself, the recently established Republic seemed disinclined to foster new debates about new identities. Things were fine as they were and anything threatening this sense of collective self-security should be ignored or allowed to suffer a slow death. 'The establishment of an efficient police force, an experienced civil service and an impartial judiciary,' as John A. Murphy remarked, 'though admirable in themselves, could hardly be hailed as the building of a new Jerusalem.' Even de Valera conceded after the election campaign of 1951: 'If I cannot say that there is a concrete plan for bringing in the six counties, then I am sure nobody else can either.'[13] The New Ireland seemed to want politicians to be politicians and artists to be artists; let politics do its pragmatic job without being lead astray by fancy visions; and let poets and painters for their part look after their own reveries to their heart's content and paint harmless self-portraits to hang in the newly constructed National Banks, Civil Service Departments and Life Assurance Companies.

This attitude was partitionist in at least two important respects. It was geographically partitionist in that it accepted the inevitability of partition as a solution to the problem of accommodating the troublesome half of the nation north of the border. But it was also partitionist in another and perhaps not unrelated sense: an intellectual sense based on the premise that the socio-political debate dealing with reality and the literary debate dealing with imaginative vision, should be kept rigidly apart.

IV: Conclusion

The consequence of this partitionism for the future of cultural journals in Ireland was quite negative. Many journals of course survived the demise of *The Bell*; but their survival was almost invariably secured by assuming either an exclusively literary identity or an exclusively sociopolitical or religious one. This is not to minimize the excellence of these journals within their specific competency; it is simply a matter of acknowledging that they increasingly tended towards specialisation. Even journals like *Studies, Doctrine and Life* or *The Furrow* inclined after the fifties almost entirely towards religious and social questions. And the sixties and seventies witnessed a new wave of high-powered, secular and socially committed magazines such as *Hibernia, Nusight, Magill, In Dublin* and so on. On the other hand, the realm of literary debate was also left to specialised journals. These divided into two distinct categories: 1) literary journals dealing primarily with poetry and 'creative' writing – *Poetry Ireland, Envoy, Irish Writing, The Honest Ulsterman, Innti, Quarterly of Ulster Poetry, Feasta, Kavanaghs Weekly, The Kilkenny Magazine, Era, Cyphers, Comhair* etc; 2) literary journals of a more critical academic nature aimed mainly at universities and libraries – *The Irish University Review, Atlantis, Threshold, Aquarius, Irish Studies* and so on.

All of these literary journals, and others besides, served the purpose of affording new generations of Irish creative writers a forum for publication and critical discussion. They also shared a common desire to eschew socio-political debate in order to concentrate on their trade of well-made fictions, to purify, as O'Faolain recommended, 'the source of art'. This apolitical commitment to the private graph of artistic sensibility, echoing the policy of the literary journals of the preceding century, is aptly conveyed in a Foreword to a 1950 issue of *Envoy* which stated that 'the younger poets' no longer need to busy themselves with national questions because they can 'take their nationality for granted'. A similar view is advanced by Robert Greacen in the journal, *Irish Writing* (No. 3, Nov. 1947), apropos of the new generation of Irish intellectuals: 'If they set store on any one quality it is on personal integrity. . . The new Irish writers seek neither to deny nor accept Harp or Sickle or Hammer . . .'

The founding of *The Crane Bag* in 1977 was an *attempt* to counter this drift towards the polarization of intellectual journals into the exclusively literary and the exclusively political. In the following passage from the first editorial, our aims were clearly expressed:

> In this journal we would hope that the creativity of art and the commitment of politics might converge to challenge the assumption that

the aesthetic and political are two mutually exclusive areas: the first a matter of the yearly visit to the gallery or concert; the second an item of daily news, but essentially other people's business. Our world is an imposition, pleasant or unpleasant as the case may be. . . . We do have a choice, however, about the way we respond to this received world. Our way can be critical or uncritical. The latter says there is nothing I can do; there are politicians to run the country for me, as there are mechanics to look after my car; I am the *protegé* of a caretaker society; if there is meaning to it all, it was there before I arrived; if there is not, then I can do nothing about it. The critical way, by contrast, challenges this acquiescence. It recognises that even if history is irretrievably past, its meaning is still in the process of becoming. It holds things at a certain distance and suspends the paralysing immediacy of facts by examining their roots and their reason for being there in the first place. Such critical freedom is what Socrates called irony: a blend of comic detachment and committed concern. Could a crane bag be for Ireland what the Socratic gad-fly was for Greece?[14]

The Crane Bag had its moments of frustration and of celebration; it produced eighteen issues between 1977 and 1986, some of which generated lively debate and others which sank like millstones into mute oblivion. I do not propose to rehearse the various fortunes of this journal, but simply to put on record this plea: We need more cultural journals in Ireland today, for without a renaissance of the kind of intellectual questioning which flourished in Ireland between 1850 and 1950, our culture will stagnate – either by uncritical reversion to tribal platitudes or by an equally uncritical immersion in the anonymous tide of modern consumerism. To juggle with the words of Pearse: cultural journals can be cleansing things and a nation which regards them as the final irrelevance has lost its sense of nationhood.

APPENDIX: A NOTE ON THE JOURNAL GENRE

The journal is neither a book nor a newspaper. This may seem all too obvious for us today. But it is interesting to recall the historical genesis of the modern journal and the way in which it came to distinguish itself as a unique genre of publication.

If we look at the etymology of the term (Old French, *diurnal*, meaning daily) – we are reminded that the journal was originally conceived as a daily record of events and impressions. In the post-Renaissance era, this conception of the daily record gave rise to two distinct kinds of journal: the *journal intime* dealing with the realm of subjective feelings and reflections; and the *journal populaire* (or *le journalisme*) dealing with the realm of objective facts.

The *journal intime* or private diary involved a highly individualised account of events and was generally registered in the first person singular. Its emergence as a common practice, particularly amongst the leisured classes, seems to have coincided with the birth of the modern era of subjectivity. This modern emphasis on subjective experience, epitomised by the *journal intime*, was a response to a combination of several different but related historical circumstances: 1) the Renaissance discovery of humanism with its central notions of personality, creativity and authorship; 2) the Cartesian and Enlightenment philosophy of the *cogito* which taught that truth begins with the subjective act of the individual knower; 3) the Reformational and Romantic insistence upon a private spiritual relationship with the transcendent; 4) the emergence of a liberal 'soul-searching' bourgeoisie with the French Revolution on the Continent and the puritan and industrial revolutions in Great Britain. All of these historical and cultural movements conspired to provide conditions favourable to the conviction that the *individual* recording of events was a meaningful practice, indeed a necessary one, for the cultivation of value in a modern world of rapidly changing circumstances.

In time the *journal intime* took a public turn; it assumed the 'published' form of a book wherein the records of one's individual feelings and fantasies were offered the possibility of communicating with other individuals in printed volumes. Thus arose the modern notion of the autonomous author addressing his/her autonomous reader in the privacy of the boudoir or garden. The most direct literary offspring of the *journal intime* was the confessional novel where the author enjoined the reader to suspend the everyday world of facts and indulge in the fiction of a *tête-à-tête* communication. In this manner, the *journal intime* progressed from a spiritual monologue to a literary complicity of shared solitude. As Walter Benjamin observes in his celebrated essay on Leskov, the birth of the novel coincided with a cultural crisis resulting from the demise of traditional beliefs. Whereas the earlier epic genres of myth, legend and oral story-telling traded on such communally shared notions as universal wisdom, truth, counsel, remembrance, tradition and authority, the novel, by contrast, was a response to the crisis of culture engendered by the very loss of such notions. 'The novelist', writes Benjamin, 'has isolated himself. The birthplace of the novel is the solitary individual, who is no longer able to express himself by giving (universal) examples of his most important concerns, is himself uncounselled, and cannot counsel others . . . the legitimacy it provides stands in direct opposition to reality (as a universally shared experience).'[15] Before the novel, literature believed in the 'moral of the story'. The novel dispensed with such universal wisdom. It represented an individual search for the 'meaning of life' no longer deemed available in the resources of a communal tradition.

But the *journal intime*, with its attendant literary form, the novel, was not the only response to the cultural transitions of the post-Renaissance era. If the Enlightenment ushered in a cult of subjective sentiment, it also recognized a quite different order of experience worthy of published record: the realm of objective fact. This attention to the objective world of empirical observation gave rise to another kind of journal: the newspaper. The newspaper sponsored a different kind of writing known today as journalism. This kind of writing did not, originally at least, take its identity from individual authors. Indeed most of the articles or news reports were anonymously recorded, the idea of personalised authorship being suspect as an indication of bias or distortion. The journalistic reporting of facts required one to describe events 'objectively' and 'neutrally'. Newspapers were generally identified not by the signature of their editors or authors, but by their geographical origin – e.g. *The London Times, The Washington Post, The Skibbereen Eagle* and so on. Furthermore, the journalistic mode of communication was not that of intimate confession (as in the *journal intime*) but that of verifiable information. 'Information', writes Benjamin, 'lays claim to prompt verifiability. The prime requirement is that it appears "understandable in itself". Often it is no more exact than the intelligence of earlier centuries was. But while the latter was inclined to borrow from the *miraculous*, it is indispensable for information to sound *plausible*.'[16]

Now, alongside these two genres of the *journal intime* and the 'journalist' newspaper, emerged a third genre – the journal as review or magazine. When we speak of a journal today we usually intend it in this third sense. The journal-magazine was, as the root arabic word *makhazan* suggests, a storehouse which records both factual and fictional experience, and which combines the resources of subjectivity (as cultivated by the *journal intime*) and objectivity (as invoked by newspaper journalism). The magazine-journal featured a miscellany of essays which carried their author's names, but whose very diversity implied that no single personal vision was being privileged. In other words, the magazine-journal would try to respond to the objective world of facts while retaining something of the imaginative richness of subjective interpretation. The publication time-span of the magazine-journal was also significant in this regard. While newspapers appeared daily and dealt with topical matters and while novels were almost 'timeless' by virtue of the unconditioned freedoms enjoyed by the artist, magazines appeared on a 'periodical' basis, that is, at regular intervals of a week, a month, every three months, every year etc. Unlike the daily intervals of newspapers, these more prolonged intervals were intended to allow the authors and the readers of the magazine articles to reflect in a measured and critical fashion upon the events recorded. The purpose was not just to view but to re-view. In other words, the magazine-journal obeyed the laws of temporal regularity and periodicity while remaining sufficiently distanced from everyday events to foster considered debate. Its aim was to invite the reader to participate in the multiple interpretations of events represented by the different essays. Indeed the very term 'essay' is perhaps significant here, for it acknowledges that the various contributions printed in a single issue of a journal are no more than a variety of *attempts* (French, *essais*) to reach a consensus. The essays of a magazine are parts in search of a whole, diverse perspectives which require the reflective response of the reader if they are to achieve any sort of overall synthesis. There is no beginning, middle or end – as in a novel. The essays represent a series of beginnings whose end is the reader. The purpose of the magazine is, therefore, *dialogue*, and by extension, *community*. This is why it seems fair to say that the possibility of a journal always excedes its actuality; it is of its nature to promise more than it can deliver.

In short, one might conclude by saying that if the artistic genre of the *journal intime* operated in terms of *individuality*, and if the journalistic form of the newspaper assumed the status of a *collectivity*, the magazine strove towards the provision of a sense of *community*; it served as a mediating link between the idioms of individualism and collectivism. This implied in turn the creation of a specific kind of writing and reading different from those solicited by artistic or journalistic literature. It is perhaps for this reason that certain social and cultural historians desiring to take the pulse of a particular period of modern history, focus on the key debates and discussions featured in magazine-journals. (A good case in point is Terence Brown's *Ireland: A Social and Cultural History (1922–1979)* which draws its material more frequently from *The Bell*, *Envoy*, *Kavanaghs Weekly*, *Studies*, *Doctrine and Life* and others, than from novels or newspapers).

14
CONCLUSION: MYTH AND THE CRITIQUE OF IDEOLOGY

'One must preserve the tension between tradition and utopia. The problem is to reanimate tradition and bring utopia closer.'

(Paul Ricoeur).

A major question arising from our studies of the transitional tension between tradition and modernity is that of the role of *myth*. The modernist break with the rhetoric of revivalism usually took the form of a *demythologizing* project. While this project provides a corrective to the conservative apotheosis of tradition – it can also be pushed to extremes. Careful discrimination is necessary.

In the field of contemporary aesthetic theory, the 'textual revolution' has occasionally yielded excessive versions of formalism, subjectivism and even nihilism. And in the human sciences, the impulse to deconstruct tradition at all costs and in every context, has been known to result in precipitate celebrations of the 'disappearance of man'[1]. In the process history itself, as the life-world of social interaction between human agents, is often eclipsed. Reduced to a 'prison house of language' (i.e. to an endless intertextual play of signifiers), the very concept of history is drained of human content and social commitment. It is deprived of its memory. It falls casualty to the amnesia of the absolute text.

In the sphere of politics, the project of demythologization has also led, at times, to a full-scale declaration of war against the past. Marx anticipated such a move in *The Eighteenth Brumaire* when he distinguished between the revolution which draws its inspiration from the past, 'calling up the dead upon the universal stage of history', and the revolution which creates itself 'out of the future', discarding the 'ancient superstitions' of tradition and letting the 'dead bury the dead in order to discover its own meaning'.[2] And Roland Barthes, in *Mythologies*, pushes the latter model even further when he canvasses the view that the political critique of myth must be motivated by 'acts of destruction'. The genuine demythologizer, he says, is one who knows not what he is for but what he is *against*. For him, 'tomorrow's positivity is entirely hidden by today's negativity'[3].

The danger of demythologizing occurs when it is pressed into the service of a self-perpetuating iconoclasm which, if left unchecked, liquidates the notion of the past altogether. Modern consciousness may thus find itself liberated into a no-man's-land of interminable self-reflexion without purpose or direction. It is not enough to free a society *from* the 'false consciousness' of tradition; one must also liberate it *for* something. And this raises the question of *myth* as a potentially positive and emancipatory project. By myth we mean a collective act of symbolic narration: a story which, in Liam De Paor's felicitous phrase, a society tells itself about itself in order to describe itself to itself – and to others[4].

The attempt to erase historical remembrance altogether results, all too easily, in a new kind of enslavement (i.e. to the blind immediacies of the present, or to abstract dreams of the future). It is a mistake to schismatically oppose the utopian impulses of modernity to the recollective impulses of tradition. For every culture invents its future by reinventing its past. And here we might usefully contrast Nietzsche's 'active forgetting' of history with Benjamin's more subtle notion of 'revolutionary nostalgia' – an active remembering which reinterprets the suppressed voices of tradition in a critical relation to modernity[5]. This latter notion entails the development of an *anticipatory memory* capable of projecting future images of liberation drawn from the past. The rediscovery of the subterranean history of the past as a 'presage of possible truth' may thus disclose critical standards tabooed in the present. And in this event, recollecting the discarded projects of tradition triggers a liberating return of the repressed. The *recherche du temps perdu* becomes the vehicle of future emancipation[6]. Herbert Marcuse spells out some of the radical implications of this *anticipatory memory* as follows:

Utopia in great art is never the simple negation of the reality principle (of history) but its transcending preservation in which past and present cast their shadow on fulfillment. The authentic utopia is grounded in recollection. 'All reification is forgetting'.... Forgetting past suffering and past joy alleviates life under a repressive reality principle. In contrast, remembrance spurs the drive for the conquest of suffering and the permanence of joy ... The horizon of history is still open. If the remembrance of things past would become a motive power in the struggle for changing the world, the struggle would be waged for a revolution hitherto supressed in the previous historical revolutions[7].

I

How does this relate to the dialectic of tradition and modernity which our studies have been exploring in the context of Irish culture?

In a recent commemorative address for Thomas Ashe (the 1916 patriot who died on hunger strike a year after the Easter rebellion), Sean MacBride accused 'many of our so-called intellectuals' of devaluing the 'concepts of Irish nationality and even the principles upon which Christianity is founded'. MacBride deplored the absence of idealism and the erosion of moral standards which were causing young people in Ireland today to despair and be cynical. Our national pride, he observed, was being corroded by the emergence of an insidious double-talk and the resurgence of the slave mentality which existed prior to 1916. 'It seems to me,' MacBride concluded, 'as if we are at a crossroads at which the choice has to be made between idealism and possibly sacrifice *or* betrayal and an abandonment of our national traditions and goals.'[8]

MacBride is quite justified in counselling intellectuals to respect the positive heritage of their tradition. He is also no doubt correct in warning against the fashionable tendency to dismiss summarily the very concepts of nationality, religion and cultural identity as so many outworn ideologies. (Indeed as the neo-Marxist critic, Frederic Jameson, remarked, 'a Left which cannot grasp the immense Utopian appeal of nationalism, any more than it can that of religion . . . must effectively doom itself to political impotence')[9]. MacBride is labouring under a misapprehension, however, if he rebukes intellectual attempts to question or reinterpret tradition as thinly-veiled forms of perfidy. Tradition can only be handed over (*tradere*) from one historical generation to the next by means of an ongoing process of innovative translation. And if tradition inevitably entails translation, it equally entails transition. The idea that there exists some immutable 'essence' of national identity, timelessly preserved and impervious to critical interrogation, is a nonsense. Tradition can only be transmitted by means of multiple translations, each one of which involves both critical discrimination and creative reinvention.

Gone are the days, fortunately, when intellectuals were expected to serve the nation by parroting simplistic formulae such as 'Up the Republic' and 'Keep the Faith' – or, north of the border, 'No Surrender' and 'No Pope Here'. Gone also, one would hope, are the days when Irish intellectuals could be branded by a government Minister as 'pinko liberals and Trinity queers', or have their works banned because they raised questions which were better not discussed (a sorry phenomenon which prompted one commentator to cite 'anti-intellectualism' among the seven pillars of Irish political culture)[10]. Irish intellectuals have been accused of almost everything, 'from elitism to indifference and from subversion to being drunk and refusing to fight. . . . Frequently these charges were trumped up because people in general, and their leaders in particular, did not take kindly to the idea of arguing with awkward customers about issues which, in the interests of peaceful existence, ought to be left alone. For the politicians and the Churches, such people were particularly troublesome . . . and the label "intellectual" was tied to their names to show that they were at best boring and at worst dangerous.'[11]

The need to perpetually re-evaluate one's cultural heritage raises, once again, the central question of *narrative*. Narrative – understood as the universal human desire to make sense of history by retelling the story of ourselves – relates to tradition in two ways. By creatively reinterpreting the past, narrative can serve to release new, and hitherto concealed, possibilities of understanding one's history; and by critically scrutinizing the past it can wrest tradition away from the conformism that is always threatening to overpower it[12]. To properly attend to this dual capacity of narrative is, therefore, to resist the polarized alternative between the eternal verities of tradition, on the one hand, and the exercise of critical imagination, on the other. Every narrative interpretation, whether it involves a literary or political reading of history, 'takes place within the context of some traditional mode of thought, transcending through criticism and invention the limitations of what had hitherto been reasoned in that tradition . . . Traditions when vital embody continuities of conflict.'[13] This implies that the contemporary act of rereading (i.e. retelling) tradition can actually disclose uncompleted narratives which open up new possibilities of understanding. No text exists in isolation from its social and historical contexts. And tradition itself is not some sealed monument, as the revivalist orthodoxy would have us believe; it is a narrative construct requiring an open-ended process of reinterpretation. To examine one's culture, consequently, is also to examine one's conscience – in the sense of critically discriminating between rival interpretations. And this is a far cry from the agonising inquest conducted by revivalists into the supposedly 'unique essence' of national identity. Seamus Deane is right, I believe, when he pleads for the abandonment of the idea of essence – 'that hungry Hegelian ghost looking for a stereotype to live in' – since our national heritage, be it literary or political, is something which has always to be rewritten. Only such a realisation can enable a new writing and a new politics, 'unblemished by Irishness, but securely Irish'.[14]

II

What is the philosophical context of the demythologizing project which so powerfully informs modern thinking? Most contemporary critics of myth have focused on its *ideological* role as a mystifying consciousness. Their approach has been termed a 'hermeneutics of suspicion' in that it negatively interprets (Gr. *hermeneuein*) myth as a masked discourse which conceals a *real* meaning behind an *imaginary* one[15].

The modern project of unmasking myth frequently takes its cue from the investigative methods developed by Marx, Nietzsche and Freud – the 'three masters of suspicion' as Ricoeur calls them. Nietzsche advanced a genealogical hermeneutic which aimed to trace myths back to an underlying will to power (or in the case of the Platonic and Christian myths of otherworldly transcendence, to a negation of this will to power). Freud developed a psychoanalytic hermeneutic which saw myths as ways of disguising unconscious desires. Thus in *Totem and Taboo*, for example, Freud identified the origin of myth as a primitive form of compensation for prohibited experience. As such, religious myths were said to represent a sort of collective 'obsessional neurosis' – a concealment of libidinal drives – through mechanisms of inhibition and sublimation. And thirdly, there was Marx who proposed a dialectical hermeneutic of 'false consciousness' aimed at exposing the hidden connection between ideological myths (superstructures) and the underlying realities of class domination exemplified in the struggle for the ownership of the means of production (infrastructures). Thus for Marx, the myth of an ideal transcendental fulfilment – whether it is formulated by religion, art or philosophy – is in fact an ideological masking of socio-economic exploitation.

Marx shares with Nietzsche and Freud the suspicion that myth conceals itself as an imaginary projection of false values. It is 'myth' precisely in the sense of illusion: that is, a deceptive inversion of the true priority of the real over the imaginary, of the historical over the eternal. Hence the need for a negative hermeneutics of unmasking. The critique of myth is described accordingly as 'the categorical refusal of all relations where man finds himself degraded, imprisoned or abandoned.'[16] And in this respect, Marx's denunciation of the mythico-religious character of the money fetish in the first book of *Capital* constitutes one of the central planks of his critique of ideology. Moreover, it is this equation of myth with the fetishization of false consciousness which animates Roland Barthes' famous structuralist critique of bourgeois 'mythologies' (where he argues that myth is an ideological strategy for reducing the social processes of History to timeless commodities of Nature)[17].*

*The negative hermeneutics of myth was by no means confined to the atheistic masters of suspicion. Many religious thinkers in the twentieth century have also endorsed the demythologising project. Indeed the very term 'demythologisation' has been frequently identified with the theological writings of Rudolph Bultmann. Bultmann held that Christianity must be emancipated from 'mythic' accretions whereby Christ became idolized as the sacrificial *Kyrios* of a saviour cult – a cult modelled on the pagan heroes of Hellenic or Gnostic mystery-rites[18]. Bultmann's

What all these exponents of the hermeneutics of suspicion have in common is a determination to debunk the ideological masking of a true meaning behind a mythologized meaning (See Appendix on 'Ideological Functions of Myth' below). While confirming the necessity for such a demythologizing strategy, we may ask if this critique is not itself subject to critique. So doing, we may recognize perhaps another more liberating dimension of myth – the genuinely *utopian* – behind its negative *ideological* dimension. Supplementing the hermeneutics of suspicion with a hermeneutics of affirmation, we may begin to discern the potentiality of myth for a positive symbolizing project which surpasses its falsifying content.[20]

III

Myth is an ideological function. But it is also *more* than that. Once a hermeneutics of suspicion has unmasked the alienating role of myth as an agency of ideological conformism, there remains the task of a positive interpretation. Hermeneutics thus has a double duty – both to *suspect* and to *listen*. Having demythologized the ideologies of false consciousness, it labours to disclose utopian symbols of a liberating consciousness.

Symbolizations of utopia pertain to the futural horizon of myth. The hermeneutics of affirmation focuses not on the origin(*arche*) behind myths but on the end (*eschaton*) opened up in front of them. It thereby seeks to rescue mythic symbols from the gestures of reactionary domination, to show that once the mystifying function has been exposed, we may discover genuinely utopian anticipations of

demythologizing is levelled against the mystification of authentic Christian spirituality. His critique casts a suspecting glance at all efforts to reduce the genuine scandal of the Cross and Resurrection to an ideological system wherein the newness of the Christian message is ignored or betrayed. Bultmann systematically exposes the manner in which the Living Word of the Gospels often degenerated into cultic myths e.g. the attempt to express the eschatological promise of the Kingdom as a cosmological myth of heaven and hell; or the attempt to reduce the historical working of the Spirit through the Church to a myth of triumphalistic power. To 'demythologize' Christianity is, for Bultmann, to dissolve these false scandals so as to let the true scandal of the word made flesh speak to us anew.

In recent years this work of theistic demythologization has been effectively developed by the French thinker, René Girard. Girard holds that the most radical aim of the Judaeo-Christian Revelation is to expose and overcome the mythic foundation of pagan religions in the ritual sacrifice of an innocent scapegoat. Imaginatively projecting the cause of all disharmony and evil onto some innocent victim, a society contrives to hide from itself the real cause of its *internal* crisis. True Christianity rejects the cultic mythologizing of the scapegoat, deployed by societies as an ideological means of securing consensus. Only by demythologizing this ideological lie of sacrificial victimage, that is, by revealing the true innocence of the scapegoat Christ, can Christianity serve as a genuinely anti-mythic and anti-sacrificial religion.[19]

peace and justice. A positive hermeneutics offers an opportunity to salvage myths from the abuses of doctrinal prejudice, racist nationalism, class oppression or totalitarianism. And it does so in the name of a universal project of freedom – a project from which no creed, nation, class or individual is excluded. The utopian content of myth differs, then, from the ideological in that it is inclusive rather than exclusive; it opens up human consciousness to a common goal of liberation instead of closing it off in the inherited securities of the *status quo*.

Where the hermeneutics of suspicion construed myth as an effacement of some original reality (e.g. will to power, unconscious desire, the material conditions of production or domination), the hermeneutics of affirmation operates on the hypothesis that myth may not only conceal some pre-exisiting meaning but may also reveal new horizons of meaning. Thus instead of interpreting myths solely in terms of a first-order reference to a predetermining cause hidden *behind* myth, it discloses a second-order reference to 'possible worlds' *beyond* myth. It suggests, in other words, that there may be an *ulterior* meaning to myths in addition to their *anterior* meaning – an horizon which looks *forward* as well as an horizon which looks *back*. Myth is not just nostalgia for some forgotten world. It can also constitute 'a disclosure of other possible worlds which transcend the established limits of our actual world.'[21]

This *epistemological* distinction between two different horizons of myth also implies an *ethical* one. Myths are not neutral as romantic ethnology would have us believe. They become authentic or inauthentic according to the 'interests' which they serve. These interests, as Habermas recognized in *Knowledge and Human Interests*, can be those of utopian emancipation or ideological domination. Thus, for example, the religious myths of a Kingdom of Peace may be interpreted either as an opiate of the oppressed (as Marx pointed out) or as an antidote to such oppression (as the theology of liberation reminds us). Similarly, it could be argued that the myths of Irish Republicanism can be used to enhance a community or to incarcerate that community in tribal bigotry. And the same would apply to a critical reading of the Ulster Loyalist mythology of 'civil and religious liberties'. Moreover, our own century has also tragically demonstrated how Roman and Germanic myths – while not in themselves corrupt – have been unscrupulously exploited by Fascist movements.

IV

The *critical* role of hermeneutics is therefore indispensable. But this does not mean that we simply reduce mythic symbols to literal facts. It demands rather that we learn to unravel the concealed intentions of myth so as to distinguish between, on the one hand, their role of ideological 'vindication' (which justifies the *status quo* in a dogmatic or irrational manner) and, on the other, their role of utopian 'exploration' (which challenges the *status quo* by projecting alternative ways of understanding our world). *Demythologizing*, as an urgent task of modern thought, must not be confused here with *demythizing*, which would lead to a reductionist impoverishment of culture[22].

The crisis of modernity is characterized by a separation of myth and reality: a separation which has led to the desacralization of tradition. But precisely because of this we need no longer be subject to the ideological illusion that myth *justifies* reality. We should no longer expect myth to provide a *literal* account of our historical environment. Indeed it is the very demythologisation of myth in this sense which permits the rediscovery of myth as *symbolic* project[23]. Having eliminated the inauthentic function of legitimating how things *are*, we are free to reveal the authentic function of myth as an exploration of how things *might be*. We begin to recognize that the very value of myth resides in its ability to contain *more* meaning than a scientific description which is, objectively speaking, true. This is what Ricoeur calls the *saving of myth* through demythologization. As he points out in our *Dialogues with Contemporary Continental Thinkers*: 'We are no longer primitive beings, living at the immediate level of myth. Myth for us is always mediated and opaque. . . . Several of its recurrent forms have become deviant and dangerous, e.g. the myth of absolute power (fascism) and the myth of the sacrificial scapegoat (anti-Semitism and racism). We are no longer justified in speaking of 'myth in general'. We must critically assess the content of each myth and the basic intentions which animate it. Modern man can neither get rid of myth nor take it at its face value. Myth will always be with us, but we must always approach it critically . . . Only then can we begin to recognize its capacity to open new worlds'[24].

What is required, then, is a heremeneutic dialectic between a critical *logos* and a symbolic *muthos*. Without the constant vigilance of reason, *mythos* remains susceptible to all kinds of perversion. For myth is not authentic or inauthentic by virtue of some eternal essence *in itself*, but by virtue of its ongoing reinterpretation by each historical generation. Or to put it another way, myth is neither good nor bad but interpretation makes it so. Every mythology implies a *conflict of interpretations*. And this conflict is, in the final analysis, an ethical one. It is when *muthos* is conjoined with *logos* in a common project of liberation for *all* mankind that we can properly speak of its utopian dimension. Whenever a myth is considered as the founding act of one particular community to the total exclusion of all others, the possibility of ideological perversion immediately arises: 'The original potential of any myth always goes beyond the limits of any single community or nation. The *muthos* of a community is the bearer of something which extends beyond its own particular frontiers; it is the bearer of other *possible* worlds. . . . Nothing travels more extensively and effectively than myth. Whence it follows that even though myths originate in a particular culture, they are also capable of emigrating and developing within new cultural frameworks. . . . Only those myths are genuine which can be reinterpreted in terms of liberation, as both a personal and collective phenomenon. We should perhaps sharpen this critical criterion to include only those myths which have as their horizon the liberation of mankind *as a whole*. Liberation cannot be exclusive. . . . In genuine reason *[logos]* as well as in genuine myth *[muthos]*, we find a concern for the *universal* emanicipation of man'[25].

We best respect the universalist potential of myth by ensuring that its utopian *forward look* is one which critically reinterprets its ideological *backward look* in such a way that our understanding of history is positively transformed[26]. The proper dialectic of *muthos* and *logos* observes both the need to 'belong' to the symbolic representations of our past and the need to critically 'distance' ourselves from them. Without the critical 'distancing' of the *logos* we would not be able to disengage the genuine utopian promise of each myth from its ideological perversions. If *muthos* is to guarantee its *utopos*, it must pass through the purgatorial detour of *logos*. But a due recognition of our sense of 'belonging' (i.e. that our understanding always presupposes a culturally situated pre-understanding) is also necessary. Without such recognition, critical reason may presume some kind of totalizing knowledge beyond the limits of human understanding. All objective knowledge about our position in a social community or cultural tradition is based on a relation of prior belonging from which we can never totally extricate ourselves. The claim to total truth is an illusion. Before we ever achieve critical distance, we belong to a history, to a nation, to a culture, to one or several traditions. In accepting this prior belonging, we accept the mediating function of mythic self-representation[27]. To renounce completely the cultural situatedness of the *muthos* is to lapse into the lie of a *logos* elevated to the rank of absolute truth. When reason pretends to dispense thus with all mythic mediations, it risks becoming a sterile and self-serving rationalism – an ideology in its own right, and one indeed which threatens to dominate our modern age of science and technology. Left entirely to its own devices, *logos* suspects everything but itself. And this is why the rational critique of myth is 'a task which must always be begun, but which in principle can never be completed'[28].

V

We return, finally, to the crucial question of *national myth*. How may we demythologize tradition while saving its myths? How are we to concretely distinguish between their ideological and utopian functions? While it is absolutely essential to subject our mythology to a hermeneutic of suspicion – as several of the studies in this book have attempted – it would be foolish to conclude that every national myth is *reducible* to the ideological function of mystification. As Tom Nairn rightly advises, even the most elementary comparative analysis shows that 'all nationalism is both healthy and morbid. Both progress and regress are inscribed in its genetic code from the start'[29]. In the *political unconscious* of Irish nationalism there also exists a utopian project which it is unjust and unwise to ignore[30]. But this utopian dimension is only legitimate to the extent that it is capable of transcending all sectarian claims (i.e. to be the one, true and only ideology) in a gesture which embraces those whom it ostensibly excludes. At a political level, one might cite here the readiness of the Forum for a New Ireland (to which all parties of Irish constitutional nationalism subscribed) to go beyond many of nationalism's 'most cherished assumptions' in order to respect opposing traditions and identities[31]. By thus demythologising the myth of a United-Ireland-in-the-morning-and-by-whatever-means, it was possible to preserve the genuine utopian aspiration of the 'common name of Irishman' – a project which pledged to cherish all the children of the nation equally.

At a literary level, we have the exploratory narratives of many contemporary Irish authors who have demythologized the insularist clichés of Irish culture in order to remythologize its inherently universalist resonances. Once a myth forgoes its power of ideological dissimulation, once it ceases to be taken literally as a force of domination, it ceases to *mystify*. Myth then no longer serves as a monolithic doctrine to which the citizens of the nation submissively conform; it becomes a symbol bearing a plurality of meanings. It is precisely the *symbolic* nature of a myth's reminiscences and anticipations which commits it to a *multitude* of interpretations[32]. No one version of a myth is sacrosanct. The worlds it discloses are possibilities to be explored rather than pre-established possessions to be restored. The positive universality of myth – which enables it to migrate beyond national boundaries and translate into other cultures – resides, paradoxically, in its very multiplicity. Here we are touching on a new understanding of myth: one we might best term *postmodern* by way of distinguishing it from both the *revivalist* apotheosis of myth as a unitary tradition and the *modernist* rejection of myth as a mystifying dogma. A postmodern approach to myth construes it as a two-way traffic between tradition and modernity, rewriting the old as a project of the new.

Joyce was no doubt one of the first to anticipate this postmodern dialectic in his reworking of the national myth of Finn. *Finnegans Wake* invites us to have 'two thinks at a time'; and as the title itself informs us, Joyce's narrative refers both to Finnegan's *death* (the term wake in Ireland means a funeral ceremony) and to his *rebirth* (that is, Finn-again-awake). Joyce deconstructs the monolithic myth of Finn, the hero of Ireland's founding mythological saga, into an infinite number of myths. (Joyce calls the *Wake* his 'messongebook'; and he thereby acknowledges that the 'national unconscious' which expresses itself in his dreams (*mes songes*) of the legendary hero, may be interpreted either as an ideological *mensonge* or as a utopian *message*). The Celtic myth of Finn and the Fianna had been invoked by the Irish literary revival and by many of the leaders of the new Republic to provide a renewed sense of cultural identity for the Irish people. Joyce knew the great power of such myths to animate the national unconscious. But he also recognized the possibilities of abuse. Joyce had little time, as we noted in our second chapter, for the sanctimonious romanticizing which characterized aspects of the Celtic Revival. He disliked its tendency to turn a blind eye to the lived experience of the present out of deference to some fetish of the past. And he fully shared Beckett's disdain for a 'Free State' which erected a commemorative statue of a dying Celtic hero in its General Post office (where the Easter Rising began) at the same time as it introduced censorship laws which banned many of its living writers. The recital of myths of the motherland to legitimate a new intellectual orthodoxy was to be treated with scepticism; for such a practice was unlikely to foster a pluralist culture respectful of the diversity of races, creeds and dialects which existed in the nation. It was in defiance of chauvinistic stereotypes of the motherland that Joyce reinterpreted the ancient Celtic heroine, Anna, as Anna Livia Plurabelle – the 'Everliving Bringer of Plurabilities'[33]. He thus opposed the *multi-minded* logic of utopian myth to the *one-minded* logic of ideological myth. *Finnegans Wake* contains not *one* dominant personage but *many* interweaving personae, not a single totalizing plot but a play of narrative metamorphosis. Similarly, Joyce's book explores not just one but many languages (he exults in its 'polyguttural' complexity), not just one but many cultural myths (alongside the Celtic and the Judaeo-Christian we find the Hellenistic, the Babylonian and the Chinese etc.) In both its form and its content, *Finnegans Wake* is a 'mamafesta' of multiple meaning. It is an open text which looks beyond the either/or antagonism of tradition versus modernity, memory versus imagination, towards a post-modern *collage* where they may co-exist.

There are many other instances of a post-modern attitude to myth to be found in recent Irish culture. To isolate just one example, one could cite how the old Irish legend of Sweeney has been reinterpreted in a wide variety of ways by writers like Flann O'Brien, Heaney, Friel and MacIntyre as well as by the film maker, Pat Murphy (in *Maeve*). Far from recycling some immutable national vision, these various rewritings of the Sweeney myth manifest a rich diversity of narratives. The retrospective allusion to indigenous mythology opens onto the prospective horizon of a multiple culture. It is because our contemporary consciousness no longer *believes* in myths as ideological dogmas that we can freely *reinvent* them as utopian symbols. Without disbelief there can be no 'willing suspension of disbelief'. Without demythologization, no remythologization.

Postmodern myth invites a plurality of viewpoints. It encourages us to reread tradition, not as a sacred and inviolable scripture, but as a palimpsest of creative possibilities which can only be reanimated and realized in a radically pluralist culture.

*   *   *

The narratives selected for analysis in this book share, with few exceptions, a common capacity to journey beyond the frontiers of Ireland while retaining the birthmarks of their origins. The works of Joyce, Beckett, Flann O'Brien, Banville, Heaney, Friel, Jordan, Murphy and le Brocquy have all responded in their particular way to the transitional crisis of Irish culture; and they have done so while simultaneously translating this crisis into the larger idioms of 'world culture'. Is this not, indeed, one of the primary aims of all narrative – to translate back and forth between the familiar and the foreign, the old and the new, tradition and utopia, reinterpreting one's own history in stories which address the challenge of change?

Appendix: The Ideological Functions of Myth

There are three main ideological functions of myth – *integration, dissimulation* and *domination*. It is only by exposing the ideological idols of myth that we can begin to let its utopian symbols speak. No contemporary consideration of myth can dispense with the critique of ideology.

Myth as Integration. Ideology expresses a social group's need for a communal set of images whereby it can represent itself. Most societies invoke a tradition of mythic idealizations which provide a stable, predictable and repeatable order of meanings. This process of ideological self-representation frequently assumes the form of a mythic reiteration of the founding-act of the community. It seeks to redeem society from the contingencies or crises of the present by justifying its actions in terms of some sanctified past, some sacred Beginning.[34] One might cite here the role played by the Aeneas myth in Roman society, the cosmogony myths in Greek society, or indeed the Celtic myths of Cuchulain and the Fianna in Irish society. And where an ancient past is lacking, a more recent past will suffice: e.g. the Declaration of Independence for the USA, the October Revolution for the USSR and so on.

Ideology thus serves to relate the social memory of an historical community to some inaugural act which founded it and which can be repeated over time in order to preserve a sense of social integration. The role of ideology, as Ricoeur has explained, is not only to extend the conviction beyond the circle of founding fathers, so as to make it the creed of the entire group, but also to perpetuate the initial energy beyond the period of effervescence. 'It is into this gap, characteristic of all situations *aprés coup*, that the images and interpretations intervene. A founding act can be revived and reactualised only . . . through a representation of itself. The ideological phenomenon thus begins very early: for domestication by memory is accompanied not only by consensus, but also by convention and rationalisation [in the Freudian sense]. At this point, ideology . . . continues to be mobilising only insofar as it is justificatory.'[35]

The ideological recollection of sacred foundational acts has the purpose therefore of both integrating and justifying a social order. While this can accompany a cultural or national revival, it can also give rise to what Ricoeur calls a 'stagnation of politics' – a process where each power reiterates an anterior power: every prince wants to be Caesar, every Caesar wants to be Alexander, every Alexander wants to hellenise an Oriental despot[36]. Either way, ideology entails a process of schematization and ritualization, a process which stereotypes social action and permits a social group to bind itself together in terms of rhetorical maxims and idealized self-images.

Myth as Dissimulation. If the schematic 'rationalizations' of ideology bring about social integration, they do so, paradoxically, at a 'pre-rational' level. The ideology of foundational myths operates behind our backs, as it were, rather than appearing as a transparent theme before our eyes. We think *from* ideology, rather than *about* it. And it is precisely because the codes of ideology function in this indirect manner that the practice of distortion and dissimulation can occur. This is the epistemological reason for Marx's denouncing ideology as the falsifying projection of 'an inverted image of our own position in society'[37]. Ideology is by its very nature an *uncritical instance* and thus easily susceptible to deceit, alienation – and by extension – intolerance. All too frequently, ideology functions in a reactionary or at least socially conservative fashion. "It signifies that what is new can be accommodated only in terms of the typical, itself stemming from the sedimentation of social experience.'[38] Consequently, the future – as opening up that which is unassimilable and unprecedented *vis-á-vis* the pre-existing codes of experience – is often translated back into the stereotypes of the past. This accounts for the fact that many social groups display traits of ideological orthodoxy which render them intolerant towards what is marginal, different or alien. Pluralism and permissiveness are the *bêtes noires* of such social orthodoxy. They represent the intolerable. This phenomenon of ideological intolerance arises when the experience of radical novelty threatens the possibility of the social group recognizing itself in a retrospective reference to its hallowed traditions and pieties.

But ideology can also dissimulate the gap between what *is* and what *ought* to be, that is, between our presently lived *reality* and our idealized self-representations.[39] By masking the gulf which separates contemporary historical experience from mythic memory, ideology often justifies the status quo by presuming that nothing has really changed. This self-dissimulation expresses itself as a resistance to change, as a closure to new possibilities of self-understanding. Whence the danger of reducing the challenge of the new to the acceptable limits of an already established heritage of meaning.

Myth as Domination. This property of ideology raises, finally, the vexed question of the hierarchical organization of society – the question of authority. As Max Weber and later Jürgen Habermas observed, social systems tend to *legitimate* themselves by means of an ideology which justifies their right to secure and retain power[40]. This process of legitimation is inherently problematic, however, in so far as there exists a disparity between the nation/state's ideological *claim* to authority and the answering *belief* of the public. Ideology thus entails a surplus of claim over response. If a system's claim to authority were fully and reciprocally consented to by those whom it governs, there would be no *need* for the persuasive or coercive strategies of ideological myths. Ideology operates accordingly as a 'surplus-value' symptomatic of the assymetry between the legitimizing *ought* of our normative traditions, on the one hand, and the *is* of our lived social existence, on the other. It is when there is no transparent coincidence between those governing and those governed, that ideological myths are deemed necessary to preserve the *semblance* of unity.

NOTES

Introduction: The Transitional Paradigm

1. As the French philosopher, Paul Ricoeur, argues: 'The ultimate problem is to show in what way history and fiction contribute, in virtue of their common narrative structure, to the description and redescription of our historical condition. What is ultimately at stake . . . is the mutual belonging together of narrativity and historicity'. ('The Narrative function', *Hermeneutics and the Human Sciences*, Cambridge University Press, 1981, p. 274).

    For a more detailed analysis of the hermeneutic philosophy of narrative and interpretation see Paul Ricoeur *Time and Narrative* (Chicago University Press, 1985); Hans-Georg Gadamer, *Truth and Method* (Sheed and Ward, 1975); Alasdair MacIntyre. *After Virtue* (Duckworth Press, 1981); and Frederic Jameson, *The Political Unconscious: Narrative as a socially symbolic Act* (Menthuen, 1981). See also Roland Barthes' comprehensive definition of narrative in his 'Introduction to the Structural Analysis of Narratives': 'The narratives of the world are numberless. Narrative is first and foremost a prodigious variety of genres, themselves distributed amongst different substances – as though any material were fit to receive man's stories. Able to be carried by articulated language, spoken or written, fixed or moving images, gestures, and the ordered mixture of all these substances; narrative is present in myth, legend, fable, tale, novella, epic, history, tragedy, drama, comedy, mime,painting, stained glass windows, cinema, comics, news item, conversation. Moreover, under this almost infinite diversity of forms, narrative is present in every age, in every place, in every society; it begins with the very history of mankind and there nowhere is nor has been a people without narrative. All classes, all human groups, have their narratives, enjoyment of which is very often shared by men with different, even opposing, cultural backgrounds.' (p. 79, *Image - Music - Text*, Fontana, 1977).

    On the relationship between narrative and the transitional crisis of a culture see Hannah Arendt's *Between Past and Future* (New York, 1954) – the French title is, significantly, *La Crise de La Culture* (Gallimard, 1972) – and in particular the Preface.

2. Desmond Fennell, 'Wanted: A Project for Ireland' in *The Irish Times*, July, 1985. See also the same author's more comprehensive treatment of this theme in *Beyond Nationalism* (Ward River Press, 1985). My own discussion of revivalism in this introduction is indebted to this work.

3. Seamus Deane, *Celtic Revivals*, (Faber, 1985), p. 15. For a critique of the Irish revivalist aesthetic see also Declan Kiberd, 'The War against the Past' in *The Uses of History*, ed. R. Garrett and A. Eyler, University of Delaware Press, 1987.

4. See Frank Kermode's useful discussion of different kinds of modernism in *The Sense of an Ending, Studies in the Theory of Fiction* (Oxford University Press, 1966), pp. 113–120, and particularly his distinction between the traditionalist modernism of Yeats and the 'schismatic' modernism of Beckett.

5. Deane, *op. cit.*, p. 13.

6. Paul Ricoeur, 'Universal Civilisation and National Cultures', in *History and Truth*, (Northwestern University Press, 1965), p. 276.

7. See our *Introduction* to *The Irish Mind: Exploring Intellectual Traditions* (Wolfhound Press, Dublin/Humanities Press, New York, 1985); and also 'The Irish Mind Defended' in *The Sunday Independent*, 26 May, 1985.

8. See Edward W. Said's proposal of a critical 'program of interference' in 'Opponents, Audiences, Constituencies' in *Postmodern Culture*, ed. H. Foster, Pluto Press, 1985, pp. 156–157: 'Non interference means laissez-faire: "they" can run the country, we will explicate Wordsworth and Schlegel. . . . Instead of noninterference and specialization, there must be *interference*, crossing of borders and obstacles, a determined attempt to generalize exactly at those points where generalization seems impossible to make. One of the first interferences to be ventured, then, is a crossing from literature, which is supposed to be subjective and powerless, into those exactly parallel realms, now covered by journalism . . . that employ representatives but are supposed to be objective and powerful.' Against this division of intellectual labour, Said proclaims the necessity of a 'sustained, systematic examination of the co-existence of and the inter-relationship between the literary and the social, which is where representation – from journalism, to political struggle, to economic production and power – plays an extraordinarily important role' (*ibid.*, p. 153).

1 Yeats and the Conflict of Imaginations

1. See the analysis of the historical philosophies of imagination in the Introduction to my *Poétique du Possible; Herménentique de la Figuration,* Beauchesne, Paris, 1984.
2. Elizabeth Cullingford, 'The Unknown Thought of W.B. Yeats' in *The Irish Mind* (edited R. Kearney), *Op. cit.*, 1984, p. 233.
3. Seamus Deane, Prefatory Note in the Field Day Theatre Company programme for Brian Friel's *The Communication Cord* (1983).
4. Seamus Deane, 'Yeats, Ireland and Revolution' in *The Crane Bag Book of Irish Studies* (ed. R. Kearney and M.P. Hederman), Blackwater Press, Dublin, 1982, pp. 139–148; and also in S. Deane's *Celtic Revivals: Essays in Anglo-Irish Literature,* Faber, 1985.
5. *Selected Prose,* ed. A.N. Jeffares, MacMillan, 1964, pp. 85–87.
6. *Ibid.*, p. 85. This conflict of interpretations, as Yeats fully realized, goes as far back as Plato, the founding father of Western metaphysics. Plato was the first to recognize the existence of two distinct and ostensibly opposed types of imagination – the 'mimetic' and the 'ecstatic'. The 'mimetic' imagination was identified with the shaping activity of the human psyche. It was treated with deep suspicion to the extent that it presumed to invent a world of images out of its own desire. This imaginary world was termed 'mimetic' because of its anthropomorphic nature, that is, because the imagination which fashioned it was deemed a threat to the authority of the Divine Demiurge who, according to Plato, was the only legitimate shaper of the world. Artists who think they are creating a new order are mistaken. In fact, they are merely 'imitating' (*mimesis*) in idolatrous fashion the divine activity of the Demiurge who first modelled nature on the Transcendental Forms (which exist beyond our historical world of time, space, matter and movement). The 'mimetic' imagination of the creative artist was condemned accordingly by Plato in the tenth book of the *Republic.* Its greatest offence was to seek to emulate the divine order of Forms with a human order of fantasies.

    In some of the later mystical dialogues such as the *Phaedrus* or *Timaeus*, however, Plato acknowledged a radically different kind of imagination which he called 'ecstatic'. This imagination was attributed to the visionary poet or holy seer. It did not invent images but received them from a sacred source beyond human experience. It was termed 'ecstatic' because it permitted man to stand outside of himself (*ek-stasis*) serving as a receptacle for transcendent visions. Rather than vainly desiring to *create* a new world in historical time, the ecstatic imagination chose to *remember* the timeless world of Divine Forms which the soul inhabited in its 'pre-existence' before it was born into this temporal world. In short, while the mimetic imagination was committed to *desire (Eros)*, the ecstatic imagination was committed to *recollection (Anamnesis)*.

7. Denis Donoghue, *Yeats,* Fontana, 1971, p. 19.

7a. See Donoghue, *ibid.* While it may appear strange at first to couple the terms 'mimetic' and 'romantic' – in opposition to the standard reading of Yeats's romanticism, by Abrams and others, as a replacing of *imitation* (the mirror) with *expression* (the lamp) – this equation is in fact justified when we consider the original platonic identification of *mimesis* with human 'images of desire' which lay claim to an autonomous life in defiance of the original source of light in the transcendental forms. It is this sense of romantic 'mimesis' which Yeats himself invokes when he endorses Mallarmé's image of the Herodiade's defiantly self-referential mirror dance: 'All about me lives but in mine own/ Image, the idolatrous mirror of my pride'; or again when he writes: 'Mirror on mirror mirrored is all the show'. Moreover, as Jonathan Culler has argued in *The Pursuit of Signs: Semiotics Literature, Deconstruction* (Routledge and Kegan Paul, 1981, pp. 162–165), the strict opposition between mirror (as derivative light) and lamp (as self-generating light) which Abrams promotes as a central motif of romanticism is ultimately unsustainable, a token of what Culler terms its 'self-deconstructive logic'.

8. *Anima Hominis* in *Selected Criticism,* ed. A.N. Jeffares, MacMillan, 1964, p. 173.

9. *Selected Prose, op. cit.,* p. 64.

10. Quoted R. Ellmann, *Yeats, The Man and the Masks,* Faber, 1949, pp. 19-20.

11. *Ibid.,* p. 141. This attitude is typical of Phase 16 as outlined by Yeats in *A Vision* pp. 138-9; 'There is always an element of frenzy, and almost always a delight in certain glowing and shining images of concentrated force'. It is this strident, querulous aspect of imagination which Denis Donoghue defines as the 'hysteria of imagination' in his *Yeats,* p. 126. The opposite Phase is 14 which Yeats has Robartes describe as that time when 'the soul begins to tremble into stillness/To die into the labyrinth of itself'. It is represented by the 'mind moving upon silence', by sacramental 'visions deeper than reverie or sleep'.

12. *Essays and Introductions,* p. 529.

13. Quoted Ellmann, *op. cit.,* p. 20.

14. *Letters,* p. 583.

15. *Ibid.,* p. 583.

16. *Trembling of the Veil,* p. 197.

17. *Per Amica Silentia Lunae* (1917), *op. cit.,* p. 133.

18. Autobiographical Writings, in *Selected Prose,* p. 194.

19. This is a typical statement of romantic idealism. See chapter 4 of my *The Wake of Imagination,* Hutchinson, 1987.

20. *Selected Prose,* p. 130.

21. *Selected Prose,* p. 113; cf. on Yeats's and Mallarmé's theory of the Eternal Imagination, Hugh Kenner, *The Pound Era,* UCP, 1917, p. 109.

22. This is 'an Ireland/The poets have imagined, terrible and gay'. As such it proved eligible for Yeats's doctrine of the Mask: 'I, that my native scenery might find

imaginary inhabitants, half-planned a new method and a new culture' (Quoted in John Unterecker's *Yeats*, Prentice Hall, 1963).

23. *Selected Criticism*, p. 133-4. It was this ability to assimilate the products of history to the designs of an erotic imagination which Pound satirized in Yeats when he wrote of him stopping to 'admire the symbol with Notre Dame standing inside it'.

24. *Trembling of the Veil*, (1922), p. 206.

25. *Selected Prose*, p. 86.

26. *Ibid.*, p. 86.

27. *Trembling of the Veil*, p. 207. Yeats finds precedents for this passive and involuntary aspect of the sacramental imagination in the examples of the priesthood of Apollo who acquired great powers from the religious meditation of his 'divine Image'; the citizens of ancient Egypt who 'assumed in contemplation, the images of their gods'; or the case of Gemma Galgani who in 1889 caused deep wounds to appear in her body by contemplating her crucifix: *Hodos Camelionis* in *Trembling of the Veil*, p. 150.

28. *Ibid.*, p. 136.

29. *Ibid.*, p. 136.

30. *Ibid.*, p. 235. And this conviction takes on even more significance when we recall Yeats's much quoted belief that 'the Celt is a visionary without scratching', for the Irish people's 'hatred of abstraction' made them deal more easily in 'visions and images', *Selected Prose*, p. 159.

31. *Trembling of the Veil*, p. 143.

32. *Ibid.*, p. 149.

33. 'Now image called upon image in an endless procession, and I could not always choose among them with any confidence, and when I did choose, the image lost its intensity, or changed into some other image.'*Ibid.*, p. 150.

34. *Ibid.*, p. 152. This statement of disaffection from the romantic imagination, made in 1922, was already prepared for some thirty years earlier when Yeats held that in various sessions with such occult spiritualists as Mathers and Madame Blatvastsky, there rose before him 'mental images which (he) could not control'. Already then in the 1890's Yeats was forced to ask the question: 'What certainty had I that (these images) which had taken me by surprise could be from my own thought'.
The following passage from *Hodos Camelias* is representative of Yeats's mystical impulse: 'When a man writes any work of genius, or invents some creative action, is it not because some knowledge or power has come into his mind from beyond the mind? It is called up by an image . . . but our images must be *given to us*, we cannot *choose* them deliberately'. *Ibid.* p. 153.

35. *Selected Prose*, p. 77.

36. *Selected Criticism*, p. 81 (on *Magic*), p. 162 (*Poetry and Tradition*).

37. *Selected Prose*, p. 82.

38. *Ibid.*, p. 84. And mythology, we must remember, is for Yeats no 'mere vanity' invented by the will but a portal to the 'Unknown' beyond the will: *Introduction to the Words upon a Window Pane, Selected Prose*, p. 214.

39. *Selected Criticism*, p. 34.

40. *Trembling of the Veil*, p. 219.

41. *Selected Prose*, p. 234.

Blake is also numbered amongst the mystic company. Yeats was particularly admiring of the prophetic poems and was, he admits, tempted to give credence to Blake's own claim that their 'author was in eternity' (*Selected Criticism*, p. 86). The visionary, as opposed to the romantic, in Blake was one of those rare poets receptive to the 'timeless memory of Nature that reveals events and symbols of distant centuries . . . the things of eternity' (*ibid*., p. 89); one of that sacramental company who followed the way of the saint, abandoning themselves to the 'wilderness to so waste the body, and to so hush the unquiet mind that, still living, they might pass the doors the dead pass daily' (*ibid*., p. 90). It was as a representative of the sacramental imagination that Yeats rapturously praised him: 'Blake represented the shapes of beauty haunting our moments of inspiration: shapes held by most for the frailest of ephemera, but by him for a people older than the world, citizens of eternity, appearing and reappearing in the minds of artists and of poets, creating all we touch and see by casting distorted images of themselves . . . ' (*ibid*., p. 23). This passage constitutes perhaps Yeats's clearest concession to the sacramental view that imagination receives images created elsewhere and is not itself their creator.

In fact, analogies between the 'ecstatic' imagination of the poet and the saint are not infrequent. Speaking of Gérard de Nerval, Yeats observes that in an earlier time 'he would have been of that multitude whose soul's austerity withdrew . . . from desire and regret' in order that they might 'reveal those processions of symbols that men bow to before altars, and woo with incense and offerings' (*ibid*. p. 51). Another example is witnessed in Yeats's appeal for a new art which would do away with the 'invention of the will' and turn instead towards more 'meditative, organic rhythms' which are the embodiment of that imagination which 'neither desires nor hates, because it is done with time' (*ibid*. p. 79). Morris, Bunyan, Dante and Paracelsus were, for Yeats, also just such 'religious artists'. The beauty of their poetry was intended to 'set us at peace with natural things', rather than creating quarrels between man and his world as would be expected of the romantic imagination. They deployed a symbolism 'by which the soul when entranced . . . communes with God and with angels' (*ibid*. pp. 109, 126).

It was through repeated meditation on the works of such sacramental poets that Yeats became sufficiently emboldened to formulate the notion of a supernatural artist who revealed himself in poetic or visionary images. Even so typical a romantic as Shelley was deemed to have partaken, on privileged occasions, of that religious Ecstasy of the Saint where the self abandons itself to a truth higher than its own creative will. Yeats begins his essay *The Philosophy of Shelley's Poetry,* by confessing that whereas he once believed that the world's destiny could best be discovered by words which gathered up the *hearts desire,* 'since then I have observed dreams and visions very carefully, and am now certain that the imagination has some way of lighting on the truth'; and furthermore, that its commandments are only 'delivered when the body is still', that is, when the heart's desire is appeased in sacramental 'vision of the divine order': that order which Shelley's platonism led him to denote as the Intellectual Beauty (*ibid*., p. 55).

42. See Terry Eagleton, 'Politics and Sexuality in W.B. Yeats' in *The Crane Bag*, Vol. 9. No. 2, 1985, pp. 139.

43. Eagleton, *op. cit.,* pp. 139-141.

44. Supportive of such a reading is the much quoted passage in *Anima Hominis* where Yeats argues that whereas the saint or sage follows the straight line to truth, the artist and poet must follow the path of the serpent that winds from desire to weariness and back to desire again. According to this view, sacramental vision could only occur when we renounce the circular self of desire and are taken up into a 'clear light and are forgetful even of our own names and actions'. (*Selected Criticism*, p. 178).

45. See for example the passage in *Selected Criticism,* p. 87 where Yeats talks of the imagination '*creating* or *revealing* for a moment what I call a supernatural artist'. See also when he wonders whether 'it is *we* or the *vision* that creates the pattern' (*ibid.* p. 179).
46. Yeats *Selected Prose,* p. 115. In a letter to Olivia Shakespeare in 1926, Yeats states that the tragic attitude most befits the aging man: "I suppose to grow old is to grow impersonal, to need nothing and to seek nothing for oneself."
47. Yeats, *Selected Prose,* p. 115.
48. Yeats, *Selected Criticism,* p. 115. This means, Yeats concludes, the the tragic-comic poet is 'known from other men by making all he handles *like himself,* and yet by the *unlikeness to himself* of all that comes before him in a pure contemplation'. Yeats, *Selected Criticism,* p. 153.
49. *Ibid,* p. 164. The twin pillars of civilization, as Yeats explains, are 'creativity/culture' and 'holiness' (*ibid.,* p. 116).
50 Quoted R. Ellmann, *op. cit.,* p. 129.

2 Joyce: Questioning Narratives

1. *Collected works of Padraig Pearse,* ed. Desmond Ryan, Dublin, 1917-22, p. 65. Quoted by Seamus Deane in 'Joyce and Nationalism' in *Celtic Revivals,* Faber, 1985, p. 94.
2. Seamus Deane, 'An Example of Tradition' in *The Crane Bag,* Vol. 3, No. 1, 1979, p. 47.
3. See Colin McCabe, *James Joyce and The Revolution of the Word,* MacMillan, 1978.
4. See Joseph O'Leary 'Joyce and the Myth of the Fall' in *The Crane Bag,* Vol. 2, No.'s 1 & 2, 1978.
4a. Mikhail Bakhtin, *Problems of Dostoevsky's Poetics,* Manchester U.P. 1984. See Paul Ricoeur's discussion of Bakhtin's concept of the 'dialogical imagination' in the modern 'polyphonic novel' in *La configuration dans le récit de fiction,* (*Temps et Récit, II,* Éd. du Seuil, Paris, 1984), pp. 144–148 and Denis Donoghue in *We Irish,* Knopf, 1986.
5. See Mark Patrick Hederman's analysis of this 'nighttime consciousness' in 'The Mind of James Joyce' in *The Irish Mind,* ed. Richard Kearney, Wolfhound Press, Dublin, 1985. See also Sheldon Brivic, *Joyce: Between Freud and Jung* (Kennikat Press, 1980) and *Joyce the Creator* (University of Wisconsin Press, 1985). For Jung's own most explicit statement on Joyce's use of the language of the unconscious see his essay '*Ulysses:* A Monologue' in *The Spirit in Man, Art and Literature* (AFK, 1984) pp. 109–135, in particular the following passages: 'The book can be read just as well backwards, for it has no back and no front, no top and no bottom. Everything could easily have happened before, or might have happened afterwards. . . . Objective and subjective, outer and inner, are so constantly intermingled that in the end, despite the clearness of the individual images, one wonders whether one is dealing with a physical or with a transcendental tape worm. . . . Ulysses wants to go on singing its endless tune into endless time. . . . What seems to be mental abnormality may be a kind of mental health which is inconceivable to the average understanding: it may even be a disguise for superlative powers of mind. . . . The distortion of beauty and meaning by grotesque objectivity or equally grotesque irreality is, in the insane, a consequence of the destruction of the personality; in the artist it has a creative purpose. . . . In the destruction of the criteria of beauty and meaning that have

held till today, Ulysses accomplishes wonders. It insults all our conventional feelings, it brutally disappoints our expectations of sense and content, it thumbs its nose at all synthesis.... It is not a matter of a single thrust aimed at one definite spot, but of an almost universal 'restratification' of modern man, who is in the process of shaking off a world that has become obsolete.... He worked on *Ulysses* in many foreign lands, and from all of them he looked back in faith and kinship upon Mother Church and Ireland. He uses his foreign stopping-places merely as anchors to steady his ship in the mainstream of his Irish reminiscences and resentments. Yet *Ulysses* does not strain back to his Ithaca – on the contrary he makes frantic efforts to rid himself of his heritage ... *Ulysses* shows how one should execute Nietzsche's 'Sacrilegious backward grasp'.... Prophets are always disagreeable and usually have bad manners, but it is said that they occasionally hit the nail on the head ... like every true prophet, the artist is the unwitting mouthpiece of the psychic secrets of his time, and is often as unconscious as a sleep-walker.... All the Dedaluses, Blooms, Harrys, Lynches, Mulligans, and the rest of them talk and go about as in a collective dream that begins nowhere and ends nowhere, and takes place only because 'no-man' – an unseen Odysseus – dreams it.... Joyce's inexpressibly rich and myriad-faceted language unfolds itself in passages that creep along in tapeworm fashion, terribly boring and monotonous, but the very boredom and monotony of it attain an epic grandeur that makes the book a *Mahabharata* of the world's futility and squalor ... the transformation of eschatology into scatology proves the truth of Tertullian's dictum: *anima naturalita christiana*.... O *Ulysses*, you are truly a devotional book for the object-besotted, object-ridden white man! You are a spiritual exercise, an ascetic discipline, an agonising ritual, an arcane procedure, eighteen alchemical alembics piled on top of one another, where amid acids, poisonous fumes, and fire and ice, the homunculus of a new, universal consciousness is distilled!'

6. Seamus Deane, 'Joyce and Nationalism', *op. cit.* p. 98.
7. G. Lukács, *The Theory of the Novel*, Merlin, London, 1971; R. Girard, *Mensonge Romantique et Vérité Romanesque*, Grasset, Paris, 1961; L. Goldmann, *Pour une Sociologie du Roman*, Gallimard, Paris, 1964. See, for instance, Goldmann's statement that the novel 'is the transposition on the literary plane of the everyday life in the individualistic society created by market production' (p. 7).
8. Milan Kundera, 'Encore sur le Roman' in *Lettre Internationale*, No. 4, Spring 1985, pp. 3–7.
9. Seamus Deane, 'Joyce and Nationalism,' *op. cit.*, p. 93. On the distinction between 'egology' and 'ecology' see Robert Scholes, *Structuralism in Literature*, Yale University Press, 1974, p. 183.
10. See S.L. Goldberg: *Joyce*, 1962, Oliver and Boyd, Edinburgh. 'For the *Portrait*, more than an autobiographical novel, or even a study of artistic alienation, is that peculiar twentieth-century phenomenon: a work of art which is at once a representative fable ... a kind of demonstration of its own significance *as* a work of art ... (the artist) expresses the external world as he understands it and at the same time expresses the very form of his understanding' (p. 51–2). But as Goldberg remarks Joyce 'could not dramatize more of the deeper vision to which Stephen is groping than is embodied in this groping itself. Hence the need for a sequel, *Ulysses'* p. 62. In *Time and Narrative* (Chicago U.P. 1984), Paul Ricoeur comments on the movement from the traditional novel to the modern (anti-)novel as follows: 'It is the reader who completes the work inasmuch as ... the written work is a sketch for reading. Indeed, it consists of holes,

lacunae, zones of indetermination, which, as in Joyce's *Ulysses*, challenge the reader's capacity to configure what the author seems to take malign delight in defiguring. In such an extreme case, it is the reader, almost abandoned by the work, who carries the burden of emplotment.' (p. 77).

11. See Jean-Michel Rabaté 'De la Hauteur à laquelle l'autorité se noue' (Joyce, Hegel et la philosophie) in *La Littérature dans la philosophie* (Lille III, 185, 1982) p. 66–68. Jung also observed in his '*Ulysses*: a Monologue', *op.cit*, p. 114: 'We behold the disintegration of Joyce's personality into Bloom, *l'homme moyen sensuel* and the almost gaseous Stephen Dedalus, who is mere speculation and mere mind. Of these two, the former has no son and the latter no father.'

12. The 'light' extinguished in Bella Cohen's reappears in Molly's bedroom window as 'as a visible luminous sign', a sort of Dantesque vision, at the end of the chapter. See W.Y. Tindall, *A Reader's Guide to James Joyce*, 1959, Thames and Hudson, London, p. 220. Molly's unequivocal affirmation of reality is an answer to Stephen's espousal of life-excluding art: 'In woman's womb word is made flesh but in the spirit of the maker all flesh that passes becomes the word that does not pass away'. Indeed, this rejection of Stephen's quest was cogently prefigured in the 'Oxen of the Sun' episode (Ch. 14) where, as we noted, the fecundity of Mrs. Beaufoy-Purefoy's child's nine-month embryonic development is contrasted with the sterility of the nine-part chronological parody of the styles of prose writing from Sterne and Swift to Carlyle and Dickens and the final decay of literature in American confusion and Billy Sunday. 'Agendath is a wasteland' as Bloom comments. Joyce seems to be suggesting that the principle of artistic creation must not ignore or despise the principle of gestatory creation. See also René Girard's critique of what he calls the *'mensonge romantique'* of desire which seeks to exclude the other and all forms of commitment to social or historical mediation in *Mensonge Romantique et Vérité Romanesque* (Grasset, Paris; 61, pp. 29–31, 42–3, 53–4).

Appendix I: Joyce and Derrida

1. Jacques Derrida, *Writing and Difference*, University of Chicago Press, 1978. See also Derrida's essay, *Ulysse, Grammaphone, L'ouie-dire de Joyce* in *Genèse de Babel* (ed. C. Jacquet, *CNRS*, Paris, 1985).

2. Mark Patrick Hederman, 'The Mind of James Joyce: from Paternalism to Paternity' in *The Irish Mind*, ed. R. Kearney, Op. cit.

3. Jacques Derrida, *Dissemination*, Athlone Press, 1981, p. 167.

4. Derrida, *ibid*, p. 92.

5. Derrida, *ibid*, p. 93.

5a. See Sheldon Brivic 'Synchronicities in *Ulysses*' in *Joyce the Creator*, University of Wisconsin Press, 1985; and *Joyce Between Freud and Jung*, Kennikat Press, 1980.

6. Colin MacCabe, *Joyce and the Revolution of the Word*, Gill & McMillan, 1979, p. 147.

7. I am indebted, for several of these references, to Deborah Reid's M.A. Thesis on Joyce 'Never Start to Finish', U.C.D. 1980.

8. cf Hederman, *op. cit.*

9. See Maud Ellmann's paper on Joyce's 'Allegory of the Fall in *The Wake*' delivered at the Zurich International Joyce conference, 1980.

3 Beckett: The End of the Story?

1. Cf. Deirdre Bair, *Samuel Beckett's Irishness* in *The Crane Bag*, Vol. I, No. 2, 1977, in particular pp. 16–19. Bair's argument is succinctly summed up in the following statement: 'Beckett had no pride in his Irishness, national identity meant nothing to him'.

2. Cf. Seamus Deane, *The Idea of Tradition* in *the Crane Bag*, Vol. 3, No. 1, 1979, p. 7.

3. This reference and several others were brought to my attention by a paper, *Samuel Beckett, James Joyce's 'Illstarred Punster'*, delivered by S.E. Gontarski at the Joyce International Congress in Zurich, 1979.

4. For a detailed account of this 'neutral' writing see Roland Barthes' analysis of modernist literature, *Writing Degree Zero*, Jonathan Cape, 1967.

4a Samuel Beckett, *Proust* (1931), Grove Press, N.Y. See also the passage in this essay where he equates solitude with the impossibility of authentic personal communication: 'Even on the rare occasions when word and gesture happen to be valid expressions of personality (i.e. the ego) they lose their significance on their passage through the cataract of the personality that is opposed to them. Either we speak and act for ourselves – in which case speech and action are distorted and emptied of their meaning by an intelligence that is not ours, or else we speak and act for others in which we speak and act a lie. . . . We are alone. We cannot know and cannot be known'.

5. Beckett's essay on Joyce appeared in the collection *Our Exagmination round his Factification for the Incamination of Work in Progress*, Shakespeare and Co., Paris, 1929, pp. 3–22.

6. For the guidelines to such an analysis see Colin MacCabe's study *James Joyce and the Revolution of the Word*, *op. cit.* Following MacCabe I first attempted to employ such a method in *Joyce on Language, Women and Politics* in *Screen*, Vol. 20, No. 3/4, 1980, pp. 124 f.

7. See my article 'Beckett: The Demythologizing Intellect' in *The Irish Mind*. *op. cit.*

7a For a more detailed analysis of the central role of Cartesian metaphysics in Beckett's novels see the first section of my article, 'Beckett: the Demythologizing Intellect', *op. cit.*

8. See Richard Coe, *Beckett*, Oliver and Boyd Ltd., 1964, p. 4.

9. For an analysis of Beckett's use of Democritus' phrase see section two of my article 'Beckett: The Demythologizing Intellect', *op. cit.*

10. See Michel Foucault, Lévi-Strauss and also the 'post-structuralist' analysis of Jacques Derrida, *La Voix et le Phénomène*, Presses Universitaires de France, 1967, translated into English as *Speech and Phenomena* by D.B. Alison, N.Y., 1972, pp. 102, 93.

11. Quoted D. Bair, *Samuel Beckett, A Biography*, Jonathan Cape, 1978, p. 191. In part two of *Molloy*, Beckett pushes this alarming argument further. Moran, a second pseudo-self of the author, is yet another writer-narrator who serves as 'agent' to some unknown and unknowable 'master' (Youdi, later to become Godot) who sends meaningless orders through his 'messenger' Gaber. Moran is commissioned to assassinate Molloy; but they cannot meet for, as Moran acknowledges, Molloy is merely his own protean fiction: 'I had invented him, I mean found him ready made in my head'. The total absence of some extra-textual space where 'Moran could bend over Molloy' is all too evident. Such an illusory

space was the prerogative of the omniscient narrators of the classical novel. It is of just such a timeless, meta-linguistic omnipotence that Moran wistfully dreams of when he asks: 'would we all meet again in heaven one day, I, my mother, my son, his mother, Youdi, Gaber, Molloy, his mother, Yerk, Murphy, Watt, Camier and the rest?' Moran himself is, however, the first to admit his inability to narrate a story capable of uniting and identifying his different pseudo-selves: 'What a rabble in my head, what a gallery of moribunds. Murphy, Watt, Yerk, Mercier and all the others. I would never have believed that – Yes, I believe it willingly. Stories, stories, I have never been able to tell them. I shall never be able to tell this one'.

12. Sartre, *Qu'est-ce que la littérature?*, Gallimard, Paris, 1948.

13. In the same essay, *Dante . . . Bruno . . . Vico . . . Joyce, op. cit.* p. 23, Beckett contrasted this definition of hell to the 'purgatorial' writing of Joyce which he defined as a 'flood of movement and vitality'. Here again one is reminded of the radical difference between the 'omnipotent writer' Joyce – 'the more he knew the more he could' – and the 'impotent writer' Beckett – 'all I can manage more than I could' (Letter to Alan Schneider in 1973).

14. See Lucien Goldmann, *Pour une Sociologie du Roman*, Gallimard, Paris, 1964; this theory has also been developed by Georg Lukács, *The Theory of the Novel*, Merlin, London, 1971 and René Girard, *Mensonge Romantique et Vérité Romanesque*, Grasset, Paris, 1961. See also discussion of this theme in the preceding chapter on Joyce.

15. Geoffrey Hartman, *Deconstruction and Criticism*, Routledge and Kegan Paul, London, 1979, p. viii.

Appendix: Writing Under Erasure

1. See Derrida's exposition of this concept of 'difference' in *Writing and Difference* (University of Chicago Press, 1978) and *Speech and Phenomena* (Northwestern University Press, 1973); see also my Appendix to *Beckett: The Demythologizing Intellect* in *The Irish Mind* (*op. cit.*), pp. 357–360.

2. This notion of the 'palimpsest' of writing is developed by Derrida in *De la Grammatologie*, Les Editions de Minuit, 1967, *Marges de la Philosophie*, Les Editions de Minuit, 1972 and *La Dissémination*, Ed. du Seuil, 1972. See Paul Ricoeur's discussion of Derrida's thesis on *La Méta-phore et la Méta-physique* in his monumental study of metaphor, La Métaphore Vive, Ed. du Seuil, 1975, translated by R. Czerny as *The Rule of Metaphor*, University of Toronto Press, 1977, pp. 280 f.

3. Frank Kermode, *The Sense of an Ending, Studies in the Theory of Fiction* (Oxford University Press, 1966), p. 94.

4. Kermode, *op. cit.*, pp. 116–117.

5. Paul Riceur, *Temps et Récit (Vol. II): La Configuration dans le Récit de fiction* (Editions du Seuil, Paris, 1984), p. 42.

6. Ricoeur, *op. cit.*, p. 48. See also Ricoeur's analysis of the dialectical rapport between the modern anti-novel and traditional narrative in *Time and Narrative* (Vol. I, University of Chicago Press, 1984). pp. 68–70 as quoted in Note 12 of our concluding study, 'Myth and the Critique of Ideology'.

4 A Crisis of Fiction

1. See in particular Brian Moore's *Answer From Limbo* and John McGahern's *Leavetaking*, both of which exemplify aspects of critical 'self-consciousness' and 'self-reflexivity'. I discuss the latter in my article 'The Crisis of Imagination', *The Crane Bag*, Vol. 3, No. 1,, 1979, pp. 64–66; reprinted in *The Crane Bag Book of Irish Studies*, Blackwater Press, Dublin, 1981.

2. See Fintan O'Toole, 'Going West: The Country versus the City in Irish Writing' in *The Crane Bag*, Vol. 9, No. 2, 1985.

2a. See *Alive Alive O: Flann O'Brien's At Swim two Birds* (ed. Rudiger Imhof, Wolfhound Press, Dublin, 1985) and Tess Harson's 'The Making of a Good Wake' in *The Sunday Tribune*, Dec. 8, 1985.

3. M.H. Abrams, *A Glossary of Literature*, p. 114, quoted by Anthony Curtis 'An Essay on the novels of Brian O'Nolan' (unpublished). Curtis describes O'Nolan appropriately, as a 'reluctant modernist . . . a home based exile of vast polarities and firm dichotomies'. Curtis argues that O'Nolan/O'Brien shared with Beckett and Joyce an uncanny ability for 'literary punning, distorted autobiography (use of persona), satire, exaggeration and expansive imagination'. I am much indebted to Curtis' analysis.

4. Roland Barthes, 'The Death of the Author' in *Image – Music – Text* (Fontana, 1977). See also Tony Tanner's 'Thomas Pynchon and The Death of the Author' in *Thomas Pynchon* (Methuen, 1982).

5. 'Novelists on the Novel' (an interview with Francis Stuart and John Banville by Ronan Sheehan) in *The Crane Bag*, Vol. 3 No. 1, 1979, p. 76. See also Stuart's article on 'Literature and Politics' in *The Crane Bag*, Vol. 1, No. 1, 1977. (Both are reprinted in *The Crane Bag Book of Irish Studies, op. cit.*).

6. *Ibid.*, p. 80.

7. 'Novelists on the Novel; *op. cit.* pp. 76–80.

8. *Ibid.*, p. 79.

9. 'Sweet Harmony' by Francis Stuart in *The Sunday Tribune*, Feb. 8, 1981, p. 26.

10. I contrast this analysis of Banville's *The Newton Letter* to Bernard McLaverty's traditional quest-novel, *Cal*, in a review article entitled 'The Nightmare of History', *The Irish Literary Supplement*, Vol. 2, No. 2, 1983, pp. 24–25. See David McCormack, 'John Banville; Literature as Criticism' in *The Irish Review*, 2, 1987.

11. See my analysis of this novel as an example of the 'critical' counter-tradition of the Irish novel in 'The Crisis of Imagination', *The Crane Bag*, Vol. 3, No. 1, *op. cit.*, pp. 69–70.

5 Heaney and Homecoming

1. Frank O'Connor, *The Backward Look*, MacMillan, London. For an informed critical discussion of this revivalist reading of Heaney see Mark P. Hederman, 'Seamus Heaney: the Reluctant Poet' in *The Crane Bag*, Vol. 3, No. 2, 1979, pp. 61–71; Blake Morrison, *Seamus Heaney*, Methuen, 1982; Tony Curtis (Ed.)

The Art of Seamus Heaney, Poetry Wales Press, 1982; Edna Longley, 'Stars and Horses, Pigs and Trees' in The Crane Bag, Vol. 3, No. 2, 1979, pp. 54–60, and 'Poetry and Politics in Northern Ireland' in The Crane Bag, Vol. 9, No. 1, 1985, pp. 26–41; Timothy Kearney, 'The Poetry of the North: a Post-Modernist Perspective' in The Crane Bag, Vol. 3, No. 2, 1979, pp. 45–54; and finally Maurice Riordan, 'Eros and History: on Contemporary Irish Poetry' in The Crane Bag, Vol. 9, No. 1, 1985, pp. 49–56. The last of these essays offers perhaps the most explicit critique of the 'mythologizing impulse' in Heaney's work. Riordan gives an historical interpretation of this impulse as a carry-over from the aesthetic of the Irish literary revival. In accordance with political efforts to establish Ireland as a nation with a distinct identity, Irish poets, Riordan argues, have frequently sought to 'restore to the national imagination an image of the greatness of the past'. This 'mythologizing tendency', he claims, 'has persisted in Irish poetry, though perhaps its explicit political-ideological function has diminished'. The basic motivation remains largely that of evoking the 'spirit of Ireland as a sustaining power, usually in the form of a goddess who is bride of the poet's imagination'. Riordan links this motivation to the historical fact that the writers of the revival 'drew their force from the ideological preparation for a patricide, in which a colonial patriarchy is rejected for the sake of the motherland'. Relating this theme to the powerful poetic motif of Cathleen Ni Houlihan, Riordan observes that 'the glimpse of, the desire for, an originary amplitude and innocence is bodied forth in a myth of Ireland as an exalted entity – to be reverenced and known, and, above all, to be reclaimed by her royal sons and heirs'. Riordan concludes that Heaney's poetry conforms to this basic traditional aesthetic of re-fusing history in forms of myth: 'it opposes to the usurping historical characters, a mythological entity . . . as if to suggest that history were the intruder'. And even where Heaney's poetry does not ignore history, it is 'hard pressed by it . . . its summons is to be the sacred ground beyond history. It is nostalgic and melancholic, sporadically ecstatic, in its hunt for lost origins, for the lost site of bliss, where the self would feel its wholeness and potency. It is, in a word, Rousseauistic, a nationalistic mutation of romanticism'. Against this mythologizing nostalgia, Riordan advocates a modern Irish poetry 'prepared to embrace the varied adventure of its becoming, the gay responsibility of making, rather than remaking, history.' I will argue that a modernist or post-modernist reading of Heaney's work exposes an irony and ambiguity in his approach to mythology; and that this approach, far from being a Rousseauistic nationalism or romanticism, does succeed in making rather than simply remaking history – the two options being, in the final analysis, inseparable.

2. Terence Brown discussing Culture and Ideology in Ireland (ed. C. Curtin, M. Kelly and C. O'Dowd, Galway University Press, 1984) in The Crane Bag, Vol. 9, No. 1, 1985, p. 90.

3. Jim Kemmy, New Hibernia, November, 1984.

4. Seamus Heaney, Preoccupations: Selected Prose 1968–1978, Faber 1980, p. 52.

5. Heaney, Preoccupations, op.cit., p. 21.

6. S. Heaney, Preoccupations, op.cit., p 55.

7. M. Foucault, Language, Counter-Memory and Practice, 1977.

8. S. Heaney, Preoccupations, op.cit., p. 56.

9. Heaney, Ibid, p. 57.

10. S. Heaney, 'Unhappy and at Home' (An Interview with Seamus Deane) in *The Crane Bag*, Vol. I, No. I, 1977, p. 63.
11. S. Heaney, *Preoccupations, op.cit.*, p. 57. Another major source for Heaney's bog poems was Anne Ross's study, *The Religion of the Pagan Celts*, in which the author identifies the emblem of the severed human head as a 'kind of short-hand symbol for the entire religious outlook of the pagan Celts' (*Ibid*, p. 59). Indeed this Celtic motif of the severed head was also to provide the Irish painter and friend of Heaney – Louis le Brocquy – with the predominant theme for his 'head series' (of Joyce, Beckett and others) in the seventies and eighties. Le Brocquy claims that the severed 'human head, the mysterious box which contains the spirit, consciousness', is the 'deepest and most persistent of all Celtic images' ('A Painter's Notes on Awareness' in *The Crane Bag*, Vol. I, No. 2, 1977). Numerous scholarly researches have been conducted on this bizarre head cult of the Celts pointing up its sacrificial import. Of particular note is the study by the French anthropologist, Clémence Ramnoux, entitled *La mort sacrificielle du roi* (1954), in which the author documents instances in several Celtic myths of how the tribal communities sought to resolve their periodic crises by resorting to rites of sacrificial bloodletting (*La mort sacrificielle du roi* in *Ogham*, tradition Celtique, 1954). And it is not difficult to adduce more contemporary examples of this cult of sacrificial martyrdom in the recent history of Irish Republicanism (See my studies on 'Myth and Martyrdom' below).
12. S. Heaney, *Preoccupations, op.cit.*, p. 58.
13. In 'Funeral Rites', Heaney sees the burial tombs of the Boyne –Knowth, Dowth and Newgrange – as offering the possibility of a tribal home for his 'dead relations'. The Boyne Valley mounds were considered legendarily to be at once the *omphalos* of the earth – its *axis mundi* – and the sacred centre of Ireland itself: the valley is situated in Meath, in Gaelic *Midhe* or middle.
14. When another poetic persona, Friel's Frank Hardy in *Faith Healer* 'returns' home in the literal sense, he discovers that such homecoming entails his own destruction. Heaney's paradoxical response to the 'terrible beauty' of the ancestral cults of blood-sacrifice is nowhere more poignantly expressed, however, than in a poem called 'Punishment', when he compares the ancient ritual practice of sacrificing young maidens to tribal deities by drowning them in bogs to the contemporary Ulster rite of tarring and shaving girls who have associated with the enemy:

> My poor scapegoat,
>
> I almost love you
> But would have cast, I know,
> the stones of silence . . .
>
> Who would connive
> In civilized outrage
> Yet understand the exact
> And tribal, intimate revenge.

In a poem called 'Strange Fruit', which immediately follows 'Punishment' in *North*, Heaney adapts the anti-lynching elegy of Billie Holiday, to repudiate his own reaction to tribal revenge: 'Murdered, forgotten, nameless, terrible/ Beheaded girl, outstaring axe/And beatification, outstaring/ What had begun to feel like reverence'.

15. S. Heaney, *Preoccupations*, *op.cit.*, p. 35.

16. *Ibid*, p. 37.

17. Jacques Lacan, *Ecrits*, 1966.

18. S. Heaney, *Preoccupations*, *op.cit.*, p. 78; see Blake Morrison's analysis of the theme of 'silence' in Heaney's poetry in *Seamus Heaney* (Methuen, 1983).

19. This characteristic tension in Heaney's work between the sanctity of home and the sceptism of homelessness is perceptively summed up by his fellow northerner Seamus Deane: 'The poet turns, entering into conversations with his family, his friends, his dead, his various personae . . . asking for manumission from his enslavement to reverence, and fearful that it will be granted. As always with Heaney, there is a paradox here. Even in his caution there is risk, and one of the delights of his poetry is to see the variety of ways in which he can pungently embody the opposing attitudes . . . "a cunning middle voice" learns to negotiate between the known and the foreign, the dialect of the local and the *lingua franca* of the world. Even in berating himself for his caution, he recognizes that he enhances the feeling of veneration for everything that is private, love-worn, ancestral by the very act of suspecting it, of chastening its easily available consolations. On the other hand, this suspicion allows him to bring in the voice of the other, peremptory world of the present, with its political crises and its alien immediacies. *Station Island's* three parts are phases in the intricate debate thus established'. S. Deane, 'A Noble Startling Achievement' in *The Irish Literary Supplement*, Spring 1985, pp. 1, 34.

20. It might be noted that Heaney's notion of homecoming as an endless circling around an origin that is no-longer or not-yet, an absent centre, a siteless site, is in tune with the basic post-modernist emphasis on cultural discontinuity and heterogeneity – what has been termed the 'crisis in cultural authority' (by Craig Owens in *Postmodern Culture*, ed. H. Foster, Pluto Press, 1983, p. 57). Heaney's overriding obsession with idioms of nomadic pilgrimage – while paying passing tribute to romantic notions of 'sacred contemporaneity' (the cultural project of uniting past and present in some quasi-mystical epiphany) – also works in the opposite direction: his poems often serve as ironic self-parodies of the orthodox Irish cultural aesthetic, with its concern to retrieve a sacred, mythic motherland. Yet Heaney is equally determined to avoid the modernist cult of aesthetic individualism. Here one finds certain parallels with the post-modern philosophy of Derrida and Foucault, the post-modern literature of Ashbery and Pynchon, or the post-modern cinema of Wenders – in particular the self-parodying homecoming motifs of *Paris, Texas*. Like Travis in *Paris, Texas*, Heaney's poetic *personae* carry with them faded photographic memories of their ancestral origins (the film's title refers to a plot of land in Paris, Texas, where Travis was conceived), but never succeed in returning home. The very quest for the lost origin is the very impossibility of ever arriving there. We have here a poetics of perpetual detour – perhaps the most signal feature of Heaney's contemporary journeywork.

21. Freud, *The 'Uncanny'* in *New Literary History* (Vol. VII, No. 3, 1976), p. 623.

22. See in particular the commentary of Freud's essay by Hélène Sixous, 'Fiction and its phantoms' in *New Literary History*, No. 7, 1976, pp. 525–548.

23. Freud, *The 'Uncanny'*, *op. cit.*, p. 622.

24. Freud, *Ibid*, p. 624.

25. Freud, *Ibid*, p. 630.

26. Freud, *Ibid*, p. 631.

27. Freud, *Ibid*, p. 634.

28. Freud, *Ibid*, p. 635.

29. Freud also offers the following personal example of his experience of the 'uncanny' as a 'repetition of the same thing' – "As I was walking one hot summer afternoon through the deserted streets of a provincial town in Italy which was unknown to me, I found myself in a quarter of whose character I could not long remain in doubt. Nothing but painted women were to be seen at the windows of the small houses, and I hastened to leave the narrow street at the next turning. But after having wandered about for a time without enquiring I suddenly found myself back in the same street, where my presence was now beginning to excite attention. I hurried away once more only to arrive by another detour at the same place yet a third time. Now, however, a feeling overcame me which I can only describe as uncanny . . . Other situations which have in common with my adventure an unintended recurrence of the same situation, but which differ radically from it in other respects, also result in the same feeling of helplessness and of uncanniness' (*Ibid*, p. 631.

30. Heaney, *Preoccupations, op.cit.*, p. 20.

31. Heaney, *Ibid*, p. 212.

32. Heaney, *Ibid*, p. 47–8.

33. It is useful to recall, in this regard, that in the original Greek myth, Narcissus was not seen as a victim of his own egoism, but as an emancipator of the aesthetic potencies of both nature and his own creative eros. Herbert Marcuse puts this point well in his *Eros and Civilization*: 'The spring and the forest respond to Narcissus' desire . . . Narcissistic Eros awakens and liberates potentialities that are real in things animate and inanimate, in organic and inorganic nature – real but in the un-erotic reality suppressed . . . In the Narcissistic experience of the world . . . the opposition between man and nature, subject and object, is overcome. Being is experienced as gratification, which unites man and nature so that the fulfillment of man is at the same time fulfillment, without violence, of nature. In being spoken to, loved, and cared for, flowers and springs and animals appear as what they are – beautiful . . . the things of nature become free to be what they are' (*Eros and Civilisation*, 1966, pp. 165–6). In 'Eros and History: On Contemporary Irish Poetry' (*The Crane Bag, op. cit.*), Maurice Riordan offers the following controversial account of the relation between sexuality and poetry in modern Irish literature: 'The sexual relationship between the poet and his subject, moreover, is not incidental or merely a conceit; on the contrary, the poet frequently uses erotic language when broaching such subjects as cultural identity, history or landscape. It is surely strange that eroticism should arise at all in relation to such subjects; that it should do so consistently seems to imply not just the political incompleteness of the nationalist revolution, but a psychological incompleteness as well (. . .) Heaney's poetry carries this eroticization of the landscape a step further . . . enacting an identity between the psyche and landscape. (Heaney's bog poems) draw up their exotic strange fruit from the bog; the deeds of men are restored to light in an assuaging rhetoric, in the voluptuous auto-erotic ease of a language that flows in vowel and consonant over tongue and tooth'. (pp. 49, 54).

34. Heaney, *Preoccupations*, p. 35.

34a Heaney, *Ibid*. p. 132.

34b Heaney, *An Open Letter*, Field Day, 1983.

35. M. Heidegger, *Being and Time* (1927), para. 40.

36. Heidegger, *Ibid*.

37. M. Heidegger, *Poetry, Language, Thought* (1971), p. 91, *et. seq.*

38. Heidegger, *Ibid*; see also M. Heidegger, *Introduction to Metaphysics* (1973), p. 127, *et. seq.*, and M. Heidegger, *Commentaries on Hölderlin* (1971), pp. 23–31.

39. M. Heidegger, *Commentaries on Hölderlin, op. cit.*

But we should not forget that for Heaney, as for Heidegger, there is also a *positive* side to the religious and mythological dimensions of poetry. The poet names what is holy, according to Heidegger, in the measure that he seeks to relocate things in the ontological play of the world's fourfold – earth, sky, mortals and gods. Heaney makes a similar point, I suggest, when he contends that poetry aspires towards a 'sacramental apprehension of things' (*Pre.* p. 90).

Such an apprehension does not serve to reinforce some racist cult of ancestral supermen; it works in the ∾pposite direction to forestall any such fascist deification of a pure, preoriginal race by enabling us to come to terms with our unconscious atavisms and thereby transform them. It demystifies the past in order to preserve its essential mystery for the present. Hence, rather than incarcerating us in the old myths of superstition and bigotry, it strains to renew myth into a liberating dimension of experience. This is surely what Heaney intends when he ratifies Patmore's maxim that 'the end of art is peace'. And this is also why Heaney's poetic reworking of local idioms – e.g. place names – assumes a significance which extends beyond the locale itself. Without such a re-formation of his communal, national or cultural origins it is hard to imagine how Heaney's work could have communicated so effectively to other nations and cultures – the Anglo-American in particular.

Heaney's foregrounding of the sacramental dimension of poetry is to be understood, therefore, not in the sense of some triumphalist bigotry which would sacrifice the humble things of this earth for the sake of an otherworldly kingdom in the future or an antediluvian golden age in the past. For Heaney to say that poetry can have a sacramental role is to say that it can help restore things to their sacred uniqueness in the present play of the world's fourfold dimensions. In an essay on art, Heidegger disclosed the way in which a simple jug could poetically re-enact this cosmic play. In *Station Island*, Section X, Heaney evokes this same restorative power of the *logos* – the play of language as a language of play. The poet writes here of an inconspicuous mug that had remained on a shelf in his home for many years, 'unchallenging and unremembered', no more significant than the 'thud of earthenware on the common table'; until one day it was rescued from its taken-for-granted role as a reified object – 'still as a milestone' – by two actors who borrowed it as a prop for a play. Beholding the actors as lovers on a stage kissing the mug and calling it their 'loving cup', the poet feels estranged from his domestic possession for the first time. But by the same token, by means of this very estrangement, he also sees the mug in all its strangeness for the first time – translated and redeemed, as it were, by the language of play:

> Dipped and glamoured from this translation
> It was restored with all its cornflower haze
>
> Still dozing, its parchment glazes fast –
> As the other surfaced once with Ronan's psalter
> Miraculously unharmed, that had been lost
> A day and a night under lough water.
>
> And so the saint praised God on the lough shore.
> The dazzle of the impossible suddenly
> Blazed across the threshold, a sun-glare
> To put out the small hearths of constancy.

This poem could be interpreted in Heideggerean terms as a translation of the unholy into the holy. The poet's act of remembrance would be understood as releasing the mug from its inauthentic existence as an anonymous object amongst objects into its own authentic 'inscape' as a play of the fourfold. The poem would then be seen as bringing together the habitually opposed claims of earth (the earthenware on the common table) and sky (the blue-eyed haze and the sun's glare), mortals (the transfiguring act of the players) and gods (the saint's celebration of the divine miracle). In this way, the creative re-play of actor and poet can be construed as liberating the mug from its familiar home into that *unheimlich* dimension which allows it to be restored to its unfamiliar, because forgotten, home – 'it reappeared . . . back in its place'. In other words, by entering the play of the poetic *logos*, the mug undergoes a sea-change into something strange and precious, it is allowed poetically to dwell.

Section X of the 'Station Island' sequence exemplifies in a concrete and unpretentious manner, the main sacramental attributes of poetic language as outlined by Heidegger – remembrance, homecoming, the naming of the holy, the piety of thinking, the presencing of the strange and the play of the fourfold. The ultimate end of such poetic language is peace. Not just the private ease of the poet, but the well-being of the entire community. For the final aim of poetry is, Heaney insists, 'to be of service, to ply the effort of the individual work into the larger work of the community as a whole' (*Pre*. p. 106).

40. Heidegger, *Ibid*.
41. Hence the curious fact that the 'joy' of homecoming is at all times tempered by 'serenity'. If, therefore, Heidegger speaks of poetry allowing us to come home, he means it not in the sense of some triumphalistic revival of the past (*Heimkunft*), but rather in the sense of an arriving which can never finally arrive: a perpetual arriving (*Heimkommen*) which preserves itself in the serene expectancy of an advent (*Ankunft*). Moreover, this problem is not confined to the individual consciousness of the poet. The poet cannot inaugurate a home-coming by himself; he needs others to listen to his language as a caring for the hidden dimensions of Being, and to take the burden of that caring upon themselves. 'Once spoken, the word slips away from the guardianship of the caring poet', affirms Heidegger, 'and so the poet must turn to the others, so that their remembrance can help the poetic word be understood, with the result that the homecoming self-appropriately transpires for each in his destined way' (*Commentaries on Hölderlin*, op. cit.). Poetry thus reveals itself as a *social* as well as *aesthetic* responsibility. And the fact that it informs society with scruples of care, serenity and anxiety ensures that all revivalist assumptions that 'home' is some pre-existing, secure tenure are exploded.
41a. In contradistinction, therefore, to an exclusively utilitarian view of language, poetic thinking allows the beauty and originality of language to come to light as it is in itself. Rather than deploying words as mere instruments or strategies, the poet invites us to dwell in language by listening to it speak. He dares language to be itself. Silence thus reveals itself as an essential dimension of language in so far as it resists all possibility of objectification. Though we can use language to objectify things in words, the Being of language itself can never be objectified in words. And this is why it is often when words fail us, when language withholds itself in silence, that we are compelled to break off our total preoccupation with things and attend to language itself as that which allows things to be in the first place. 'Where is language itself brought to word?', asks Heidegger. 'Strangely

enough, there where we cannot find the right word for something which concerns us. . . . Thus, we let that which we mean or intend acquiesce or rest in the unspoken and thereby, without properly reflecting about it, pass through moments in which language itself has touched us, fleetingly and from afar, with its presencing' (*On The Way to Language*, 1971).

42. M. Heidegger, *On The Way to Language*, *op.cit.*, p. 152. See also L.M. Vail, *Heidegger and The Ontological Difference* (1972), pp. 169f.

43. M. Heidegger, *Poetry, Language, Thought*, *op.cit.*, p. 226. In a study entitled *Language in the Poem*, Heidegger expands his analysis of '*homecoming*' as poetic estrangement in a commentary on Georg Trakl's verse, 'Something strange is the soul on the earth'. He makes quite clear that he understands the term 'strange' (*fremd*), not in the sense of occult escapism, but as a concrete existential experience open to all human beings who specifically seek to dwell poetically in the innermost, and for that reason frequently unknown, being of things:

'The word we are using – the German '*fremd*' . . . really means – forward to somewhere else, underway toward –, onward to the encounter with what is kept in store for it. The strange goes forth, ahead. But it does not roam aimlessly, without any kind of determination. The strange element goes in its search toward the site where it may stay in its wandering. Almost unknown to itself, the 'strange' is already following the call that calls it on the way into its own. The poet calls the soul 'something strange on the earth'. The earth is that very place which the soul's wandering could not reach so far. The soul only *seeks* the earth; it does not flee from it. This fulfills the soul's being: in her wandering to seek the earth so that she may poetically build and dwell upon it, and thus may be able to save the earth *as* earth (*On the Way to Language*, *op. cit.*, p. 163).

See also Heidegger's analysis of Trakl in *Language* in *Poetry, Language, Thought*, *op. cit.*, pp. 187–210; and his analysis of Rilke in *What are Poets For* in *Poetry, Language, Thought*, *op. cit.*, pp. 89–142.

44. All quotations from Celan are from Michael Hamburger's translation *Paul Celan: Poems*, Carcanet New Press, Manchester, 1980.

6 The Language Plays of Brian Friel

1. *The Man from God Knows Where*, Interview with Brian Friel by Fintan O'Toole, *In Dublin*, No. 165, Oct. 1982, p. 21.

2. *Ibid*. p. 21.

3. *Ibid*. p. 22.

4. *Ibid*. p. 20.

5. *Ibid*. p. 21. See *The Crane Bag Book of Irish Studies op. cit.* pp. 10–12.

6. *Ibid*. p. 23.

7. *Ibid*. p. 23.

8. *Poetry, Language, Thought*. by Martin Heidegger. Trans. A. Hofstadter, Harper and Row, 1971, p. 215 (. . . 'Poetically Man Dwells' . . .).

9. Heidegger, *ibid*, p. 134 ('What are Poets for?').

10. Friel's diary entries for May 29 and June 1, 1979, quoted by Richard Pine in *The Diviner: The Art of Brian Friel* (Lilliput Press, 1988).

11. *The Man from God Knows Where*, *op. cit.*, p. 22.

12. *Ibid*. p. 22.

13. Quoted by Richard Pine, *op. cit.*

14. Quoted by Richard Pine, *op. cit.*

15. *The Man from God Knows Where*, op. cit. p. 23.

16. *Complete Works of Oscar Wilde* (Collins, London, 1949), p. 1023.

17. 'Anglo-Irish Playwrights and the Comic Tradition' by T. Kilroy in *Crane Bag*, Vol. 3, No. 2, 1979.

17a Interview with Tom MacIntyre by Ciaran Carty in 'Arts Tribune', *The Sunday Tribune*, 8 Sept., 1985.

18. *Dialogue* by Ciaran Carty, Arts Page, *Sunday Independent*, Oct. 24, 1982.

19. 'Word and Flesh: A View of Theatre as Performance' by D. McKenna in *Crane Bag*, Vol. 6., No. 1, 1982.

20. Brian McEvera in *Fortnight* Magazine, No. 215, March '85, pp. 19–21.

21. Edna Longley, 'Poetry and Politics in Northern Ireland' in *Contemporary Cultural Debate, The Crane Bag*, Vol. 9, No. 1, 1985, p. 28.

22. John Wilson Foster, 'The Landscape of the Planter and the Gael', in the *Canadian Journal of Irish Studies*, Vol. 1, No. 2, Nov. 1975, quoted Longley, *op. cit.*

23. Longley, *op. cit.*, p. 29.

24. John Andrews and Brian Friel, *'Translations* and *A Paper Landscape:* Between Fiction and History' (with a preface by Kevin Barry) in *The Forum Issue* of *The Crane Bag*, Vol. 7, No. 2, 1983, pp. 118–125.

25. *Poetry, Language, Thought*, op. cit. p. 226 (. . . 'Poetically Man Dwells' . . .).

26. In part III of the *Essay*, entitled 'Words of Language in General', Locke used his 'historical, plain method' of empiricist rationalism in order to overcome 'the artifice, fallacy . . . and cheat of words' (III, x) caused by the traditional notions of a natural or ontological language, and to replace it with a pragmatic interpretation of language based on the commonsense correlation of words with empirical sensations. 'All words', Locke argued, 'are taken from the operations of sensible things' (III, i). He maintained that these operations were best appreciated by 'those minds the study of mathematics has opened' (Locke, *Works*, Vol. VIII). Language can be exploited in the domination of the logos of Being by the logic of science, for 'the making of *Species* and *Genera* is in order to generalise names' (III, vi). Locke wished to abolish the confusion of uncertainty spawned by mystical or metaphysical doctrines of language (e.g. Boehme's belief in the 'signatures of things', the 'language of nature . . . which is a secret, a mystery granted by the grace of God'). He promoted instead a *conventionalist* theory of naming which argued that there is no essential or intrinsic relationship between being and words, only an arbitrary rapport *imposed* by men for reasons of ease, order, efficacy and utility – what he called 'the improvement of understanding'. Rejecting all ontological models of naming in favour of a representational model, Locke insisted that 'the same liberty also, that Adam had of affixing any new name to any Idea, the same has one still. . . . But in communication with others, it is necessary, that we conform the ideas (i.e. common sensible ideas) we make the Vulgar Words of any language stand for, to their known proper significations, or else to make known what new signification we apply to them' (III, v). 'The signification of sounds', Locke affirms accordingly, 'is not natural, but only imposed and arbitrary' (III, iv). Locke's exclusive emphasis on scientific objectivity compelled him to jettison the ancient doctrine that some etymological alliance could obtain between language and nature; he had no time for the etymologist's reverence for language as a remembrance of the hidden *origins* of meaning or community (See Hans Aarleff, *From Locke to Saussure, Essays on the Study of Language and Intellectual History*, Athlone, London, 1982, pp. 66–9, 82–3).

For Locke, language was merely a tool for the attainment of certain and certi-fiable knowledge. Words were legitimate in so far as they were useful and useful in so far as they enabled men to 'range (things) into sorts, in order of their naming, for the convenience of comprehensive signs . . . so that we may truly say, such a manner of sorting things is the Workmanship of Men' (III, vi).

Speaking of how such Enlightenment positivism serves to reduce man's rich sense of temporal and historical being to a manageable 'picture', William Spanos, the Heideggerean critic, talks appositely of 'a flattened out, static and homogeneous Euclidean space – a totalized and ontologically depthless system of referents (a *map*) – if the objectifying consciousness is positivistic. . . ." (See *Deconstructive Criticism*, by V. Leitch, Hutchinson University Library, 1983, p. 74).

27. *Anthropologie Structurale*, Paris, 1958; see also *Structuralism and Since*, Oxford U.P. 1979, edited by John Sturrock.

7 Tom Murphy's Long Journey into Night

1. Cf. Tom Murphy, *Collected Plays,* Vol. 1, *(The Gigli Concert, On the Outside, Sanctuary Lamp, A Whistle in the Dark)* Gallery Books, Dublin, 1983.

2. See my article on 'Language Play: Brian Friel and Ireland's Verbal Theatre' in *Studies*, Spring, 1983, pp. 20–56.

3. Christopher Murray, 'The Art of Tom Murphy' in the Abbey Theatre Program to *The Gigli Concert*, September, 1983. I am also grateful to Murray for several of the above quotations. See also Murray's informative article on Tom Murphy in 'The Contemporary Irish Writers Series', 7, in *Ireland Today*, No. 997, April 1983; and his specially edited issue of *The Irish University Review* (Spring 1987) devoted to the work of Tom Murphy. This issue includes very illuminating articles by Fintan O'Toole and Patrick Mason on *The Gigli Concert*.

4. Quoted Fintan O'Toole, 'Going West: The Country versus The City in Irish Writing', in *The Crane Bag*, Vol. 9, No. 2, 1985.

5. *Ibid*. Fintan O'Toole offers the following commentary on the central role played by the Abbey Theatre in this Revivalist project: 'The notion of the peasant and of the country which the peasant embodied was not a reflection of Irish reality but an artificial literary creation, largely made in Dublin, for Dubliners. It was a political image of the countryside which helped to create a sense of social cohesion in a country which was trying to define itself over against England. Since the revival centred around the Abbey Theatre it was not enough to simply create peasants of the mind, creatures of the imagination. The Abbey had to literally create a company of peasants to act the peasant plays which made up two thirds of its early repertoire. It had to create an imagined country in the heart of the city. It had to turn Dublin clerks and civil servants into western peasants'.

The dramatic transposition of urban to rural life required that modern Dubliners had to be convinced that what they were viewing on the Abbey Stage were *real* peasants (and not simply idealized fictions). And this resulted in the Abbey's use of ultra-naturalistic scenery featuring *real* three-legged stools, creels of turf or spinning wheels beside the fireside. The pretence that the Abbey was a theatre of real peasants in the heart of the city meant that 'for a Dublin audience, which was often no more than a generation removed from the countryside, a visit to the Abbey was a travelogue into its collective past' *(Ibid.)*. But this pretence also served, ironically, to re-enforce certain colonial stereotypes of the Irish

peasant as a charming and fanciful Celt, 'a dreamer of dreams' unadulterated by
the pressures and exigencies of modern urban existence. By continuing to
romanticize the golden age of rural peasantry, the national literary revival thus
occasionally interiorized, despite itself, the patronizing imperial views of the
former British colonizers:

'The charm and naturalness seen by the (Revival) writers in the Irish west is in
its turn reproduced as a literary creation and is recognised at the heart of the
Empire as the genuine essence of Ireland. The Irish identity which has been
'revived' over and against England is an identity which fits in well with one
aspect of colonial paternalism. The Abbey presented itself in such a way as to
allow it to be patronised, creating a strong identification between the peasant and
childishness, and, for England, an identification between Ireland and
childishness. . . . Their language is the language of the British imperialist talking
about the wild savages of the jungle – naive, animal-like, part of the landscape,
outside of history – and the fact that it was not seen as such is a mark of how
effectively the revival had nationalised colonial attitudes, internalising a process
which belonged to the colonial mentality and selling it back to the outside world
as a reflection of Irish reality. The appeal of the peasant-as-child was an appeal
to an imagined past, freezing and fossilising the country as an unreal category, a
safe and conservative myth'*(ibid.)*. Fintan O'Toole shows how Tom Murphy's
play *Bailegangaire* (1986) serves to parody and subvert such stock revivalist
motifs in his review article of the play (gallery, 1986) in *The Irish Review*,
2, 1987.

6. Lecture at the Royal Dublin Society, Un. 1984, quoted by Richard Pine in *The
   Diviner: The Art of Brian Friel* (The Lilliput Press, forthcoming).
7. Quoted by Claudia Harris in *The Irish Literary Supplement*, Spring, 1985,
   p. 39.
8. Seamus Heaney in an Interview with Seamus Deane, 'Unhappy and at Home' in
   The Crane Bag, Vol. 1, No. 1, 1977, and in *The Crane Bag Book of Irish
   Studies op. cit.*
9. See my 'Heidegger and the Possible', *(Philosophical Studies,* Vol. xxvii, 1980,
   pp. 176–195); 'Heidegger, le possible et Dieu' in *Heidegger et la question de
   Dieu* (edited by Richard Kearney & J.S. O'Leary, Grasset, Paris, 1980,
   pp. 125–168); and my *Poétique du Possible op. cit.*
10. Perhaps even Murphy's uncompromising defence of the three-hour duration of
    The Gigli Concert against those 'condescending, begrudging' critics (his terms)
    who recommended it be cut by an hour, itself revealed the author's conviction
    that the artist is, almost by his very nature, condemned to challenge the
    conformist expectancies of 'public opinion'. Murphy particularly resented the
    assumption that plays be written according to a standardized two-hour formula
    (with time 'for a quick dinner beforehand and a drink afterwards'). The work of
    art, he retorted, has its own laws of time and space. Of course, Murphy's
    turbulent relation with his critics is incidental to the nature of his work. But since
    everything Murphy writes – and *The Gigli Concert* is certainly no exception – is
    written, after the manner of O'Neill or O'Casey, from the 'blood, sweat and tears'
    of the author's personally felt experience, this relation is perhaps not altogether
    irrelevant an analogy for the defiant Murphyesque anti-hero incorrigibly at odds
    with society. (Moreover, these remarks on Murphy's individualistic repudiation
    of the collectivity are in no way intended to diminish his fidelity to the theatrical
    community itself. Directors, actors and audiences have all borne witness to his
    deep commitment to the communal act of collaboration – be it with the Druid or

Abbey companies – which is the hallmark of great drama).

11. Since the completion of this article Murphy wrote *Bailegangaire* (1986) a play which develops many of the themes of *The Gigli Concert* and his early dramas: in particular, the soul destroying constraints of contemporary Irish society and the power of creative fiction and story telling to conquer in spite of all.

8   Nationalism and Irish Cinema

1. Luke Gibbons, 'Lies that tell the Truth: History and Irish Cinema' in *The Crane Bag*, Vol. 7, No. 2, 1983. I use the term 'Irish Cinema' in a general sense to refer to films made *in* Ireland *about* Ireland (but not necessarily by Irish directors or actors etc).
2. Gibbons, *ibid*.
3. Gibbons, *ibid*.
4. Quoted by Kevin Rockett, 'Irish Cinema: Notes on some Nationalist Fictions' in *Screen*, Vol. 20, Nos. 3/4, 1979, p. 118.
5. Kevin Barry, 'Cinema and Feminism' in *The Furrow*, 1985, p. 244.
6. Neil Jordan, Interview with Colm Toibín in *In Dublin*, No. 152, 1982.
7. John Boorman, Interview with Ray Comiskey in *The Irish Times*, 1981.
8. Neil Jordan, Interview with Ray Comiskey in *The Irish Times*, May 11, 1982.
9. Neil Jordan, *ibid*.
10. Thomas Mann, *Dr. Faustus*, for a further discussion of this theme see my 'Beyond Art and Politics' in *The Crane Bag*, Vol. I, No. 1, 1977.
11. Kevin Barry calls these synchronic motifs, which cut across the diachronic narrative plot, 'discarded images' in his article 'Discarded Images: Themes of Narrative in Cinema' in *The Crane Bag*, Vol. 6, No. 1, 1982, pp. 45–52, which includes an analysis of Joe Comerford's *Travellers*, scripted by Neil Jordan.
12. Neil Jordan, *Irish Times* interview, *op. cit.*
13. Jordan, *ibid*.
14. Pauline Kael, *Deeper into Movies*, Warner Books, New York, 1969, p. 343.
15. Barbara O'Connor, 'Aspects of Representation of Women in Irish Film' in the *Media and Popular Culture* issue of *The Crane Bag*, Vol. 8, No. 2, 1984, p. 79; See also on this theme 'Is Television Drama Ideological?' by Helena Sheehan, *The Crane Bag*, Vol. 9, No. 1, 1985, pp. 79–83.
16. Barbara O'Connor, *op. cit.*, p. 79.
16a. For an extended analysis of this theme see my article, 'The Iphigeneia Complex in Recent Irish Cinema', in *Studies*, Spring, 1984.
17. Luke Gibbons, *op. cit.*, p. 150. See also L. Gibbons, 'Romanticism in Ruins: Developments in Recent Irish Cinema' in *The Irish Review*, No. 2, 1987; and *Cinema and Ireland* by L. Gibbons, K. Rockett and J. Hill, Croom Helm Ltd, 1987.
18. Philip Marcus, *Standish O'Grady*, Lewisburg, 1970, p. 35 (quoted by Gibbons).
19. Standish O'Grady, *History of Ireland*, 1881, p. 51 (quoted by Gibbons). See also Fintan O'Toole's article, 'Going West: The Country versus the City in Irish Writing' in *The Crane Bag*, Vol. 9, No. 2, 1985. O'Toole writes: 'For the last hundred years, Irish culture and in particular Irish writing has been marked by the dominance of the rural over the urban, a dominance based on a false opposition of the country to the city which has been vital to the maintenance of a conservative political culture in the country. The Irish literary revival of the turn of the century was not a rural phenomenon. It was created in a metropolitan

context for a metropolitan audience. Yet it helped to create and sustain an image of rural Ireland as an ideal which fed into the emergent political culture of Irish nationalism.'

20. Gibbons, *Lies that Tell the Truth*, *op. cit.*, pp. 150–151.
21. Pat Murphy, interview in *Iris*, June, 1984.
22. Gibbons, *ibid.*, p. 151. See also Murphy's 'Open Letter', *Circa*, 1987.
23. Gibbons, *ibid*, p. 153. On the dominance of verbal over visual discourse in Irish Culture, see Gibbons, 'Word and Image: Film and Irish Writing' in *Graph*, 2. Spring 1987, pp. 2–3.
24. Barbara O'Connor, *op. cit.*, p. 80.
25. O'Connor, *ibid*.
26. See Luke Gibbons, 'Ideology and the Media' in *Workers Life*, Vol. 4, No. 6, 1983, p. 19.
27. O'Connor, *op. cit.*, p. 83.

9 An Art of Otherness: A Study of Louis Le Brocquy

1. Conor Joyce, 'Louis le Brocquy' in *Circa* art magazine, No. 22, May/June 1985, p. 32.
2. Louis le Brocquy, 'A Painter's Notes on Ambivalence' in *The Crane Bag*, Vol. 1, No. 2, 1977, p. 69; reprinted in *The Crane Bag Book of Irish Studies, op. cit.*, p. 152.
3. Le Brocquy, *ibid.*
4. Le Brocquy, 'Notes on Painting and Awareness' in *Louis le Brocquy*, edited by Dorothy Walker, Ward River Press, 1981, p. 135.
5. Roland Barthes, *Mythologies*; quoted by Denis Donoghue in *The Arts Without Mystery*, The British Broadcasting Corporation, 1983, p. 137.
6. Quoted Richard Ellmann, *James Joyce*, Oxford University Press, p. 393. As Joyce remarks in *Finnegans Wake*: 'every person, place and thing in the chaosmos of Alle was moving and changing every part of the time'; so that the text constitutes a multiplicity of 'forged palimpsests'.
7. Le Brocquy, 'A Painter's Notes on his Irishness', in *The Recorder*, Vol. 42.
8. Quoted Ellmann, *op. cit.*, p. 597.
9. Herbert Marcuse, *The Aesthetic Dimension,* Beacon Press, Boston, 1978.
10. Le Brocquy 'Notes on Painting and Awareness', *op. cit.,* p. 135.
11. Le Brocquy, *ibid.*, p. 146.
12. Marcuse, *op. cit..*, p. 13.
13. *Ibid.*, p. 22. Marcuse's spirited defence of the otherness of art was shared by several of his humanist-Marxist colleagues in the Frankfurt School of Social Research – in particular Adorno and Horkheimer. This defence has been most cogently developed in recent years by the art critic Peter Fuller who has consistently attacked all attempts by both orthodox Marxism and bourgeois conservatism to reduce the aesthetic dimension of art to the utilitarian functions of ideology or consumerism. Fuller sums up his position in a manifesto entitled 'Towards a Materialist Aesthetic': 'The aesthetic dimension which I uphold implies the rejection of . . . the simplistic equation of art with the so-called technologizing ethos of modern times. It calls for the refusal of the visual ideology of contemporary capitalism — the publicity syndrome — which is also frequently evidenced in certain left-wing ideologies of art. This refusal affirms the existence of a reality *other-than-this-one* which I believe is anticipated by the

"aesthetic dimension" which can find expression in authentic painting, sculpture and design.' Peter Fuller, 'Towards a Materialist Aesthetic' in *Penser L'Art Contemporain: Bulletin de la Biennale de Paris,* 1980, p. 158. One might also note here some curious similarities between le Brocquy's paintings and the modern continental philosophies of deconstruction –particularly those of Heiddegger, Merleau-Ponty and Derrida – which attempt to reinstate the alterity and ambivalence of meaning which the logocentric bias of traditional western thought has consigned to oblivion. Logocentrism is to philosophy what classical realism is to art – that is, an attempt to reduce the multiplicity and mystery of being to a single centralizing and controlling perspective (the *logos*). Heidegger seeks to deconstruct this logocentric prejudice of classical thinking, based on the reduction of human experience to a linear non-contradictory consciousness, in order to rediscover the essential strangeness (*Unheimlichkeit*) of Being as a presencing which absences, as a giving (*Es Gibt*) which recedes. Indeed, it is significant that Heidegger looks to modern poets and painters as the best guides or witnesses to this suppressed dimension of ontological otherness. Derrida also urges philosophy to take its 'deconstructive' lead from modern literature and art in its disclosure of the disseminating character of language as an endless play of multiple meaning. And Merleau-Ponty, another exponent of Heideggerian *Destruktion*, concludes his celebrated study of painting, *Eye and Mind*, by suggesting that what we call artistic inspiration should be understood as a response to the irreducible ambivalence of being: 'There is truly inspiration and expiration of Being, action and passion so scarcely discernible that one no longer knows what sees and what is seen, what paints and what is painted. One says that a man is born at that instant when that which was but a virtual visibility at the heart of the maternal body makes itself visible for itself and for us. The vision of a painter is a perpetual birth.' Merleau-Ponty, *Eye and Mind* in *Phenomenology, Language and Sociology*, Heinemann, London, pp. 28—312. Le Brocquy's paintings are powerful aesthetic testaments to this dual inspiration and expiration of Being which defy our accredited modes of perception.

14. Marcuse, *ibid* pp. 35, 39.

15. Le Brocquy, interview with Harriet Cooke in *The Irish Times* quoted by Dorothy Walker, *op. cit.*, p. 69.

16. But le Brocquy is not the only modern painter to speak about this enigmatic reciprocity of aesthetic interiority and otherness. Max Ernst declared that the task of the painter is to 'discern that which sees itself through him'. Similarly, Paul Klee described how he used to experience the trees of a forest perceiving him and speaking to him as he painted them, concluding: 'I think that the painter should be transpersed by the universe rather than wish to transperse it . . . I wait to be submerged and to submit; and I paint in order to emerge'. See my essay, 'Phénoménologie et Péinture' in *Penser L'Art Contemporain,* Bulletin de la Biennale de Paris, Paris, 1980, pp. 117–129.

17. Le Brocquy, 'Notes on Painting and Awareness', *op. cit.,* p. 139.

18. Le Brocquy, *ibid.*, pp. 147–9.

19. Quoted by John Russell in his introduction to *Louis le Brocquy, op. cit.,* p. 16; See also le Brocquy's remark to Harriet Cooke: 'Where an artist is concerned his own personality should not be imposed but overcome,' *ibid.*, p. 39.

20. Seamus Heaney, 'Louis le Brocquy's Heads' in *Louis le Brocquy, op. cit.,* p. 132. Referring specifically to his Joyce images, le Brocquy elaborates as follows on this paradox of painting as an emergence of the *other* through the suspension of the *self*: 'Is there an archeology of the spirit? Certainly neither my will nor my

skill has played any essential part in these studies. For the fact is that many of them emerged entirely under my ignorant left hand – my right hand being for some months immobilized in plaster. So it would appear that no dexterity whatever was involved in forming these images, which tended to emerge automatically, so to speak, jerked into coherence by a series of scrutinized accidents, impelled by my curiosity to discover something of the man and, within him, the inverted mirror image of my own experience.' (Quoted Dorothy Walker, *op. cit.,* p. 60).

21. Le Brocquy, 'A Painter's Notes on his Irishness', *op. cit.*
22. See Dorothy Walker's essay in *Louis le Brocquy, op. cit.,* p. 44. She writes: 'Two aspects of Celtic culture may still be said to inform Irish art in the twentieth century: one is the head image and the other is the cyclical abstract linearity of form and structure. Le Brocquy's head images, although single images centrally placed on the canvas, have nothing to do with a Renaissance dimension of centrist order. On the contrary, the image defies its central placing by floating in an indeterminate space between planes. This effect is sometimes accentuated by the artist's device of placing the central image within two faintly delineated squares, one unfinished at the top and the other unfinished at the bottom. The artist has invested this nebulous space not just with the memory or recreation of one man, but with one man from time immemorial. In the barely palpable evidence of a human image, a human presence moves slowly forward to the surface of the painting from unimaginable depths of time'.
23. Le Brocquy, 'Notes on Painting and Awareness', *op. cit.,* pp. 147–9.
24. Quoted Vivian Mercier, 'James Joyce as Medieval Artist' in *The Crane Bag,* Vol. 2, Nos. 1 & 2, 1978, p. 11; reprinted in *The Crane Bag Book, op. cit.,* pp. 161–168.
25. Le Brocquy, 'Notes on Painting and Awareness', *op. cit.,* p. 152.
26. *Ibid.,* p. 139.
27. Le Brocquy, 'A Painter's Notes on Ambivalence', *op. cit.,* p. 69.
28. *Ibid.*
29. *Ibid.*
30. Dorothy Walker, *op. cit.,* p. 45.
31. Patrick Collins, 'A Celtic Art?' Interview with Aidan Dunne in *The Crane Bag,* Vol. 5, No. 2, 1981; and reprinted in *The Crane Bag Book of Irish Studies, op. cit.,* pp. 920–925.

10 Myth and Martyrdom I

1. Paul Ricoeur, 'Universal Civilization and National Cultures' in *History and Truth* (North Western University Press, Evanston, 1965), pp. 271–286.
2. These passages are quoted by David George, 'These are the Provisionals', in *The New Statesman,* No. 19, 1971.
3. 'An Interview with Seamus Twomey' in *The Crane Bag,* Vol. 1, No. 1, 1977; reprinted in *The Crane Bag Book of Irish Studies* (Blackwater Press, Dublin, 1981), pp. 107–113.
4. See C.C. O'Brien *States of Ireland* (Panther, 1974), p. 287: 'And in Padraig Pearse's mind and those of some other notable Irish patriots, the sufferings of the Irish (Catholic) people were in a particular sense one: the sacrifice of Irish patriots was analogous to the sacrifice of Christ; and the resurgence of the national spirit that such a sacrifice could set in motion was analogous to the resurrection

of Christ. The timing of the rising for Easter was no coincidence'. Unfortunately, Dr. Cruise O'Brien does not go on to analyse the *meaning* of the analogy.

5. Eamonn McCann, *War and an Irish Town*, Pluto Press, 1980, pp. 9, 13.

6. Mircea Eliade, *Myths, Dreams and Mysteries* (Fontana, London, 1968).

7. Oliver McDonagh, *States of Mind: A Study of Anglo-Irish Conflict, 1780–1980* (Allen and Unwin, 1983), p.13.

8. See Redmond Fitzgerald, *Cry Blood, Cry Erin*, (Vandal publications, 1966) p. 112. The title of this popular history of the Rising is itself representative of the widespread conception of this event in terms of a 'blood-letting' myth. For the other references and quotations in this section see in particular Roger McHugh's comprehensive Anthology *Dublin 1916* (Arlington Books, London, 1966). See also G.F. Dalton's critique of the symbols of the Irish tradition of blood sacrifice in 'To The Goddess Eire' in *Studies*, Winter 1974, p. 343–354.

9. See Augustin Martin's detailed discussion of this symbol in 'Reflections on the Poetry of 1916: To make a Right Rose Tree', *Studies*, 1966; and G.F. Dalton, 'To The Godess Eire', *op. cit.*, p. 349f.

10. Daniel Corkery, *The Hidden Ireland* (Gill, Dublin, 1967). See also the preface by Tom Kinsella and Sean O Tuama to their translation of the 'poems of the dispossessed', *An Duanaire* (Dolmen Press, 1980).

11. Quoted by Edgar Holt in his *Protest in Arms*, p. 141.

12. Lennox Robinson, *Four Aspects of Change* quoted in the McHugh Anthology, *Dublin 1916, op. cit.* pp. 338–350.

12a Quoted by Augustin Martin, *op. cit.* See also Joyce Kilmer's *Easter Week:* 'There was a rain of blood that day/red rain in gay blue April weather/It blessed the earth till it gave birth/to valour thick as blooms the heather./Romantic Ireland is not old/for years untold her youth will shine/her hearth is fed on Heavenly bread/the blood of martyrs is her wine'.

13. W.B. Yeats, *The Trembling of the Veil* (Werner Laurie, London, 1922), pp. 53–4.

14. *Ibid.* pp. 145–150.

15. See also the final stanza of Yeats's verse-play *The Death of Cuchulain:* 'Are those things that men adore and loathe/their sole reality?/What stood in the Post Office/with Pearse and Connolly?/What comes out of the mountain/where men first shed their blood?/who thought Cuchulain till it seemed/he stood where they had stood'? Similarly, in Eoin Neeson's biography of Michael Collins we hear this Republican hero praised as one 'who has been admitted to the company of heroes stretching from Cuchulain to Hugh O'Neill and Parnell'.

16. Yeats was by no means an isolated 'poetic' spokesman of this mythic dimension of the Republican movement. In a poem called *Situations* George Russell proclaimed that Pearse had 'turned all life's water into wine' and that MacDonagh had been 'by death redeemed'; he concluded his panegyric with the sententious claim that 'Life cannot utter things more great/Than life can meet with sacrifice'. Eva Gore-Booth, writing of another Easter hero, Francis Sheehy-Skeffington, declared that he was not alone when he died 'for at his side does that scorned Dreamer stand/Who in the Olive Garden agonized'. And in the same vein, Sean O'Casey caricatured the mythological trappings of the uprising as follows: 'Cathleen Ní Houlihan, in her bare feet is singing, for her pride that had almost gone is come back again. In tattered gown and hair uncombed she sings, shaking the ashes from her hair, she is singing of men that in battle array . . . march with banner and fife to the death, for their land. . . . The face of Ireland twitches when the guns again sing, but she stands ready, waiting to fasten around

her white neck this jewelled story of death, for these are they who will speak to her people for ever; that Spirit that had gone from her bosom returns' (Sean O'Casey, *Autobiography*). See also Frank O'Connor's recognition of the mythic nature of the Rising in *An Only Child:* 'It was only in the imagination that the great tragedies took place . . . the impossible and only the impossible was law . . . then the real world began to catch up with fantasy' (quoted McHugh, *op. cit.*).

17. Sean O'Faoláin, *Vive Moi* quoted in the McHugh Anthology, *op. cit.* pp. 369–386.

18. 'Interview with Seamus Twomey', *The Crane Bag*, Vol. 1, No. 2, *op. cit.*

19. Jûrgen Moltmann, *Theology of Hope*, (SCM Press, 1967). Rudolph Bultmann argues in a similar vein in *The Theology of the New Testament*: 'To understand Jesus' fate as the basis for a mythic cult, and to understand such a cult as the celebration which sacramentally brings the celebrant into such fellowship with the cult-divinity that the latter's fate avails for the former as if it were his own – that is a *Hellenic* mystery idea.' Rudolph Bultmann, *The Theology of the New Testament* (SCM Press, 1952).

20. Mircea Eliade, *Patterns in Comparative Religion* (Sheed and Ward, London, 1958). for an analysis of the 'reactualizing myths' of blood-sacrifice, see Eliade, *Myths, Rites, Symbols* (Vol. 1, Harper, 1975), pp. 253–255. For a feminist critique of the sacrifice myths see: M. Condren, 'Death and Patriarchy' in *Women's Spirit Bonding* (eds. Valver and Buckley) Pilgrim Press, 1984; *The Cult of Death in the Easter Rising* (forthcoming). See also N. Jay, 'Sacrifice as remedy . . . ' in *Immaculate and Powerful* (ed. C. Buchanan), Beacon Press, 1985; Edna McDonagh, 'Dying for the Cause: An Irish Perspective on Martyrdom' in *Between Chaos and New Creation*, Gill & McMillan 1968.

21. Eugen Fink, *Spiel als Weltsymbol* (Stuttgart, Kohlhammer, 1960).

22. Paul Ricoeur, *The Symbolism of Evil* (Beacon Press, Boston, 1969), pp. 162–3.

23. Max Scheler, *Ressentiment* (Schocken Books, New York, 1972).

24. See Sartre, *Sketch for a Theory of the Emotions* (Methuen, 1962) and *The Psychology of Imagination* (Citadel press, 1972); see also my analysis of Sartre in *Modern Movements in European philosophy* (Manchester University Press, 1985).

25. Ricoeur, *The Symbolism of Evil, op. cit.*, p. 5. See also Mircea Eliade, *Myths, Dreams, Mysteries*, p. 27:'It seems that myth itself, as well as the symbols it brings into play never quite disappears from the present world of the psyche – it only changes and disguises its operations.' We might add at this point that the credibility of our attempt to identify a mythological dimension in Ulster terrorism does not presuppose a belief in a Jungian collective Unconscious, Herderian Racial Memory or Yeatsian Anima Mundi. Mythic archetypes of behaviour and thought are as likely transmitted by means of actual and narrated experience as by some form of transhistorical or innate inheritance. It is enough for the Provisionals to have known and heard of the 1916 martyrs and these to have known and heard of the Fenian rebels and these of the heroes of ancient Ireland etc. for the mythic experience of sacrificial terror to perdure and recur.

11 Myth and Martyrdom II

1. Bobby Sands, *One Day in my Life* (Pluto Press, London, 1983), pp. 117–118.

2. Sean MacBride, *Introduction* to *One Day in my Life, op. cit.*, pp. 7–21.

3. See, for example, reports by Cardinal Tomás Ó Fiaich and Tim-Pat Coogan,

author of *On The Blanket* (Ward River Press, Dublin 1980).

4. H-Block Christmas Document, 1979, compiled by Dennis Faul and Raymond Murray (whose defence of the prisoners never prevented them from continually condemning the IRA's use of violence). In this document the authors make the following plea: 'Let all the Irish family . . . respond to this new threat of hunger by Britain with loud and endless protests against British tyranny' – the allusion here being to the great Irish famine of the 1840's and 50's where millions died due to the continued exportation of grain by the British after the potato crops had failed.

5. Tim Pat Coogan, *On The Blanket, op. cit.*, p. 15. I am indebted to Mr. Coogan's detailed research on the Republican prison campaigns for much of the material in the following analysis.

6. Quoted Coogan, *op. cit.*

7. Quoted Coogan, *op. cit.*

8. Garret Fitzgerald's famous 'flawed pedigree' attack on Mr. Haughey on the eve of his election as Taoiseach in 1980 merely reinforced this curious status in allowing Haughey to play the coveted dual role of leader and victim. This ambivalence which appeals so much to the Irish political psyche, is perhaps the secret of Charles Haughey's success. If our minds gave assent to the moral reasoning of Conor Cruise O'Brien, our hearts ran with the dark horse 'Charlie'. Which went some way to explaining why Dr. O'Brien failed to be re-elected and was soon editing the *Observer* 'over there' while Mr. Haughey decided our political future 'over here'. Charles Haughey's term as scapegoat greatly contributed to his earning a term as prime minister of the Irish Republic. It might also be remembered that Neil Blaney, a Fianna Fáil colleague of Mr. Haughey also accused in the arms trial, went on to be elected as a European Deputy several years later. Moreover, it is possible that the Peace Movement's inability to maintain their initial momentum and support stems from the fact that they rapidly became *prize winners* of prestige and success thereby forfeiting their original *sacrificial role as victims of violence*.

9. Quoted Coogan, *op. cit.*

10. *Ibid.* See also Sean MacBride, *Introduction* to *One Day in my Life, op. cit.*, pp. 14–16, and the Faul and Murray H-Block document, *op. cit.*, where the authors write: 'The problem of prisoners is the problem of peace in Northern Ireland. The evidence of the growth in the number of prisoners, from 712 in 1969 to 3,000 prisoners in 1979, is due to the political conflict involving Northern Ireland and Great Britain. The British handling of H-Block has blighted hopes for peace for years to come. . . .'

11. Quoted by Coogan, *op. cit.*, pp. 177–8.

12. Quoted by MacBride, *op. cit.*, pp. 11–12.

13. *The Irish Press*, 22 January, 1979.

14. Paul Durcan in *The Cork Examiner*, 2 September, 1980.

15. See the statement of the former IRA leader, Seamus Twomey, that 'From all wars peace has sprung. Peace has never been built on anything else but violence.' 'Interview with Seamus Twomey' in *The Crane Bag*, Vol. 1, No. 2, 1977, P. 23, reprinted in *The Crane Bag Book of Irish Studies* (Blackwater Press, Dublin, 1981), pp. 107–112.

16. Statement by IRA Army Council spokesman talking to Ed Maloney in *Magill*, Dublin, September, 1978, p. 27.

17. For further analysis of this sacrificial logic see my *Myth and Motherland* (Field Day pamphlets, 5, Derry, 1984) and 'Terrorisme et Sacrifice, Le Cas de

L'Irlande du Nord' in *Esprit* (Paris, April, 1979).

18. See Ed Maloney's interview with IRA Army Council Spokesman, *Magill, op. cit.*. It is surely no accident that several bombing campaigns followed immediately upon statements by the British government to the effect that the terrorists had been effectively quashed. See *Magill* article on the IRA, Sept. 1980, p. 27: 'We have not managed to match last year's performance this year. . . . But we are totally confident that we can overcome these short term problems. The British are sliding into their 1977 mistake of predicting our defeat. They're fighting a statistical war, we're not. We're fighting a political war. The Brits are saying the Provos are beaten, operations are down, there's less poundage of explosives used, four soldiers less have died this year, etc. That's a false confidence and that's OK with us because we will wreck it when we choose to.' See also the statement by Gerry Adams, IRA leader: 'In December Mason said he would squeeze out the IRA like a tube of toothpaste. The IRA replied with a bombing offensive and the toothpaste congealed.' (*Hibernia*, December, 1978, p. 25).

19. MacBride, *op. cit.*, p. 14.

20. For legal and statistical details see MacBride, *op. cit.*, pp. 14–20.

21. For a detailed analysis of the myths and ideologies of the Protestant tradition in Ulster see the third set of *Field Day pamphlets* (Nos. 7, 8, 9, Derry, 1985) by Terence Brown, Marianne Elliott and Robert McCartney; and Desmond Bell's, 'Contemporary Cultural Studies in Ireland and the Problem of Protestant Ideology' in *The Crane Bag, Irish Ideologies*, Vol. 9, No. 2, 1985. Bell offers the following reservations: 'Loyalism as an ideological *practice* amongst the Protestant working class does not primarily take the form of an unswerving electoral support for political representatives who proclaim a conditional loyalty to a British state seen as defending Protestant interests via various political guarantees and policies. Rather its potency resides in a set of cultural practices – to which the Orange parade is central – concerned with the public display of the symbols of Protestant identity. This display is often interpreted as being solely triumphalist in intent. These marches are, as they always have been, about the staking of symbolic claims to territory i.e. where you can or cannot 'walk'. But, they are also about the celebration of a sense of belonging. The names of the bands inscribed on the colourfully decorated drums of the marchers proclaim a loyalty to community and Ulster protestant identity, rather than to any distant polity.'

22. The flaming straw dummy of Lundy was annually suspended (on 18 September) from the statue of the victorious governor Walker overlooking the subordinated Catholic Bogside. The rite still continues despite the fact that the provisional IRA exploded the Loyalist memorial to the victorious Walker. It should also be mentioned that if extreme Loyalist ideology and rhetoric occasionally invoke the theme of christian martyr (as for example Ian Paisley's naming of his Belfast church 'The Martyr's memorial'), it is 'martyr' taken in its literal etymological sense of 'witness', and more precisely of a chosen witness to the power, glory and wrath of God, rather than to his suffering and passion.

23. Manuel de Diéguez, reply to my *Esprit* article, *op. cit.*

12 Faith and Fatherland

1. For details and statistics on these changes in the religious attitudes of Irish youths, see Peader Kirby, *Is Irish Catholicism Dying?* (Mercier Press, Cork,

1984); John J. O'Riordan, *Irish Catholics, Tradition and Transition* (Veritas, Dublin, 1980); Liam Ryan, 'Faith under Survey' in *the Furrow*, January, 1983; Ann Breslin and John Weafer, 'Survey of Senior Students' Attitudes towards Religion, Morality, Education 1982' (available from the Council for Research and Development of the Irish Bishops' conference, Maynooth, Co. Kildare); Bernadette MacMahon, 'A Study of Religion among Dublin Adolescents' in *Religious Life Review* (Vol. 23, No. 107, 1984).

2. See Patrick Corish, *The Origins of Catholic Nationalism* (A History of Irish Catholicism, Vol. III, No. 8), Gill, Dublin, 1968, p. 57.

3. James McEvoy, 'Catholic Hopes and Protestant Fears' in *The Crane Bag*, Forum Issue, Vol. 7, No. 2, 1983, pp. 90–105.

4. Quoted by Padraig O'Malley, *Uncivil Wars*, Blackstaff Press, 1983.

5. Lévi-Strauss, *Tristes Tropiques* (Atheneum, New York, 1971). See also on this subject of religious myths and nationalism, my *Myth and Motherland*, (Field Day publications, No. 5, 1984).

6. Uinseann MacEoin, *Survivors* (Dublin, 1980), p. 242; quoted by Margaret O'Callaghan, 'Religion and Identity: The Church and Independence' in *The Crane Bag*. The Forum issue, Vol. 7, No. 2, 1983, pp. 65–76. I am indebted to Margaret O'Callaghan for several of the quotations and arguments used in this chapter.

7. O'Callaghan, *ibid*.

8. O'Callaghan, *ibid*.

9. O'Callaghan, *ibid*.

10. O'Callaghan, *ibid*.

11. Quoted Terence Brown, *Ireland: A Social and Cultural History – 1922-79*, (Fontana, 1981).

12. See Dermot Moran, 'Nationalism, Religion and the Education Question', in *The Crane Bag*, The Forum Issue, Vol. 7, No. 2, 1983, pp. 77–85.

13. See John A. Murphy, 'Further Reflections on Nationalism' in *The Crane Bag*, Vol. 2, No.'s 1/2, 1978; reprinted in *The Crane Bag Book of Irish Studies*, (Blackwater Press, Dublin, 1981), pp. 304–312.

14. 'Minorities in Ireland' report prepared by the Irish Council of Churches advisory forum on Human Rights. See *The Irish Times*, 5th September, '85.

13 Between Politics and Literature

1. For the research material used or quoted in this first section of our study I am indebted to Barbara Hayley's exhaustive study of the journals of this period, 'Irish Periodicals from the Union to the Nation' in *Anglo-Irish Studies*, II, 1976, pp. 83–103. See also Patrick Rafroidi's comprehensive list of Irish nineteenth century journals in *Ireland and The Romantic Period* (Colin Smythe, London, 1980).

2. Hayley, ibid.

3. As Hayley also points out it was the professional, clerical and university *intelligensia* who produced these journals, however popular their base of support. An illustrative case in point is the resounding success of the *Dublin University Magazine*, founded by Trinity College graduates in 1833 and surviving for over forty years. Hostile to any hint of pro-Catholic liberalism on the part of its fellow Protestants, the manifesto of this journal was uncompromisingly provocative and bellicose: 'We are conservatives: and no feeble vacillation shall

dishonour our steady and upright strength. We cannot assent to the suspicious friendship that would counsel an impotent moderation, where vigour and intrepid activity point to rough collision' (cited Hayley, *ibid*).

4. Seamus Deane in *Two Decades of Irish Writing* (ed. Douglas Dunn, Manchester, Carcanet, 1975), p. 8.

5. Another noteworthy cultural journal which combined non-sectarian political and literary interests in the pursuit of a cross-communal national identity was the *Irish Monthly Magazine of Politics and Literature*, founded in 1833, which addressed its new generation of enlightened readers as follows: 'We come not to support Whig or Tory. . . . We shall, in our philosophy, in our politics, in our fun, even in our vituperation and satire, be Irish – and purely Irish . . . (our) cause is that of the Nation – not of sect or party, but of the entire people of Ireland' (cited Hayley, *ibid*).

6. Hayley, *op. cit.* p. 93.

7. F.S.L. Lyons, *Ireland Since the Famine* (Wiedenfield and Nicolson, 1971), p. 244.

8. Lyons, *op. cit.* p. 46.

9. See Terence Brown, *Ireland: A Social and Cultural History, 1922–79 (Fontana, 1981)*, pp. 120–129. I am indebted to Brown's extensive research for much of the material in this section.

10. For a detailed analysis of the cultural debates between the *Irish Statesman* and D.P. Moran and the *Catholic Bulletin* see Margaret O'Callaghan's thesis on *Language and Identity: The Quest for Identity in the Irish Free State 1922–1932* (U.C.D., 1981).

11. Quoted by Terence Brown, *op. cit.* p. 121.

12. Brown, *op. cit.* p. 205.

13. Quoted by Ronan Fanning, *'The Four-Leaved Shamrock. Electoral Politics and National Imagination in Independent Ireland'* (The O'Donnell Lecture, 1983, University College Dublin).

14. Editorial, *The Crane Bag*, Vol. 1, No. 1, 1977; reprinted in *The Crane Bag Book of Irish Studies*, *op. cit.* For further analysis of the new cultural journals emerging in Ireland in the eighties see my 'Postmodern Ireland', *The Clash of Ideas* (ed. M. Hederman, Gill and MacMillan, 1987).

15. Walter Benjamin, *'The Story Teller, Reflections on the Works of Nikolai Leskov'* in *Illuminations* (Jonathan Cape, 1970), p. 87.

16. Benjamin, *op. cit.* p. 89.

14 Myth and the Critique of Ideology

1. See in particular the structuralist and post-structuralist philosophies of Michel Foucault, Jacques Lacan and Jacques Derrida. For a detailed critique of this tendency see J. L. Ferry and A. Renault, *La Pensée 68: Essai sur l'anti-humanisme contemporain*, (Gallimard, Paris, 1985). See Derrida's defençe against such charges in our *Dialogues with Contemporary Continental Thinkers*, Manchester University Press, 1984, pp. 123–126.

2. Karl Marx, *The Eighteenth Brumaire of Louis Bonaparte* (1852), Unwin Brothers, London, 1926, pp. 24–26.

3. Roland Barthes, *Mythologies*, Paladin, 1973, pp. 157–8.

4. Liam de Paor, *The Peoples of Ireland*, Rainbow Press, Dublin, 1986.

5. See Terry Eagleton, 'Capitalism, Modernism and Postmodernism' in *New Left*

Review, No. 152, 1985, p. 64; and also *Walter Benjamin: Towards a Revolutionary Criticism*, Verso, London, 1981.

6. Herbert Marcuse, *Eros and Civilization*, Beacon Press, Boston, 1955, p. 19, and also Barry Katz, *Herbert Marcuse: Art of Liberation*, Verso, 1982, pp. 102, 153.

7. Herbert Marcuse, *The Aesthetic Dimension*, Beacon Press, Boston, 1978, p. 73.

8. Sean MacBride quoted in *The Cork Examiner*, 27th July, 1985.

9. Frederic Jameson, *The Political Unconscious: Narrative as a Socially Symbolic Act*, Methuen, 1981, p. 298.

10. Basil Chubb, *The Government and Politics of Ireland*, Landman, 1982, pp. 21–33.

11. Dick Walsh 'Come on the Intellectuals' in *The Irish Times*, June 20, 1985.

12. See Walter Benjamin, 'Theses on the History of Philosophy' in *Illuminations*, Fontana, p. 57. Paul Ricoeur's definition of a literary tradition in *Time and Narrative* as an interplay of innovation and sedimentation is also most instructive here. The term tradition, suggests Ricoeur, should be understood not as the 'inert transmission of some dead deposit of material but as the living transmission of an innovation always capable of being reactivated by a return to the most creative moments of poetic activity'. Tradition must thus be seen as a sedimented history of innovations. But by the same token, innovation remains relative to sedimentation in the sense that it remains a form of behaviour governed by rules. 'The labour of imagination', as Ricoeur notes, 'is not born from nothing. It is bound in one way or another to the tradition's paradigms. But the range of solutions is vast. It is deployed between the two poles of servile application and calculated deviation, passing through every degree of "rule-governed deformation" . . . the possibility of deviation is inscribed in the relation between sedimented paradigms and actual works. Short of the extreme case of schism, it is just the opposite of servile application. Rule-governed deformation constitutes the axis around which the various changes of paradigm through application are arranged. It is this variety of applications that confers a history on the productive imagination and that, in counterpoint to sedimentation, makes every narrative tradition possible' *(Time and Narrative*, Vol. I, Chicago University Press, 1984, pp. 68–70).

13. Alasdair MacIntyre, *After Virtue*, Duckworth Press, 1981, p. 206.

14. Seamus Deane, *Heroic Styles: The Tradition of an Idea*, Field Day pamphlets 4, Derry, 1984, p. 18.

15. See Paul Ricoeur, *The Conflict of Interpretations*, Evanston, Illinois, 1974; *An Essay on Interpretation*, Yale University Press, 1970, and 'The Critique of Religion' in *The Philosophy of Paul Ricoeur: An Anthology of his work*, ed. C. Regan and D. Stewart, Boston, 1978, p. 215. See also my essay, *Religion and Ideology: Ricoeur's Hermeneutic Conflict* in *Irish philosophical Journal*. Vol. 2, No. 1, 1985.

16. Karl Marx and Fredrich Engels, *On Religion* (Moscow, 1955), p. 50.

17. Roland Barthes, *Mythologies*, *op. cit.*, pp. 109–159.

18. Rudolf Bultmann, *The Theology of the New Testament*, S.C.M., London, 1952, pp. 295f. And also Rudolf Bultmann & Karl Jaspers, *Myth & Christianity: An Inquiry into the possibility of Religion without Myth*, Noonday Press, 1958, p. 15f.

19. René Girard, *Le Bouc Emissaire*, Grasset, Paris, 1982 in particular the chapter 'Qu'est-ce qu'un mythe?' pp. 36–37. See also my 'René Girard et le mythe comme bouc émissaire' in *Violence et Verité: Colloque de Cérisy autour de*

René Girard, Grasset, Paris, 1985, pp. 35–49.

20. On this distinction between utopia and ideology see Karl Mannheim, *Ideology and Utopia*, Routledge and Kegan Paul, 1936; Frederic Jameson, 'The Dialectic of Utopia and Ideology' in *The Political Unconscious, op. cit.*; and Paul Ricoeur, 'Science and Ideology' in *Hermeneutics and the Human Sciences*, ed. J. B. Thomspon, Cambridge University Press, 1981, pp. 222–247. See also note 26 below.

21. Paul Ricoeur, 'Myth as the Bearer of possible worlds' in *The Crane Bag*, Vol. 2, 1978; reprinted in my *Dialogues with Contemporary Continental Thinkers, op. cit.*, pp. 36–45.

22. On these distinctions between the 'justificatory/explanatory' and 'exploratory/symbolic' functions of myth, and the critical procedures of *demythologization* and *demythization* see Paul Ricoeur, *The Symbolism of Evil*, Harper and Row, 1967 and 'The language of Faith' in the *Union Sem. Quart. Review*, 28/1973. See also T. Van Leeuwen's lucid commentary in *The Surplus of Meaning: Ontology and Eschatology in the Philosophy of Paul Ricoeur*, Rodopi, Amsterdam, 1981, pp. 146 forward. Karl Jaspers also has some interesting remarks on this subject in his essay, 'Myth and Religion' in *Myth and Christianity, op. cit.* For example: 'Mythical thinking is not a thing of the past, but characterizes man in any epoch. . . . The myth is a carrier of meanings which can be expressed only in the language of myth. The mythical figures are symbols which, by their very nature, are untranslatable into other languages. . . . They are interpreted only by new myths, by being transformed. Myths interpret each other. . . . Only he has the right to demythologize, who resolutely retains the reality contained in the cipher language of the myth. . . . We should seek not to destroy, but to restore the language of myth' (pp. 15–17).

23. Ricoeur, *The Symbolism of Evil, op. cit.*, p. 5: 'Demythologization works on the level of the false rationality of myth in its explanatory pretension'.

24. Ricoeur, 'Myth as the Bearer of possible worlds', *op. cit.*, p. 39.

25. Ricoeur, *ibid*, pp. 40–44. See also Mircea Eliade in *Myths, Rites and Symbols*, Vol. I, Harper, 1975, and in particular the sections entitled, 'The Corruption of Myths' (pp. 109–122) and 'The Fallacy of Demystification' (pp. 120–123).

26. On this dialectic between ideology and utopia see my 'Religion and Ideology' *op. cit.* pp. 48–50; also the section on 'mythe et logos' in my *Poétique du Possible*, Beauchesne, Paris 1984, pp. 190–198; and my interview with Ricoeur entitled 'The Creativity of Language' in *Dialogues with Contemporary Continential Thinkers, op. cit.*, pp. 29–30. Here Ricoeur suggests the possibility of a complementary dialectic between the retrospective horizon of ideology and the prospective horizon of utopia.

27. Ricoeur, 'Science and Ideology', *op. cit.* 243.

28. Ricoeur, *Ibid*, p. 245; see also Ricoeur's study of the Habermas/Gadamer hermeneutic debate on this question in 'Hermeneutics and the Critique of Ideology' in *Hermeneutics and the Human Sciences, op. cit.*, pp. 63–100. See my application of the *muthos/logos* dialectic to Irish culture in *Myth and Motherland*, Field Day Pamphlets, 5, 1984.

29. Tom Nairn, *The Break-up of Britain*, New left Books, 1977, p. 298).

30. Hence the limitations of the "traditional Marxian negative hermeneutic for which the national question is a mere ideological epiphenomenon of the economic". Frederic Jameson, *The Political Unconscious, Narrative as a socially symbolic Act, op. cit.*, p. 298.

31. See John Hume's opening address where he declared that the Forum was not a

'nationalist revival mission' and that one of the reasons for the failure to resolve the national problem up to this may have been due to an inability to place the creation of a New Ireland 'above some of our most cherished assumptions.' *(Proceedings of the New Ireland Forum*, Vol. I, Dublin Castle, 1984).

32. Paul Ricoeur, *The Symbolism of Evil*, *op. cit.*, p. 168.
33. See the analysis of Joyce in my *Myth and Motherland*, *op. cit.* and in my 'Mythos und Kritik' in *Das Keltisches Bewusstsein*, Dianos-Trikont, Munich, 1985.
34. Mircea Eliade, *Myths, Dreams and Mysteries*, Fontana, 1968, p. 23: 'Myth is thought to express the absolute truth because it narrates a sacred history; that is, a transhuman revelation which took place in the holy time of the beginning. . . . Myth becomes exemplary and consequently *repeatable*. . . . By *imitating* the exemplary acts of mythic deities and heroes man detaches himself from profane time and magically re-enters the Great Time, the Sacred Time'. See Chapter 10 above, 'Myth and Martyrdom I'.
35. Ricoeur, 'Science and ideology', *op. cit.*, p. 225.
36. Ricoeur, *ibid.*, p. 229.
37. Ricoeur, *ibid.*, p. 227.
38. Ricoeur, *ibid.*, p. 227.
39. See the chapter 'Faith and Fatherland' in this book and also my *Myth and Motherland*, Field Day pamphlets, 5, Derry, 1984, (republished in *Ireland's Field Day*, Hutchinson, London, 1985).
40. Jurgen Habermas, *Legitimation Crisis*, Beacon Press. 1973.